RECENT PHILOSOPHY

Volume Two: *From Bentham to Dewey*

Étienne Gilson *and* Armand A. Maurer, C.S.B.

CLUNY
Providence, Rhode Island

RECENT PHILOSOPHY

CLUNY EDITION, 2023

This Cluny edition is a republication, in part, of *Recent Philosophy: Hegel to the Present* (forematter and Parts Three and Four), originally published by Random House Inc., in 1966.

…………

For this Cluny edition, citation and reference styles
have been updated and developed, as needed,
for the purposes of clarity and accessibility.

For more information regarding this title
or any other Cluny Media publication,
please write to info@clunymedia.com, or to
Cluny Media, P.O. Box 1664, Providence, RI 02901

◈ VISIT US ONLINE AT WWW.CLUNYMEDIA.COM ◈

ISBN (paperback) | 978-1685952082
ISBN (hardcover) | 978-1685952150

NIHIL OBSTAT: Eduardus A. Synan, *censor librorum deputatus*
IMPRIMATUR: PHILIPPUS F. POCOCK, *archiepiscopus coadiutor torontinus*

Cover design by Clarke & Clarke
Cover image: Giorgio de Chirico, *La matinée angoissante*,
1912, oil on canvas
Courtesy of MART, Italy

CONTENTS

PART FOUR: *American Philosophy* (Armand A. Maurer)

INTRODUCTION TO
A History of Philosophy

THIS *History of Philosophy* is intended as an introduction to philosophy itself. The approaches to philosophy are many, but if one aims to give the reader, beyond mere factual information, a genuine philosophical formation, the historical approach becomes a necessity. Much more important than knowledge about philosophy is a true notion of what it is to philosophize. And what better way is there to learn to philosophize than to observe the great philosophers of the past? If one has the understanding and the patience to follow the discussions of Plato, Aristotle, Thomas Aquinas, or Kant, he cannot fail to appreciate what it means to philosophize. And, equally important, he will have a standard of philosophical excellence that will deter him from confusing a shabby piece of philosophy with one that is first-rate.

Those who take philosophy seriously must have some knowledge of its history, because philosophy is a collective enterprise in which no one can pretend to take part unless he is first properly introduced. Before playing a game, one must learn its rules, must even practice for a long time under the coaching of some expert. The same can be said of the future philosopher, or of any educated man who wishes to share in a philosophical discussion without incurring ridicule. In our own day, philosophy is to be found everywhere; it is hardly an exaggeration to say that it dominates our political life, since Hegel, Marx, and materialistic scientism provide some of our greatest political powers with the ideology they need to justify their actions. At the very least, an equally well-thought-out ideology is necessary to meet this challenge and, if possible, submit it to a rational critique.

Why is its history a necessary introduction to philosophy? Because philosophy is actually a continuous chain of philosophers who have conducted in the West, for twenty-five centuries, a sort of conversation on the ultimate problems the human mind can ask. What stuff is reality made of? How did it come to be? What is the place of man in the universe? How is knowledge possible? Can we form a sensible opinion concerning our future destiny? Whatever our answer to such questions, it is bound to be a philosophical one. Even to say that they should not be asked and that, anyway, they cannot be answered, is to take a big philosophical chance. These questions, and others like them, have been discussed by countless philosophers, among whom there is at least one point of agreement: that a definite technique be adhered to by all those who want to share in this collective inquiry. First defined by Socrates, followed by Plato and Aristotle, this technique can be found at work in all philosophical doctrines. Two faults will at once disqualify any newcomer to the inquiry: one is not to have learned the technique of philosophical discussion; the other is to want to share in the dialogue without adequate knowledge of the history of philosophy. In the words of the French critic Albert Thibaudet: "Experience shows that during these twenty-five centuries, no self-taught man, no mind uninformed about the work of its predecessors, has been able to make any valuable contribution to philosophy."

A history that aims to make readers feel at home in the great family of philosophers should be neither an accumulation of proper names and dates, which would be better provided by dictionaries and encyclopedias, nor a mere juxtaposition of philosophical doctrines, which would amount to a succession of unrelated monographs. To avoid the first defect, we had to decide which philosophers would be singled out for detailed examination and, within each particular philosophy, what parts of it should be presented. Choice entails arbitrariness; in some cases, other choices could have been made with equal justification. The only rules we have tried to observe were not to omit any really great doctrine and never to mention one of which not enough could be said to relate it to some definite philosophical position. The second defect has been avoided, we hope, by our effort to relate every great doctrine to those with which it was vitally linked. Here, again, enough had to be said to achieve philosophical intelligibility without burdening our history with purely dogmatic considerations.

The last remark leads us to a further question. How should this *History* be used? The answer cannot be the same for all classes of readers. Students will have their teachers to help them make their own selection according to the various kinds of philosophical studies they are engaged in. The only general hypothesis we can visualize is that of the reader who is free to make whatever use of the book he thinks best. To him our advice would be, first, to read the *History* in a rather cursory way so as to gather a general picture of the growth of philosophical doctrines within any one of the four main periods into which it has been divided. A second reading should be both selective and exacting, with the reservation, however, that after making his own choice of the particular philosophy he intends to study more precisely, the reader will not submit it to a hasty criticism. As a rule it takes much more cleverness to understand a philosophy than to refute it. Moreover, no doctrine should be discussed on the basis of its interpretation by any historian, whose role is merely to introduce the reader to the study of the writings of the philosophers themselves. Last, not least, one should always keep in mind that, since philosophy is about ultimate problems, each particular doctrine is determined by its particular way of approaching such problems.

The slightest deviation in the understanding of philosophical principles brings about important differences in the conclusions. In critically assessing a philosophy, therefore, the greatest attention should be paid to its initial data. To discuss a philosopher's conclusion without understanding his principles is a waste of time. However, one will never regret the time and care devoted to a detailed examination of what a philosopher calls philosophy, of the method he advocates and uses in discussing its problems, and, more important still, of his own personal way of understanding these principles. If as much time were spent meditating on our own philosophical ideas as is devoted to refuting those of other philosophers, we would probably realize how much more important it is to set forth truth than to fight error. Hopefully, this *History* will convey to its readers a positive notion of philosophical wisdom, conceived as a never-ceasing effort to deepen the understanding of the first principles of human knowledge. We have planned the *History* as a guide for those who need an introduction to a very wide field of historical information and philosophical speculation. If, as we would like to think, the readers of this *History* want to continue beyond it to some exploring of their own, we trust that they will find themselves at least proceeding in the right direction.

The present general history of philosophical doctrines in the Western world falls naturally into four Parts, and therefore into four volumes: I. *Ancient Philosophy*; II. *Medieval Philosophy*; III. *Modern Philosophy: Descartes to Kant*; IV. *Recent Philosophy: Hegel to Dewey*. The distribution of the materials within each Part is dictated by the variations in philosophical thinking itself during the course of centuries, in its way of approaching problems as well as in its mode of expressing them. Even so, the emphasis is always on the doctrinal content of each particular philosophy. Biographical and bibliographical information is limited to what is needed to embark on a personal study of any one of the philosophers, schools, or periods represented. For indeed the very substance of a history of philosophy is philosophy itself. That is why, so far as possible, everything in these four volumes is made to serve this truth.

Étienne Gilson

PREFACE TO
Recent Philosophy

THE philosophical unity so visible in Europe at the time of the Reformation and still perceptible during the seventeenth and eighteenth centuries began to disintegrate in the early years of the nineteenth century. The accession of new languages to the status of scientific languages, the rise of nationalistically minded generations of philosophers, the progressive multiplication of the professors of philosophy, many of whom became philosophical writers, created a new historical situation. Descartes wrote his *Meditations* in Latin, so they were read at once in the whole of civilized Europe; one hundred years later, Condillac could not read Locke in the original, and when Kant published his masterwork in German, it remained for many years a sort of mystery philosophy chiefly known from summaries, interpretations, and even criticisms. It is therefore almost unavoidable to take into account the nationalities of the philosophers in the nineteenth century and, up to a point at least, to order their doctrines accordingly.

The method followed in the preceding sections of this history has not been modified. We wanted to avoid the danger of turning a history of philosophy into an encyclopedia of proper names and dates. It was therefore necessary to eliminate many philosophers for the sole reason that too little would have been said about them for it to make philosophical sense. In such cases, arbitrariness is unavoidable; we can only apologize for it.

Similarly, the temporal limit assigned to this history deserves comment. In principle, it was intended to cover the philosophy of the nineteenth century and of the first third of the twentieth. A few exceptions were made in order to include two or three contemporaries whose doctrines have assumed a recognized importance in the Western philosophical world. It was felt that their places should at least be marked, pending the time when an objective assessment of their work becomes possible. Specialized histories of today's philosophy in some particular countries will direct the readers to appropriate sources of information.[1]

PART THREE

ENGLISH PHILOSOPHY

by Armand A. Maurer

XVI.

Utilitarianism

ENGLISH philosophy in the eighteenth century was dominated by the two towering figures of Locke and Newton. The former laid the groundwork for the empiricism that culminated in Hume; the latter inspired the century with the vision of the universe as a Great Machine designed and set in motion by God, and with a scientific method whose astounding success in physics seduced philosophers to apply it to their own subject. With Hume all the implications of Locke's principles became apparent: phenomenalism in the theory of knowledge, associationism in psychology, hedonism in ethics, skepticism in metaphysics, agnosticism in religion, and liberalism in politics. Nor was it only in England that the full force of Locke's ideas was felt. On the continent the influence of "the wise Locke," as Voltaire called him, can be seen in the sensism of Condillac (1715–1780) and the other French *philosophes*.

The philosophical reaction to the empirical and skeptical movement initiated by Locke came through Thomas Reid (1710–1796), the founder of the Scottish school of philosophy. Reid tried to restore metaphysics to its rightful position by showing that the human mind can (now more than the appearances of things; endowed with the power of common sense, it can immediately grasp first principles concerning reality itself. The revival of metaphysics in Europe was begun by Sigismond Gerdil (1718–1802), who developed a Christian philosophy along the lines of Malebranche, with echoes of St. Augustine and St. Thomas Aquinas.

It is against the background of this eighteenth-century struggle between empiricism and a nascent metaphysical spirit (whose history has already been told in Volume III of *A History of Philosophy*)[1] that we can best understand the philosophical movement known as English utilitarianism.[2] The utilitarians left no doubt as to their position in the debate: they resolutely attacked the budding metaphysics of Reid and his common-sense school and returned to the empiricism traditional in England since the time of Francis Bacon. The weakness of Reid's metaphysics, compromised as it was by large concessions to empiricism, made the victory of the utilitarians all but certain. The final assault came in 1865 with John Stuart Mill's refutation of the philosophy of Sir William Hamilton, who combined the Scottish philosophy of common sense with Kantianism.[3] Mill dealt the death blow to the philosophy of common sense and once more established empiricism as the reigning philosophy in England. Like all philosophical victories, however, Mill's was short-lived. In the last third of the nineteenth century utilitarianism itself was eclipsed by the rising tide of idealism. Although utilitarianism left a permanent mark on English thought, it no longer survives as a philosophical school.

Utilitarianism, then, was in its ascendancy during the first two-thirds of the nineteenth century. Although its origins have been traced back to Hume, the real founder of the school was Jeremy Bentham (1748–1832). Its greatest philosopher was John Stuart Mill (1806–1873). James Mill (1773–1836), the father of John Stuart and disciple of Bentham, passed on Benthamism to his son.

None of the leading utilitarians held a university post. They were not academic philosophers but men engaged in the practical professions—law, public administration, or government—and their main interests lay in the theory and practical reform of morality, private and public. The England of their day was undergoing the profound upheaval of the Industrial Revolution and reforms were badly needed in economics, politics, law, and education. To these practical problems the utilitarians turned their attention; but beyond their solution they sought a single principle that would give coherence and unity to their many ethical notions. This they found in the principle of utility—that an action is good insofar as it contributes to the greatest happiness of the greatest number of people. Here was the guiding light of all their thinking, the firm foundation of all their reforms.

The formulation of this principle and of simple laws of the mind (for example, the law of the association of ideas as expounded by David Hartley)[4] convinced the utilitarians that at last the moral sciences could be made truly scientific—a goal toward which Locke and Hume had been working. Newton had shown how, through the use of the experimental method, physical laws could be discovered that would render intelligible a vast number of natural phenomena. Now it appeared that a universal practical science of morality could be established by applying the Newtonian method to the phenomena of man's conduct as an individual and social being. By means of a few simple laws of human nature and conduct this science would make it possible to explain the details of moral phenomena by a synthetic and deductive method, analogous to that of Newtonian physics. Moreover—and this was the main point to utilitarianism—this knowledge would give the moralist and political theorist power to reform man and society, as the knowledge of the laws of physics secures the domination and control of nature.

It is from this perspective that we can best appreciate the work of the utilitarians. Jeremy Bentham's new "art-and-science" of legislation, with its emphasis on the role of observation and experiment, mathematical calculation of pleasures and pains, and logical method, all for the purpose of reshaping society, falls within this pattern. But the most serious effort to justify the utilitarian extension of the Newtonian method to the moral sciences is J. S. Mill's *Logic*. As we shall see, Mill attempts to make these sciences deductive and demonstrative, along the lines of Newtonian physics, while adhering to a rigid phenomenalist theory of knowledge. The failure of Mill's logic brought to an end the fondest hopes of utilitarianism.

Jeremy Bentham

logic of the will

Educated as a lawyer, Bentham practiced his profession for a short time; but he became so disgusted with the injustices and inadequacies of British law that he decided to devote all his energies to its reform.[5] It was not a thing of perfection, as Blackstone claimed, but cumbrous, uncertain, partly unwritten, slow, and expensive. The result was widespread suffering among the people. His life-long aim was to reform the legal structure of England and to correct other social abuses, thus leading men to greater happiness.

The legal and social reforms Bentham had in mind were not superficial but reached down to the very foundations of morality. Thus he was bound to come to grips with basic ethical problems. Inspired by the French philosopher Helvétius, he set out to create a new science, the science of law, which would direct the art of legislation somewhat as the science of anatomy directs the art of medicine. As the doctor heals his patient using the theoretical science of anatomy, so the legislator secures the happiness of all the people by employing the science of law. The art of legislation embraces all men's action and aims at their total happiness; hence it should be based upon the all-embracing science of law.

But what is law? This is how Bentham imagines its birth. There was a time when men existed without laws, obligations, rights, or crimes. The actions of men, however, were fraught with many consequences, some of which were evil, and this gave rise to the first notions of morals and legislation. The strongest men in the group wanted to stop these mischievous actions, which they called crimes. The declaration of their will, expressed by an outward sign, received the name of law.[6] A law, then, is a command issued by a superior; and since a command is an act of the will, law is a product of will. More precisely, "A law may be defined as an assemblage of signs declarative of a volition conceived or adopted by a *sovereign* in a state, concerning the conduct to be observed in a certain *case* or class of persons, who...are...subject to his power..."[7]

This definition makes it clear that Bentham's notion of law is voluntaristic; law, in his view, is not the expression of man's reason but of his will. This assigns law to man's highest faculty, in Bentham's estimation, for he placed the will above the intellect. In obvious dependence on Hume, he makes the understanding the slave of the will and passions. Bentham's definition of law is also nominalistic. A law is said to be "an assemblage of signs" (in other words, a sentence) expressing the will of the sovereign. It is a legal fiction, a "fictitious entity," like all language, except the names of bodies. There are no natural laws; there are only uniformities and propensities in nature. If we describe such a uniformity or propensity, we state *what is*, not *what ought to be*, and only in the latter case do we state a law. For example, if we say that parents are inclined to look after their children, we state a fact; but if we say that parents ought to look after them, we express the will of the legislator and consequently a law.[8]

If there is to be a science of law, it must have a logic of its own; and since law is an expression of will, this must be, according to Bentham, a logic of the will. Classical logic is a logic of the understanding, or *noology*. This deals with sentences that assert something to be a fact, and with the various kinds of argumentation. The logic of the will, which Bentham proposes to call *thelematology*, has to do with sentences expressing volition; for example, "My will is that you kill the robber." Commands (for example, "Kill the robber") and questions (for instance, "Is the robber killed?") are also utterances expressive of the will, and they must also be dealt with by the logic of the will. *Nomography*, the most important branch of thelematology, has to do with the language used by superiors to direct the conduct of inferiors. *Deography* deals with the language expressing the will of inferiors to superiors; *pothography* treats of the language expressing the will of an equal to an equal.[9]

The possibilities of the new logic of the will excited Bentham's imagination. As yet no one had explored the language of the will, though he considered its cultivation essential to the science of law and to the business of government. He saw himself as the pioneer in charting this virgin territory. To this end he proposed to make a complete code of law, a *pannomon*, to be based on an entirely new system of logic comprising both a logic of the understanding and a logic of the will. More fundamental still, he projected an analysis of the principal relations between thought and language, and the establishment of the main principles of universal grammar. This would necessarily involve him in metaphysics—"genuine metaphysics, of which Locke was in a manner the inventor...which teacheth the signification of words, and the ideas which they signify..."[10]

Like his projected model prison, the *Panopticon*, on which he spent so many fruitless years, this vast undertaking—which appears so modern to us in the age of linguistic analysis—was never completed. Some sections of it were published; others remain among the unprinted manuscripts that Bentham left for the perusal of future paleographers.

the greatest happiness principle

It should now be clear that Bentham's interest in philosophy is thoroughly pragmatic. Knowledge has meaning for him only to the extent that it can be put into practice; knowing must be inextricably bound up with doing. Unless a science has some use and subserves an art, it is valueless. Thus the logic of the will claims his attention only because it can be used in the art of legislation. The purpose of this art, in turn, is to relieve men of the miseries of life and thus to secure their happiness. The legislator, like the physician, relieves men's sufferings but on a vastly greater scale. All the arts aim to secure men's happiness; the art of legislation is supreme because it can work more effectively than the others for "the greatest happiness of the greatest number." Happiness, then, is the end of all the arts and sciences. When Bentham classifies them in his Encyclopedical Tree, he places eudaemonics at their head as the master-art-and-science of happiness, with all the others contributing to it.[11]

That men should always act for the greatest happiness of the greatest number of people is Bentham's primary ethical principle. It is his golden rule for the legislator and his general standard of all conduct. Bentham describes it as "a principle constituting not only a rational foundation, but the only rational foundation, of all enactments in legislation and all rules and precepts destined for the direction of human conduct in private life."[12]

At first Bentham called his golden rule "the principle of utility." He found the term "utility" in Hume's *Principles of Morals* and used it to mean the capacity of a thing to give pleasure. Later he became disenchanted with the term. Cannot something be useful for a bad end as well as for a good one? "Utility" does not express the true end of human action, which is pleasure and exemption from pain. Since, according to Bentham, pleasures blended together constitute happiness, he adopted the more precise phrase "the greatest happiness principle" to describe his primary principle.[13]

The notion that we should act for the greatest happiness of the greatest number of people was not original with Bentham. It seems to have first appeared in a work of Francis Hutcheson, and from there it was quickly taken up by other ethical treatises. We find it, for example, in Helvétius, Beccaria, and Priestley.[14] None of these moralists, however, built his entire system on it, as Bentham did. When he first read the phrase "the greatest happiness of the greatest number" in Priestley's *Essay on Government* it burst on him with all the force and light of a revelation. Henceforth this was the guiding principle of his whole thought.

Like all first principles, the greatest happiness principle cannot be demonstrated. Bentham assumes it as a postulate, indeed as the only one in his ethical system. In deciding all ethical questions (determining whether something *ought to be*), and in justifying all moral sentiments, he appeals solely to this principle. His only other assumption is the existence of the material world. In settling questions of fact (determining whether something is), the final court of appeal is experience or observation of this world.[15]

In interpreting the principle of greatest happiness Bentham acknowledges the help of Helvétius and Beccaria. He learned from Helvétius that happiness is a blending of a number of individual pleasures. Thus he defines happiness as a whole uniting several pleasures: "The distinction between pleasure and happiness, is, that happiness is not susceptible of division, but pleasure is. A pleasure is single—happiness is a blended result, like wealth."[16]

Pleasures and pains are the basic facts of human experience. Bentham gives them the general name of "interesting perceptions"; that is to say, sensations that affect us, arousing our interest or concern. We are completely under their sway; they are both guides for our moral judgments and determining causes of what we actually do:

> Nature has placed mankind under the governance of two sovereign masters, *pain* and *pleasure*. It is for them alone to point out what we ought to do, as well as to determine what we shall do. On the one hand the standard of right and wrong, on the other the chain of causes and effects, are fastened to their throne. They govern us in all we do, in all we say, in all we think: every effort we can make to throw off our subjection, will serve but to demonstrate and confirm it.[17]

Bentham lists the simple pleasures as follows: pleasures of sense, wealth, skill, amity, good name, power, piety, benevolence, malevolence, memory, imagination, expectation, association, and relief. Correspondingly, there are pains of privation, sense, awkwardness, enmity, ill name, piety, benevolence, malevolence, memory, imagination, expectation, and association. He does not think it possible, however, for someone to decide what is pleasant or painful for another; everyone has to determine this for himself. It is not up to the legislator to settle this but only to secure the well-being of the citizens in what they judge to be pleasure and absence of pain.

All the pleasures and pains listed above are self-regarding, except those of benevolence and malevolence, which are extra-regarding. An extra-regarding pleasure or pain affects the pleasure or pain of another person; a self-regarding one does not. Bentham is well aware that men often act selfishly, that self-regarding interests frequently prevail over social instincts. But he himself deplored this; he not only praised benevolence but he gave a good example of it in his own conduct. Benevolence in his view is the supreme utilitarian moral virtue. He writes in his *Principles of Morals* that "the dictates of utility are neither more nor less than the dictates of the most extensive and enlightened (that is *well-advised*) benevolence."[18] We are as naturally inclined to benevolence as to self-seeking, but the inclination to the former is weaker, and consequently the legislator should do all he can to encourage it. Wise legislation will curb the tendency to self-seeking when it conflicts with the common good[19]; it will strive to harmonize self-interest and public interest. We can see from this that Bentham has no sympathy with the egoistic hedonism of Hobbes. While recognizing a strong inclination in men to seek their own pleasure, and approving of it, he thinks that in the loner run this can be made to coincide with their native tendency to work for the greatest happiness of the greatest number.

But how are we to judge what is the greatest happiness of the greatest number? How are we, in other words, to evaluate pleasures and pains? Bentham does not think they differ in quality but only in quantity—a point, as we shall see, for which he is criticized by John Stuart Mill. In a classic statement of philistinism Bentham declares, "Prejudice apart, the game of push pin is of equal value with the arts and sciences of music and poetry."[20] This reduction of the differences of pleasures and pains to the quantitative order makes it possible for him to submit them to a mathematical calculus, and thus to make ethics objective and scientific.

Following Beccaria, he distinguishes between four elements or dimensions of pleasure or pain, considered by itself and as affecting an individual: (1) intensity; (2) duration; (3) certainty, or uncertainty; and (4) propinquity, or remoteness. To these he adds three other dimensions. Considered in relation to pleasures and pains that may follow it, a pleasure or pain varies in *fecundity* (the chance of its being followed by sensations of the same kind; that is, by pleasures if it be a pleasure, by pains if it be a pain), and *purity* (the chance of its being followed by sensations of the opposite kind; that is, by pains if it be a pleasure, by pleasures if it be a pain). If pleasure or pain is viewed in its effect on more than one individual, we must consider its *extent* (the number of those affected).[21]

With the analysis of pleasures and pains into these dimensions, Bentham hopes to give scientific rigor to his maxim of the greatest happiness of the greatest number. He works out in great detail the rules for a "moral arithmetic" that will enable one to calculate whether or not he should do an act, the standard being the balance of pleasure over pain. The legislator should use this calculus in framing laws, the judge in deciding the punishment for a crime.[22]

This turns the moralist and legislator into calculators, and virtue into a kind of mathematics. Socrates is right: vice is ignorance, virtue is knowledge.

> Vice may be defined to be a miscalculation of chances: a mistake in estimating the value of pleasures and pains. It is false moral arithmetic; and there is the consolation of knowing that, by the application of a right standard, there are few moral questions which may not be resolved, with an accuracy and a certainty not far removed from mathematical demonstration.[23]

Here is the triumph of the mathematical method in ethics! And yet, not quite. Bentham realizes how difficult, if not impossible, it would be completely to mathematicize the sciences of law and ethics. How can one accurately estimate all the pleasurable or painful results of his actions for himself and for others? How can one calculate the results of the actions of others? The method of calculation sets up an ideal that we should strive to attain, but in practice we must often fall short of it. More serious still, Bentham confesses that pleasure itself is not measurable. We need an instrument by which to measure it, as we need a thermometer to measure heat and a barometer to measure air pressure. "Money," Bentham declares, "is the instrument for measuring the quantity of pain or pleasure. Those who are not satisfied with the accuracy of this instrument must find out some other that shall be more accurate or bid adieu to politics and morals."[24]

This debasement of ethics to a monetary calculus is the price Bentham was willing to pay in order to establish it as an objective science. Not all utilitarians, however, had such a narrow view of human nature and happiness. John Stuart Mill for one—admirer of Bentham though he was—deplored his limited perspective. He writes of Bentham: "...no one, probably, who, in a highly instructed age, ever attempted to give a rule to all human conduct, set out with a more limited conception either of the agencies by which human conduct *is*, or of those by which it *should* be, influenced."[25] Mill's aim was to broaden and deepen utilitarianism and to put it on a more humane basis, without however abandoning its greatest-happiness principle.

John Stuart Mill

Among the friends and disciples of Bentham was James Mill, a dour Scotsman who, after studying Greek at Edinburgh, came to London to follow journalism.[26] There he met Bentham, and became the most loyal articulate exponent of his ideas. His most significant contribution to Benthamism was to lay its psychological foundation by his *Analysis of the Phenomena of the Human Mind.* This work was not particularly original; its main ideas were taken from Locke and Hume, as they were developed in the associationist psychology of David Hartley. Sensations are said to be the basic facts of experience; these leave traces or images in the mind called simple ideas. Complex ideas are formed through the association of simple ideas. The experience of identity is that of a series of sensations and ideas held together in memory.

By his phenomenalist and associationist psychology James Mill opposed the common-sense realism of his fellow Scotsman Thomas Reid. He was saying in effect to Reid and the whole Scottish commonsense school: Hume was right and you are wrong; we have no metaphysical intuitions of a reality lying behind our sensations and ideas. And if there are no metaphysical intuitions, neither are there any moral ones. We have no moral faculty by which we immediately perceive or intuit moral principles. These must be justified empirically, by considering their consequences for the pleasure and pain of mankind. Thus Mill's excursus into psychology aimed to bolster Bentham's utilitarian ethics.

Following Hartley, James Mill revived the mechanistic view of the mind, making the conditions governing the workings of the mind similar to those controlling the behavior of matter. The mind is passively controlled by its environment, its ideas and affections being mechanically determined by external stimuli. Education is a matter of conditioning the child so that he will make the right association of ideas, respond correctly to motives, and choose the course of action that leads to the greatest happiness of the greatest number.

These were the principles according to which James Mill personally educated his eldest son, John Stuart, with a view to making him a perfect utilitarian and a worthy successor of Bentham and himself.[27] The elder Mill put his son through a rigorous course in the classics, history, political economy, Aristotelian logic, and other miscellaneous subjects, so that at the age of fourteen he had acquired as broad an education as a university graduate.

As John Stuart Mill tells us in his *Autobiography*, this early training was in reality a course of Benthamism. When he finally read Bentham himself at the age of fifteen, the ground had been well laid, and he seized on the principle of utility as "the keystone which held together the detached and fragmentary components of my knowledge and beliefs." He had now a philosophy of life, and even, "in one among the best senses of the word, a religion; the inculcation and diffusion of which could be made the principal outward purpose of a life."[28] It was to this creed that he devoted all his thought and energy. At the age of sixteen he founded a small philosophical club, which he called the Utilitarian Society, to discuss and propagate the ideas of Bentham and his father. The term "utilitarian" was not original with him; it had been used occasionally by Bentham and others. It was John Stuart Mill, however, who popularized it as the name for Bentham's philosophy and for his own reformulation of Benthamism.

That Bentham's philosophy might need recasting was beyond the wildest imagination of the young Mill. In his twentieth year, however, its necessity was forcefully brought home to him by an event entirely unforeseen by either himself or his father. He had been raised as the living embodiment of Benthamism—that is to say, of a philosophy that made happiness or pleasure the sole aim of life. He suddenly discovered that he was not happy. He had been educated for happiness, but happiness had eluded him. He could not imagine the achievement of any of the Benthamite projects—the reform of law, institutions, or ideas—bringing him happiness. Disillusioned and despondent, he was close to despair. Under his father's tutelage he had cultivated his intellectual powers; he had learned to analyze and to classify objects, to reason and to dispute; but he had not developed his capacity for feeling and loving. His had been an arid and severe education, reflecting the character of the man who had imposed it on him. Did it not also reflect the narrow-heartedness of Bentham's philosophy? As Mill gradually recovered from his mental depression he realized that this philosophy would have to be recast if it were to be a true guide to happiness.

the greatest-happiness principle recast

In his essay *Utilitarianism* Mill makes it clear that he has no intention of abandoning the greatest-happiness principle. There must be "one fundamental principle or law, at the root of all morality," one ultimate standard of conduct, and this is the principle of utility. According to this principle, "actions are right in proportion as they tend to promote happiness, wrong as they tend to produce the reverse of happiness. By 'happiness' is intended pleasure, and the absence of pain; by 'unhappiness,' pain, and the privation of pleasure."[29] Hence pleasure and freedom from pain are the only things desirable as ends; everything desirable is desirable either for its inherent pleasure or because it promotes pleasure and prevents pain.

So far Mill is merely repeating Bentham; but he advances considerably beyond him in his treatment of the kinds of pleasure. Defending utilitarianism against the charge that it belittles human nature by making pleasure the supreme end of life, he insists that the utilitarians distinguish between pleasures. They rate pleasures of intellect, feelings, and imagination much higher than those of mere sensations. True, they generally place the superiority of mental pleasures over bodily ones in the incidental advantages of the former; for example, in their greater permanence, safety, and inexpensiveness. But Mill thinks that he can stand on "a higher ground" and distinguish pleasures by their intrinsic natures. The principle of utility admits of *kinds* of pleasures, some of which are intrinsically more desirable and valuable than others. In short, pleasures differ in quality, and not only in quantity.

Bentham, on the contrary, taught that one pleasure is intrinsically as good as another; as Mill formulates the famous Benthamite dictum, "quantity of pleasure being equal, push-pin is as good as poetry."[30] This is what Mill denies when he insists that there is a qualitative as well as a quantitative difference between pleasures. Poetry holds a particularly lofty place in his scheme of values, since it helped him to recover from his mental depression. Through Wordsworth's poems he was introduced to a new world of feeling and beauty, "a source of inward joy, of sympathetic and imaginative pleasure."[31] The game of push-pin cannot rival this in pleasure, no matter how often or how long it is played.

What is meant by saying that pleasures differ in quality? What makes one pleasure more valuable than another simply as a pleasure? Mill gives no intrinsic criterion by which to judge the quality of pleasures, but only an empirical guide: "Of two pleasures, if there be one to which all or almost all who have experience of both give a decided preference, irrespective of any feeling of moral obligation to prefer it, that is the more desirable pleasure."[32] That pleasure is superior in quality which the majority of experienced persons prefer, even though it may be accompanied by a greater amount of discontent than another pleasure. Now most people who have enjoyed the pleasures of mind and body give a marked preference to the former: "No intelligent human being would consent to be a fool, no instructed person would be an ignoramus, no person of feeling and conscience would be selfish and base, even though they should be persuaded that the fool, the dunce, or the rascal is better satisfied with his lot than they are with others." Happiness, then, should not be confused with content; these are two very different notions. A person with a low capacity for happiness is more easily satisfied than one with a higher capacity; the more highly endowed person will always feel that his happiness is imperfect. And yet he would not want to sink to a lower grade of existence, even if this would mean greater content and satisfaction. In short, "it is better to be a human being dissatisfied than a pig satisfied; better to be Socrates dissatisfied than a fool satisfied."[33]

In speaking of grades of existence Mill introduced a new dimension into utilitarianism. He based man's ultimate end, or happiness, not only on the psychological experience of pleasure and pain, but also on the ascent of man to a higher level of existence. Thus he inserted into his ethical theory an ontological factor unrecognized by Bentham. Bentham never realized, Mill complained, that man is "capable of pursuing spiritual perfection as an end; of desiring, for its own sake, the conformity of his own character to his standard of excellence, without hope of good or fear of evil from other source than his own inward consciousness."[34] This goes far beyond Bentham's narrow hedonism, and even beyond Mill's own statement in his *Utilitarianism* that pleasure and freedom from pain are the only things desirable as ends. He is now telling us that nobility of character and an upright conscience are also ends to be cultivated for their own sake. He even adds that in some cases we should sacrifice our own happiness and that of others for the sake of nobility of character. But if happiness is not the sole end of our actions, it is the final justification and controller of all the ends we pursue. If we strive for nobility of character it is only because this "would go further than all things else towards making human life happy, both in the comparatively humble sense of pleasure and freedom from pain, and in the higher meaning of rendering life, not what it now is almost universally, puerile and insignificant, but such as human beings with highly developed faculties can care to have."[35]

Thus Mill did not abandon utilitarianism, but neither Bentham nor his father would have recognized the doctrine with his modifications. He learned during his mental crisis that the direct pursuit of happiness is fruitless. If we want to be happy, we must fix our minds on some object other than our own happiness: "Paradoxical as the assertion may be, the conscious ability to do without happiness gives the best prospect of realizing such happiness as is attainable."[36] Paradoxical indeed, that happiness, the *summum bonum*, should not be our direct and conscious objective but that it should be reached as a concomitant of other ends! But then, Mill is not telling us to renounce working for the happiness of mankind. He is telling us not to concentrate on our own happiness, but to devote ourselves to the happiness of others; even, if necessary, to sacrifice our own for the sake of theirs. Then happiness comes to us in the greatest measure possible. Utilitarianism, then, does not teach a selfish egoism. Mill insisted that its morality is as lofty and altruistic as that of any religion. Indeed, it demands nothing less than the golden rule of Jesus Christ: to do as you would be done by, and to love your neighbor as yourself.

In thus transforming the utilitarian principle Mill reacted against Benthamism and in general against the arid, superficial rationalism of the eighteenth century. He himself was educated according to the spirit of this century and he never consciously revolted against it. But he came to recognize its one-sidedness and he deliberately opened himself to the new winds of doctrine abroad in the first half of the nineteenth century. As a corrective to Bentham, who epitomized in his eyes the spirit of the previous century, he recommended the reading of Coleridge, the leading English representative of German philosophy, he saw in "the Germano-Coleridgian doctrine" "the revolt of the human mind against the philosophy of the eighteenth century. It is ontological, because that was experimental; conservative, because that was innovative; religious, because so much of that was infidel; concrete and historical, because that was abstract and metaphysical; poetical, because that was matter-of-fact and prosaic."[37] To the partial truth of Bentham must be added those of Coleridge—"the two great seminal minds of England in their age."[38] Mill did not go so far as to accept Coleridge's claim that the human mind knows *a priori* truths—a claim made by German philosophers since Kant and by Reid and Hamilton. As we shall presently see, he agreed with Locke that all knowledge is generalized experience. But he found some value even in the idealistic theory of mind; at least it challenged the shallow sensism of Condillac and his school prevalent in Europe during the eighteenth century and it opened the way for a general much-needed renewal of philosophy.

logic and the moral sciences

Mill's first major contribution to this renewal was his famous *System of Logic*, which he published in 1843 after a labor of ten years. In turning his mind to logical problems he was not abandoning his primary interest in ethics and politics or diverting himself from his purpose of social and political reform in England. He intended in his *Logic* to lay a firm foundation for the moral sciences and for institutional reform, bad institutions (he tells us in his *Autobiography*) being the result of false philosophy.[39] Thus the main purpose of the *Logic* is to be found in the last chapter (VI) "On the logic of the Moral Sciences." This was in fact one of the first chapters Mill worked on; only after dealing with the theory of the moral sciences did he write the central chapter (III) on induction and the methods of the physical sciences. Hence Mill's theory of induction must be seen against the background of his preoccupation with moral and social philosophy.

James Mill, in his *Essay on Government*, defended the Benthamite thesis that political science was a deductive science; from a single principle of human nature, namely that men always act from self-interest, he tried to deduce the whole theory of government. Macaulay criticized this method of arriving at political conclusions as *a priori* and out of touch with the actual political experience of men. He himself advocated what he called the Baconian approach to political science: it should use the inductive method and rest its case solely on the observation of political facts rather than on principles of human nature.

In this debate John Stuart Mill does not agree with Macaulay that the science of politics, or for that matter any of the moral sciences, can be constructed purely inductively, by a mere generalization of experience. Whether it is a question of ethology (the name Mill gives to the science of the formation of character) or sociology (the science of man in the social state), a purely empirical method will not yield valuable results. In physical science, such as chemistry, planned experiments can be made, but not in the moral sciences. Moreover, human actions are too complex in their causes and effects to permit any sure conclusions by way of generalization from experience. We cannot be certain that unknown factors are not playing a role. In social affairs "Plurality of causes exists in almost boundless excess, and effects are, for the most part, inextricably interwoven with one another."[40] Consequently, induction by simple observation is inapplicable to the sciences of human affairs.

A simple generalization, moreover, will yield a description but not a scientific explanation. Mill illustrates the difference between a description and an explanation by the work of Kepler and Newton. On the basis of his observations Kepler described the movement of the planets as elliptical, but Newton was able to show why they moved in this way by his theory that their motion combines a centripetal force toward the sun and a projective force away from it. If the moral sciences are to be truly scientific, on the model of Newtonian physics, they must contain not only general descriptions but also explanations in terms of the laws of human nature. In short, they must be deductive sciences, inferring moral and social phenomena from causes.

On this point Mill concurs with Bentham and his father; but he is critical of their attempt to deduce all moral and social phenomena from one single law of human nature—that men always act for their own interests. Such an "abstract and geometrical deductive method" is inapplicable to social matters, which are highly complex and contain a conflict of human tendencies. It is simply not a fact that self-interest is the only motive of men's actions.[41]

The method Mill advocates for the social sciences is an adaptation of the "concrete deductive method" used, for example, in astronomy and physics. By this method an effect is inferred from all the causal laws on which it depends (as Newton explained the elliptical movements of the planets by the concurrence of the laws of centripetal and projectile force). Mill has no doubt that the actions and feelings of men in their social state are entirely governed by the laws of psychology and ethics.[42] Sociology, then, like astronomy should be a predictive science; it should be able to calculate *a priori* how men will act or feel in society from a knowledge of all the laws and circumstances influencing them. Actually, this is impossible owing to the great number of relevant agencies and circumstances affecting any social phenomenon. All that the sociologist can do is to predict tendencies in human behavior, not actual facts.[43]

Mill also makes room in social science for Comte's "inverse deductive method." This consists of generalizations from history, verified by deduction from the laws of human nature.

In his insistence on the predominantly deductive character of the moral and physical sciences Mill firmly opposes the experimentalism of Francis Bacon. Owing chiefly to the work of Newton, Mill finds that "A revolution is peaceably and progressively effecting itself in philosophy, the reverse of that to which Bacon has attached his name. That great man changed the method of the sciences from deductive to experimental, and it is now rapidly reverting from experimental to deductive."[44] Mill does not mean at all to deny that he is an experimentalist, in the sense of holding that all scientific knowledge is grounded in experience. The deductive method praised by him has no room for *a priori* intuitions of first principles or laws. In his view the only objects of intuition (that is to say, of knowledge that is not the result of reasoning) are our own feelings and mental acts. All other knowledge is the consequence of induction. Even the laws that science uses to deduce effects are reached by induction; and after these laws have been formulated they are subject to rigorous verification in experience. Experience, then, stands at the beginning of the scientific process and also at the end. Mill does not disagree with Bacon on this point, but rather on the necessary role played by deductive reasoning in giving a scientific explanation of phenomena. Mill believes he can reinstate "the deductions which Bacon abolished," because he knows better than Bacon how to establish the rules of experimental inquiry by which the laws of nature are inductively acquired and the results of scientific deduction are verified by experience.

Mill's *Logic*, then, defends the deductive and explanatory character of science without yielding to the rationalist claim that the premises of deductive reasoning are known *a priori*. These principles of reasoning are the result of induction from experience. Mill's problem was to show, within the context of his associationist psychology according to which all knowledge is constructed from atomic sensations and feelings through the laws of association, that induction does not lead to a mere enumeration and arrangement of facts but to true causal laws of nature.

In order to solve this formidable problem Mill was forced to reinterpret the logic of induction. In the simplest terms induction is "generalisation from experience." It is the operation of the mind "by which we infer that what we know to be true in a particular case or cases, will be true in all cases which resemble the former in certain assignable respects."[45] Underlying every induction is the assumption that the universe is governed by general laws and follows a uniform course; that what happens in nature will, if the circumstances are similar, happen again. In short, induction presupposes the universal law of causation, which Mill defined as "invariability of succession...between every fact in nature and some other fact which has preceded it..."[46] Paradoxically, Mill maintained that this law, which is assumed in every induction, is itself the result of induction. It is not self-evident or known *a priori*; it itself is a generalization from experience.

But what scientific value has such an induction? Does it result in a well-established truth or only in a probability? The answer to this question is of the utmost importance, for the law of causation is a necessary condition for the truth of all inductions, and if it is not certain no inductive inference is.

The law of causality, according to Mill, is an example of what Bacon calls "induction by simple enumeration." This type of induction is based solely on the uniformity of experience; it is a "generalization of an observed fact from the mere absence of any known instance to the contrary."[47] For example, men thought for many centuries that all swans were white, never having encountered black ones. The fallibility of such an inference is clear enough; only one instance to the contrary destroys the truth of the conclusion. Usually this kind of induction yields nothing but "empirical laws" or descriptions, not "true laws of nature." But Mill argues that in some remarkable cases it may amount practically to proof. Examples are the law of causality, the laws of contradiction and excluded middle, and the principles of arithmetic and axioms of geometry. Because of their broad basis in experience, these most universal truths "are duly and satisfactorily proved by that method [of induction by simple enumeration] alone, nor are they susceptible of any other proof."[48] Thus the law of causality is among the most certain and firmly established truths; it is not contradicted by any known fact and it is coextensive with all human experience. However, this does not warrant our extending the principle beyond the range of our experience. "In distant parts of the stellar regions, where the phenomena may be entirely unlike those with which we are acquainted, it would be folly to affirm confidently that this general law prevails, any more than those special ones which we have found to hold universally on our own planet."[49]

How are these special laws of nature established? Not by induction by simple enumeration (their basis in experience is not broad enough for that), but by a scientific induction, whose rules Mill explained at some length. In this type of induction accuracy and precision are achieved by the use of the experimental method. One generalization is corrected by another; a narrower and weaker conclusion acquires added strength by being deduced from a wider and stronger one. All natural laws are supported by the fact that they are deducible from the law of causality; and this law in turn is confirmed by them. In this way both the natural and moral sciences can arrive at more than mere empirical generalizations; they can establish true causal laws of nature and the mind that serve as the foundation for true deductive inferences in these sciences.

evidence for theism

The extraordinary education Mill received from his father did not include religious instruction. A rationalist and agnostic, James Mill passed on to his son his own negative attitude toward religion. He taught him that nothing can be known about the origin of the world, and that if there is a God he is certainly not the omnipotent and absolutely wise being described by orthodox religion. In his *Autobiography*, John Stuart writes:

> I am thus one of the very few examples, in this country, of one who has not thrown off religious belief, but never had it: I grew up in a negative state with regard to it. I looked upon the modern exactly as I did upon the ancient religion, as something which in no way concerned me.[50]

The advantage, in Mill's eyes, of this neutral position with regard to religion is that he can treat it "as a strictly scientific question," testing its assertions "by the same scientific methods and on the same principles as those of any of the speculative conclusions drawn by physical science." In short, God, like man and society, can be the object of scientific investigation. Convinced that the rules of scientific evidence are the only ones capable of yielding knowledge, he proposes "to consider what place there is for religious beliefs on the platform of science, what evidences they can appeal to, such as science can recognize, and what foundation there is for the doctrines of religion considered as scientific theorems."[51]

The only conception of God consistent with science, according to Mill, is monotheism. The prescientific, uncultivated mind tends to attribute the various phenomena of nature to a number of gods. Science, however, shows that the world is one connected system, one united whole governed by universal laws, so that if the scientifically trained man believes in God he is not likely to believe in more than one. And indeed, no scientific truth contradicts the notion that a creative will is at the origin of all natural phenomena. The question is: is there any evidence to prove the existence of such a will? Weighed in the scientific balance, what is the value of the customary proofs for the creation and government of nature by God?

At the outset Mill ruled out all *a priori* proofs for the existence of God. The *a priori* method, which "infers external objective facts from ideas or convictions of our mind" is unscientific. This eliminates at one stroke the Cartesian proof based on our idea of God and also the Kantian argument from the feeling of obligation or duty.

There remain the *a posteriori* proofs, all of which are scientific by their method according to Mill, but only one—the argument from design—has any real cogency. He rejects outright the argument for a first cause. If this proof were valid, he says, everything we know would have a cause of its existence. We could then argue that the world, the aggregate of all we know, has a cause to which it is indebted for its existence. But Mill insists that it is not a fact of experience that everything we know has a cause. We know two factors in nature, one permanent, the other changeable. The permanent factors, according to the current physics, are matter and force; the changeable ones are appearances or physical events. Now it is a matter of experience that every event is the effect of a previous event, but not that matter and force are caused by anything. Having no experience of their beginning to exist, we have no reason to think their existence was caused. Consequently:

> The phenomena or changes in the universe have indeed each of them a beginning and a cause, but their cause is always a prior change; nor do the analogies of experience give us any reason to expect, from the mere occurrence of changes, that if we could trace back the series far enough we should arrive at a primeval volition.[52]

Those who accept the argument for a first cause believe that we can delve beneath appearances to the essence and "true cause" of reality, "the cause which is not only followed by, but actually produces the effect." In other words, the validity of the first-cause argument presupposes the knowledge of ontological or efficient causes, and not simply that of phenomenal or physical ones; and, as we have seen, Mill does not think we are capable of this.[53]

The mere existence of the world, then, does not bear witness to God. Does the design we observe in nature point to him? Mill thought the argument from design, when properly stated, is truly scientific, conforming to the rules of inductive reasoning, but in his estimation its cogency is usually overrated. Paley, for one, put the case much too strongly with his example of the watch. Observing the similarity between products of nature and human art, Paley concluded that they have a similar cause, namely intelligence. If we found a watch on a lonely island, we would infer the presence of a human being. Now we find in nature things very similar to watches—for example, human eyes—which are even more ingeniously made than human artifacts. So we may infer that they too are products of an intelligence, and of one that is more than human.

The weakness in this analogy, according to Mill, is that we know by direct experience that watches are made by men, and it is this fact, rather than any indication of design in the watch, that leads us to infer the presence of human intelligence whenever we encounter one. We have no similar experience of the divine intelligence's production of nature.

To this weak analogy (which Mill does not consider to be a true inductive argument) he adds a real induction that considerably strengthens the ease for theism, while not settling it beyond all doubt.[54] There is no mere similarity between the works of human intelligence and the products of nature; there is a resemblance with respect to the special characteristic that we have learned from experience depends on an intelligence, namely ordination of parts to an end. The parts of the eye, for example, have in common the remarkable property of subserving vision. The particular combination of organic elements that we call an eye had, in each instance, a beginning in time, and therefore it had a cause. The number of instances in which this combination occurs is far greater than is required by inductive logic to exclude chance. Hence the rules of induction enable us to conclude that all the parts of the eye were brought together by a cause common to them all. Can we go further and infer that this is a *final* cause, that the combination of parts originates from an intelligent will? Mill does not think this conclusion is so certain. By 1868, when he was writing his essay on *Theism*, he was acquainted with the law of the survival of the fittest, proposed by Darwin in *The Origin of Species* (1859), and he thought this law might account for the wonderful mechanism of the eye and the fact of sight. Mill was obviously intrigued by the Darwinian hypothesis, but he was not inclined to accept it as the total explanation of design in nature. It is not inconsistent, he said, with the notion of creation, though it would greatly weaken the evidence for creation if it were proved true. He left it to the future to decide the question, concluding that for the present it is more probable that the contrivances in nature are due to a creative intelligence.

Granting design in the world and the probability of the existence of a designer-God, what can be known of his attributes? All the evidence points to his finite power. The presence of evil in the world and the use of means to an end imply limitation of power. If the designer of nature could achieve his end by his mere word, why use means? There is no reason to think that God created matter and force, the two great elements in the universe, but only that he introduced order into them. Clearly, Mill's God is closer to Plato's demiurge than to the creator of Christian tradition.[55]

Nothing in nature proves its author's omniscience. He must have more than human intelligence, hut his knowledge and skill need not be infinite. Nor is it necessary to think that his designs are always the best possible; indeed, we find many defects in nature.

Mill sees abundant evidence of God's benevolence. The designer of nature seems to desire the pleasure of his creatures, but his main purpose was not a moral one. He simply intended the limited duration of the world, with species and individuals. He wants "to keep the machine going," and pleasure was designed for this purpose. Pleasure results "from the normal working of the machinery"; pain appears to be accidental, the consequence of God's being hampered by the material he had to work with. As for divine justice, there is no indication of it in the universe.

Can man hope for a life after death? Mill did not think there is any scientific evidence either proving or disproving immortality. The usual argument against an afterlife is based on the admitted fact that mental operations depend on the working of the brain—a material, perishable organ. But Mill insists that feelings and thoughts are of an entirely different nature from matter, and hence the destruction of the latter may not entail that of the former. Mill is a phenomenalism holding that sensation, feeling, and thought are the only realities we directly know. What we call matter is something inferred from them; in Locke's words, it is "the permanent possibility of sensation." Because possibilities of sensation come and go, we are not warranted to conclude that our mind also does.[56]

While thus leaving open the possibility of an afterlife, Mill finds no evidence that there actually is one. We naturally tend to believe in a life after death, but this is because we desire to live forever. We do not like to give up existence, but there is no reason to think we must not. Nevertheless, there is no harm in hoping for immortality; on the contrary, this hope may be satisfying and useful in our lives. And there is some reason for hoping: have we not seen that there probably is a God who has great power over us and who is good? Mill did not go as far as William James, who asks us, in his *Will to Believe*, to believe beyond the evidence. Belief, for Mill, must always be rational, strictly based on evidence. But, anticipating James, he stressed the beneficial consequences of the notion of an afterlife, and at least held out hope that it is true.

Such are Mill's main religious positions. They are entirely within the bounds of natural religion, strictly controlled by rational evidence. He does not rule out the possibility of a divine revelation, but in his view the only possible evidence for such a revelation would be miracles, and, with Hume, he dismisses these as incredible. But even without a supernatural sanction, religion is still possible, for nature gives us some reason for thinking there is a God who, though finite in power and knowledge, is the organizer and governor of the world. A great admirer of Auguste Comte and his religion of humanity, Mill was nevertheless critical of his hasty rejection of theism. In his early years Mill was entirely in agreement with Comte's project to eliminate God from religion and to establish a positivist religion of humanity.[57] In later life, however, he inclined to the view that Comte's program is neither theoretically nor practically sound.[58] Given the present state of science and society, we cannot rule out the possibility of the existence of God or deny the utility of theism for the betterment of humanity. Whatever the future may bring, Mill was convinced that in his own day his views on God were "excellently fitted to aid and fortify that real, though purely human, religion which sometimes calls itself the Religion of Humanity and sometimes that of Duty." To a religious devotion to the cause of mankind, theism "superadds the feeling that in making this the rule of our life we may be co-operating with the unseen Being to whom we owe all that is enjoyable in life."[59]

Bentham and Mill did not hold academic positions; they propagated utilitarianism not through university lectures but through private discussions and their numerous writings. Utilitarianism came to the universities and received academic recognition through Mill's disciples, the chief of whom was Alexander Bain.

A Scotsman like Mill, Bain taught natural philosophy at the University of Glasgow from 1845, and logic at the University of Aberdeen from 1860 to 1880.[60] In these universities he challenged the declining Scottish school of philosophy with his empiricism and utilitarianism. He collaborated with Mill in the writing of his *Logic*, wrote a logic book of his own, and several influential works in psychology. Bain is chiefly known for his work in psychology. While adopting the associationist psychology of Hartley and the two Mills, he considerably modified it by stressing the active role of the emotions and will in mental formation and in the psychic processes. Not content with the older explanation of mental life as the result of a passive, mechanical association of sensations and ideas, he insisted on the activity and spontaneity of the mind. Through the influence of the German school of physiology he used physiological data as an approach to the study of the mind—an approach criticized by J. S. Mill. Thus Bain was the initiator of physiological psychology in England.

Less closely associated with the utilitarian school was Henry Sidgwick, professor of moral philosophy at Cambridge.[61] His best-known work, *Methods of Ethics*, divides ethical systems into egoistic hedonism, universalistic hedonism or utilitarianism, and intuitionism. Rejecting the first, he tries to work out a synthesis of the latter two. The weakness of Mill's system, he says, is its attempt to establish what men ought to desire from what they actually do desire. From the fact that men actually desire pleasure alone it cannot be shown that the general happiness of mankind is desirable, in the sense of "ought to be desired." Anticipating G. E. Moore's criticism of Mill, Sidgwick pointed out the confusion in the utilitarian's use of the word "desirable"; it sometimes means "ought to be desired," sometimes "can be desired."[62] Sidgwick found a surer basis for the greatest happiness principle in intuitionism—which was Mill's *bête noire*. This system grounds ethical principles on rational intuitions or insights rather than on empirical inductions. According to Sidgwick, the principle that I ought to pursue the happiness of all men, not only my own, is guaranteed by an intuition whose clarity and certainty are as great as those of the axioms of mathematics. Sidgwick was here consciously returning to the earlier intuitional school of English ethics, particularly as represented by Clarke, and he was opening utilitarianism to the influence of Kant and the German idealists—the very men whose ethical ideas, as embodied in the systems of Green and Bradley, were to bring about the collapse of utilitarianism at the end of the century.

XVII.

Philosophy of Evolution

THE appearance of Charles Darwin's *The Origin of Species* in 1859 was a momentous event in the history of science and of philosophy. His biological theory of natural selection revolutionized the scientific view of nature as radically as did Newton's physics in the seventeenth century, and it effected a comparable upheaval in philosophy. As Josiah Royce said, "With the one exception of Newton's 'Principia,' no single book of empirical science has ever been of more importance to philosophy than this work of Darwin."[1] Darwin himself foresaw the repercussions his theory of evolution would have on philosophy. One of his early notebooks contains the prophetic statement that it would affect the whole of metaphysics.[2]

The revolution in ideas for which Darwin, among all the nineteenth-century evolutionists, was primarily responsible is best seen against the background of the conception of natural history that prevailed in the seventeenth and eighteenth centuries. This conception was well formulated by John Ray (1627–1705), English naturalist and theologian, and one of the founders of systematic natural history. According to Ray, "the number of true species in nature is fixed and limited and, as we may reasonably believe, constant and unchangeable from the first creation to the present day."[3] He offered this not only as the conclusion of science but also as the general opinion of the philosophers and the teaching of Scripture. Did not God finish his works of creation in six days; and what does this mean except that he completed the number of species for all time? The naturalist, then, does not have to discover the origin of species; this raises no scientific problem for him. He has but to describe and classify them. Neither does the naturalist have to explain the structures and properties of natural species by means of natural causes. These can be accounted for by the purposes God had intended them to serve when he created them. Everywhere in nature structure is adapted to function (the eye, for example, has been created for seeing), which is a clear proof of God's wisdom and providence.

The Swedish naturalist Carolus Linnaeus (1707–1778) gave classical expression to the immutability of species in his famous dictum: "The number of species is the same as the number of forms created from the beginning." This assumption underlies his natural method of classifying species. He was forced to retract his dictum when confronted with evidence that a hybrid form could reproduce itself. He then made the momentous concession that "it is possible for new species to rise within the plant world."[4] Species, in short, are "the daughters of time."

This concession played into the hands of the Comte de Buffon (1707–1788), who challenged the Linnaean natural method of classification. Buffon, whom Darwin calls "the first author who in modern times has treated [evolution] in a scientific spirit,"[5] saw no absolute boundaries between species or even a definite line separating the animal from the vegetable kingdoms. He wrote that "the Creator's hand seems not to have been opened in order to give existence to a determinate number of species, rather it seems to have thrown forth at one and the same time a world of creatures related and unrelated, an infinity of harmonious and contrary combinations, a perpetuity of destructions and renewals."[6] Buffon also criticized the appeal to final causes in natural science. The naturalist, he says, should not ascribe the habits and mechanisms by which birds build their nests to the design of the creator; he should assume "that they depend, like every other animal operation, on number, figure, motion, organization, and feeling." Indeed, we cannot be sure that every structure or character in nature has some utility for man or for other creatures.

By the end of the eighteenth century the idea of organic evolution was gaining in popularity, bolstered by the accumulation of more and more scientific evidence. Darwin's grandfather, Erasmus Darwin (1731–1802), put forward evolutionary suggestions, anticipating Lamarck's notion that an animal's organs have been shaped through their use and disuse in adapting itself to its environment, and also his grandson's doctrine of natural selection. Jean Baptiste Lamarck (1744–1829), the most important figure in the history of evolution before Charles Darwin, saw life as possessing an inner perfecting principle or drive, constantly assuming forms of greater complexity and ascending to higher levels. Thus evolution accomplishes an immanent purpose to perfect creation.

Charles Darwin

Darwin at first held the traditional view that species are unchangeable, but on his return from the scientific expedition on the Beagle in 1836 he began to change his mind on the matter.[7] "At last gleams of light have come," he wrote to a friend, "and I am almost convinced (quite contrary to the opinion I started with) that species are not (it is like confessing a murder) immutable."[8] The initial stimulus for his theory of organic evolution of species by natural selection came from his reading Malthus' *An Essay on the Principles of Population*. Malthus theorized that living beings reproduce at a geometric rate, outstripping the increase in food production, with the result that there is a constant struggle for existence. It struck Darwin that under these circumstances organisms with favorable variations would tend to be preserved while those with unfavorable ones would be destroyed. The result would be the formation of new species. This is the gist of the Darwinian theory of evolution through natural selection—a theory that he presented so forcefully and for which he marshaled such a wealth of evidence that on the whole he convinced the scientific world.

We are not here concerned with Darwinism as a scientific theory, or with the controversy over its scientific merits that broke out immediately and has lasted to our own day.[9] What is of interest to us are the philosophical implications Darwin saw in his theory. He made no pretension to be a philosopher or to have given much systematic thought to problems of religion and morals, but occasionally and somewhat reluctantly he spoke out on these subjects. These statements are part of the legacy of Darwin and they influenced the course of subsequent philosophy.

When Darwin was writing *The Origin of Species* he was strongly convinced of the existence of God as the author of nature. It is extremely difficult, or rather impossible, he wrote in his *Autobiography*, to conceive of the immense and wonderful universe as the result of blind chance or necessity. He felt compelled to look to a first cause, with an intelligence analogous to that of man, to account for the order in the universe. As time went on, however, this conviction grew weaker in him. If, as he fully believed, the mind of man developed from a mind as low as that of the most insignificant animal, how can it be trusted when it draws such lofty conclusions? "I cannot pretend," he concludes, "to throw the least light on such abstruse problems. The mystery of the beginning of all things is insoluble by us, and I for one must be content to remain an Agnostic."[10]

The fact was that, with the establishment of natural selection as the main agency of evolution, Darwin felt that there was no longer any need of God as the designer of the universe. If a divine intelligence were directing the course of evolution, causing the variations in form and structure that give rise to new species, what reason would there be for natural selection? Natural selection is the law according to which organisms develop their specific forms; to posit an agency outside this law, Darwin wrote to his friend Lyell, an intelligent cause that preconceives and ordains its results is a bit of "theological pedantry." Only in its theological phase of development could biology find room for an extra-scientific principle of design in the universe. Now that the scientific law of evolution is known, the notion of a designer-God is superfluous.[11]

In Darwin's view this undermines William Paley's argument for the existence of God based on design in nature.[12] In his *Natural Theology* (1802) Paley argued that if we found a watch on the ground, we would have to admit that it was made by an intelligent being, for we see that its parts have been constructed and put together for the purpose of telling time. Purpose and design can be accounted for only by an intelligence. Even if the watch were produced by another watch, and that by another *ad infinitum*, a designing mind would still be needed to explain the purpose exhibited by the watch. Now nature manifests even more wonderful design than works of art, as is evident in the case of the eye. The parts of the eye, like those of a telescope, serve a specific purpose. There must, then, be an intelligent creator of nature. We cannot admit that a "principle of order" acting blindly and without choice can account for the order in nature. Order is the adaptation of means to an end, and we have no experience of an unintelligent principle producing such an adaptation. Hence we are forced to conclude that there is an intelligent creator of the order of nature.

This argument resembles in some respects the traditional Greek and medieval Christian approaches to God through the order and providential governance of the world. It is significantly different from them, however, in that it is set in the narrow framework of modern classical mechanism. Paley did not offer a metaphysical proof of the existence of God, as this was understood in pre-Newtonian days, but a "physico-theological argument." On the strength of the analogy of the watchmaker and his watch he argued that the living "mechanisms" in nature have been designed by a supreme intelligence. This presupposes that the species of plants and animals have designs in the narrow sense in which a watch has one; moreover, that these species are fixed and invariable both in their structures and functions, and that as a consequence they have special and final purposes that can be discovered by us.

In this form the argument is vulnerable to Darwin's criticism. In the light of his theory of natural selection the universe is not static or closed; living beings are not fixed and invariable in their structures and activities but constantly changing and developing in their struggle for existence. Hence they cannot be said to have purposes fixed for all time. So there is no need to assume that they have been specially created for such purposes. They can be explained genetically by the laws of natural selection and adaptation to environment. Darwin concludes in his *Autobiography*:

> The old argument from design in Nature, as given by Paley, which formerly seemed to me so conclusive, fails, now that the law of natural selection has been discovered. We can no longer argue that, for instance, the beautiful hinge of a bivalve shell must have been made by an intelligent being, like the hinge of a door by man. There seems to be no more design in the variability of organic beings, and in the action of natural selection, than in the course which the wind blows.[13]

This conclusion was distressing to Darwin. He confessed that he was not content to view this wonderful universe as the result of brute force. He had no intention "to write atheistically." Law rules "the machine of the world," and this would seem to imply a lawgiver. But he was loath to accept a God who would impose on nature the law of natural selection, with its wasteful proliferation of random variations, its ruthless elimination of the unfit, and its immense suffering. Unable to make his way out of this dilemma, he lapsed into agnosticism in his later years.

Scientists from Darwin's day to our own have protested that the theory of evolution does not eliminate from nature design or purpose in every sense of the word. Thus his friend Asa Gray commented that, while rejecting the idea of design, Darwin was constantly bringing out the neatest illustrations of it.[14] Even the agnostic Thomas Huxley, who agreed with Darwin that he could find no evidence of purpose in nature, conceded that evolution is compatible with a wider notion of teleology than that known to the pre-evolutionists. He wrote:

> The teleology which supposes that the eye, such as we see it in man, or one of the higher vertebrata, was made with the precise structure it exhibits, for the purpose of enabling the animal which possesses it to see, has undoubtedly received its death blow. Nevertheless, it is necessary to remember that there is a wider teleology which is not touched by the doctrine of Evolution, but is actually based upon the fundamental proposition of Evolution. This proposition is that the whole world, living and not living, is the result of the mutual interaction, according to definite laws, of the forces possessed by the molecules of which the primitive nebulosity of the universe was composed.[15]

According to this broader teleological view, "the original plan of the universe was sketched out…the purpose was foreshadowed in the molecular arrangements out of which the animals have come." Thus, while the scientists were adding to the data of the question whether there is design and purpose in nature, they were not answering it definitively. And this is only as it should be, for the question is more properly religious and philosophical than scientific.

Regarding the immortality of the human soul, Darwin had no settled convictions. But he acknowledged the strength and quasi-instinctiveness of the belief, adding that it has acquired new force from the almost unanimous opinion of scientists that the sun and planets will eventually grow too cold for life. "Believing as I do," he continues, "that man in the distant future will be a far more perfect creature than he now is, it is an intolerable thought that he and all other sentient beings are doomed to complete annihilation after such long-continued slow progress. To those who fully admit the immortality of the human soul, the destruction of our world will not appear so dreadful."[16]

In his *Descent of Man* Darwin devotes several chapters to the evolution of man's intellectual and moral powers, thus contributing to evolutionary ethics and to the budding social science of the nineteenth century. He proposes that natural selection is the main agency of the development not only of man's physical structure but also of his intellectual and moral powers. He sees no fundamental difference between the mental faculties of man and those of the higher mammals.[17] These differ only in degree, and their improvement is due mainly to natural selection. The most intellectual individuals and tribes tend to survive, and thus the intellect of the human species gradually improves. And as man's intellectual powers develop, so too do his social instincts. Living with others, he takes pleasure in their company, feels sympathy for them, and wants to perform services for them. Thus he acquires a moral sense or conscience, which Darwin regards as the most important difference between man and the lower animals. With Kant, he calls man's sense of duty his most noble attribute. The moral sense is the feeling of shame and remorse at choosing to act for self-interest rather than for the good of the group. Once this moral sense arose in man's primitive ancestors it developed by natural selection, the tribe with the greater spirit of patriotism, obedience, courage, and sympathy proving victorious over others. Hence, by the elimination of the less fit "the standard of morality and the number of well-endowed men...everywhere tend to rise and increase."[18]

While emphasizing the role of natural selection in the social progress of primitive peoples, Darwin recognizes that in civilized countries the process of the elimination of the unfit has been checked by the humane treatment of the sick, poor, and insane. The weak members of civilized societies are allowed to propagate their kind, though "this must be highly injurious to the race of man." Far from deploring this humanitarianism, however, Darwin sees it as evidence of a "higher morality," whose golden rule is: "As ye would that men should do to you, do ye to them likewise."[19] He does not reconcile this Christian precept with the harsh morality of natural selection, nor does he seem to feel the need to do so. He leaves us with the contradiction of a "higher morality" that in its humanitarian tendencies partially supplants the natural law of the survival of the fittest and to that extent does not conduce to man's benefit.

Darwin takes issue with the utilitarianism of J. S. Mill for holding that the "greatest happiness principle" is the foundation of morality. According to Darwin, it is only a secondary guide to conduct. Men do not always act with a consciousness of pleasure; they often act impulsively, from instinct or long habit. The general good is not happiness or pleasure but "the rearing of the greatest number of individuals in full vigor and health, with all their faculties perfect, under the conditions to which they are subjected." Hence "the general good or welfare of the community, rather than the general happiness," is the standard of morality.[20]

Herbert Spencer

Spencer is noteworthy as the first English philosopher who systematically exploited the evolutionary ideas in biology that were growing in popularity in the mid-nineteenth century.[21] Philosophy was now joining hands with the sciences of living beings—an event that was to prove as momentous for its development as was its marriage with mathematics and physics in the days of Descartes and Newton. Unfortunately Spencer, the minister of this new union in England, was not of the philosophical caliber of Descartes, Leibniz, or Kant; but greater philosophers of evolution, notably A. N. Whitehead, Samuel Alexander, and Henri Bergson, were on the horizon.

Spencer received a formal education in neither science nor philosophy; largely self-taught, he boldly ventured into both of these fields and produced a well-knit system which he expounded in his ten volumes of *Synthetic Philosophy*.

From his earliest writings the notion of evolution and progress dominated his thought. Even before the publication of Darwin's *The Origin of Species* he was an evolutionist, having been won over to the Lamarckian idea that organisms evolve by striving to adapt themselves to their environment and by passing on the modifications in their structures to their progeny. Through Schelling he came to envisage the evolution of life as a movement of ever-increasing differentiation, organization, and individualization. The German embryologist K. E. von Baer confirmed him in this view by his law that an organism while developing passes from a state of homogeneity to one of heterogeneity. Like Darwin he reflected on the Malthusian theory of population and concluded that mankind was undergoing a "struggle for existence," resulting in "the survival of the fittest"—phrases of his coinage that have often been used to sum up Darwin's conception of evolution. It was Darwin, however, and not Spencer who formulated the theory of natural selection.

While Spencer read and drew upon all the evolutionary literature of his day, he was not primarily concerned with the scientific hypothesis of organic evolution. His ambition was far greater than Lamarck's or Darwin's; he was looking for a philosophical law of evolution that would explain alike the genesis of the inorganic and organic world. In other words, he aimed to establish a philosophy of evolution. Such a philosophy, in his view, would unify a great number of facts discovered in the sciences, and it would lay down the first principles from which they could be deduced. Thus it would fulfill the role of all philosophy, which is to unify the data of the special sciences. Knowledge progresses by becoming more general and more unified. The lowest kind of knowledge is un-unified knowledge of particular facts. Science is partially unified knowledge, its highest branches achieving the widest generalizations that embrace the narrower truths of the more special sciences. Philosophy is completely unified knowledge. Its truths are the most universal of all and they comprehend and consolidate the widest generalizations of the sciences.[22] Nothing short of this most general philosophical knowledge would content Spencer. Beyond the data of the sciences he sought the law governing the development of the whole universe and all its parts, and beyond this he aimed to discover the first principles from which this law could be deduced.

An ambitious project indeed! But Spencer felt that he could carry it through because to him the universe, for all its complexity, consisted of nothing but matter and motion or force. Even ideas and feelings are forms of force, which can be transformed into physical force, and vice versa. The universe, as Newton saw, is a vast machine whose workings are thoroughly determined by law. What has been added since Newton's day is the awareness of the all-pervasiveness of evolution and change in the universe. Why should it not be possible, within the mechanistic framework, to discover the general law according to which all evolution and change take place, changes alike in the inorganic and organic realms?

In his first book, *Social Statics* (1850), Spencer made his initial attempt to state the principle of organic evolution, or, as he then preferred to say, of progress. The development of an individual organism was described as consisting in an advance from simplicity to complexity, and from independent like parts to mutually unlike parts. This formula was then extended to the evolution or progress of civilization, which Spencer conceived as a natural and necessary fact. "Progress, therefore, is not an accident," he wrote optimistically, "but a necessity. Instead of civilization being artificial, it is a part of nature; all of a piece with the development of the embryo or the unfolding of a flower. The modifications mankind have undergone, and are still undergoing, result from a law underlying the whole organic creation; and provided the human race continues, and the constitution of things remains the same, those modifications must end in completeness...so surely must man become perfect."[23]

A more abstract formula was needed, however, if the law of evolution was to be extended to inorganic phenomena, such as the development of the solar system and the earth. Spencer thought he had found this in von Baer's statement of the progress of an organism from a homogeneous to a heterogeneous state. In an essay of 1857 entitled "Progress: Its Law and Cause" this becomes the very essence of evolution. In its primary stage life is a uniform substance; later it exhibits differentiation, with contrast of parts and functions. Organic progress, then, "consists in a change from the homogeneous to the heterogeneous." Moreover, this law of organic progress is the law of all progress. In the development of the solar system, of the earth, of life on its surface, of society, government, tools, commerce, language, literature, science, and art, "this same evolution of the simple into the complex, through successive differentiations, holds throughout."[24] Spencer insisted that the current conception of progress as consisting of changes that increase human happiness is largely erroneous. This is a teleological notion of progress; it concerns progress insofar as it bears upon our happiness, without telling us what it is in itself. It gives us the shadow without the substance, the accompaniments without the reality.

All of these notions reappear in Spencer's definitive treatment of evolution in his *First Principles*, the first volume of his *Synthetic Philosophy*. In this work, however, change from the homogeneous to the heterogeneous is no longer considered to be the essence of evolution but only one of its secondary characteristics. Its primary features are found in the behavior of matter and motion, the basic constituents of the universe. Matter tends to become integrated or pressed together more compactly. Motion, on the other hand, tends to become dissipated or scattered. Spencer found an illustration of this ready to hand in the nebular hypothesis, which postulates that the matter of the solar system was once uniformly scattered but later was contracted to form compact spheres. In the course of integration the original motion of the nebulous mass was dissipated as heat. As a result of this transformation the sun and its planets became heterogeneous, coherent, and definite bodies. Development in every order of reality, from the lowest to the highest, from the formation of the earth to the growth of human language and religious art, follows the same pattern and moves in the same direction of increasing heterogeneity, coherence, and definiteness. Thus the law of evolution can be formulated as follows: "Evolution is an integration of matter and concomitant dissipation of motion; during which the matter passes from a [relatively] indefinite, incoherent homogeneity to a [relatively] definite, coherent heterogeneity; and during which the retained motion undergoes a parallel transformation."[25]

This empirical generalization, arrived at by induction, is not the end of Spencer's quest. We still do not know why all classes of phenomena evolve according to this law, or how the various characteristics of the evolutionary process are connected with each other. Until we reach a deeper law, an underlying philosophical principle from which the law of evolution can be deduced and which unites all of its constituent truths, we fall short of the completely unified knowledge that constitutes philosophy.

This philosophical principle Spencer called "the persistence of force." By this he meant that force (which he conceived as the most ultimate phenomenon, underlying even the phenomena of matter and motion) remains unalterable in quantity. Thus it is a philosophical counterpart of the scientific hypothesis of the conservation of energy. As the ultimate principle, the persistence of force cannot be demonstrated; it can only be assumed as the most fundamental and general truth implied in all experience. From this single primary law Spencer thought he could deduce all the phenomena of process and evolution, and thus show their necessity "down to the accelerated fall of a stone or the recurrent beat of a harp-string."[26]

We cannot here follow all the steps of Spencer's complicated deduction. Let it suffice to indicate how he derives from the law of the persistence of force the tendency in evolution toward increasing heterogeneity. A homogeneous body, he argues, necessarily tends to lose its homogeneity when it is acted on by a force. This is because a force produces different changes throughout a uniform mass owing to the fact that the parts of the mass stand in different relations to the force. For example, if a bar of iron is struck, the blow has a different effect on its different parts. Moreover, if the parts of a homogeneous aggregate are exposed to different forces, they are of necessity differently modified. Thus a species will not remain uniform but it will tend to take on different forms by being exposed to different environments. This shows that homogeneity is not a stable condition; heterogeneity is bound to result from the application of force. And once heterogeneity has set in, other characteristics of evolution necessarily follow. External forces will act similarly on similar parts and differently on different parts. Segregation will follow, similar parts tending to gather together in one place and unlike parts tending to be separated out. Differentiation, integration, and definiteness also appear as a result of the segregation of parts.

Will these changes go on forever? Will nature evolve, increasing in heterogeneity, differentiation, and integration, world without end? Spencer thinks that evolution in this direction is not an infinite process. After a time a state of equilibrium is reached, as we see in the case of our solar system, in the lives of animals and men, and in the development of a civilization. After a period of stability, dissolution sets in, in which we observe changes that are the direct opposite to those characteristic of evolution. But dissolution and death are not ultimate; there is no universal death. After dissolution evolution recommences. Thus the universe is in perpetual flux, passing from evolution to equilibrium to dissolution, and from dissolution again to evolution.[27]

All this Spencer regarded as not only inductively established but also as demonstrable by deduction from the principle of the persistence of force. This principle is given as the necessary reason for the phenomena of evolution. We should not suppose, however, that we can fathom the *real* cause of evolution. Our knowledge remains on the level of phenomena, without reaching reality itself. The nature and origin of the laws of evolution are a mystery forever transcending the human mind.

The scientist, philosopher, and religious thinker, each in his own way comes face to face with this mystery of an unknowable reality underlying knowable phenomena. The scientist groups phenomena under laws of ever-increasing generality, but he finally reaches a limit beyond which he cannot go. Thus Newton explained the movements of the planets by the law of gravitation, which is within our mental grasp. But as he himself confessed, we cannot comprehend the real force of gravitation; this remains a mystery. So it is with all scientific generalizations: they inevitably merge into the inconceivable and unknowable.[28] The philosopher, for his part, agrees with common sense that there is a reality beneath appearances, a reality that is unknowable in itself. He proves, moreover, that there exists an Absolute or Unconditioned Reality by showing that it is presupposed by our knowledge of the relative, conditioned, and phenomenal.[29] So the philosopher is certain of the existence of an ultimate reality or God, though he must acknowledge that its nature is unknowable. To Spencer, however, it is not quite as unknowable as Kant's noumenon. The Absolute manifests itself to us in everything we know, but especially in the idea of force, which, as we have seen, is the most basic of all notions. The Absolute can be described as a force that remains constant throughout all the changes in the evolving universe, a power unlimited by time or space. This same infinite power, transcending knowledge, is the primary object of religious belief. It is clear, then, that science, philosophy, and religion recognize the existence of an unknowable power or force lying beyond appearances, and in this common recognition they are harmonized and reconciled.[30]

evolutionary ethics

Spencer's philosophical system culminates in an ethics in which he applies his evolutionary laws to the problems of human conduct. He hoped in this way to secularize ethics, showing that moral laws can be established on a purely natural basis without an appeal to supernatural authority. At the same time he intended to make ethics scientific by determining the general laws governing the behavior of men both as individuals and as members of society.

If there has been an evolution of structures and functions throughout the ascending scale of animal life, there must also have been an evolution of human conduct, that is to say, of purposive acts about which we make moral judgments. In the lower forms of life many actions are done at random, without conscious pursuit of an end. During the course of evolution the distinction between purposeless and purposeful acts arose by degrees. Animals, and finally men, came to determine their acts more consciously with reference to objects to be pursued or escaped. Those better equipped to adjust their acts to ends were able to survive longer, "which constitutes the supreme end."

The evolution of conduct, however, does not only bring with it a better adjustment of acts to ends so as to prolong life; it also increases the amount of life, or the sum of vital activities of an individual. In short, it augments the life of the individual both in its length and breadth. "Each further evolution of conduct widens the aggregate of actions while conducing to elongation of it."[31] At the same time evolution extends the life of the species in both of these directions, for example by improving the care and discipline of offspring.

Conduct is not completely evolved when there is a perfect adjustment of acts to ends subserving individual life and the rearing of offspring. Generally when one individual successfully adjusts itself in these respects it causes other individuals of the same species or of a different species to be ill-adjusted. Individuals and groups constantly interfere with each other in the struggle for existence. Competition prevents the prolongation and heightening of life for all members of a species or for all species.

Conduct that if perfectly evolved is such that adjustments of acts to ends by some does not necessitate non-adjustments by others. Thus the predatory life of savages is imperfectly evolved, since it fosters antagonisms between members of the same group and between different groups. Conduct can reach the limit of evolution only in permanently peaceful societies. Only as war decreases and dies out can there be perfect adjustment of some that does not hinder perfect adjustment of others. Beyond this, further advance is possible by the members of a society giving mutual aid in adjusting their acts to ends.[32]

This evolutionary view of conduct enabled Spencer to answer the age-old problem of what constitutes a good or bad act. An act is good to the degree that it is evolved, bad to the degree that it is not evolved. A perfectly evolved act is one that is well-adjusted to prolong and enrich life in the individual, in his offspring, and in his fellowmen. An act that is low in the evolutionary scale (and to that extent bad) is one that tends to diminish or destroy life in these three classes.[33]

This assumes that life is worth living; that evolution is not a mistake but a blessing. And this in turn rests on the assumption that life on the whole brings more pleasure than pain. If life in the main resulted in more pain than pleasure, no one would call it good. Pleasure, then, is the ultimate good; it is that which makes life good and makes the conduct conducive to life good. Thus in the end Spencer's evolutionary ethics joins the hedonism and utilitarianism of Bentham and Mill. Like them he maintained that conduct is good or bad according as its aggregate results, to self or others or both, are pleasurable or painful.[34]

The remarkable feature of Spencer's ethics, however, is not its hedonism or utilitarianism; it is the notion that man's moral nature and conscience are products of organic evolution, and that moral progress is an extension of cosmic and organic progress and is subject to the same inexorable law. The law of progress is everywhere the same and binds everything with the same necessity. Inscribed in the very structure of things, "Progress is not an accident, not a thing within human control, but a beneficent necessity."[35] We could not wish for a better expression of the nineteenth-century myth of inevitable progress, a myth that was shaken only by the catastrophe of the First World War.

The progress of society (which Spencer called super-organic evolution) follows the general rules of evolution in the biological realm. Just as the struggle for existence is necessary in this realm to insure the survival of the fittest, so competition among individuals and races is required to develop mankind. It is hardly surprising to see Spencer adopt Adam Smith's *laissez faire* policy in economics and politics; free enterprise, without interference from the government, should bring the greatest benefit to the state. The progress of humanity depends on the stern law of the elimination of the unfit, on "a continuous overrunning of the less powerful or less adapted by the more powerful or more adapted, a driving of inferior varieties into undesirable habitats, and, occasionally, an extermination of inferior varieties."[36] As we have seen, Darwin drew the same harsh conclusion from his theory of natural selection. For Spencer as for Darwin, man's intellectual and moral powers are improved by competition and by the extermination of the less intellectual and moral races.

If this is true, is not the law of the jungle the highest moral code for man? Is not ruthless competition, unbridled individualism, elimination of the weak and unfit the best means of social progress? To Thomas Huxley this is the logical outcome of an ethics based on evolution, and precisely for this reason he rejected such an ethics out of hand. After passing through a Spencerian stage, he came to deplore the adoption of the struggle for existence as the model for social progress. "Social progress," he declares, "means a checking of the cosmic process at every step and the substitution for it of another, which may be called the ethical process; the end of which is not the survival of those who may happen to be the fittest...but of those who are ethically the best.... The ethical progress of society depends, not on imitating the cosmic process, still less in running away from it, but in combating it."[37] And indeed Spencer himself was repelled by the harsher implications of applying natural selection to ethics. Like Darwin, he believed that, although social progress in the barbaric past resulted from the struggle for survival, in the future it would be achieved by "the quiet pressure of a spreading industrial civilization on a barbarism which slowly dwindles."[38]

Emergent Evolutionists

Spencer's evolutionary philosophy enjoyed an immediate popularity in England and America—a sure sign that it was a congenial expression of the spirit of the time. The nineteenth century believed in the inevitability of progress through the working out of the laws of nature and society. Spencer gave voice to this conviction by his notion of evolution as an impersonal process rigidly controlled by law and automatically leading to higher stages of existence. He attempted to deduce evolution from the mechanical principle of the persistence of force; even life, the human mind, and society were in his view the inevitable results of the interaction of cosmic forces. Man is not a free, active, controlling agent in nature, but a passive product of his environment.

Some of the first and most stringent critics of the Spencerian attitude toward evolution were the American pragmatists.[39] Like Spencer, they were profoundly influenced by Darwinism, but they could not accept his mechanistic and deterministic evolutionary system. To Chauncey Wright, one of the founders of pragmatism, Spencer was but a second-rate metaphysician who presumed to know ultimate truths and who wasted his time with useless abstractions. Had he been a true positivist, Wright claimed, he would have realized that scientific laws are the result of induction and consequently that they are only probable. Under these circumstances it is impossible to predict all future events from their antecedents; "accidents" or novelties can arise, such as self-consciousness or the use of the voice in social communication. C. S. Peirce, another member of the Pragmatist circle, maintained that to a consistent evolutionist the laws of nature themselves are the result of evolution and hence they are not absolute but limited. In opposition to Spencer he argued that there exists "an element of indeterminancy, spontaneity, or absolute chance in nature."[40] Although at first a great admirer of Spencer, William James, like Peirce, came to loath his finished, deterministic philosophy which was closed to all true novelty and left no room for human effort in the bettering of life.

The most powerful attack on Spencerian evolutionism, however, came from Bergson. After some years of strong attraction to Spencer's system, Bergson rejected it as an attempt to understand the past by appealing to concepts and laws of the present, which are themselves products of evolution. Spencer imagined that the same laws held in prehistoric times as today, and thus he tried to reconstruct evolution with fragments of its product. To "the false evolutionism of Spencer"—which consists in cutting up present reality, already evolved, into little bits no less evolved, and then recomposing it with these fragments, thus positing in advance everything that is to be explained, Bergson opposed "a true evolutionism, in which reality would be followed in its generation and its growth."[41] This is the Bergsonian "creative evolution," according to which life is inventive and unpredictable spawning new forms in its evolutionary advance that were not eternally foreordained to appear.

Bergson's doctrine of creative evolution has already been treated in Part II of the present volume of the *History of Philosophy*. These few remarks about it are necessary to provide the background for the emergent evolution of the English philosophers Lloyd Morgan and Samuel Alexander. Inspired by Bergson, they reacted similarly to his mechanistic theory of evolution, stressing the element of novelty in the evolutionary process.

lloyd morgan

Morgan was well qualified to speak out on the subject of evolution.[42] After studying biology under Thomas Huxley, he engaged in scientific research and made valuable contributions to animal psychology. In later life he gave full scope to his interest in philosophy, developing a phenomenalist theory of knowledge and a natural philosophy in which evolution plays a central role.

The term "evolution" is ambiguous in Morgan's opinion. In the older sense it meant the unfolding of what was already contained in nature, the simple appearance of what before was hidden from view. In the newer sense of the term (which Morgan accepted as his own) "evolution" means the coming into existence of something genuinely new. This novelty is no mere "resultant" or product of antecedent forces in nature, calculable before the event, as Huxley claimed. It is an "emergent," unpredictable before its actual occurrence.[43] Morgan did not deny the presence of resultants in evolution, but he insisted that evolution is not constituted solely of them; there are also emergents. Resultants account for the continuity in the evolutionary development, emergents for its creative advance.

According to Morgan, the evolutionary development of nature takes place by stages or leaps, new qualities and relations springing up that cannot be anticipated from previous ones. Critical turning-points are reached in the ascending course of events, when new qualities emerge that are inexplicable by the naturalists. The quality of life appeared at a critical stage of the organization of matter; mentality or mind supervened at a definite point in the evolutionary advance of organisms. What the naturalist describes as a new emergent quality can also be viewed as a new system of relations in nature. The term "life" signifies the totality of vital events, and in vital events there is a new system of relations not found in physico-chemical events. Similarly, there is a new system of relations in mental events not found in vital events. The very substance and integral unity of events on any level are determined by the kind of systematic relations that obtain in them. The universe can be described as a four-dimensional space-time system of relations, with three main stages in its evolutionary development: matter, life, and mind.

In Morgan's view this is as far as a purely scientific and naturalistic investigation of evolution can go. Physics does not ask questions about the primal cause of evolution; by its very nature it is agnostic. As a metaphysician, however, Morgan finds it necessary to assume the existence of a divine author of the evolutionary process. The whole creative advance of nature points to a spiritual and personal God who reveals himself progressively in its ascending stages.

samuel alexander

Alexander was less a scientist than his colleague Lloyd Morgan, but he was more a philosopher.[44] With him, emergent evolution reaches the status of a comprehensive metaphysical system. This system keeps close contact with the empirical sciences, making use of the biological doctrine of evolution and the concept of space-time, currently developed in relativity theory. But this is not to be wondered at, for according to Alexander metaphysics is itself a science, different from the other sciences not so much in its method as in the comprehensiveness of its subject matter. Like Spencer, he regarded philosophy as a generalization of the particular sciences. Its subject matter is the totality of the universe seen in its pervasive features, such as space, time, and the categories.

The biological doctrine of evolution brought to philosophy a new awareness of the importance of time for an understanding of reality. The temporal dimension of the universe was given scant attention by the absolute idealists Bradley and McTaggart. For them time is not real but merely an appearance. Protesting against the depreciation of time by philosophers Bergson insisted that concrete time is the very stuff of our lives, and that time cannot be interpreted in spatial terms. Alexander also took time seriously; but in opposition to Bergson he found time unreal apart from space. According to him, it is not time that is the stuff of the universe but the combination of space-time. Taken separately time and space are mere abstractions. In the concrete they are so interwoven and interdependent that one is unintelligible without the other. All space is temporal and all time is spatial. There is no moment of time that does not include a point of space, and no point of space occurs except at a definite moment of time. Consequently, there are no such things as points of space or moments of time in themselves; there are only "point-instants" which make up a continuum of space-time.

There is a certain resemblance between this doctrine and the relativity theory of Minkowski and Einstein, which makes time a fourth dimension. With relativity theory, mathematical physics advanced to the state where, to use Minkowski's words, "From henceforth space in itself and time in itself sink to mere shadows, and only a kind of union of the two preserves an independent existence."[45] But whatever inspiration Alexander may have derived from current mathematical and physical theories, his doctrine of space-time is thoroughly metaphysical and only indirectly related to the scientific notion. He conceived of space-time as the primal matter or stuff of all things, the matrix out of which they are made. Infinite in itself, it is the cloth out of which all finite things or events are cut. Alexander did not mean that space-time is material in the ordinary sense of the word, for in this sense matter is a derivation of space-time, as is everything finite, including mind and even the Deity. It is "material" in the more basic sense of being that from which all things arise or have their origin. Like the absolute of the monistic idealists, to which Alexander compared it, space-time embraces the whole of reality; what we experience as finite beings are but its empirical variations or changing configurations. These latter are indeed real in themselves, but they can also be called appearances of space-time, a falling off from its perfection, and ultimately unreal because of their finiteness.

Within the bosom of space-time perfections have emerged in an ascending scale: materiality first of all, then life, and finally mind. The creative impulse generating these perfections comes from time, which assumes the predominant role in Alexander's system. Time stands in relation to space somewhat as the creative mind or spirit stands in relation to the material of a work of art. "As the work of art is the fusion of spirit and matter in finite ingredients, so within this space-time, which is below fusion, there is an element which corresponds to spirit and one which corresponds to matter, and these are respectively time and space. Time is, as it were, the mind to which the body is space."[46] In even more abstract terms, evolution is the result of the movement of time through space. Alexander explained this difficult notion as follows. A point in space can be occupied by a succession of instants. This successive occupation of a point by instants of time is what is meant by motion. Since points in space are ceaselessly being occupied by new instants of time, the universe is a vast system of motions; indeed, space-time can be described as pure motion. Thus the universe and everything in it is historical; it is a universe of motion and of events.[47] The spatio-temporal universe is by its nature a universe in motion, and through the creative impulse of time it is a developing and growing universe.

Where does God fit into this conception of the universe? At first sight, because of its infinite creativity we may be tempted to regard space-time as the deity. But Alexander pointed out that space-time does not answer the usual description of the God of religion. It is not an object of religious emotion or worship; at best it arouses our intellectual admiration. Can the metaphysician discover a being corresponding to the object of religious experience? The highest quality that has come to birth in the universe up to the present is mind or consciousness. But there is good reason to believe that this is not the final product of space-time. Because it is infinite we can be sure that space-time is pregnant with a still higher quality, and this is what we call deity. Deity is "the next higher empirical quality to mind, which the universe is engaged in bringing to birth."[48] Hence God is not an actually existing being, unless we consider him to be space-time with its nisus toward deity. Then God is identical with the whole world and deity is his ideal quality. What this quality is we have no way of knowing. But this much is certain: the deity that emerges in time is a product of time and essentially involved in time. It is not a timeless, transcendent being. Neither is it a finished and completed being, for infinite time will always be in throes of giving it birth. Deity is not a finite quality, like mind, but an infinite ideal toward which the universe is tending but which will never be fully realized.

This is indeed a remarkable deity to offer the religious man for worship! We may well wonder if it is a more suitable object of religious experience and faith than space-time. Certainly it evokes our intellectual admiration but, contrary to Alexander's claim, it is not likely to arouse our religious passion. How can one worship a godhead that, like our own mind, is a creature of time and inextricably bound up with it? There is a certain romantic and poetic force in Alexander's conception of the universe and God, but its bold and fanciful speculation is far from convincing. It is no wonder that the next generation of English philosophers will show such an antipathy to metaphysics. To them this branch of philosophy will be most vividly portrayed by the fantastic speculations of men like Morgan and Alexander and the absolute idealists whom we shall study in the next chapter.

XVIII.

Idealism

SPENCER and the utilitarians who were considered in the previous two chapters tried to solve the philosophical problems of their age with the principles of empiricism and mechanism inherited from the eighteenth century. As empiricists, they scorned ontology and tended toward skepticism regarding the major issues of religion. On the question of the existence and nature of God they were either agnostics or deists, and throughout their thinking they showed but scant regard for those spiritual realities that had been the dominant principles in traditional philosophies.

It is to the credit of John Stuart Mill that, while remaining within the empiricist tradition, he recognized its narrowness, especially in its Benthamite form. His essay on Coleridge, written in 1830, is eloquent testimony that he, with other Englishmen of his time, was eagerly looking for a deeper and more satisfying philosophy of life. The essay prophesies, moreover, that Coleridge will play a leading role in shaping such a philosophy of the future. Mill saw in Coleridge a traditionalist thinker who aligned himself with the German metaphysicians in reacting against the empirical and mechanistic philosophy of the eighteenth century. One of the great seminal minds of the age, he was the man who both reaffirmed Platonism in England and introduced into it German idealism.[1]

SAMUEL TAYLOR COLERIDGE

Coleridge did not begin as an idealist.[2] While a student he was attracted to the empiricism of Locke and Newton, and more especially to its offspring, the associationist psychology of David Hartley. In his admiration for Hartley, whom he called "that great master of Christian Philosophy," he named his first son David Hartley Coleridge. In an outburst of enthusiasm for Hartleianism, he wrote to his friend Southey, "I am a complete necessitarian, and understand the subject as well as Hartley himself, but I go farther than Hartley, and believe the corporeality of *thought*, namely that it is motion."[3]

Coleridge, however, did not remain content with Hartley's reduction of thought and imagination to the mechanical association of sensations and ideas. It was not long before he completely rejected the Hartleian psychology and the whole empirical system on which it rests. If Hartley is correct, he contends in his *Biographia Literaria*, the acts of mind and will are necessary consequences of external stimuli and products of a blind mechanism. These faculties are entirely passive, incapable of controlling and determining our thoughts and affections. Ideas prove to be nothing more than "diminished *copies* of configurative motion," and the soul itself loses its reality, becoming a merely abstract entity. In that case how can we explain such non-mechanical acts as the invention of the watch, Lord Byron's composition of *Childe Harold*, or indeed the production of a system of philosophy?[4] What is more, the consequences of Hartley's system are destructive of morality and religion, for "the existence of an infinite spirit, of an intelligent and holy will, must, on this system, be mere articulated motions of the air."[5] The proofs of God's existence and attributes advanced by "the excellent and pious Hartley" in the second part of his *Observations on Man* are certainly not derived from, or in keeping with the materialistic principles of the first part!

The basic fallacy of Hartley and other empiricists, according to Coleridge, is the opinion that there is nothing in the intellect that is not previously in the senses. They forget Leibniz's important qualification, "except the intellect itself." Believing that all experience arises through impressions from without, they conceive the human mind as something passive, completely controlled by external circumstances. This is contrary to the facts discovered by any man who obeys the Socratic injunction "Know thyself." Such a man finds that the mind is no mere "lazy Looker-on on an external world," but that it actively molds and shapes the world it knows.[6] For this reason one should begin philosophizing with an affirmation of self-existence. He should avoid the mistake of Spinoza, who began with a substance and not with an act, with an *it is* rather than with an *I am*. For what after all is philosophy, Coleridge exclaimed, but I-thinking?

For this approach to philosophy Coleridge had been prepared by his reading of the Platonists. As a youth, even before entering the university, he had been captivated by the philosophy of Plotinus. Later, he read Plato, delved more deeply into Plotinus, and studied Proclus. As the years went by he turned to the works of such Renaissance Platonists as Ficino, Pletho, and Giordano Bruno. He also read with great admiration the Cambridge Platonists of the seventeenth century and the medieval Platonist Scotus Erigena, whose *De Divisione Naturae* he annotated.[7]

A crucial stage in Coleridge's philosophical development began with his reading of the works of Immanuel Kant. In 1798 he traveled to Germany to acquire a first-hand knowledge of Kantianism. We have his own account of the overpowering effect Kant had on his mind:

> The writings of the illustrious sage of Koenigsberg, the founder of the Critical Philosophy, more than any other work, at once invigorated and disciplined my understanding...the clearness and evidence of the Critique of Pure Reason; and Critique of Judgment, of the Metaphysical Elements of Natural Philosophy, and of his Religion within the bounds of Pure Reason, took possession of me as with the giant's hands.[8]

Of the German philosophers not only Kant but also Fichte and Schelling, and in lesser degree Hegel, Lessing, Herder, Goethe, and Schiller influenced his thinking. None of the opinions of the German idealists, however, were accepted without criticism, and eventually Coleridge passed beyond all of them in his philosophical journeying. But his debt to the German idealists remained considerable. Historians dispute whether his mature philosophy was shaped more by English Platonism or by German idealism; none denies, however, that these two streams of idealism are merged in his philosophy.[9]

Coleridge's ambition in his philosophical maturity was to revive metaphysics after its long eclipse by empiricism and mechanism, and thereby to rescue religion and morals from their deplorable state. The thesis that dominates his thinking is that there can be no true religion without a sound metaphysics, and that true metaphysics both serves and supplements religion.

Coleridge's mature philosophy is a metaphysics (or "spiritual realism" as he himself called it) that unites the emotions, will, and intellect in the search for being and truth. "The term Philosophy," he says, "defines itself as an affectionate seeking after the truth; but Truth is a correlative of Being."[10] Being itself is a pure and infinite act (*actus purissimus*). As an infinite act, being is not known by the discursive understanding. This, with its logical abstractions and arguments, operates in the areas of the lesser sciences, such as physiology and economics. The act which is being is discerned by the higher power of reason. Reason is also the source of our ideas of God, freedom, immortality, and moral duty. Such ideas have a regulative function, as in Kantianism, but they are also living truths that provide an insight into reality itself, into the noumenal world lying beneath appearances. For instance, the idea of God "is the true source and indispensable precondition of all our knowledge of God."[11]

Accordingly, Coleridge's approach to being and God is not *a posteriori* but *a priori* and ontological. He does not deny all value to the cosmological proofs of God's existence, including Paley's argument from design, but he regards them not as cogent arguments but rather as illustrations of what is involved in the idea of God.

By the analysis of truth Coleridge, following Schelling, arrives at the notion of God as an absolute spirit in which there is an identity of subject and object. For Coleridge there is no act of knowledge without a knowing subject and a known object. The main question is which of these two is the primary, the self as the subjective pole of experience or reality as its objective pole? The empiricists have taken the objective side as primary and have explained the self and consciousness in terms of it. The transcendentalists, according to Coleridge, more correctly give the primacy to the subjective ego, maintaining a coincidence of the object with this and affirming the identity of subject and object in an absolute self-consciousness.

In his argument for a self-conscious absolute, Coleridge contends that a mediate or dependent truth must depend on one that is immediate and independent, and that all dependent truths derive their certainty from one that is absolute. This absolute, Coleridge further contends, cannot be an object which is dependent on a subject as its antithesis. Absolute truth is not located in either a subject or an object taken separately, but in a being in which both are identical.

The being containing such an identity is for Coleridge a spirit, self, or self-consciousness, which becomes a subject only through its constructing an objective world for itself. This objective world has actual existence only in the one self-consciousness that constructs it. Absolute and infinite, this consciousness manifests itself primarily in the affirmation of itself, in the *SUM* or I AM. God's primary revelation of himself in his absolute being is in terms of existence, in "the great eternal I AM."[12] This affirmation is the final as well as "the fundamental truth of all philosophy." "We begin," says Coleridge, "with the I KNOW MYSELF, in order to end with the absolute I AM. We proceed from the SELF, in order to lose and find all self in GOD."[13]

Coleridge's philosophical odyssey never came to a definite end; his restless mind was "growing and accumulating to the last." Like many other of his ambitions, his projected system of philosophy remained an unfulfilled dream. Nevertheless his aim as a philosopher is clear enough, and what he accomplished appropriately earned him the title of the founder of nineteenth-century English idealism.

Idealism Goes to College

The first diffusion of German idealism in England was largely the work of poets and essayists like Coleridge and Carlyle and not of academic philosophers. A few isolated professors in the universities showed the influence of Kant and the post-Kantians in the first half of the nineteenth century, but it was only in the second half that their revolutionary impact was felt in academic circles. This was preceded by a long period of assimilation, in which their writings were translated into English, commented on, and variously interpreted and accommodated to native English ways of thinking.

It is to be expected that Kant's works were the first to be translated.[14] Some of his moral and political essays were put into English in the last decade of the eighteenth century. His *Critique of Pure Reason* was first translated in 1838. But Kant by himself failed to satisfy the metaphysical yearnings of the new generation of philosophers. They were aspiring to an ontology or doctrine of being, an approach to the truly real or thing-in-itself, and the Kantian critical epistemology placed this beyond their grasp. Some of the first academic idealists, such as John Grote (1813–1866) and James Ferrier (1808–1864), professors respectively at Cambridge and St. Andrews, were critical of the agnostic side of Kant's philosophy, which was stressed in the phenomenalistic interpretation of Sir William Hamilton. They were looking for a full metaphysical idealism, and this they found not in Kant but in Hegel.

The man primarily responsible for introducing Hegel into England and thus preparing the way for the great flowering of Hegelianism at the end of the century was James Stirling, a Scottish doctor who came under the influence of Carlyle and abandoned his profession to pursue philosophy.[15] In 1869 he published his important *Secret of Hegel*, which combines translated selections from Hegel's *Logic* and *Encyclopedia* with a long deduction of the categories. To Stirling, the whole of modern philosophy culminates in Hegel as Greek philosophy reached its peak in Aristotle.

In academic circles one of the pioneers in promoting Hegelianism was Benjamin Jowett (1817–1893), professor at Balliol College, Oxford. Jowett is famous for his translation of Plato's *Dialogues*; far less known is his interest in German idealism. After spending the summers of 1844 and 1845 in Germany, he returned to England full of enthusiasm for Hegel. Through his encouragement a group of students at Oxford undertook the study of Hegel, sowing the seed that was to yield a rich harvest in the writings of the Oxford professors, T. H. Green and his more famous Hegelian disciples, F. H. Bradley and Bernard Bosanquet. The Scotsman Edward Caird (1834–1908) also imbibed German idealism at Oxford from Jowett and then taught it at the University of Glasgow. With his brother John Caird (1820–1898) he made this university a center of German idealism, supplanting by this the philosophy of Sir William Hamilton.

Because of the direct influence of Green on Bradley and Bosanquet, a word should be said about his manner of interpreting German idealism. Green's most important work, the *Prolegomena to Ethics*, begins by accepting the Kantian dictum "the understanding makes nature."[16] This dictum means for Green that the understanding is not a part or a product of nature but rather the principle that constitutes the objective world of experience. The reality or objectivity of this world implies a permanent order of relations, and such an order is impossible without a transcendental ego that, in being conscious of itself, objectifies itself in the world.

While accepting Kant's doctrine of the transcendental ego, Green rejected the Kantian notion of a thing-in-itself. Kant distinguished between the form and the matter of nature, the form having its origin in the understanding and the matter originating in a source that, being alien to the understanding, remains unknown. By the form of nature Kant meant those relations by which phenomena are connected in a unified world of experience; by the matter of nature he meant pure sensations as yet undetermined by these relations. Nature in its formal aspect is, then, the work of the understanding, while in its material aspect it is the work of unknown things-in-themselves which act in some mysterious way upon us. But in Green's view this Kantian doctrine introduces an unintelligible bifurcation into nature. If the noumenal world lies beyond our experience, is it not isolated and independent of it? And if this is so, how can sensations, or the matter of experience, be intelligibly related to that world as effects to their cause?

Accordingly, Green abandoned the Kantian doctrine of a real thing-in-itself and adopted Hegel's doctrine that reality is intelligible and therefore logically rational. There is, then, only one world for Green, and this is the intelligible world of experience—a world constructed by thought in the act of revealing itself to us. This world is not the product of our finite individual mind, for it can never grasp the universe in the totality of its relations. Rather, it is constituted by an absolute self or God, who is eternal and omniscient. The finite self or ego has its origin in the absolute consciousness and it possesses the same nature as that consciousness; the human consciousness is but a progressive reproduction in time of the eternal consciousness of God. Through this reproduction God communicates himself to man, and man achieves his moral end.

The moral order of the universe demands that we fulfill all the potentialities of our ego; yet we can never hope to realize ourselves to the extent of equaling God in goodness or knowledge. We can fulfill ourselves at best by identifying our interests with those of the society in which we live. "It is in fact only so far as we are members of a society, of which we can conceive the common good as our own, that the idea [of moral good] has any practical hold on us at all.... Each has primarily to fulfill the duties of his station."[17] These themes of Green appear, with modifications, expansions, and developments in the works of his disciple, F. H. Bradley.

Francis Herbert Bradley

idealistic ethics

A pupil of Green, Bradley published his *Ethical Studies* seven years before his professor's *Prolegomena to Ethics*.[18] The *Ethical Studies* was an epoch-making work, the first attempt to overthrow the hedonist and utilitarian ethics then in vogue by means of German idealism.

It is natural, Bradley says, for the moralist to ask, Why should I be moral? The moralist rightly assumes that we act virtuously in order to attain an end, that morality implies a good to be done or realized. Now this good cannot be external to myself, because I realize it through my virtuous actions, that is, through actions which are not mere means to the good but are good themselves. The moral good, then, must be the realization or fulfillment of myself. Indeed, the only object we can really desire, Bradley argues, is our own self, for anything desired as such is an object within our thought and therefore identified with ourself.[19] The question now remains: what is the self that we aim to fulfill by moral action?

Hedonists tell us to act only for pleasure. But pleasure is not the self; it is a state of the self, either one particular state or a collection of particular states. If the hedonists are right, then, the self that we try to realize is a mere state or collection of states of the self. But the true self is not a collection or aggregate; it is a whole that *has* states or feelings. Moral action aims at realizing or fulfilling this true self, not merely the "empirical self." Such an end Bradley sees affirmed by the ordinary decent and serious man, who holds before his mind an idea of perfect happiness which is not that of a series of discontinuous states but of a unity or system in which particular goods subserve one whole.

The true self, then, which we realize through virtuous action is not a series or collection of feelings or states, as the hedonists maintain, but a whole. This, Bradley maintained, is an infinite whole. At first sight it may seem nonsensical to say that we are infinite. But Bradley argued that our knowledge of ourselves as finite establishes our infinitude. How could our mind be aware of its limitation unless it knew something of non-limitation, that is to say of infinity? It would be as impossible as that a man should know that he is inside a room without knowing something about the outside. The whole, then, that I as a moral agent must fulfill is an infinite one. No doubt I am finite and limited, but there is an infinity in me that is never quite myself. In other words, I am at once finite and infinite, and hence I am in a state of contradiction. The moral life consists in the elimination of this contradiction by progress toward my identification with the infinite.

The problem to be solved, then, is how, being limited and consequently not a whole, I can extend myself so as to be a whole. Bradley's answer is that I must become my true self through membership in a whole. When this is achieved my private self ceases to exist and becomes a function of a moral organism. In this organism I am not a mere private self. Insofar as I become moral this self ceases to exist. "I am morally realized," Bradley writes, "not until my personal self has utterly ceased to be my exclusive self, is no more a will which is outside others' wills, but finds in the world of others nothing but self."[20] In other words, perfect self-realization is reached only when my personal will is made wholly one with the infinite whole.

This throws light on Bradley's quarrel with utilitarianism. The utilitarian seeks pleasure for pleasure's sake; not exclusively his own pleasure, to be sure, but the maximum pleasure of all sentient organisms. But the notion of maximum pleasure is contradictory. There is no greatest pleasure, for pleasure is never more than a passing feeling or a series of feelings, either of which is finite and consequently never finished or realized. The basic error of the hedonist or utilitarian is the substitution of a particular satisfaction or collection of particular satisfactions for man's final end, which is always a universal good, namely the satisfaction of oneself as a whole.[21]

When he says that the moral good is a universal good, Bradley makes it clear that he is not asserting a mere abstract, formal principle, such as "Duty for duty's sake." A principle of this sort, being without content, is for him an idle and useless abstraction, giving no information about what we ought to do. It is no good to tell us to do our duty for duty's sake if we do not know what our duty is. Bradley, following Hegel, is here criticizing the ethical formalism of the Kantian system, though he concedes that his statement does not do full justice to that system.[22]

It is clear that, according to Bradley, the self cannot be realized by a series of particular pleasures or by an abstract universal law. For him, as we have seen, self-realization is possible only when the individual enters into the broader life of an organic whole, such as the family or state. The individual can find himself only by becoming a function in the social organism, "a heart-beat in its system." And this is possible only if he makes his will one with the general will of the social body and takes up his duties as required by that will.

Alan achieves moral perfection, then, by submitting his will to a will superior to his own, which imposes both a law and an obligation upon him. Only in this way does he acquire a *good will*, which his moral conscience tells him is alone morally good. This is not a private "natural" will, because it does not depend on one's own likes and dislikes; it is, in short, an objective and not a subjective will. It is also a universal will, standing above all individual men and ruling them all alike. It is, finally, a real will, a will of living human beings, and nor an unreal abstraction. In the language of Hegel, it is a "concrete universal," above and yet within all its particulars and existing only insofar as they exist.[23]

At the heart of this ethical theory is the notion of society as an organic whole that is more than the sum of the individuals it contains. The utilitarian ethics presupposes that a society is nothing but the sum of its members, and that the members are just as real outside the whole as they are within it. Their relations to each other within the society are accidental and external to their being. But for Bradley an individual human being unrelated to other men is a fiction. An individual is never an isolated self; he is what he is "because of and by virtue of the community in which he lives." Hence his relations to others are not external and accidental; they are internal and essential to his being.

Because a man is by his nature a member of a social group, such as a family or a state, he must look to these social organisms—and especially to the laws, institutions, and customs of the state—to discover his duties. He must identify his will with the moral spirit of the community in which he lives and judge accordingly. "If a man is to know what is right," Bradley says, "he should have imbibed by precept, and still more by example, the spirit of his community, its general and special belief, as to right and wrong."[24]

But is there no higher moral good for Bradley than the actual morality of the society in which we may happen to live? Do we fully realize ourselves by conforming to its will as expressed in its laws and spirit? Bradley, while advocating social conformism, by no means restricts the moral good to that which is actually realized in society. He grants that there is a higher ideal not fully realized there. It is true that when a man has performed his duties and filled his place as a member of his family, society, and state, he has in the main realized his "good self." But then further claims are made on him, "claims beyond what the world expects of us, a will for good beyond what we see to be realized anywhere." Some of these new and higher demands are nonsocial; for example, the aspirations to truth in science and beauty in art. Others are social ideals, such as love, honor, and purity, which are not found fully realized in society.

Consequently, over and above the real morality of our society there is a higher "ideal morality" to which we ought to aspire. Only through this morality will our "ideal self" be fulfilled. Yet the higher ideal morality must be grounded in the real morality of social life. Bradley does not suggest that we give up the moral values of our community for some utopian or superhuman morality. Rather, he regards the common ethical norms as the foundation of the higher morality. "The highest type we can imagine," he says, "is the man who, on the basis of everyday morality, aims at the ideal perfection of it, and on this double basis strives to realize a non-social ideal."[25]

This ideal is, of course, never perfectly realized. No matter how good men become, they will always discern new heights to be climbed, and feel themselves obliged to tend to an ideal that always eludes their grasp. Indeed, if this ideal were ever reached, morality itself would disappear. A morally perfect man would no longer be obliged to tend to perfection, and without obligation there is no morality. Thus morality is self-defeating because it involves a contradiction. It demands that we strive to realize the ideal good, but its realization would be the end of morality. As a moral being, then, man himself is a contradiction.

Finding himself in this awkward dilemma because of his ethics of obligation, Bradley escapes it through transcending morality by means of religion. Hegel provides him with the key. We know that our true self is not really a contradiction, but rather a unity or whole. By the very fact that a man feels or knows the contradiction within him he *ipso facto* rises above it. For "Unless man was and divined himself to be a whole, he could not feel the contradiction, still less feel pain in it, and reject it as foreign to his real nature."[26] Here morality ends and religious faith takes over. What is a pure ideal for ethics is a reality for faith. The object of faith is an infinite, divine reality, in which the ideal good is perfectly realized. And through faith we are reconciled to this infinite reality and become one subject with it. Man finds and fulfills himself perfectly in God and in the supra-moral organism of the Kingdom of God.

appearance and reality

Throughout Bradley's *Ethical Studies* there is a constant appeal to certain metaphysical notions, such as "reality," "the real self," and "relation," but their full explanation and justification is lacking. There the author is aware of a skirting of metaphysical issues in order to focus attention on moral problems. Only later, in *Appearance and Reality*, does he come to grips with metaphysics itself and clarify the underlying presuppositions of his ethics.

Metaphysics is a serious business for Bradley, as it was for his mentors the German idealists. Yet instead of constructing a system of metaphysics, he attempts to give his readers only a glimpse of the nature of reality as a whole, as distinct from its manifold appearances. At the outset he urges his readers to adopt a skeptical attitude toward all the preconceptions and first principles which traditional builders of systems have asserted. Only after such a therapeutical skeptical inquiry will they be ready for the positive work of metaphysics.[27]

The first preconception Bradley examines is the Lockean distinction between primary and secondary qualities. Secondary qualities, such as color and sound, are thought by Locke and his followers to be mere appearances of reality; only the primary qualities of extension and the other spatial aspect of things belong to reality itself. Bradley is willing to grant that secondary qualities are only appearances; but he questions whether extension is real. The same arguments proving the unreality of color and sound can be applied to the spatial aspects of things. It is argued that a thing appears colored only when perceived by an eye, and it appears differently colored to different eyes. Hence, if the thing were really colored, reality would contradict itself. "We assume," Bradley writes, "that a thing must be self-consistent and self-dependent. It either has a quality or has not got it. And, if it has it, it cannot have it only sometimes, and merely in this or that relation. But such a principle is the condemnation of secondary qualities."[28] But is the ease of extension any different from that of color? The spatial aspects of things are also perceived in relation to a sense organ, and they appear differently to different perceivers. Indeed, primary qualities are presented and perceived as one with secondary qualities. Hence both are infected by the same contradiction and relativity.

Throughout this argument Bradley assumes that reality is self-consistent and self-dependent; in other words, that the contradictory and the relative fall short of the perfection of reality. Enunciated on the first page of *Appearance and Reality*, this Hegelian principle underlies Bradley's whole discussion and virtually assures its conclusion.

Applied to the distinction between a substance and its qualities, this principle once again shows that we are dealing not with reality but with mere abstractions. We say that a lump of sugar is a thing, and that it has the properties of being white, hard, and sweet. The sugar *is* all of these, but it is difficult to know what *is* means in this context. The sugar is not any one of these qualities taken by itself; it is not merely white or merely hard. Nor is the sugar the sum total of its qualities, for they are many and diverse, whereas the reality of the sugar lies in its unity: it is one thing. We are baffled and want to know what the reality of the sugar might be besides its various attributes, and yet we cannot find the unity of that reality in the attributes.

Perhaps the sugar is nothing more than its qualities in relation to each other. But the relations between the qualities are not the qualities themselves: "to be related to hardness" is not identical with whiteness. Perhaps the relation of whiteness to hardness is a reality independent of the qualities. But we must then ask: what relates the relation to the quality? We must posit another relation for this, and so on to infinity.

Bradley's conclusion regarding relations is of great importance for his metaphysics: "The attempt to resolve the thing into properties, each a real thing, taken somehow together with independent relations, has proved an obvious failure. And we are forced to see, when we reflect, that a relation standing alongside of its terms is a delusion."[29]

A relation is either a nonentity, and then qualities are not really related; or it is a reality, and then there is no intelligible way to relate the relation to the qualities.

Thus the attempt to understand things in terms of qualities and their relations lands us in contradiction—which is a sure sign that we are not dealing with reality but with appearance. We cannot think of qualities without relations: qualities are always related to each other as different or similar. And neither can we think of relations without qualities, for without them there would be nothing to relate. But this relational way of thinking necessarily involves contradictions and consequently it has to do only with the world of appearance.

Turning to the concepts of space and time, motion, causality, and substance, Bradley finds that they all involve relations and the inconsistencies inherent in relations; they are, accordingly, appearances and not realities. Even the self dissolves on examination into a number of feelings and states, without a permanent center that can be identified as the person. In his ethics Bradley speaks of "the true self" that is to be realized and actualized; it is now clear that this self is in fact only an appearance. He does not deny that the self, like space, time, and causality, exist, in the sense that they fall within our experience. What he insists on is their failure to measure up to the perfection of reality because of their lack of consistency and intelligibility.

Human thought itself comes under Bradley's criticism as illusory because it is essentially discursive and relational. In its perfect form thought is judgment, and judgment always involves a relation. When we judge, Bradley says, we predicate an idea or adjective of a reality.[30] For example, when we affirm, "A horse is a mammal," the subject (horse) is a reality and the predicate (mammal) is an adjective, distinct from the subject and added to it. Hence rational thinking is necessarily caught up in the dualism of subject and predicate and their relation. Thought craves for something better than this; it wants to transcend the distinction between subject and predicate and reach the unity and wholeness of reality, but it cannot do this without destroying its own nature. In short, thought itself belongs to appearance and not reality.

But are we condemned forever to a contradictory world of appearances? Is there no way to go beyond appearances to reality? Bradley thinks there is, not by means of thought but through feeling and emotion. Feeling is the most basic of all our experiences; it is more primitive than conscious intelligence with its clear-cut abstractions, divisions, oppositions, and relations. We immediately feel reality as a "blurred and confused totality" in which differences are present but felt as a unity or whole.[31] Thought supervenes and breaks up the wholeness of reality with its neat divisions into (for example) subject and object, and truth and error. This divisive and abstractive work of the intellect is necessary, but it turns the undivided wholeness of reality into a multiplicity of contradictory appearances.

Feeling, then, is the criterion of reality. "Nothing in the end is real," Bradley says, "but what is felt, and for me nothing in the end is real but that which I feel.... The real, to be real, must be felt."[32] What is more, reality is identical with feeling or "sentient experience." Thought distinguishes between the feeling subject and the felt object, but for pure feeling there is no such division; there is just the experience of a completely undifferentiated feeling. Hence Bradley's conclusion: "Sentient experience, in short, is reality, and what is not this is not real."[33]

This conclusion, however, is diametrically opposed to that of the traditional associationist psychologists, according to whom experience comes to us in bits and pieces of sensation which are then united to form complex ideas. Bradley is saying that our primitive experience is the feeling of a "blurred whole" in which the intellect makes "apparent" divisions into quality, quantity, subject and object, and so on. At about the same time William James was expressing the similar idea that our conscious experience begins with the awareness of a "buzzing confusion." Bradley acknowledged the similarity, but denied any indebtedness to James. Before reading James, he said, Hegel taught him the revolutionary doctrine of "feeling as a vague *continuum* below relations."[34]

It was with Hegel's guidance, too, and not with James', that Bradley developed the metaphysical aspect of this doctrine of feeling in his *Appearance and Reality*. As a metaphysician Bradley identified reality with feeling, but not with my feeling or yours. The distinction between mine and yours is the work of relational thinking, and consequently it belongs to appearance and not to reality. Reality is an Absolute, a single, harmonious, all-embracing system, whose content is feeling or sentient experience. My private feeling is but an aspect of this total experience; it is included within it, and hence Bradley could say that "what I feel *is* the all-inclusive universe."[35] But my experience does not exclude that of others, all of which are likewise embraced in the total experience that is the universe.

As a mere aspect of the Absolute, my feeling gives me an imperfect taste of its riches. We can be sure that the Absolute is infinitely richer than any experience we presently enjoy. But Bradley insists that it is not of a different nature from our sentient experience; it is but more of the same kind.

In the Absolute, all differences and oppositions are present but perfectly reconciled. Nothing is lost in it; all finite perfections are in the Absolute but transformed in its perfect unity. The differences of all the items of experience are sublimated and resolved in it; for example, the difference between appearance and reality, between the particular and the universal, and between thought and reality. Even the difference between truth and error, and between good and evil disappear in the Absolute. These are seen to be different aspects of the same reality. Thus error is really truth, though partially and imperfectly understood.[36] Evil serves the good and exists for its sake. The Absolute itself rises above the opposition between good and evil; hence it transcends morality and must be called super-good and super-moral.

Similarly, the Absolute is super-personal. Of course, possessing all perfections, it has personality in the highest degree. But personality is not the highest mode of experience. The notions of "self" and "person" are limited and exclusive; they do not include the non-self and the non-personal. The Absolute, on the contrary, is the whole of reality, embracing in its unitary experience all finite perfections. Consequently, it is not God, as he is usually depicted by religion. The Deity and religion are but aspects of reality and therefore appearances; they must be transcended to reach the oneness of the Absolute.[37]

When considering Bradley's moral doctrine, we saw that for him morality involves contradictions that are reconciled only by religion. Now it is apparent that religion itself must be surmounted in order to gain the harmony and consistency of the Absolute. Metaphysics takes over where religion leaves off and opens the way for our complete self-realization in the Absolute. For the Absolute is our final end, the goal of all our striving. Alone perfectly real, it gives value and reality to everything else. Only in it, then, do we completely realize our nature and find our true selves. Salvation, in short, comes through metaphysics.

The Absolute, however, can be described as spiritual. It is on this note—which Bradley calls the essential message of Hegel—that he closes his *Appearance and Reality*. Reality is at the opposite pole of the barely mechanical: "Outside of spirit there is not, and there cannot be, any reality, and, the more that anything is spiritual, so much the more is it veritably real."[38]

Bernard Bosanquet

Bradley's friend and follower Bernard Bosanquet shared with him the essentials of absolute idealism.[39] Though he was less original and critical than Bradley, his interests and erudition were wider, and he extended the doctrine to areas scarcely touched upon by Bradley, such as the theory of the state and aesthetics. These two men, with John McTaggart and a host of lesser idealistic lights, dominated the philosophical scene in England at the turn of the century.

the value of the individual

At the outset of his Gifford Lectures, *The Principle of Individuality and Value*, Bosanquet dispels any illusions his reader may have that absolute idealism is a philosophy alien to life and experience. It does not take refuge in any ivory tower apart from the facts of life (no great philosophy, he adds, does this); nor, like religion, does it conceive the Absolute as a heaven to be known and enjoyed in a future life. It is concerned with the experience of the concrete universe, just as much as, and indeed more than, the empiricism of a man like William James. Bosanquet praises James for refusing to construct a philosophy aloof from the world of concrete personal experiences; but he criticizes him for ignoring the largest and deepest experiences in life.[40] Bosanquet wants to be more genuinely empirical than the usual run of empiricists, accepting not only partial, finite experiences, but also the absolute experience which alone gives meaning and value to them. His idealism, then, like that of Bradley, identifies reality with experience—not with the multiplicity of particular experiences but with one absolute experience of which finite experiences are but fragments.

The experience of the Absolute to which Bosanquet refers is not reserved to a few practiced metaphysicians. In a rudimentary and unreflective way we all experience the Absolute; in a sense we even experience it more fully than anything else, because it is present in everything, in all we do and suffer: "the open secret of the Absolute confronts us in life, in love, and in death."[41] This experience is of a power deep within us, but it is also outside of us and greater than ourselves. This power drives us, finite beings though we are, to want something above ourselves, to seek a good that is not ours alone but belongs to the whole universe. To illustrate this, Bosanquet appeals to the truly noble man, who does not value himself as an isolated person. He feels that he has been entrusted with a gift that he must use for the good of others. He does not seek his own pleasure or satisfaction but looks to the society of which he is a member and works for its good. Only what contributes to this good is of value to him. What matters is not his private destiny but "the thing to be done, known, and felt; in a word, the completeness of experience, his contribution to it, and his participation in it."[42]

If this is true, the finite self as such has no value. It is incomplete and imperfect, a fragment of a whole in which it must lose itself in order to find itself. The self feels within it the opposition between what it is and what it wants and ought to be. It is finite but it yearns for infinity; it is divided and multiple but it longs to be whole and united; it is in turmoil but it wants to be at rest. It can overcome this inner opposition only by transcending itself and entering into the unity and peace of the Absolute. Thus transfigured, the self achieves a kind of immortality: not a personal immortality, for the self as we now know it disappears; but it remains in a new and transcendent form in the eternal reality of the Absolute.

But how can we be certain of the reality of the Absolute? Following Hegel, Bosanquet bases his conviction of its reality on "the positive and constructive principle of non-contradiction—in other words, the spirit of the whole." Our finite experiences (for example, in the physical world, logic, morality, and religion) are contradictory and unstable. We are forced to the conception of the Absolute from the imperfection of all these data: "This, then, is the fundamental nature of the inference to the absolute; the passage from the contradictory and unstable in all experiences alike to the stable and satisfactory, the βέβαιον."[43] In short, without the Absolute no finite experience has meaning or gives complete satisfaction.

The Absolute, then, is the ideal implied in all experiences; it is the goal to which they all tend and in which they find their full satisfaction. But this ideal is real, for it alone makes experience possible. It does not, strictly speaking, *exist*, for existence is a successive appearance in space and time. In saying that the Absolute is real, Bosanquet means that it is "the total of stability or satisfactoriness"[44]—terms that indicate that he conceives the Absolute not as the supreme existent or being but as the ultimate value.

It is hardly surprising, then, that Bosanquet does not describe the Absolute as a self or person. The self is other than the non-self; hence it is limited and partial, whereas the Absolute is the whole of reality. Personality belongs to the realm of existence and appearance, which the Absolute includes but transcends. Accordingly, the Absolute is not the God of religion, who is depicted in terms drawn from human personality. The Absolute is supra-personal; it is the all-comprehensive and self-harmonious system, embracing all partial and contradictory appearances in a state of perfect reconciliation.

Although Bosanquet refuses to call the Absolute a person, he does call it an individual. At first sight this is puzzling, because we tend to think of an individual as a member of a class, and hence as "not being some one else." In this sense the Absolute is obviously not an individual, for it is the whole of reality. It includes the "otherness" implied in this use of the term "individual," but it transcends it by its completeness and perfect unity. But Bosanquet points out that there is a more profound meaning of individuality than this. Individuality is essentially a positive conception: it means wholeness, completeness, and integrity. In this sense we speak of a human being as a great individual because his nature is so full and so thoroughly integrated, "so vital and so true to itself, that, like a work of art, the whole of his being cannot be separated into parts without ceasing to be what it essentially is."[45] This is an ideal toward which finite human beings strive and which they attain in some degree, but no one of them completely measures up to it. There is only one ultimately complete and integral individual, and this is the Absolute.

In this sense, an individual is a world of its own, a self-contained and self-sufficient system whose parts are thoroughly integrated with each other and with the whole. Another name for such a world or system is "a concrete universal." This is different from an abstract universal, such as a genus or species, which contains only the likenesses of things while leaving out their diversities. A concrete universal includes the entire concrete nature of all the individuals it contains, their differences as well as their similarities; but it contains them in harmonious unity in which contradictions and differences ultimately disappear, whereas an abstract universal is but a fragmentary aspect of what in actuality is an integrated totality.[46]

One of the main oppositions that is removed in the Absolute is that between thought and reality. Following Hegel, Bosanquet shows that these are ultimately one, and that they are both ruled by the same law of non-contradiction. By "thought" he means not only abstract judgment and inference, but all forms of experience, including sense knowledge, intellectual cognition, love, emotion, and practical activity. In every form of experience there is a "passage of a being or content beyond itself, in a word, ideality, adjustment, or the universal."[47] Hence all finite experiences point to the Absolute; only philosophy takes as its explicit object the whole of reality. All assertions tell us something *about* reality; only philosophy pretends to speak of the nature of reality as a whole. Philosophy differs in this respect from science, because science concerns only an aspect of the universe, in abstraction from the rest. The mechanistic theory of evolution, for example, is only a partial view of the world; while contributing to the construction of a general theory of the world, it is not the exclusive basis of such a theory. Philosophy, on the other hand, concerns the universe as a whole—that is to say, in its individuality as a concrete universal. It views the universe as a system or organism in which all partial aspects—even those that are contradictory, such as the beautiful and the ugly, and the good and the bad—are seen to be reconciled in a higher unity.

It is Hegel's dialectic, therefore, that has laid the basis for Bosanquet's method of philosophy. This method, in brief, shows how contradictory experiences lead us to a higher form of experience in which the contradiction is removed. For example, one day we experience a thing as beautiful, and another day, in another light or in another mood, we experience the same thing as ugly. If this seems contradictory, it is because we have not given attention to the partial nature of these experiences. If we were to consider their different circumstances they would be seen not to contradict each other. The difference between beauty and ugliness would still remain, but they would not be in conflict. While retaining their difference they would be experienced as harmonious elements in a total system. Thus experienced, beauty would take on a fullness of meaning that would preclude our ever saying that it is ugly.[48] Thus it is by appealing to "the spirit of the whole," which is the same as the principle of non-contradiction, that we are able to reach reality in its concrete universality and individuality. Accordingly, there is but one criterion of truth and reality, and this is non-contradiction.[49]

theory of the state

It should now be clear that Bosanquet's monistic idealism follows the main lines of Hegelianism. He conceives the Absolute, or Ultimate Individual, as immanent in matter and acting upon it, causing living beings and, finally, human minds to evolve from it. These minds are finite individuals, limited "worlds" in which the Absolute has dispersed itself in order to reveal its infinite riches, but they now yearn to return to the Absolute in order to recover their lost unity. The human spirit is engaged in an adventuresome Pilgrim's Progress in quest of the Absolute, in which alone it will find itself.

The return to the Absolute is accomplished in successive stages. Individuals transcend their particular worlds and complete each other through the collective consciousness of society, of which the state is the highest form. But this does not satisfy their infinite aspirations. Further progress toward the Absolute is made through the products of civilization, especially through science, philosophy, art, and religion. In the present section we shall consider briefly Bosanquet's theory of the state; in the final section we shall see the role he assigns to art and aesthetic experience in the search for the Absolute.

As in his metaphysics, Bosanquet's main objects of criticism in his social and political philosophy are the English empiricists. According to him, Bentham, Mill, and Spencer took a superficial view of the individual and his relation to society. They regarded the individual and society as they *prima facie* appeared to be and thus failed to reveal their true nature. At first sight, individuals appear to be independent, self-satisfied, and self-willed, each isolated from and even opposed to the others in his innermost being. Their coming together in society is but an external and artificial association. Even when they are altruistic, they regard their neighbors as "others." According to this view, the individual is more important and more real than society, which is nothing but a collection or association of individuals.

A deeper and truer view of society, according to Bosanquet, is that it is a living organism or organization. In an organization, individuals are not casually juxtaposed to each other, as they are in an association; they are determined and controlled by the general idea or plan of the organization. Consider the difference between a crowd and an army. A crowd thinks and acts as a mere mass. An idea may pass from one man to another, resulting in common action, but the level of intelligence and responsibility of the crowd is, as a rule, very low. The "mind of a crowd" is not a true "social mind." An army, on the other hand, is an organized group or system bound together by a controlling idea, which is embodied in its structure and which determines the movements and relations of its members. This illustrates a society or organization, in contrast to a mere association, which is exemplified by a crowd.[50]

Bosanquet finds a parallel to the empiricists' explanation of society in their psychological theory of the association of ideas. In the empiricist account of the mind, ideas are associated with each other simply because we expect to find them together. For example, the engine's whistle makes us think the train is going to start. These ideas are naturally independent, and their connection in our mind expresses nothing essential to their nature. If they are separated they will not be seriously affected. But the mind, like society, cannot be accounted for as a mere association. It must be seen as an organization, in which ideas cohere in an organized system of thought. In this system one dominant idea controls and harmonizes all the others. Such a completely organized mind is, of course, an ideal that is not realized in human thought. In a human mind there is no one thoroughly organized and unified system of ideas. There is rather a multitude of such systems in various degrees of connection, indifference, and opposition to each other.[51]

It is along these lines that Bosanquet wants us to conceive society. It is not a casual or habitual association, but a natural grouping of men organized and systematized by a dominant idea or plan and possessed of a true social mind. There are many such groupings in society at large, each relatively, though not absolutely, closed and self-complete. The state is the widest society or organization. It is the one society with absolute power to harmonize, by force if necessary, all the subordinate societies within it so as to ensure the good life of all its citizens.

In his early writings Bosanquet looked forward to a world state embracing all communities and nations, and ensuring peace and harmony throughout the globe, but he thought it improbable that this ideal would soon be realized. With the founding of the League of Nations after the First World War, his hopes were raised that a world state was at last imminent. In the fourth edition of his *Philosophical Theory of the State* (1923), he appended a note: "I hope and am fully confident that we will soon see the accomplishment of these things."[52]

We have still to discover, however, in what the reality of society and the state consists. As we have seen, Bosanquet finds an analogy between the organized structure of minds and the organized structure of society; but he goes further and insists that they are really "the same fabric." A social whole is a social mind, and it has the same basic structure as the mind of an individual; that is to say, it is an organic system of ideas. Consider, for example, a school. The reality of the school consists of certain living minds—teachers, pupils, manager, parents—connected in a certain way. The institution is the meeting point of these minds bound together in a single system. The external appearance of the school is but the outward aspect of this spiritual organism in space and time.[53]

But not only is society endowed with a social mind; it also possesses a general will. This is not the sum total of the particular wills of the members of society, as the empiricists claim; it is a real universal will that aims at a truly common interest or good. It was this general will that Rousseau described, though somewhat faultily, in his *Contrat Social*.[54] In Bosanquet's interpretation, inspired by Hegel, Green, and Bradley, the general will is "the ineradicable impulse of an intelligent being to a good extending beyond itself, in as far as that good takes the form of a common good."[55] Through union with the general will the individual overcomes the limits of his "trivial and momentary self"; he enters into a deeper communion with himself and realizes his true self in the social self.

In society, then, a man is more himself than he is as a mere individual. He is also freer, for liberty means "being able to be yourself." Liberty is not a negative notion—a mere absence of constraint, as Bentham, Mill, and Spencer would have us believe. It consists in harmonizing the various conflicting desires and impulses of our will, and this is achieved by identifying our will with the general will of society. Through voluntary obedience to the laws and other constraints of society we gain a higher type of liberty: "In all social co-operation, and in submitting even to forcible constraint, when imposed by society in the true common interest, I am obeying only myself, and am actually attaining my freedom."[56]

Thus the state is a more perfect whole than the bare individual. It realizes more perfectly the notion of the individual as a concrete universal, and hence it is a more authentic manifestation of the Absolute. In it and through it, human beings acquire a more complete individuality by achieving their liberty and value. Social life—above all, life in the state—is a necessary stage in their progress toward the Absolute; but they must pass beyond it if they are to reach their goal.

aesthetics

Alone among his contemporaries in England, Bosanquet gave considerable attention to aesthetics, in the main following Hegel and Croce. Goethe and Ruskin to a lesser extent were influential in shaping his views on art and beauty. His interest in this subject was due to the fact that he saw in the experience of the beautiful a stage in man's pilgrimage to the Absolute, different from that of philosophy.

The philosopher seeks the satisfaction of thought by creating a complete and harmonious system of ideas that will account for all the relevant facts. On the other hand, the man who adopts the aesthetic attitude satisfies his feeling by embodying it in an object. In its simplest form, aesthetic experience is a pleasant feeling. But to be truly aesthetic, this feeling must have an object in which it becomes "organized," "incarnate," or "plastic."[57] The object of an aesthetic experience is not a real thing as known by conceptual knowledge (for instance, a cloud as a mass of cold wet vapor), but one of the numerous appearances of things chosen from nature or produced by an artist as imaginatively perceived. Hence there are two main elements in the experience of the beautiful: feeling and its object, and these are, respectively, the soul and body of the experience. There is also an aesthetic experience of ugliness, the opposite of beauty. In this case there is an embodiment of feeling in an object, but the embodiment is frustrated and incomplete. The essence of ugliness is the failure fully to express feeling in an object.[58] As error is partial truth, and evil is imperfect good, so ugliness is partial beauty.

Bosanquet agrees with Croce that the aesthetic attitude is basically one of expression. It involves contemplation or intuition, but this includes from the start a creative element, so that expression and intuition are inextricably interwoven. There is always an object before us to contemplate when we adopt the aesthetic attitude, but this object is the expression or embodiment of a feeling.

At first sight it may seem that the experience of the spectator of beauty and that of the creative artist are basically different; the former simply enjoys the contemplation of beauty in nature or art, while the artist actively creates a work of beauty. But Bosanquet assures us that their aesthetic experiences are fundamentally the same. Like the artist, the spectator enters into his object and is absorbed and carried away by it. The feeling of the spectator is simply a lower degree of the creative artist's; the spectator's attitude is merely a faint analogue of the creative rapture of the artist.[59]

Thus the experience of beauty is identical with that of art: it is the concentration of one's feeling "into an image which is at once its essence and its utterance." "Beauty, in other words," Bosanquet continues, "lives in the creative imagination, and there alone; and art is nothing more and nothing less than the experience which we call beauty."[60]

Bosanquet praises Croce for grasping the fundamental truth that beauty is "for the mind and in the mind." There is no beauty in the full sense in a physical thing that is unperceived and unfelt. We attach beauty to it by embodying our feeling in it, somewhat as we attach color and sound to it by perceiving it. Croce comes under his criticism, however, for making beauty a quality of the mind alone and relegating its physical embodiment to a secondary and incidental position. In Croce's view, this embodiment is only for the sake of the permanence and communication of the aesthetic experience. The inward vision of the artist, or his intuition, is the only expression of the aesthetic feeling. Strictly speaking, external media, such as clay, metal, or sound, are superfluous. Bosanquet, on the contrary, insists that the artist does not work "in the bodiless medium of pure thought or fancy."[61] The embodiment of feeling is essential to the artist's aesthetic experience and adds to it. Bosanquet writes:

> Croce says, indeed, that the artist has every stroke of the brush in his mind as complete before he executes it as after. The suggestion is that using the brush adds nothing to his inward or mental work of art. I think that this is false idealism. The bodily thing adds immensely to the mere idea and fancy, in wealth of qualities and connections. If we try to cut out the bodily side of our world, we shall find that we have reduced the mental side to a mere nothing.[62]

The opposition between Bosanquet and Croce on this point results from their different conceptions of the external world. For Croce, this world is not real at all, and therefore art cannot enter into it or in any way be concerned with physical processes or media. It is only by way of metaphor that we speak of a picture, statue, or printed poem as a "work of art." Bosanquet, on the other hand, recognizes in a sense the reality of the external world. While not conceding to the realists that it exists independent of experience, he will have no part in an idealism that makes it merely a state of mind. He insists that natural objects are experienced as external, concrete existences, and hence that there are various external media in which the creative imagination yearns to express itself.[63] Indeed, an artist thinks and feels in terms of his medium: "it is the peculiar body of which *his* aesthetic imagination and no other is the peculiar soul."[64]

As a consequence of this, Bosanquet takes issue with Croce on the question of the subjectivity or objectivity of beauty. Croce argues that beauty is subjective and unreal because it is relative to each individual; but Bosanquet calls this "the hoariest of fallacies."[65] If an experience varies relatively with the variation of conditions, we can be sure that the experience points to reality. In fact, the experience of beauty is not purely subjective. As we have seen, it necessarily implies an object, and the more harmonious and integral the object the more satisfactory is the aesthetic experience. The beauty of a work of art does not consist solely in the subjective satisfaction of the artist or spectator, but also in the satisfactoriness of the object itself. A perfect work of art, such as a painting by Turner (Bosanquet's preferred painter), gives us a more lasting and harmonious satisfaction than a mediocre one. There are objective criteria, therefore, by which to judge beauty. An aesthetic experience is satisfying to the degree that it is stable, because it does not quickly satiate; coherent, because its object has a logical and harmonious structure; and universal, because it can be shared by everyone having an adequate aesthetic education.[66]

Thus beauty is subject to the same law of experience as truth and reality. Like them, it obeys the impulse toward unity and coherence, or "the positive spirit of non-contradiction." By this supreme law "every fragment yearns towards the whole to which it belongs, and every self to its completion in the Absolute, and of which the Absolute itself is at once an incarnation and a satisfaction."[67]

the reaction against monistic idealism

Monistic idealism, taught by Bradley and Bosanquet in England and by Royce and Creighton in the United States, came under the attack of the pragmatists, the realists, and the personal idealists in both countries. Since we consider the first two groups in other chapters, we need not here dwell at length on their reasons for rejecting the idealism of the Absolute. Suffice it to say that pragmatists such as James, Dewey, and Schiller were repelled by the conception that reality is ultimately one, and that the world of everyday life, with its diversity and change, its failures, errors, and evils, is, if not illusory, at least nothing but appearance. The pragmatists subordinated thought to action; it is in this world that men must act, struggling against its real imperfections and evils to achieve a better and more intelligent human life. Thus the pragmatist is an inveterate pluralist. James writes: "There is no possible point of view from which the world can appear an absolutely single fact. Real possibilities, real indeterminations, real beginnings, real ends, real evil, real crises, catastrophes, and escapes, a real God, and a real moral life, just as common-sense conceives these things, may remain in empiricism as conceptions which that philosophy gives up the attempt either to 'overcome' or to interpret in monistic form."[68]

This implies the rejection of Bradley's theory of internal relations, which maintains that nothing is completely understandable without its relations to other things; in short, that only the whole of reality is intelligible and real. In the pragmatist's view, relations can be external to the related terms and just as real as them. To take an important example, James considered time not only as real but as the form of all real things.

Like James, the English neo-realists G. E. Moore and Russell taught the externality of relations, in opposition to Bradley. But they went beyond the American pragmatist when they applied the notion of external relation to knowledge. In their view, the relation of reality to knowledge is not contained in the nature of reality; in other words, reality is independent of knowledge or experience.

The personal idealists took issue with Bradley and Bosanquet on still another ground. While accepting their basic idealistic position, the personalists argued that monistic idealism fails to do justice to the reality and value of the finite self or person. By subsuming the human person within a supra-personal Absolute, Bradley and Bosanquet denied him his distinctive liberty, finality, and immortality. Writing in 1894, Andrew Seth Pringle-Pattison reproached Bradley with introducing Spinozistic monism into English philosophy and called for the re-establishment of the notion of the "impervious self."[69] The same year, the young John Ellis McTaggart, in an article in the *Revue de Métaphysique et de Morale,* made the same point against Bradley.[70] In 1904, James Ward[71] edited a collective volume entitled *Personal Idealism,* in which the authors supported the personalist movement against monistic idealism. It is an indication of the close connection between English and American philosophy that at the same time in the United States a similar struggle was taking place between the personalist idealists Bowne and Howison and the absolutists Royce and Creighton.

In England both Ward and McTaggart rejected Bradley's notion of an impersonal and supra-personal Absolute of which finite selves are mere appearances. Insisting on the irreducible value and reality of the human person, they conceived the Absolute as a concrete whole or society, whose members are finite persons. Ward thought of these persons as spiritual monads, each of which is an active subject of experience and a center of self-determination. Together they form an objective whole (*totum objectivum*) arranged in an ascending scale of perfection. At the peak of this hierarchy is God, an infinitely good and powerful spirit, the creator of all monads below him and coordinator of all their experiences.

McTaggart shares with Ward his personalist idealism but not his theism. For him, too, all reality is spiritual. The primary parts of this spiritual world are selves or persons, and the secondary parts are perceptions. As primary and original elements in the universe, selves are uncreated and immortal, so there is no need to posit a creator. Nor does the universe require a God to account for its order; the causal laws that bind the substances of the universe together are eternally written into their being. McTaggart does not find the notion of God contradictory, but he sees no reason to affirm his existence. Even if there were a God, he would not be all-powerful or perfectly good; the presence of evil and imperfection in the universe is incompatible with a God with these attributes.

Since every person is fundamentally different from every other, one cannot be contained in another. Hence finite selves cannot be merged into an all-embracing personal God or even into a supra-personal Absolute. But the totality of spiritual substances or selves does constitute one universe. This is a single substance or Absolute, conceived as an organic system of persons bound together by universal laws and especially by the emotion of love. The universe can be considered as a unity of substance or as a multiplicity of parts, but McTaggart thinks the latter view is more fundamental. He does not reject the notion of an Absolute, but his inveterate pluralism leads him to emphasize the manifold elements of the universe rather than its substantial unity.

The idealism of McTaggart differs from that of Bradley and Bosanquet not only in its pluralism, personalism, and atheism, but also in its disregard of concrete experience and its insistence on the possibility of deducing *a priori* the attributes of being. Once he is assured of the existence of the world through perception, he tries to determine by pure deduction the nature of existence as a spiritual organism of interrelated selves. As a consequence, his philosophy has the appearance of an austere and precise logical system—in Bradley's famous phrase, "an unearthly ballet of bloodless categories." Its coldness and abstractness is tempered only at the end, when McTaggart strikes the note of love as the binding force between persons. This love, which he extols as man's greatest good, is to find its perfection in another life, when men will be drawn together by a force "so direct, so intimate, and so powerful that even the deepest mystical rapture gives us but the slightest foretaste of its perfection."[72] Thus, as so often happens in the history of philosophy, logicism ends in mysticism.

XIX.

Pragmatic Humanism: F. C. S. Schiller

AT the beginning of the twentieth century, English philosophy was dominated by the Anglo-Hegelians, the chief of whom were F. H. Bradley and Bernard Bosanquet. Their absolute idealism and monism set the prevailing tone of philosophical discussion. In the first decades of the century, however, voices were raised in protest against their exaltation of "pure thought" to the neglect of methods of thinking in accord with common sense and the empirical sciences. Attempts were made to bring English philosophy back to its traditional realism and empiricism, which had been eclipsed through the importation into England of German idealism. In the next chapter we shall be concerned with the revolt of the English realists against absolute idealism. In the present chapter we shall consider F. C. S. Schiller, one of its first and most trenchant critics, who combined an empirically minded idealism with pragmatism.[1]

Although Schiller claimed that he arrived at his pragmatic position independently, not having begun to read William James until he was twenty-seven, there can be no doubt that his association with the American pragmatist deeply influenced his thinking. After obtaining his M.A. at Oxford, he traveled to the United States and continued his studies at Cornell. During his four years in the United States (from 1893 to 1897) he began a friendship with James that lasted until the latter's death in 1910. After Schiller's return to England, they corresponded and wrote laudatory reviews of each other's works. Although James thought that Schiller's approach to pragmatism was more subjectivistic and individualistic than his own, he found a basic agreement between them.[2] Both put their pragmatisms to the same use in destroying absolute idealism in their respective countries, James combating the idealism of Josiah Royce, and Schiller particularly that of F. H. Bradley. Schiller also shared with the American pragmatists (with the exception of C. S. Peirce) a distaste for formal and symbolic logic, advocating a more human and personalized logic, as Dewey did in the United States.

pragmatism as humanism

While associating himself with the pragmatic movement begun by Peirce and carried on by James and Dewey, Schiller had little liking for the name "pragmatism." It was, he thought, too obscure, technical, and unattractive. He wrote to James that pragmatism "is not the final term of philosophic innovation: there is vet a greater and more sovereign principle now entering the lists of which it can only claim to have been the forerunner and vicegerent."[3] This principle Schiller calls humanism. While not dissociating the word from its historical sense of excellence of literary style (barbarism of style, he says, has reached colossal heights with Kant and Hegel) and anti-scholasticism, Schiller above all means by humanism a certain philosophical perspective and spirit.[4] The humanist in philosophy always takes into account the human aspect of the problem he is considering. He does not begin with a bare dehumanized abstraction, such as the Absolute, the Universal Ego, Pure Being, or the Idea, which leaves out the richness and variety of human experience. Rather, he starts with man's integral nature, with its complex interests, desires, and emotions, and he aims at the complete satisfaction of this nature. As James points out in his review of Schiller's contribution to *Personal Idealism*, the latter's philosophy is a "re-anthropomorphized universe"; or, as Schiller prefers to say, a "re-humanized universe."[5]

Schiller sums up the spirit of philosophical humanism with Protagoras' saying, that man is the measure of all things. This principle—which Schiller calls "the truest and most important thing that any thinker ever has propounded"—means that man determines his own experience.[6] Man is an ineradicable factor in the world of his experience; that world is not completely intelligible unless the individual human being, with his habits of knowing, stock of information, desires, and interests, is taken into account. But does it not contradict the commonsense notion of the independence of the external world to say that this world is determined by man? Schiller will not allow that this is so. As we shall see, he thinks that the common-sense notion has great pragmatic value, but that this notion is compatible with the recognition that the real world is determined to some extent, and perhaps totally, by human experience.

One of the subjects that Schiller is most insistent to humanize is logic. He is critical of traditional formal logic, as taught, for example, by Aristotle, and also of the newer symbolic and mathematical logics, because they abstract from the material content of propositions and attempt to draw truths from pure forms. Does not the meaning of any statement depend on the person, time, and place in which it is made? Cannot one and the same form take on different meanings in different contexts? To isolate forms of thought from their material content, Schiller urges, is to lose contact with the actual thinking of men and the problems they have to solve. Logic cannot be divorced from psychology or the empirical sciences; it should reflect the actual processes of our thinking and not attempt to be a calculus independent of the operations of our brain in concrete situations. In short, logical rules should rest on the observation of psychical facts; they should not be *a priori* laws that dictate to facts. "Humanist logic," Schiller writes, "...challenges all the earlier logics, and accuses them of a false and foolish intellectualism, which has ignored and abstracted from all the characteristic operations of real thinking, and substituted a whole system of fictitious notions of abstraction. These have severed logic from its natural setting in the human mind, estranged it from human psychology, and delivered it over, bound hand and foot, to artificial and artful conventions of language. Thus has logic been made into a word-game—or rather into a series of such, since their conventions could be infinitely varied—which had no relation whatever to the acquiring and assuring of knowledge, nor any bearing on the progress of the sciences."[7]

Schiller's criticism of the Aristotelian doctrine of definition is a good illustration of the difficulty he finds with formal logic. A definition, according to Aristotle, comprises the genus or class in which an object is located, and the specific differences that differentiate that object from other members of the genus. Each individual has but one essence, and this is made known by its definition. But, Schiller protests, such a formal definition is completely alien to the way we actually know. It presupposes that we really know the essences of things and their essential properties. This is indeed what we are trying to find out, but we do not know them at the beginning of our inquiry; our initial definitions are only provisional, and they have to be modified as our knowledge increases. And we never come to an end of our investigation of the properties of things, so that even if they had essences we would not be able to know them. Moreover, a given object can be defined in several ways; no one definition exhausts its attributes. Depending on our purpose, we select certain properties of the object and formulate its definition. Thus in actual practice, essences and definitions are necessarily plural, variable, relative, and never absolute. Science needs and devises definitions that are flexible, corrigible, and adapted to a specific use; and such definitions formal logic does not provide. In short, formal logic "never descends to earth and has no concern with real definitions or real knowing."[8] Schiller directs similar criticisms against Aristotle's formal handling of propositions and syllogisms.

This effort to humanize logic is but one aspect of a wider program of reform embracing the whole theory of knowledge. Schiller sees this theory as dominated in his day by an intellectualism centered on abstractions and "pure thought," without regard for real processes of knowing. To bring epistemology down to earth, humanism must be applied to it, and this application is what Schiller means by pragmatism. Thus pragmatism is nothing but the extension of humanism to the theory of knowledge. It is that part of humanism dealing with the method of evaluating truth.[9]

the making of truth

The realist claims that there are facts independent of the processes by which they are known. Knowing facts makes no difference whatsoever to them. Truth is possessed when we know that there is a perfect correspondence between the fact as it is in itself and outside our knowledge, and the fact as it appears in our knowledge.

To Schiller these statements involve insuperable difficulties. If facts are really independent of our knowing processes, they must transcend them; how, then, can they be known by and in these processes? Furthermore, how can an independent fact be apprehended by a subjective activity that is largely, if not wholly, arbitrary; and this without making any difference to facts?

The absolute idealist introduces the notion of "an eternal ideal of truth." But this ideal is also supposed to be independent of us and our doings, and consequently it leads to the same difficulties as the realist position on truth. Indeed, it adds to them, because now we have to know the correspondence between our human knowledge and the absolute ideal, which, just because it is perfect, cannot be fully known by us. "Absolute truth, therefore, as conceived by absolutism, is not merely *useless* as a criterion of *our* truth, because we do not possess it, and cannot compare it with our truth, nor estimate where and to what extent our truth falls short of its 'divine' archetype.... It is positively *noxious*, actively disruptive of the whole notion of truth, and pregnant with self-destructive consequences."[10]

The fundamental mistake of the realist and absolute idealist is to disregard the human element in truth. They assume that truth is something independent of human interests, desires, satisfactions, hopes, and purposes; in other words, something that can be analyzed in purely intellectual terms, without regard for man's volitional life. They fail to see that truth comes into existence through human effort and activity, and that human action is always psychologically conditioned. As a result, they overlook the fact that truth is not independent of ourselves or discovered ready-made, but is something made by us in order to fulfill some human need.

Like the American pragmatists, Schiller points out that the search for truth always begins with a problem that we are interested in solving. Rational inquiry is purposive; it grows out of a concrete situation as a means of satisfying some human want. Truth and falsehood have meaning only in relation to the satisfaction of this want. "'True' and 'false,'" he writes, "are definable in terms of the purpose of the inquiry. Whatever is found to thwart or defeat this purpose is called 'false,' whatever is taken to forward it and to lead it to a satisfactory and successful conclusion is voted 'true.'" Consequently, truth and falsehood are valuations, like good and evil. Truth is a kind of good; it "is simply the good or end aimed at in knowing."[11]

Schiller encounters the same difficulty as James in trying to clarify the sense in which truth is a good or an end. Like James, he claims that a true idea is one that works or is useful, but he is not very precise in defining the utility that is the criterion of truth. He makes it clear that he does not consider truth to be equivalent to usefulness. All truth must work and be useful, but not everything that works or is useful is *ipso facto* true. A lie may serve a useful purpose in a given situation, but that does not make it true. We must take into account all the consequences of an assertion and judge its claim to truth by them and not by just any good result it may have. An assertion is true if it is satisfactory in the long run and conducive to the ultimate harmony of human life.[12]

In every case, we do not arrive at truth by passively observing objects but by actively manipulating them and experimenting with them. Every judgment is an experiment which must be tested by acting upon it. For example, if I assert, "This is a chair," I have some purpose in mind; perhaps I desire to sit down or to buy a chair. "This" denotes an arbitrary selection of a part of a given whole. In order to test my assertion that this is a chair, I try to sit in it. If it is really a chair my test succeeds, if it is an hallucination it fails. Unless I act and experiment, I never know for sure whether "this" is a chair or only a false appearance of one.

For Schiller, then, truth is made by human operations on the data of experience. It consists in verification, which, as the word indicates, is "truth-making." It goes without saying that this is a continuous and progressive activity; knowledge grows in extent and trustworthiness by successful functioning and by assimilating fresh material into existing bodies of knowledge. Not only are fresh facts assimilated; they also transform: "The old truth looks different in the new light, and really changes." There is no absolute truth, except in the sense of an ideal still to be reached, a completion of the making of truth, when no further questions are asked and no incentive is given to remake the old truth.[13]

the making of reality

Remarkable as is Schiller's contention that truth is not so much a discovery as a product of human activity, the consequence he draws from it is still more paradoxical: reality itself is a creation of knowledge, so that the making of truth is at the same time the making of reality.

Schiller recognizes that in equating the making of truth with the making of reality he is following in the footsteps of Hegel. In Schiller's view, however, Hegel spoiled his "great idea" of the identity of the thought process with the cosmic process by conceiving thought as eternal and above the evolution of reality in time.[14] This puts the real events of history outside of the order of the eternal Dialectic of the categories and makes the former mere illustrations of the latter. It also misconceives the process of thought by emptying it of all the actual, concrete thinking of men. Thought becomes a dehumanized, absolute ideal entirely incapable of engendering the real, concrete cosmic process. In the perspective of the pragmatic theory of knowledge espoused by Schiller, this process is a product of the actual thinking of human beings.

But in what sense does thought engender reality? In answering this question Schiller distinguishes between *subjective* and *objective* making of reality. Subjectively we make reality in the sense that, by thinking, facts become real *for us*; objectively we make reality to the extent that our thinking affects reality in its very existence.[15]

Considering first the subjective making of reality, Schiller regards this as a necessary consequence of the pragmatic theory of knowledge. This theory holds that the immediate object of experience is not a real fact; a fact becomes real for us when we evaluate it as such. What we immediately experience is a meaningless chaos, the stuff out of which real facts will be made. It may even include errors, illusions, and hallucinations. By experimenting, we come to distinguish real facts from those that are unreal. Thus we select real facts from among many possible ones; and this selection is highly arbitrary and individual, involving not only our ideas but also our desires, interests, and emotions. Some people will not face unpleasant facts or do so only by constraint. Others tend to postulate ideal realities or to extend reality to console themselves. We can neglect facts, ignore them, exclude them from our lives, and so they really tend to become unreal for us. Truly, then, we can say that our real world is the product of our own making.[16]

But are there no objective facts—hard, plain facts independent of our knowledge and interests? From the pragmatic viewpoint an objective fact would be one that is completely satisfactory and that raises no problem. This is an ideal toward which we are striving but which we have not yet reached. What today seems to us the "real world" may someday seem unreal in contrast to a superior reality. Even the real external world that common sense regards as independent of ourselves and as having existed before we were born is nor an objective fact. It is a postulate of high pragmatic value (like the axiomatic principles of identity and causality)[17]; it explains our experience and can be acted on with great success. It is not, however, an original datum of experience.[18]

Granted that we make reality subjectively, or relative to ourselves, do we also make it objectively, in its very existence? Schiller's right even to raise this problem has been questioned.[19] Does not his pragmatist epistemology preclude the existence of a reality independent of thought? How then can he entertain the notion of a making of reality that is not subjective but affects its very existence?

Valid as this objection is from the standpoint of philosophical realism, in Schiller's view it does not touch his own humanist position. He denies that he is an out-and-out idealist. Reality, for him, is not purely mental and reducible to experience, though it is always related to experience. The real world is an *ex-*

perienced world, and therefore it is related to thought; but thought also needs a *real* world of some sort in order to have real knowledge. So there must be a real world that is relatively, though not absolutely, independent of the mind. Thus, Schiller attempts to rise above both idealism and realism. These he regards as outworn labels; the truths they express can be subsumed in the superior doctrine of philosophical humanism.[20] He feels that it is perfectly legitimate from this lofty vantage point to examine both the subjective and objective features of experience (as William James did before him), and to ask whether thought makes reality objectively, in its very existence.

In the case of the knowing subject it is obvious that knowledge makes a real difference to him. Knowing brings about a real change in the knower, a real enlightenment of his ignorance, and since he is a part of reality he plainly alters or makes his own reality by knowing. But what about the other pole of the cognitive process, the object known? Is it altered by being known, and consequently made by this process? Common sense would have us believe that there are facts independent of experience which we discover, and to which our knowing makes no difference. But once we adopt the pragmatist view of knowledge we have to admit that there is no discovery of reality that does not involve an alteration of it. Knowing is but one aspect of a process that is completed by acting, and our actions are bound to change reality. The reality we know always responds to our knowledge of it, and it is thereby altered. This is obvious in the case of our knowledge of human beings and animals; they are aware of our observations of them and alter their behavior accordingly. But even inanimate things are sensitive to our knowledge and manipulation, and as a consequence they undergo real changes. Schiller suggests that there is a primitive awareness even in the inanimate world (pan-psychism); it, too, takes notice of our knowing and is altered by it.[21]

To what extent can we change reality by knowing and handling it? In principle we should assume that it is completely plastic and re-makable for our purposes. To think otherwise, as William James has shown, is to shut ourselves out from many goods that we might realize if we only have faith in their possibility. To act effectively, we should assume that no facts are unalterable and inflexible.[22]

Are we then to think of ourselves as creators? By no means. We do not make reality out of nothing. There is a "primary reality" that we do not make but that underlies all of our knowledge and action. This ultimate reality is a formless, indeterminate matter (*hulé*). Like Kant's *Ding an sich*, on which it is obviously modeled, this primal reality is not an object of experience, for it is completely indeterminate; we infer its existence as a necessary condition of knowledge and action. It is the plastic, determinable stuff of the universe, the primitive chaos that is molded and shaped by experience.[23]

Are we the only agents who make reality? There are aspects of the universe that we who live in the present cannot claim to have made. Are these original features of the universe, or have they been determined by processes analogous to those by which we make reality? Schiller thinks the latter alternative more plausible. He considers the universe, with its present laws of nature (which are more or less stable habits of acting), to be the consequence of an evolution whose course has been shaped by many agents in continuous interaction. Among these agents he postulates one (or perhaps more than one) whose part in shaping reality has been so preponderant that we may almost call him a creator.[24] The God (or gods) thus postulated is not quite a creator, because he is not omnipotent or infinite. Like Renouvier, Mill, and James, Schiller has no use for a God who is all-powerful; would not such a God render superfluous our own efforts to remake the world? A limited deity, who needs man's co-operation, but on whom he can also call in time of trouble, is the one most satisfactory from the pragmatic point of view.[25] Like ourselves (on whom he is obviously modeled), such a God not only makes reality by his thinking but at the same time struggles to bring himself into existence. The process of making reality is, for him as it is for us, identical with the process of making himself.

conclusion

Schiller is a lonely figure in English philosophy. He was surrounded by no circle in England sharing his ideas and interests, nor did he leave an outstanding pupil to carry them on after his death.[26] The American pragmatists were almost alone in offering him understanding and sympathy. In his own country he had to withstand the assaults of both the absolute idealists and the new realists, especially G. E. Moore and Bertrand Russell, who opposed pragmatism as vehemently as they did idealism. It is hardly surprising that Schiller, having spent a lifetime as a David combating the Goliaths of absolute idealism in England, retired to the United States and passed his few remaining years in its more congenial atmosphere.

Schiller's main significance in the history of philosophy does not lie in his pragmatism. Although he began his own humanistic pragmatism more or less independently of James and Dewey, he does not rival them in originality or influence. His importance is rather in his determined opposition to German absolute idealism, in the forms it took in the British universities at the turn of the century. He waged a bitter struggle against its bloodless abstractions and strove to restore philosophy in England to its traditional empiricism and humanism. Throughout his writings he insists that the human element must be taken into account in philosophy; that thinking must be seen not as "pure thought" but as a kind of human activity, psychologically motivated and serving the interests of the whole man. From this point of view, he could not have chosen a better label for his philosophy than "Humanism."

That Schiller was not more successful is due to the fact that he chose to oppose absolute idealism with the weapons of idealism. What are his "making of truth" and "making of reality" but humanized forms of Hegelianism? Despite his criticism of German idealism, its influence pervades his philosophy. His gesture toward realism is half-hearted. He never conceived reality as independent of mind; at most he granted a relative independence to it. But does not this concession sit poorly with his basic idealist tenets? To break the spell of idealism in England a new philosophical atmosphere had to be created. A new point of departure had to be found and new methods of procedure in philosophy had to be forged. This was the work of the realists we shall study in the next chapter.

XX.

Return to Realism

THE revival of realism in England in the early decades of the twentieth century was owing chiefly to G. E. Moore and Bertrand Russell. In Chapter XXV we shall consider the movement away from idealism initiated at about the same time by the American New Realists and Critical Realists. Moore and Russell rebelled in their own way against the idealism dominating the contemporary philosophical world, and they and their disciples created the new methods and set the philosophical tone that have prevailed in English philosophy to our day. These men did not simply return to the realism of the classical English empiricists or of the Scottish school of common sense. While continuing in some respects the older types of realism, they were engaged in a truly creative work, in which even the idealism they combated played a constructive role. There are traces of Bradley's influence, for example, on Whitehead, Russell, and Wittgenstein. English philosophy had been too long under the dominance of Bradley's idealism to forget the experience. As Whitehead says, "Philosophy never reverts to its old position after the shock of a great philosopher."[1]

G. E. Moore

Russell has vividly described his own and Moore's reaction against Bradley's idealism and the leading role Moore played in it. Referring to Moore, Russell writes: "He took the lead in rebellion, and I followed, with a sense of emancipation. Bradley argued that everything common sense believes in is mere appearance; we reverted to the opposite extreme, and thought that *everything* is real that common sense, uninfluenced by philosophy or theology, supposes real. With a sense of escaping from prison, we allowed ourselves to think that grass is green, that the sun and stars would exist if no one was aware of them, and also that there is a pluralistic timeless world of Platonic ideas. The world, which had been thin and logical, suddenly became rich and varied and solid."[2]

It was to Russell, however, that Moore owed his initiation to philosophy. When Moore went to Cambridge in 1892 to study the classics, he hardly knew that there was such a thing as philosophy.[3] His interest in the subject came through his friendship with Russell, who was two years his senior at the university. In his *Autobiography* Moore recalls Russell's inviting him to tea, to meet the idealist James McTaggart. In the course of the conversation McTaggart expressed his view that time is unreal. This seemed so monstrous a statement to Moore that he could not restrain himself from arguing against it. On this and similar occasions Moore acquitted himself so ably in philosophical discussion that Russell advised him to add philosophy to his course in classics. Thus began a career that was to play a major role in altering the direction of philosophy in England.

This new direction was toward the analysis of language. Moore did not dispute the generally accepted opinion that there is such a thing as metaphysics or that it deals with reality. Indeed, he always considered that the most important and interesting task of philosophy is to give a general description of the universe as a whole. Yet he himself was not aroused to philosophize by problems concerning the world but by puzzling statements of philosophers. "I do not think," he writes, "that the world or the sciences would ever have suggested to me any philosophical problems. What has suggested philosophical problems to me is things which other philosophers have said about the world or the sciences."[4] He frankly admitted that he did not understand many of the statements of the philosophers, and if he did understand them he often questioned whether the philosophers had satisfactory reasons for thinking their statements were true. Hence philosophy, as he practiced it, tended to be mainly the clarification of the meaning of philosophical statements and the examination of the reasons given for them. Since these reasons were stated in propositions, what he was chiefly concerned with was not reality itself but the language or thought of the philosophers.

the refutation of idealism

In one of his first essays, "The Refutation of Idealism" (1903), Moore examines some of the puzzling statements of the idealists and finds them completely false.[5] In later life he criticized this essay and abandoned some of its views, but it is remarkable for the effect it had on English philosophy. It not only initiated the realist movement but, perhaps equally important, it introduced contemporary philosophers to Moore's distinctive philosophical style, which has been copied by so many of his followers, especially at Cambridge. The main features of his procedure are the careful and even meticulous delineation of the point at issue, and the analysis of philosophical statements by appealing to common sense and the ordinary use of language.

According to the idealists, Moore says, the universe is very different from what it seems. Chairs and tables appear to be lifeless and unconscious, but idealists claim that the whole universe is spiritual and endowed with intelligence. He does not pretend in his essay to settle the question whether reality is spiritual or material. But he does think he can show that the propositions on which idealists rest their claim are completely false. Idealism, then, may still be true, but it has not been proved to be true. The common sense view that the universe is material may well be, and likely is, correct.

The basic proposition of idealism disputed by Moore is that *to be is to be perceived* (*esse* is *percipi*). All idealists, he says, hold this in some sense, and from it they deduce their conclusion that reality is mental in character. They argue, for example, that whatever is, is an object of thought, and consequently that thought enters into the nature of all reality.

But is it true that *esse* is *percipi*? In Moore's view, the statement is highly ambiguous, and when this ambiguity is cleared up by a careful analysis of all the terms its falsity is evident.

Does the formula mean that *being* is identical with *being perceived*; that *yellow*, for example, is identical with the *sensation of yellow*? If so, the terms would be synonymous and the proposition would be a barren tautology. Moreover, it would be self-evident, in need of no proof. Idealists can hardly intend this; and yet they have not understood the implications of saying that *to be perceived* is in some way different from *being*.

True, some idealists recognize a distinction between a sensation or an idea and its object, but they insist that they form an inseparable unity. There is no real difference between them; they are so connected in an "organic unity" that they cannot be legitimately abstracted from each other. But Moore objects that this is an attempt to hold two contradictory positions at the same time. These idealists assert that *esse* and *percipi* are distinct while treating them as if they were not. They fall into the basic error of idealism, which is to affirm and deny that *being* and *being perceived* are distinct.

Some idealists claim that the object is only the content of a sensation or idea. The sensation or idea is a whole with two inseparable aspects: content and existence. Moore thinks that this view can be disproved by a correct analysis of the statement "one thing is the content of another." We say that blue is the content of a blue flower, meaning that blue is a quality of the flower. But blue clearly does not have this relation to consciousness. We do not speak of a "blue consciousness." According to Bradley, the object is the content of consciousness in the sense of being *what* we assert to exist, in distinction to consciousness which we assert is *that* which exists. Moore retorts that surely blue is not in this sense the content of the sensation of blue, for it is not the whole of what is said to exist; in this sense consciousness is also part of the content.

The correct analysis of a sensation or idea, in Moore's view, distinguishes between consciousness as the element common to all sensations and ideas, and the object of consciousness. One of these is not identical with the other. There exists an awareness of blue. This is what we know when we know that the sensation of blue exists. And this awareness is something unique and utterly different from blue. It has, moreover, a perfectly distinct and unique relation to blue. This relation is not that of a things or substance to its content, nor of one part of a content to another part. It is the relation of consciousness to its object. For example, when I have a sensation of blue I am sure that I am aware of *blue*, not that its content is blue. In short, blue stands in relation to my awareness as its object.

If this is true, there is no problem of how we are to get outside the circle of our own ideas and sensations. "Merely to have a sensation is already to *be* outside that circle. It is to know something which is as truly and really *not* a part of *my* experience, as anything which I can ever know." Moore concludes: "When, therefore, Berkeley supposed that the only thing of which I am directly aware is my own sensations and ideas, he supposed what was false; and when Kant supposed that the objectivity of things in space *consisted* in the fact that they were 'Vorstellungen' having to one another different relations from those which the same 'Vorstellungen' have to one another in subjective experience, he supposed what was equally false. I am as directly aware of the existence of material things in space as of my own sensations; and *what* I am aware of with regard to each is exactly the same—namely that in one case the material thing, and in the other case my sensation does really exist."[6]

defense of common sense

Thus Moore takes his stand against idealism in the name of common sense, rejecting any philosophical opinion that is plainly contrary to it. To him, the common-sense view of the world is in certain fundamental respects absolutely true. He has no doubt, for example, that his own body and other material things really exist in space and that he has experiences of perceiving and dreaming. Neither does he question the fact that the world existed in the past, before he was born. Moreover, he is certain that he is not the only one who knows facts of this sort. Many human beings beside himself have similarly perceived their own and other bodies in space and have experienced sensations and dreams.[7]

Although Moore is absolutely certain of all these propositions, he does not claim to understand them completely. They are in need of philosophical analysis, and he is sometimes skeptical of what their correct analysis is.[8] But he insists that they have an ordinary meaning—one that everyone, including philosophers, knows—and in this sense the propositions are wholly true. He will not concede to Bradley that, taking them in their natural and ordinary meaning, they are partially false. As we ordinarily use language, a statement that is partially false is not said to be true. But the propositions in question are true. Hence they cannot be partially false; they must be wholly true.[9]

What are we to say to idealists who assert that material bodies and space and time are unreal? If their statement is taken in its most natural and proper meaning, it follows that no philosophers have ever existed, for a philosopher is a human being with a body that has lived on the earth for a time. Hence the idealists' statement is incompatible with the existence of the philosopher who makes it! Furthermore, philosophers constantly allude to other philosophers. They speak of themselves in the plural, as *we*, implying that there are other human beings beside themselves who have bodies and who live on the earth. It is the height of absurdity for philosophers to speak with contempt of common-sense beliefs; by their statement they acknowledge the truth of at least some of these beliefs. If they say that these are beliefs of common sense, they must say that they are true, since the proposition that they are beliefs of common sense logically entails the proposition that many human beings, beside the philosopher himself, live on the earth and have beliefs of this sort.

In appealing to common sense as a touchstone of truth Moore is following in the footsteps of Thomas Reid, whose works he read. Like the Scottish philosopher he regards the views of common sense as more solidly grounded than those of philosophy, so that the latter should be rejected if they manifestly contradict the former. Unlike Reid, however, he does not look for an explanation of the origin of our common-sense beliefs in the constitution of our nature as it has been created by God. He is content to take these beliefs as self-evident facts without examining their source.[10]

By a common-sense belief Moore means one that is universally accepted and constantly assumed to be true; for example, the belief in the existence of material things. He does not think that the belief in God or a future life, though held by an enormous number of people, passes this test, because many do not believe in them. Beliefs once generally held and now abandoned also fail to measure up to the standard of common sense. We can recognize a belief of common sense by the force with which it appeals to us and by the fact that its denial leads to inconsistencies. Thus Hume contradicts himself when he says that we cannot know any external facts, but that in ordinary life we cannot avoid believing that we do. Does this not imply that he does know many ordinary facts of the external world, such as that other men exist beside himself who resemble him in their beliefs and actions?[11]

Common sense statements, such as "this pencil exists," are so certain that they cannot be disproved, and they are so evident that they do not need to be proved. There are no more certain premises by which they could be proved false, and they are much more certain than any premise that could be advanced to prove that they are true. If I raise my hand and say, "Here's a hand," how can I prove the statement? It is not possible or necessary that I do so. I have conclusive evidence that a hand exists, and consequently that an external object exists. Does my inability to prove the existence of my hand mean that I must accept it merely on faith? Not at all; the statement is true on the evidence furnished by my hand.[12]

As a criterion of the truth of statements Moore appeals not only to common sense but also to ordinary language. He often points out to his reader that he already knows the meaning of common words like "real" and "time," and that he knows how to use them in sentences. He insists that philosophers should be guided by the ordinary use of everyday language. They should not use words in a way inconsistent with this use. Moore himself often appeals to ordinary language to justify his own way of speaking, and he criticizes those who go against the common use of terms. Thus he complains that Bradley misuses the word "real" when he denies that time is real; as we ordinarily use the word we would call time real.[13] Inconsistency with the ordinary use of words indicates that a philosophical doctrine is badly expressed and that it is likely to be absurd.[14]

Moore's concern with ordinary language is not to insure grammatical correctness; this he leaves to the grammarian. He defends everyday language because it is an indication of our common beliefs. What we ordinarily say is a sign of what we commonly hold to be true, and consequently our ordinary language can be used as a guide to common sense. Ultimately it is common sense that is the touchstone of truth. Moore's point was already made by Reid when he wrote apropos of a confusion of terms in Berkeley and Hume: "But there is reason to distrust any philosophical theory when it leads men to corrupt language, and to confound, under one name, operations of the mind which common sense and common language teach them to distinguish."[15]

perception and sense-data

Moore's defense of common sense statements rests on the fact that they have an ordinary or natural meaning which nobody—not even philosophers—can fail to know. Taken in this sense, everyone, including philosophers, must acknowledge them to be true. But this does not mean that the philosophical analysis of these propositions is certain. Indeed, Moore thinks that on certain important points no philosopher as yet has been able to analyze them correctly.

A case in point is the proposition "material things exist." Everyone knows this statement to be true, and yet philosophers differ greatly in their analysis of it. Moore's analysis leads to simpler propositions of the type: "I am perceiving a human hand," which in turn lead to even more simple propositions such as "I am perceiving this" and "this is a human hand." Analyzing the latter proposition, Moore arrives at two important conclusions: (1) The subject of the proposition is a sense-datum—in the present case a patch of color of a certain size and shape; (2) the sense-datum is not identical with the hand but merely represents it. Consequently, the analysis of propositions of this type ends with the existence of sense-data, which are themselves incapable of further analysis.

Moore holds it as certain that we do not directly perceive material objects but only "sense-data"—a term, incidentally, that he introduced into philosophy.[16] Material objects are only indirectly perceived by means of these data. Moore's reason for saying this is that we plainly do not see a hand in its entirety but at most a certain part of its surface. Indeed, it can be doubted if what we directly perceive is identical with the surface of the hand. If several people look at a hand, each sees it from a different position and under different environmental conditions, so that what each actually sees is different. What each sees is a patch of color of a different shade, size, and shape. And yet all would agree that they see the same hand. This shows that there is one material object that all see, but that this object is distinct from the sense-data by which all see it.

Although Moore never doubted the existence of sense-data, he wavered as to their nature and their relation to physical objects on the one hand and to perception on the other. Is the sense-datum I see when I look at a hand a part of the surface of the hand? While considering this possible, he sees grave objections to it. Because the sense-datum of one person seeing the hand is different from, and incompatible with that of another person seeing the same hand, we would have to say that the surface has simultaneously many inconsistent qualities. Moreover, when we see a thing double, or have a "double image" of it, we have two sense-data of its surface, and these cannot both be identical with the surface.

If the sense-datum is an entity distinct from the surface, we have to face the grave problem of its relation to the surface. Is the surface the source or cause of the sense-datum? Is the sense-datum the appearance or manifestation of the surface? How can we be sure of the answers to these questions? Indeed, on this supposition how can we know anything about the physical object itself? It would seem that we could only know the sense-datum. The same difficulty arises if, with Mill, we define material things as "permanent possibilities of sensation." If this were true, "the sense in which a material surface is 'round' or 'square,' would necessarily be utterly different from that in which our sense-data sensibly appear to us to be 'round' or 'square.'"[17]

Moore confesses that he is equally perplexed as to the relation of sense-data to the one perceiving them. As we have seen, in an early paper entitled *The*

Refutation of Idealism he tried to show that Berkeley's principle *esse* is *percipi* is unfounded. His analysis of the principle convinced him that "in no case does it follow from the fact that a thing of a certain kind exists that that thing is perceived."[18] Later he made an exception in the case of pains, after-images, and all sense qualities. He was strongly inclined to agree with his critic C. J. Ducasse that the *esse* of a sense-datum is *percipi*—"that it is as impossible that anything which has the sensible quality 'blue,' and more generally, *anything whatever which is directly apprehended,* any *sense-datum,* that is, should exist unperceived, as it is that a headache should exist unfelt."[19] But he never abandoned his opinion that the *esse* of a material thing is not its *percipi.* A toothache, he writes, certainly cannot exist without being felt, but the moon certainly can exist without being perceived.[20]

Moore never succeeded in solving to his satisfaction the problems to which his notion of sense-data led him. In one of his last comments on these problems he acknowledges a strong inclination to assert two incompatible things: that the sense-data we directly perceive are subjective and hence not identical with physical surfaces, and that we do directly perceive these surfaces. "I am completely puzzled about the matter," he says with characteristic simplicity and candor, "and only wish I could see any way of settling it."[21] But he never abandoned the notion of sense-data that landed him in this inextricable dilemma.

being and reality

We have seen that the analysis of "material things" in the proposition "material things exist" leads ultimately to sense-data as the direct objects of perception. There remains the analysis of the other part of the proposition, the verb "exists." Moore takes great pains to examine the notion of existence and the related terms "being," "reality," and "fact." In several essays this analysis is prompted by Bradley's contention that time exists but is not real. Is this not a contradiction? Are reality and existence two different properties, so that one can, without contradiction, say that something exists but is not real?

The reason Bradley asserts that appearances exist though they are not real seems to be that they can be thought and talked about. But Moore questions whether this is a good reason for ascribing existence to something. If we entertain a false belief, there really is no such thing as what we believe in. It does not exist or have being. It is possible to think of things that do not exist; for example, a round square or a chimera. Being is the property of what we believe in when our belief is true, and which does not belong to what we believe in when our belief is false. In short, what has being or exists is an object of true knowledge. This is the most fundamental property denoted by the term "being" or "existence."[22]

This definition of being in terms of belief comes as a surprise from a philosopher who defends the independence of being from thought. It indicates how deeply idealism was ingrained in the English philosophy of this period. A more realistic description of the property of being follows. Whatever exists or has being, Moore says, belongs to the universe or is a constituent of it. The universe itself is the sum of all things that exist, including what has existed in the past and what will exist in the future.

According to Moore all the constituents of the universe fall into three classes: (1) particulars, (2) facts, and (3) universals. Particulars are individual things such as lions and bears. Facts are the class of entities expressed by a clause beginning with "that" or by the corresponding verbal noun; for example, "that lions exist" or "the existence of lions." Facts are truths—not in the sense of true beliefs but the objects of these beliefs. By universals Moore does not mean abstract ideas, insofar as they are mental acts, but the objects of these acts; for example, the number two or the property of being nearby. Moore insists that truths and universals are not dependent on our mind, nor are they in our mind as our acts of thinking are. There may be two things, and the number two, even when no one is thinking of them. The same is true of the relation *nearby*.

While it is usual to speak of particulars as existing, it is hardly normal to say that facts exist. We say that "lions exist" but not that the fact "that lions exist" exists. For this reason Moore hesitated at first to identify existence and being. He was inclined to restrict existence to particular things, and to say that they alone exist while the other constituents of the universe only have being. Later he thought it more likely that this is just a grammatical difference and that existence and being really designate the same property of being a constituent of the universe. He doubted if particulars have any kind of reality that truths and universals do not have.[23]

The upshot of this is that the terms "being," "existence," and "reality" are equivalent; they designate that something exists or is a constituent of the universe. Moore points out that we most commonly use "real" in contrast to "imaginary." For instance, we call bears real animals and centaurs imaginary ones. This is but another way of saying that bears exist and centaurs do not.

Do fictions of the imagination have no being at all? We ordinarily do not say that centaurs exist. We seem to contradict common sense if we say they do. And yet Moore wonders if, in one sense, we must not say they exist or have being. When we imagine a centaur we are not imagining nothing but something. As an object of the imagination, a centaur *is*, although this is not the proper meaning of the term. Moore thinks that this unusual and improper sense of the term may have misled Bradley to say that time exists but is not real. To refute Bradley, then, it is enough to point out that this would make time something imaginary; that temporal sequences would not be constituents of the universe.[24]

Although Moore speaks of existence as a property, he has grave doubts as to the propriety of saying it really is a property or predicate. Linguistic analysis inclines him to the Kantian conclusion that existence is not a predicate. Because the propositions "tame tigers exist" and "tame tigers growl" have the same grammatical form, it might be thought that "exists" is a predicate like "growl." But there is good reason to think that this is not so. We can say, "All (or most) tame tigers growl," but hardly "All (or most) tame tigers exist." Again, we can say, "Here's a tame tiger and he growls," but it is redundant to say, "Here's a tame tiger and he exists." This indicates that "exists" is not the usual sort of property or predicate. Yet, it is surely significant to say, "Tigers exist." The contrary is possible—that no tigers exist. Consequently, the fact that they do exist is meaningful. Moore suggests that what we mean (at least in part) when we point to something and say, "This exists," is that a certain sense-datum that we are perceiving is "of" a physical object. Thus when we point to a book and say, "This exists," we mean, "This sense-datum is of a physical object." "This exists" can also be said significantly of the sense-datum itself.[25]

ethical views

Moore wrote two books on moral philosophy: *Principia Ethica* (1903) and *Ethics* (1912). Although he preferred the latter as the more mature expression of his views, the former is his most famous book and it has exercised a powerful influence on subsequent ethical thought in England.

The main problem of ethics, Moore says, is to answer the question "What is the meaning of the term 'good'?" In everyday language we call many different things good. What characteristic do they have in common that is designated by this word? In *Principia Ethica* he is convinced that goodness is a unique and indefinable quality of things. Like the notion of yellow, the notion of goodness is simple and incapable of being defined in more elementary terms. If a person does not already know what goodness is, you can no more explain it to him than you can tell him what yellow is if he has not perceived it. But "Every one does in fact understand the question 'Is this good?' When he thinks of it, his state of mind is different from what it would be, were he asked 'Is this pleasant, or desired, or approved?' It has a distinct meaning for him, even though he may not recognize in what respect it is distinct. Whenever he thinks of 'intrinsic value,' or 'intrinsic worth,' or says that a thing 'ought to exist,' he has before his mind the unique object—the unique property of things—which I mean by 'good.' "[26]

If the notion of goodness is simple, how can the philosopher analyze and elucidate it? Moore thinks this can be done by showing how it differs from other notions that resemble it and with which philosophers have often confused it. Most ethical writers, in his view, have failed to recognize the unique character of goodness. They have equated it with some natural quality like pleasure, or with some metaphysical reality like the Absolute or the will of God. This is to commit what Moore calls the "naturalistic fallacy." This fallacy is "the contention that good *means* nothing but some simple or complex notion, that can be defined in terms of natural qualities."[27] The result of this error is the proliferation of naturalistic and metaphysical systems of ethics, all of which misconceive the meaning of goodness.

Moore finds hedonism the most widespread naturalistic ethics, especially as taught by Bentham and Mill, and by Moore's contemporary Henry Sidgwick. Hedonists are guilty of the fallacy of identifying goodness with pleasure. Mill, for example, equated the good with the desirable, which he thought could be discovered by finding out what men actually desire. Convinced that they desire pleasure alone as an end, he concluded that the only good is pleasure. But this is to regard the word "desirable" like the word "visible." It is to think that just as we can discover what is visible by finding out what is seen, so we can discover what is desirable by finding out what is desired. But as an ethical term "desirable" does not mean "what can be desired"; it means "what ought to be desired" or "what is good to desire." This cannot be revealed by examining the actual desires of men, some of which are obviously bad. Nor is pleasure the only object we desire for its own sake; even Mill admitted that some men want virtue or money for their own sakes.[28]

As for systems of ethics based on metaphysics, Moore finds that they also commit the naturalistic fallacy in the wide sense of describing the supreme good in terms of reality. Metaphysicians differ from naturalists in connecting goodness with some supersensible reality, such as the Absolute Substance or Self. But like the naturalists they fail to see that the proposition "this is good in itself" is unique in kind and hence incapable of being reduced to any assertion about reality. Ethical questions, such as, "what ought to be?" and "what ought we to do?" cannot be answered by metaphysical statements about what exists.

Kant did not fall into the usual mistake of metaphysicians of allowing his view of reality to influence his judgment of what is good. His ethics is based on the Moral Law, the knowledge of which is obtained independently of metaphysics. Nevertheless, Moore accuses him of committing the naturalistic fallacy because he identified goodness, or "what ought to be done," with the commands of free will. He equated "this is good" with "this is willed," thus basing moral goodness on a moral imperative or command. Moral obligation is conceived as analogous to legal obligation, with the sole difference that whereas the source of legal obligation is earthly, that of moral obligation is heavenly. Yet it is clear that an authority obliges us to obey only because what it commands is good, not because it commands. Hence the property of being commanded or willed is not the quality of goodness.[29]

Having disposed of fallacious attempts to define goodness, the last two chapters of the *Principia Ethica* take up questions of practical ethics such as "What ought we to do?" and "What things are intrinsically good?" Contrary to intuitionists, Moore does not regard the goodness of moral laws as self-evident. A moral law is simply a statement that a certain kind of action will have good effects. Consequently, its goodness has to be confirmed or refuted by investigating its consequences. In this, Moore agrees with the utilitarians. Like them, he insists that it is our duty to do that which will cause more good in the world than any possible alternative. In short, an act is a duty if it produces more good than harm. Since it is impossible to be certain about the consequences of our actions, moral laws are not certain; but there is a high probability that certain types of actions, such as lying and murder, will result in bad effects. Individuals are bound to obey such established laws even though they may think that in a particular case more good may come from breaking them. The general probability that that kind of action is wrong is of more weight than the individual's judgment. In cases covered by no general rule, "the individual should rather guide his choice by a direct consideration of the intrinsic value or vileness of the effects which his action may produce."[30]

Turning to the problem of what things are intrinsically good, Moore says that they are those, if they existed all by themselves, whose existence we would still judge to be good. He sees little difficulty in identifying them. "By far the most valuable things, which we know or can imagine, are certain states of consciousness, which may be roughly described as the pleasures of human intercourse and the enjoyment of beautiful objects. No one, probably, who has asked himself the question has ever doubted that personal affection and the appreciation of what is beautiful in Art or Nature, are good in themselves..."[31] On the other hand, it is evident that the enjoyment of what is ugly or lascivious, or the consciousness of pain, are great evils. In determining matters of this sort, as everywhere in his philosophy, Moore gives the final word to common sense.

Bertrand Russell

While studying at Cambridge in the 1890s Russell came under the sway of his Kantian and Hegelian professors James Ward, G. E. Stout, and James McTaggart, and for a few years he was won over to absolute idealism.[32] The logical rigor of Bradley's system captivated him, and the notion of an ideal Absolute afforded some compensation for the loss of his religious faith, which occurred at the age of eighteen. His idealism, however, was short-lived. Toward the end of 1898 he rebelled against Kant and Hegel, following the lead of G. E. Moore. With the feeling of being released from a subjective prison, he now believed in the reality of space and time, of sense qualities, and even of instants, points, numbers, and universals. As the years passed he considerably modified this naïve and Platonic realism. In his own words: "Gradually, Occam's razor gave me a more clean-shaven picture of reality."[33] But he never abandoned his conviction that facts are independent of the knowledge we have of them.

Russell concurs with Moore not only in this basic tenet of realism, but also in the belief that the aim of philosophy is to answer the question "what is there in the world and what is it like?" Neither thinks philosophy can stop short of metaphysics, because it is orientated toward the understanding of reality. It is true that both are much preoccupied with language and its analysis, but they do not regard this as an end in itself. As philosophers they look beyond language to its meaning and to the basis of its truth in the structure of the world. This accounts for Russell's vehement dislike of the later phase of the philosophy of his pupil Ludwig Wittgenstein. The later Wittgenstein and his followers (whom we shall consider in the next chapter) center philosophy on the study of language, as though the philosopher should try to understand sentences and not the world. Russell comments that this would make philosophy "at best, a slight help to lexicographers, and at worst, an idle tea-table amusement."[34] He is also critical of some Logical Positivists (especially Neurath, Hempel, and the early Carnap) for trying to divorce the world of language from the world of fact. Russell himself wants to take his place in the long line of Western philosophers, from Thales onward, who dedicated themselves to "that grave and important task" of understanding the world. True, he is not as optimistic as most of them as regards the possibility of success in this undertaking, but he considers even the failures of philosophers as so much material for their successors and an incentive to new effort.

Russell also agrees with Moore that the proper method of philosophy is analysis, but his method of analysis is quite different from that of Moore. Whereas Moore analyses philosophical statements by appealing to common sense and ordinary language, Russell strives to make analysis scientific by employing rigorous logical techniques. In short, he advocates and practices a logical analysis.[35] He has nothing but contempt for the cult of ordinary language that has sprung up among contemporary linguistic analysts in the wake of Moore's philosophy. This school considers the language of daily life, without any technical terms or changes, to be sufficient for philosophy—a view, he says, that makes philosophy trivial and perpetuates among philosophers the muddle-headedness of common sense. He himself wants philosophy to be close to science and to share in its precision, and this requires a technical method of procedure and an exact vocabulary. For the purpose of logical analysis Russell, with Whitehead, worked out in the *Principia Mathematica* a perfect logical language.

The divergence between Moore and Russell on the nature of analysis reflects the difference in their early interests and education. Moore came to philosophy from the classics, which gave him a fine appreciation of language in its ordinary usage, while Russell's early training emphasized mathematics. Obsessed by the problem of certitude from boyhood, he thought he had found his desired certainty in pure mathematics. As he was taught it, however, it failed to dispel all his doubts, and he looked about for a way to perfect it by giving it a more secure foundation. The search for the foundations of mathematics led him to logic. With the help of the Italian mathematician Peano he found a way to reduce mathematics to logic—a reduction described in *Principia Mathematica*. Not content with eliminating all essential difference between mathematics and logic, Russell then proceeded to reduce philosophy itself to logic. As he pursued philosophy, he became convinced that "every philosophical problem when it is subjected to the necessary analysis and purification, is found either to be not really philosophical at all, or else to be, in the sense in which we are using the word, logical."[36] In short, logic and not metaphysics is the key to philosophy; indeed, for him as for Leibniz, logic is the essence of philosophy. This accounts for Russell's preoccupation with problems of logic, and also for the name he gave to his philosophy. From a metaphysical point of view he calls it a realism, but he prefers to describe it as Logical Atomism, from the type of logic on which it is grounded.[37]

logical atomism

While lecturing on Leibniz' philosophy at Cambridge in 1898 Russell became convinced that it is based on a fallacy in logic, namely that every proposition attributes a predicate to a subject. The same notion, he thought, developed with greater logical rigor, underlies the monism of Spinoza, Hegel, and Bradley. For, if all propositions have the subject-predicate form, those ascribing a relation to a subject assert some property of it. Thus relations are reduced to intrinsic properties of the related terms, and ultimately to a property of the whole that they compose. The inevitable consequence of this doctrine, which Russell calls "the axiom of internal relations," is that reality is one and plurality is merely appearance.[38]

Nothing revolted Russell more than this denial of pluralism. Monism appeals to the mystic; but, he insists, the mathematician, scientist, and man of common sense must be a pluralist; and pluralism demands that relations are not intrinsic properties of things. This is particularly clear in the case of asymmetrical relations; that is, relations that hold between A and B but not between B and A. Consider, for example, the relation *earlier*. "If A is earlier than B," Russell writes, "then B is not earlier than A. If you try to express the relation of A to B by means of adjectives (i.e., properties) of A and B, you will have to make the attempt by means of dates. You may say that the date of A is a property of A and the date of B is a property of B, but that will not help you because you will have to go on to say that the date of A is earlier than the date of B, so that you will have found no escape from the relation. If you adopt the plan of regarding the relation as a property of the whole composed of A and B, you are in a still worse predicament, for in that whole A and B have no order and therefore you cannot distinguish between 'A is earlier than B' and 'B is earlier than A.' "[39]

Thus the existence of asymmetrical relations shows that relations cannot, at least in all cases, be reduced to the intrinsic properties of things. Relations are often, and perhaps always, real components of the universe, linking things together in space and time. Since asymmetrical relations are found in all series (not only in those of mathematics, but also in those involving space and time and many other important features of the actual world) this world ceases to be a mere appearance or illusion once the reality of relations is granted. Reality is no longer an undifferentiated unity, but a complexity of many items linked together in temporal and spatial order by real relations. Consequently, the discovery of the reality of relations removes all logical grounds for supposing the world of sense to be illusory, as the Hegelians believe it to be.[40]

What are the basic components of the universe? In his early writings Russell, like Moore, divides all entities into two classes: particulars and universals. Particulars are the subjects of predicates or the terms of relations; universals are the predicates (i.e., qualities) and relations possessed by particulars. In this early theory, Russell held that both particulars and universals are real. His reason for distinguishing between them is that particulars cannot occupy more than one place at one time, whereas universals, being independent of time, can exist simultaneously in several places.[41] Russell later eliminated particulars as real entities, but he retained the reality of universals (both qualities and relations). In this new view, to which we shall have occasion to return, particulars are nothing but "compresent bundles of qualities."

In Russell's language, a *fact* is not a particular thing; it is a thing with a certain quality or relation. Napoleon, for example, is a thing and not a fact, but it is a fact that Napoleon was ambitious or that he was married to Josephine. Facts are objective or independent of our beliefs about them. Not so the propositions we assert about them; these involve thought. A *proposition* is a form of words that may be either true or false; in other words, it is what may be significantly asserted or denied. A true proposition is one that corresponds to a fact. Thus Russell writes: "What an asserted sentence expresses is a *belief*; what makes it true or false is a *fact*, which is in general distinct from the belief. Truth and falsehood are external relations, that is to say, no analysis of a sentence or a belief will show whether it is true or false. (This does not apply to logic and mathematics, where truth or falsehood, as the case may be, follows from the form of the sentence…)."[42]

Russell recognizes two basic types of propositions: those asserting that a thing has a certain quality (for example, "This is red"), and those asserting that a thing has a certain relation (for example, "This is before that"). Such propositions are the most simple of all. Because they enter into complex propositions in a way analogous to that in which atoms enter into molecules, they are called "atomic propositions," while those into which they enter are called "molecular propositions." Conjunctions such as *if*, *or*, *and*, *unless* are indications of molecular propositions.[43]

Corresponding to atomic propositions are "atomic facts." These are the simple properties and relations of simple things that are asserted by atomic propositions.[44]

Russell acknowledges his debt to his pupil Wittgenstein for the "principle of atomicity," which is the basis of linguistic analysis. Wittgenstein states the principle as follows: "Every statement about complexes can be analyzed into a statement about their component parts, and into those propositions which completely describe the complexes."[45] As we shall see, Wittgenstein later gave up the belief in atomic facts and with it the principle of atomicity. Although Russell also found difficulties with it in his later works, he still thinks it defensible in a modified form.[46]

Another doctrine of the young Wittgenstein that strongly influenced Russell in his early writings was that "a proposition is a picture of the facts which it asserts." He calls this the basic point of Wittgenstein's *Tractatus Logico-Philosophicus*. As a map is similar in structure to the region about which it conveys information, so a linguistic assertion has a form resembling that of the fact it asserts. Suppose, for example, you see a fox eat a goose, and then say, "The fox ate the goose." The original event was a relation between a fox and a goose, which is represented by the sentence forming a relation between the word "fox" and the word "goose," namely that the word "ate" comes between them.[47] After accepting this Wittgensteinian view for a time, Russell now feels very doubtful "that a true proposition must reproduce the structure of the facts concerned."[48] Nevertheless, he believes that "partly by means of the study of syntax, we can arrive at considerable knowledge concerning the structure of the world."[49] There is often, in explicit language, a structural resemblance between a sentence and what it asserts, but this is not a necessary condition for its truth. What is fundamental for the truth of a proposition is that it correspond to a fact. Russell is critical of James and Schiller for asserting that minds create truth or falsehood. "They create beliefs," he retorts, "but when once the beliefs are created, the mind cannot make them true or false, except in the special case where they concern future things which are within the power of the person believing, such as catching trains. What makes a belief true is a *fact*, and this fact does not (except in exceptional cases) in any way involve the mind of the person who has the belief."[50]

In thus asserting the independence of facts from the beliefs we have of them, Russell is a realist. He does grant, however, that the *structure* of facts to some extent can be deduced from the logical form of language. On this point he betrays his early Hegelian training. In his own words, he aligns himself with "a very distinguished party" among whom he numbers Parmenides, Plato, Spinoza, Leibniz, Hegel, and Bradley.[51] Thus Russell's empiricism is tempered with a degree of idealism, according to which the *a priori* knowledge of logical forms can lead to a knowledge of the structure of the physical world.

Beyond this service of logic to philosophy, Russell also demands from the logical theory of descriptions the definition of existence, the most elusive metaphysical notion.

the theory of descriptions

Basic to this theory is the distinction between names and descriptions.[52] A name is a word designating a particular thing or person; for example, Sir Walter Scott. A description is a phrase of the form "a so-and-so" (for example, "a man") or "the so-and-so" (for example, "the author of *Waverley*"). The former is an ambiguous, the latter a definite, description.

An important difference between names and descriptions is that a name cannot occur significantly in a proposition unless there is something that it names, whereas a description is not subject to this limitation. Thus I can say "I met Jones," but not "I met a unicorn," because "unicorn" is not the name of an existing animal. However, we can form true and significant propositions involving descriptions that describe nothing. I can say, for example, "The golden mountain does not exist." Under the influence of Meinong, Russell at first believed that because we can make meaningful statements about such objects as golden mountains and unicorns they must subsist "in some shadowy Platonic world of being." Later, through his theory of descriptions, he was able to eliminate this world. "The essential point of the theory," he writes, "was that, although 'the golden mountain' may be grammatically the subject of a significant proposition, such a proposition when rightly analyzed no longer has such a subject."[53]

The key to the elimination of descriptive phrases from propositions is the propositional function. By this Russell means an expression containing one or more variables, such that, when values are given to them, the expression becomes a proposition. Thus, "*x* is human" is not a proposition but a propositional function, for as long as *x* is undetermined it is neither true nor false; but when a value is assigned to *x* it becomes a true or false proposition.

Using a propositional function Russell analyzes the proposition "the golden mountain does not exist" as follows. "The propositional function 'x is golden and a mountain' is false for all values of x." That is to say, whatever is substituted for *x*, the proposition is false. Similarly, the statement "Scott is the author of *Waverley*" becomes on analysis: "For all values of *x*, 'x wrote *Waverley*' is equivalent to 'x is Scott.' " Thus the descriptive phrases "golden mountain" and "author of *Waverley*" can be eliminated from propositions and there is no need to suppose that they represent existing things.

More generally, the theory of descriptions is used to clarify the meaning of existence itself. It is meaningful to assert existence of descriptions, but hardly of names; we can say "The author of *Waverley* exists," but not "Scott exists." Russell's reason for this is that because a name must name something it is redundant to add "exists" to it. But there may not be an entity corresponding to a description, so it is significant to assert existence of it. For example, it makes sense to say, "The author of the *Iliad* and *Odyssey* exists," for it is possible that he does not exist. Of course, the statement is still meaningful if we substitute "Homer" for "the author of the *Iliad* and *Odyssey*," but then we are using "Homer" not as a name but as an abbreviated description.[54]

Now, as we have seen, descriptions of which existence can be asserted are either ambiguous or definite. An example of the former is "A man exists," of the latter "The author of *Waverley* exists." "A man exists" is equivalent to "The propositional function 'x is human' is sometimes true." In other words, there are one or more names that can be substituted for *x* in this propositional function, resulting in a true proposition. "The author of *Waverley* exists" means, "There is a term *c* such that '*x* wrote *Waverley*' is always equivalent to 'x is *c*.'" In this way Russell eliminates existence from existential propositions. Existence is simply "a case of a propositional function being true of at least one value of the variable."[55] In this view, the basic meaning of the word "existence" is the assertion that a propositional function is sometimes true or that it is possible.

G. E. Moore protests in the name of common sense against this reduction of existence to a property of a propositional function. Does not ordinary language permit us to attribute existence to individuals as well as to descriptions?[56] Russell does not deny this, but for him the ordinary use of language is not the criterion of good grammar. In his view it is simply bad grammar to say, "That exists." Although we talk of the existence of an individual, existence cannot be one of its properties because it adds nothing significant to the notion of an individual and it cannot conceivably be denied of an individual.[57]

If Moore and Russell are at loggerheads over this matter it is because the former appeals to common sense whereas the latter uses logic as the key to philosophy. To say that particular things do not exist offends common sense and ordinary language but not logic, because logic is concerned with the forms of thought and nor with the existence of things. As Russell says, "The logician, as such, does not know of the existence of Socrates or of anything else."[58] It is understandable, then, that Russell the logician should regard the existence of particulars as meaningless and reduce existence to a purely logical property. This is an excellent illustration of his dictum that "the point of philosophy is to start with something so simple as not to seem worth stating and to end with something so paradoxical that no one will believe it."[59]

between materialism and idealism

Russell's view as to the nature of knowledge and consciousness underwent an important change during the year 1918. At first he agreed with Brentano's analysis of sensation into three elements: act, content, and object. In the interest of simplicity he soon dropped the distinction between content and object, but he still regarded sensation as a cognitive act by which we are aware of something. The direct relation of the knowing subject to the known object he called "acquaintance" or "awareness." Knowledge by acquaintance was distinguished from knowledge by description, the former having for its object sense-data and by introspection probably our own minds, the latter being an indirect cognition of an object through a judgment or inference, as when we know Sir Walter Scott as the author of *Waverley*.[60]

Long reflection on William James' essay "Does 'Consciousness' Exist?" convinced Russell that this view of sensation and consciousness was erroneous. Try as he might, he could not by introspection observe himself as a knowing subject but only mental events, and much less could he observe the minds of other people. So he concluded that the notion of a subject, though necessary for grammar, is in fact a logical fiction and not a reality. And if there is no subject, there can be no awareness as a cognitive act relative to an object. Accordingly, Russell ceased to think of sensation as a kind of knowledge, and with this he dropped the notion of physical sense-data as distinct from sensation. As we have seen, Moore's thought underwent a similar development.

In this new view, the sensation we have when we see a patch of color is identical with the patch of color, and it is no more cognitive in character than the color. It is a mental occurrence, or part of a mind, when it is linked with other occurrences in a chain of mental events. On the other hand, it is a physical occurrence, or part of the physical world, when it is grouped with other events as its causal antecedents. Hence the stuff of which mind and matter is composed is neither mental nor material in itself but is neutral to both. It becomes mental in one arrangement and material in another. This theory, called "Neutral Monism," was suggested by Ernst Mach and developed by William James and the American New Realists.[61]

The theory of Neutral Monism delighted Russell with its simplicity. It enabled him to eliminate mind and matter as entities or substances and to view them simply as logical constructions. Thus at one stroke he bridged the gulf between the psychic and physical worlds and removed the age-old opposition between materialism and idealism. If this theory is correct, mind is not reducible to matter (as the materialists claim), nor is matter reducible to mind (as the idealists think). There is but one "stuff" of which both are made, and which in one context is called mental and in another is called material.

Searching for the basic components underlying both mind and matter, Russell came to adopt the view of his friend Whitehead, that both the physical and psychic world are composed of events, an event being defined as "something having a small finite duration and a small finite extension in space"; or, in conformity with the theory of relativity, "something occupying a small finite amount of space-time." Matter is nothing but a convenient word to designate certain causal laws concerning events—laws such as those established by the physical sciences. Mind is a convenient shorthand for laws governing events in the living brain—the laws, for example, formulated by psychology. Since events in the region of the brain and in the external world are basically the same, "In a completed science," Russell writes, "the word 'mind' and the word 'matter' would both disappear, and would be replaced by causal laws concerning 'events,' the only events known to us otherwise than in their mathematical and causal properties being percepts, which are events situated in the same region as a brain and having effects of a peculiar sort called 'knowledge-reactions.'"[62]

Events, however, are not simple and unanalyzable. Each event is a "complete bundle of compresent qualities." For example, a flash of lightning is a complex of qualities, including brightness, similarity (to other lightning flashes), and spatio-temporal relations. When all the qualities of an event have been enumerated, it is fully defined as a particular. This was the view of Leibniz, and Russell adopts it as his own. Socrates, for instance, is a bundle of qualities with definite spatiotemporal relations. In this interpretation a subject-predicate proposition, such as "Socrates is snub-nosed," states that a certain quality, named by the predicate, is one of the bundle of qualities named by the subject. Every quality in the bundle can also be present in other particulars. Thus the quality of humanity, belonging to Socrates, also belongs to Plato. In itself a quality is one; the multiplicity of instances of it results from the addition of other qualities. Hence qualities are universal; their individuation is owing to the unique combination in which they are present.[63]

Sensations are also events, but they have no cognitive status; they are only causes of knowledge. What then is knowledge? Russell uses the word in various senses, but always as designating something more than mere sensation. Its simplest meaning seems to be noticing or perceiving, which involves among other things giving one's attention to some aspect of the sensible environment and thus isolating it from the rest. Other forms of knowledge are consciousness and true belief based on evidence, memory, or inference.

An important difference between knowledge and sensation is that the former is usually distinct from its object whereas the latter never is. According to Neutral Monism, seeing and what is seen are identical; but there is a duality between knowing and what is known. Thus my perception of a chair is the knowledge of an object distinct from the act of perceiving. Common sense would have us believe that we directly perceive physical objects, but Russell argues that we have direct awareness only of mental data. He writes that "what we perceive is part of the stuff of our brains, not part of the stuff of tables and chairs, sun, moon, and stars."[64] We have to infer from our sensations the existence of events in the physical world. These events are not totally unknown, like Kant's things-in-themselves, but there is always an element of incompleteness and uncertainty in our knowledge of them. To some extent we can know their structure in space and time, though we must remain agnostic regarding their possession of qualities similar to those of the sensations by which we perceive them.[65]

retreat from pythagoras

With his usual facility of phrase Russell describes his philosophical development as "a gradual retreat from Pythagoras."[66] Like the Greek philosopher-mathematician, he cultivated mathematics in his early years with a religious and even mystical fervor. Mathematics appeared to him to be a world of ideal being and supreme beauty where the spirit could delight in objects that are more than human. In comparison the humdrum life of nature and man seemed drab and impure.

This exultation in pure mathematics sustained Russell through the first decade of the century when he was engaged with Whitehead in writing the *Principia Mathematica*. It was the well-spring of all his work in mathematical logic, which is his most enduring contribution to human thought. Disillusionment came when Wittgenstein convinced him that mathematics consists of nothing but tautologies. Now the whole of mathematics seemed trivial to him, and its subject matter lost the superhuman status that once evoked his reverence. He could no longer find mystical satisfaction in contemplating mathematical truth.

Having lost the God of his youth and the Platonic mathematical heaven of his middle age, Russell turned—not without regret—to the human and animal world as the only one of intrinsic value. Social, political, religious, and educational problems increasingly occupied his attention, and a long series of articles and books on these subjects have flowed, and continue to flow, from his active pen. His guiding ideas in these works stem from nineteenth-century liberalism and humanitarianism, of which his godfather John Stuart Mill was a leading exponent.

Russell's general ethical position is close to Mill's utilitarianism.[67] At first he adopted G. E. Moore's view that "good" is an indefinable notion, and that we know *a priori* that such things as happiness, knowledge, aesthetic experience, have intrinsic value. Later he abandoned this opinion, partly through the influence of Santayana's *Winds of Doctrine*. He now derives the notion of "good" from desire, defining a morally good act as one that is most likely to bring about the most general satisfaction of desires. Since pleasure or happiness is what is most commonly desired, Russell is broadly in agreement with hedonism. Thus he approves of Henry Sidgwick's principle that we ought to aim at maximizing pleasure, with the qualification that some pleasures are inherently preferable to others, such as the enjoyments of intelligence and aesthetic experience.

Accordingly, the truth of ethical propositions is not determined by their correspondence with facts of perception but by emotions and feelings. An act is right if it arouses an emotion of approval, wrong if it arouses one of disapproval. Whether it is approved or disapproved depends on the kind of effects it is thought to have. We approve of an act if we believe that its effects will be good; that is to say, that they will give rise to the feeling of enjoyment or satisfaction. Russell insists that on this theory ethics contains statements that are true or false and not merely optative or imperative, but its basis is one of emotion and feeling. Thus he proposes an "emotive theory" of ethics that retains the truth value of ethical judgments. In the next chapter we will see A. J. Ayer reject the meaningfulness and truth of such judgments because they are expressions of emotion and unverifiable in sense experience.

Alfred North Whitehead

When Russell came to Trinity College, Cambridge, in 1890, Whitehead had already been there ten years, first as an undergraduate and then as a teaching Fellow.[68] Whitehead found in Russell a brilliant student of mathematics and later a friend and collaborator in writing the *Principia Mathematica*. He recalls in his *Autobiographical Notes* that in those days Russell was a great factor in his life. "But," he adds, "our fundamental points of view—philosophic and sociological—diverged, and so with different interests our collaboration came to a natural end."[69]

The divergence between these two philosophers, so alike in their logical and mathematical thinking, is visible in their reactions to their boyhood education. In their pre-university years both received a solid training in the classics, which Whitehead was to treasure all his life and Russell was to reject as mainly a waste of time. Sympathetic contact with the ancient civilizations of Greece and Rome and with medieval culture gave Whitehead a breadth of historical vision forever closed to his younger colleague. Both were raised in Christian homes, Whitehead responding positively to his religious upbringing and making religion a central feature of his philosophy, Russell reacting negatively and adopting an intransigent antireligious stand.

Whitehead's career falls into three main periods. The first, extending to 1910, was almost exclusively given over to mathematics and logic. From his undergraduate days he had been interested in philosophy and read widely in it, but he did no creative philosophical thinking until he separated from Russell and joined the science faculties of the University of London and the Imperial College. This began his second period, which lasted from 1910 to 1924. During his London sojourn he published his first philosophical works, all of which deal with the philosophy of natural science, with special reference to the new developments in physics. These include *An Inquiry Concerning the Principles of Natural Knowledge*, *The Concept of Nature*, and *The Principle of Relativity*. He reached his philosophical maturity and produced his greatest works in speculative philosophy (notably *Process and Reality*) during the third period of his life, which began at the age of sixty-three, when he moved to the United States and became Professor of Philosophy at Harvard.

Whitehead's original impulse to philosophize came from the momentous changes that were taking place in mathematical physics during the first decades of the century, particularly through Einstein's theory of relativity and the quantum theory. Whitehead realized the importance for philosophy of these developments in physics. He felt that philosophy should keep close to science and respond to its demands; it is not one of the special sciences with its own small area of abstractions to investigate, but a general survey of the sciences for the purpose of harmonizing and completing them.[70] Hence the philosophy of any era will be conditioned by its physics. With the passing of the Newtonian mechanics and the advent of relativity and quantum theory, the classical systems of modern philosophy are outmoded; philosophers have to make a fresh effort to assimilate the new evidences of the sciences and to elaborate a basis for them in a general system of reality. This is what Whitehead set out to do, first in his London period when he founded a philosophy of nature that took into account twentieth-century physics, and then in his American period when he constructed a metaphysics that in its boldness of speculation and depth of vision rivals some of the greatest in the history of philosophy.

the new physics and philosophy

In his precious *Dialogues of Alfred North Whitehead*, Lucien Price has recorded the verbal comments of Whitehead on the revolution that took place in physics around the turn of the century. "We supposed," he said, "that nearly everything of importance about physics was known. Yes, there were a few obscure spots, strange anomalies having to do with the phenomena of radiation which physicists expected to be cleared up by 1900. They were. But in so being, the whole science blew up, and the Newtonian physics, which had been supposed to be fixed as the Everlasting Seat, were gone. Oh, they were and still are useful as a way of looking at things, but regarded as a final conception of reality, no longer valid."[71]

According to Newton's mechanistic view of the universe, space is an eternal, unchanging receptacle containing material bodies, each of which has a definite mass, shape, and motion. Essential to this picture of the universe is the notion that a material body at any given instant of time occupies a determined location in space, so that it can be fully described by saying that it is *here* in space and *here* in time without reference to other regions of space or periods of time. Whitehead calls this the property of "simple location."[72] A material body, so conceived, can be divided by a division of the volume of the space it occupies, but not by a division of the time in which it exists. It is fully itself throughout its temporal duration and at any instant of time. In other words, the lapse of time is an accident and not of the essence of the material thing. Thus, according to this mechanistic theory of nature, the universe is a succession of instantaneous configurations of matter.[73]

A heavy blow was dealt to classical physics by the advent of the relativity theory. According to this theory, the location of a body in space and its date in time vary with the position of the observer's instrument. There is no absolute point in space or unique present instant of time; spatial and temporal relations have different meanings according to the different positions of observers. In short, (to use Whitehead's language) there is no "simple location" in space or time by which to describe a material particle.[74]

Newtonian physics was further shaken by the quantum theory. In the older physics natural events were explained in terms of the continuous local motion of material particles. The quantum theory postulates that locomotion is discontinuous in space and time; for example, the orbit of an electron is now regarded as a series of detached positions and not as a continuous line. These discontinuities in nature demand a basic revision of our concept of matter.

Does this mean that the Newtonian concepts are simply incorrect? Not at all, according to Whitehead. They have a limited value in expressing the facts of experience, but they do not tell the whole story. They are abstractions that leave out of account other important aspects of nature as it concretely presents itself to us. Error arises when these abstractions are taken to be concrete reality itself. The mistaking of the abstract for the concrete Whitehead calls the "Fallacy of Misplaced Concreteness," and he was constantly on the alert to point out instances of this fallacy both in science and philosophy. He protests, with Bergson, against the distortion of nature by the concepts of mechanistic science and philosophy, but he does not agree with the French philosopher that this distortion is due to the nature of the intellect. The fallacy of misplaced concreteness is not a vice inherent in our faculty of knowing but is accidental to it.[75]

Another instance of this fallacy arising out of mechanistic physics, but philosophical rather than scientific, is the distinction between substance and its primary and secondary qualities. This theory, begun by Galileo and elaborated by Descartes and Locke, distinguishes between bodies and the characteristics we observe in them. Some of these characteristics, called primary qualities, are real attributes of bodies; examples are length and quantitative mass. Others, called secondary qualities, are sensations with which the mind clothes external nature; for instance, colors, sounds, and smells. But if this theory is true, Whitehead says, "bodies are perceived as with qualities which in reality do not belong to them, qualities which in fact are purely the offspring of the mind. Thus nature gets credit which should in truth be reserved for ourselves: the rose for its scent: the nightingale for his song: and the sun for his radiance. The poets are entirely mistaken. They should address their lyrics to themselves, and should turn them into odes of self-congratulation on the excellency of the human mind. Nature is a dull affair, soundless, scentless, colourless; merely the hurrying of material, endlessly, meaninglessly."[76]

This division is called by Whitehead the "bifurcation of nature." On the one hand there is the nature apprehended by the senses: the greenness of trees, the song of the birds, the warmth of the sun; on the other there is the nature that causes our awareness of these objects: a system of molecules and electrons that so affect the mind that it produces the awareness of sense qualities. Between these two natures is the mind, which receives the influence of the molecular world and from which in turn flows the world we actually perceive.[77]

Whitehead admits that the separation of secondary qualities from the physical world is of practical advantage to the scientist. Concentrating his attention on the factors in nature that can be measured, such as length and mass, he avoids the extreme difficulty of relating perceived qualities like redness and warmth to the movement of molecules. And yet, for all its efficiency this conception of the universe is unbelievable. Instead of taking nature in its concrete unity and trying to establish the interrelations of its parts, it divides it into a reality and an appearance that are related only through a mind. These are obviously abstractions, but modern philosophy has been ruined by mistaking them for concrete realities. Since the seventeenth century, philosophers have been juggling these abstractions as though they were handling realities themselves. Some have been outright dualists, accepting matter and mind as on equal terms; others have been monists, either putting mind inside matter or matter inside mind. All have been guilty of the fallacy of misplaced concreteness because they mistook the abstractions of the mechanistic view of the world for concrete reality.[78]

If this is true, the task of the philosopher at the present time is clear enough. He should not disregard the message of modern science; it has much to tell him that is of the greatest importance for his work. But he should recognize the inherently abstract and limited character of any scientific pronouncement and not take it for the whole account of nature. In short, he must be a "critic of abstractions." Nature as we experience it is a concrete whole or organism, and it is the task of the philosopher to seek the "larger generalities" that characterize this whole. This is what Whitehead sets out to do in his speculative philosophy, which he aptly calls a "philosophy of organism." His goal is an ambitious one: it is no less than the elaboration of a metaphysical system that will elucidate the general categories necessary for classifying and determining reality as a whole. But he embarks on this venture not as a dogmatist who thinks he can say the final word on the subject, but as an adventurer who is well aware "how shallow, puny, and imperfect are efforts to sound the depths in the nature of things."[79]

the furniture of the universe

The advent of modern physics makes it necessary for the philosopher to recast his notion of what Whitehead calls "the furniture of the universe." Gone is the concept of absolute space filled with subtle ether and containing permanent bits of matter in motion. Matter must now be conceived as energy, and energy is sheer activity. The universe is a process within which we can discern particular processes or events. The key notion in Whitehead's new interpretation of reality is "process" or "event"—terms that express the dynamic character of matter as revealed by contemporary science. An event is anything that actually happens or occurs in nature. Hence Whitehead calls it an "actual occasion" or "actual entity." By this he does not mean that there are self-identical entities or substances in nature to which things happen. A thing or entity is nothing but a happening or occurrence. In short, a thing is what it does.[80]

An event occurs at some place and time, but not at a point in space or at an instant in time. Points and instants are, like space and time themselves, abstractions from the concrete occurrences in nature. Each event is spread out over space and time and consequently it has spatial and temporal extension. Since space and time are inextricably interwoven, it is more correct to speak of an event as having a spatiotemporal extension. Another important characteristic of events is that they extend over each other. For example, the endurance of the Great Pyramid is an event that overlaps many goings-on of briefer duration in Egypt. Every event, no matter how small its extension, extends over other events that are contained in it as parts, and it itself is contained as a part in other events that extend over it. Accordingly, the universe is a web or network of events, each of which is a unit, but intimately connected with other events. This interconnection of events is not something external to them, like the external relations between bodies in mechanistic physics, or between impressions in the philosophy of Hume; the relations binding events together enter into their very being, with the result that events cannot be completely described without them. In this view, nature is an organic unity in which every event has some bearing on everything else. "Any local agitation shakes the whole universe. The distant effects are minute, but they are there."[81] In a sense, then, "everything is everywhere at all times. For every location involves an aspect of itself in every other location. Thus every spatio-temporal standpoint mirrors the world."[82] Whitehead is here using the language of Leibniz; and indeed his events, like Leibnizian monads, reflect each in its own way the whole universe. They differ from these monads, however, in that they are not windowless but open to each other's causal influence.

Events are not permanent but continuously move forward in time. Strictly speaking they cannot be said to change, for this would imply that they are enduring entities underlying movement, whereas in fact they are identical with movement and progression. They can be said to change only in relation to subsequent events into which they pass. Since the world is made up of such transitory events, it is in continual movement and flux, prior events passing into subsequent ones and conditioning them in the creative advance of nature.[83]

Through sense perception we experience the passage of events, but at the same time we become aware of permanent features in them. Amid the flux of events we recognize objects that retain their identity throughout the event and that can be repeated in other events. Examples are a particular shade of red or a particular tune. Whitehead calls these permanent factors in nature "objects," and our awareness of them "recognition." Events are not recognized because they happen but once; they are simply apprehended. Recognition is the awareness of an object that retains its identity and can repeat itself.[84]

Accordingly, there are two basic kinds of entity in nature: events and objects. Events account for the movement and fluidity of nature, objects for its permanence and uniformity. The characteristics of objects are directly contrary to those of events. Events are continuous, objects are discrete. Events are concrete and particular, objects are abstract and universal. They are abstract because in themselves they are not in space or time; they have spatial and temporal dimensions only insofar as they enter into events. They are universal because they can recur in many events.[85]

Whitehead distinguishes between many different kinds of objects, among which are sense objects, perceptual objects, and scientific objects. Sense objects are sensible qualities such as colors, tastes, and sounds. These are of the utmost importance for science; situated in events, they are the whole basis of our knowledge of nature. Perceptual objects are the ordinary objects of common experience; for example, chairs, tables, trees. A perceptual object is defined as "an association of sense-objects in the same situation."[86] The object that is recognized is simply the permanence of this association. Perceptual objects are either illusory or non-illusory; if the latter, they are called physical objects. Scientific objects, such as atoms, molecules, and electrons, are unlike physical objects in that they are not directly perceived; they are abstractions inferred from physical objects because of their capacity to express the causal characters of events. Whitehead insists that these scientific abstractions are not merely conceptual; insofar as they are true, they exhibit the nature of physical reality.[87]

Objects have no actual existence outside of events. Redness, for example, actually exists only insofar as it is the quality of a definite occurrence in nature. Whitehead does not admit the actual existence of universals, such as redness. As we shall see, in his later writings he locates universals (now called "eternal objects") in the mind of God; but in this condition they are merely possibilities and not actualities. They become actual by entering into the composition of events. The entering of an object into an event Whitehead calls "ingression." Events for their part lay hold on appropriate objects. This grasping of objective features in one event by another event is called "prehension." An actual entity appropriates to itself elements in its environment that are suitable to it, and this activity of appropriation or prehension formally constitutes the entity. Thus Whitehead defines an event as "the grasping into unity of a pattern of aspects [i.e., objects]."[88] The coming into being of an event is a "concrescence"; that is to say, a growing into unity of a number of objects.

In the process of concrescence an entity absorbs only those elements in other entities that are suitable to it. It selects certain ones and excludes others as irrelevant to it. This implies that the entity has a "subjective aim" or end that it is striving to realize. It also implies that at least in some primitive way it experiences or "feels" its environment. Its act of prehension, Whitehead says, is an act of feeling and even an emotion. Thus an actual entity "is a process of 'feeling' the many data, so as to absorb them into the unity of one individual 'satisfaction.'"[89]

Whitehead also describes actual beings as "drops of experience" or "occasions of experiences"—a notion already expressed by William James but without the systematic elaboration given to it by Whitehead. The latter stresses the self-creative character of each pulsation of experience. An actual entity, thus viewed, is not a static reality but an experiencing subject that creates itself through its experiences. Since the subject emerges into actuality in the process of self-creation, Whitehead prefers to call it a "superject." "An actual entity," he writes, "is at once the subject experiencing and the superject of its experiences."[90]

Whitehead is not saying, any more than James, that all experience is conscious of itself. There is a basic unconscious experience in everything, in men as well as in the lowest forms of nature, a taking into account of other things that is below the level of reflective awareness.[91] Consciousness (which, as James already pointed out, is not an entity but a function or activity) is a heightened intensity of subjective experience.[92] Intellectual *apprehension* in men is but a developed form of *prehension*, and it should be conceived along the same lines. That is to say, the knowing subject (or superject) grasps the objective data presented to it and creates itself in the process of assimilating that data.

Thus Whitehead's theory of knowledge is a realism, formulated in direct opposition to that of Kant. "The philosophy of organism," Whitehead writes, "is the inversion of Kant's philosophy. *The Critique of Pure Reason* describes the process by which subjective data pass into the appearance of an objective world. The philosophy of organism seeks to describe how objective data pass into subjective satisfaction, and how order in the objective data provides intensity in the subjective satisfaction. For Kant, the world emerges from the subject; for the philosophy of organism, the subject emerges from the world—a 'superject' rather than a 'subject.'"[93]

In this passage Whitehead calls his philosophy a "philosophy of organism," as he usually does in his later writings. This emphasizes his view that all actual entities, from highly developed and complex living beings to electrons, are organisms; that is to say, concrete events with enduring patterns or structures that have arisen through a process of self-creation. Nature is not a dull, dead affair, as the mechanists believe; it is warm-blooded and living. It has evolved to its present state, but its evolution has not been a mere change, purposeless and unprogressive, as the mechanistic philosophy of evolution claims. The emergence of novel organisms is a creation of new values in nature, and their emergence is the result of a striving to achieve definite aims or purposes.[94] In proposing this philosophy of organism Whitehead is trying to meet the demands of the theory of evolution, as before he strove to take into account the scientific theories of relativity and quantum.

creativity and god

In the last phase of his philosophy Whitehead constructed a metaphysics that deepened and developed ideas in his earlier, cosmological period, and laid down the most general categories for the interpretation of our experience.[95] All that can be done here is to explain his ultimate category of "creativity" and the role of God in the fashioning of the universe.

As we have seen, each actual entity in the universe arises through an act of self-creation; it is a process of becoming and this in virtue of its own activity. Common to all actual entities, therefore, is self-causation or creativity. Each actuality is a particular form of this general activity. In saying this Whitehead does not mean that creativity exists apart from individual actualities, that there is a general creative process distinct from this or that particular creative process. Creativity is found in every actual entity, and each of them is a particular accidental embodiment of it; but apart from them it is only an abstraction. To conceive it as an actual entity would be to commit the fallacy of misplaced concreteness. The concrete is the particular actual entity; the ultimate category or abstract universal embodied in the concrete is creativity.

Thus creativity is the bond linking the many concrete entities in the universe into a unity. In short, it is the reason why it is a *universe*. "It is that ultimate principle by which the many, which are the universe disjunctively, become the one actual occasion, which is the universe conjunctively. It lies in the nature of things that the many enter into complex unity." Creativity is also the principle of novelty. "The 'creative advance' is the application of this ultimate principle of creativity to each novel situation which it originates."[96]

Whitehead likens creativity to Aristotelian primary matter because, lacking all definite character of its own, it is wholly indeterminate to the forms it can assume. It differs from primary matter, however, in that it is not a passive receptivity to form but a creative activity that begets and produces its particular embodiments. It also bears a resemblance to the primordial chaos from which the cosmos emerges in Plato's myth in the *Timaeus*, although this is a receptacle of forms rather than the efficient principle of their emergence.[97]

Creativity is the basic activity and efficacy underlying all the actual existences in the universe. It is not only common to all of them but it is the ultimate ground and reason for their existence. As the ultimate explanation of the universe, Aristotle posited an unmoved mover, Christians a transcendent creator, monists like Spinoza an Absolute, but these are actual entities. Whitehead's ultimate ground of the universe, creativity, is not itself an actually existing being; it exists only in its individual instances or creatures. It is real, but its reality is not that of an actually existing being; rather it is the real potentiality or power of engendering new actual beings.[98]

As the ultimate ground of existence, creativity cannot be explained or accounted for. It is an irrational element or surd in the universe. Does this mean that the notion of God is superfluous in Whitehead's metaphysics? Not at all. God is not needed to explain creativity or the existence itself of the world, but he is required to account for the definite character this existence takes in actual beings. Hence God is one of the formative elements in the universe, though not its transcendent creator.

How does God exercise his formative role in the universe? As we have seen, an actual entity is a growing together or concrescence of objects into a novel unity. This process is directed by a subjective aim or concept. Where does this concept come from? What governs the concrescing activity and determines the definite character it takes? Actual entities prior to it in time cannot perform this function; as objects they can enter into the new entity but they cannot decide what its definite form will be. There must be a unique, eternal actual entity which is the primordial source of the subjective aims governing the activities of ordinary actual entities. This "principle of concretion"

Whitehead calls God.[99] In this view, God does not create the world from nothing; his precise role is to provide the concepts directing events and thereby to give definiteness to them.

As the principle of concretion God envisages all the possible subjective aims or concepts that can be realized in the universe. Because he eternally views these data, they are called "eternal objects." As such, they have no necessary reference to actual beings in the temporal world; they are pure essences conceptually known or "felt" by God, and they are neutral with respect to their ingression into the physical world. However, they *can* ingress into this world, and when they do actual beings are said to participate in them. For example, a red flower participates in the essence "redness." That eternal objects actually ingress is due to the urge God feels to realize them and to the definite selection he makes for such ingression.[100]

The Platonic cast of Whitehead's metaphysics is nowhere more evident than in his doctrine of eternal objects, which he calls "Platonic Forms." As he interprets these Forms, they are not created by God, but neither do they exist outside of his knowledge of them. God, he writes, "does not create eternal objects; for his nature requires them in the same degree that they require him.... The general relationships of eternal objects to each other, relationships of diversity and of pattern, are their relationships in God's conceptual realization. Apart from this realization, there is mere isolation indistinguishable from nonentity."[101]

When we consider God as conceptually envisaging pure abstract eternal objects, we are thinking of him in his "primordial nature." In this nature he is, like other actual entities, a process of self-creation, an instance of creativity, differing from other instances because he is primordial, transcendent, timeless, and eternal. But there is more to God than this. His original nature is but one aspect of his complete being. He not only abstractly conceives the unlimited possibilities of things but he actively enters into the creative process of the world and shapes and forms it by the ingression of his eternal objects. This secondary function of God reveals his "consequent nature" as a being immanent in the world and assisting it in its creative advance. But God cannot immerse himself in the world without being affected by it. His encounter with the world enriches his own conscious experience; its creative advance furthers his self-development. Thus the universal principle of relativity, according to which everything has a bearing on everything else, applies to God as well as to the temporal world. He is engaged in the world and is active in every event; so too every event has a repercussion on him and calls forth a reaction from him.[102]

This brings us to the culminating theme of Whitehead's metaphysics, namely immortality. Temporal events (including human lives) perish but they do not lapse into sheer nothingness. They cease to exist "subjectively," as processes or activities, but they endure "objectively," that is to say as completed, past facts that enter into the composition of subsequent events. A clear instance of this is an event that runs its course and then is held as an object in the memory of succeeding generations. The event is said to have "objective immortality." Events are not subjectively immortal, but they are objectively immortal in the sense that they are incorporated into new events and particularly into the ever-growing experience of God. With tender care and patience he saves whatever of value occurs in the world. "He saves the world as it passes into the immediacy of his own life. It is the judgment of a tenderness which loses nothing that can be saved. It is also the judgment of a wisdom which uses what in the temporal world is mere wreckage."[103]

civilization

Whitehead's adventuresome mind delved into many areas besides those of mathematics, logic, cosmology, and metaphysics. Some of his most brilliant books and essays deal with the more concrete problems of society, the philosophy of history, education, and religion. A constant preoccupation in these works is the notion of civilization. What is civilization? When is an individual or a society civilized? What forms has civilization taken in history and what are their relative merits? These and similar questions are touched upon in his later writings, especially his *Adventures of Ideas*.

Whitehead regards civilization as the quality of perfection of human life. The good life, the life of "ultimate good sense," is the civilized life. Every civilization aims at "fineness of feeling," and at its peak it realizes a certain type of perfection. Hence the importance of analyzing the ideal of civilization and of studying and evaluating its concrete realizations in history.

While emphasizing the great difficulty involved in defining the notion of civilization, Whitehead suggests as a general definition that a civilized society exhibits the five qualities of Truth, Beauty, Adventure, Art, and Peace. Since these values are among the eternal objects conceived by God, it is clear that he is thinking of civilization as a complex or pattern of eternal values—a kind of Platonic Form—capable of ingression into the temporal world. The degree to which it is realized in human life determines its grade of civilization.

Truth, the first quality of civilization, does not apply to reality in itself, but to an appearance in relation to reality. For example, a man in himself is not true, but his reflection in a mirror can be said to be truthful. In general, truth is defined as "the conformation of Appearance to Reality."[104] In human experience the two outstanding examples of truth are the conformity of sense perception and propositions to reality.

In estimating the value of a proposition Whitehead considers not only whether it is true but more especially whether it is interesting or has an "emotional lure." Statements of matter-of-fact are important, but Whitehead is not satisfied with them. More significant are the judgments of value made by the philosopher. Because science limits itself to factual knowledge and to the laws governing facts, Whitehead rates it below philosophy as an ingredient of civilization. The Chinese, Persians, Greeks, and Romans made great strides toward civilization without much accurate scientific knowledge. Philosophy, on the other hand, is essential to civilization because it makes us aware of the meaning and value of life. It enables us to organize both facts and values in terms of general ideas, and it offers us the lure of the ideal, enticing us to rise above what is to what might be.

Another essential element of civilization is beauty. This Whitehead defines as the perfection of harmony, the mutual adaptation of the factors in an experience.[105] As we have seen, the concrescence of an event is governed by a subjective aim or end; when this aim has been attained by the harmonious blending of the factors in the event, beauty results. Beauty reaches its greatest intensity when such harmonious arrangements are enriched by interwoven and patterned contrasts. Discord, destructiveness inhibit the attainment of the aim of an experience, and this is evil. Goodness is not a quality distinct from beauty; it is found, however, only as a qualification of reality and not of appearances. This is why art, which concerns appearances, does not aim at goodness but only at beauty.

Art is a medium by which men strive to express the eternal ideals of beauty and truth in perishable forms. Works of art refresh and relax the spirit; they also stimulate new ideas and fresh emotions. Another service art renders to civilization is to make men aware of their creative powers. The beauty of nature overpowers man with its splendor; works of art give him a heightened sense of his humanity. "A million sunsets will not spur on men towards civilization. It requires Art to evoke into consciousness the finite perfections which lie ready for human achievement."[106]

Both art and civilization need the spirit of adventure. Has not Whitehead told us that life is activity and self-creation? The stream of life does not stand still; it either advances or declines. If it is to go forward, men must embark on adventures, not only facing physical dangers but more especially adventuring in the realm of ideas. The great civilizations of the past were the work of creative imagination and the spirit of adventure. When these flagged, the civilizations became decadent. Today, as the world passes into a new stage of its existence, it is not enough to know what past cultures have achieved. Like the Greeks, we must be speculative, adventurous, eager for novelty; without these qualities we cannot meet the new problems of our day and carry forward the work of civilization.[107]

The final quality Whitehead assigns to civilization is peace. This is no passive condition or anesthesia. It is a positive experience based on deep metaphysical insight into the harmony and permanence of the supreme values of life. It raises a man above his own narrow self-interests and gives him a glimpse of eternity. Its effect on his emotions is to calm the turbulence that inhibits effective action. The man who has gained peace of soul is not overwhelmed by evil or tragedy; he is incited to overcome them and "to aim at fineness beyond the faded level of surrounding fact."[108] Tragedy is not in vain; it is an inevitable factor in the creative advance of the universe and contributes to its greater good. To understand this, to experience permanence and harmony amid pain, frustration, loss, and tragedy, is peace.

XXI.

Language and Metaphysics

IF F. H. Bradley were alive today he would survey the panorama of contemporary English philosophy with disappointment. Having "a high opinion of the metaphysical powers of the English mind," he encouraged his colleagues at the turn of the century to undertake a comprehensive study of first principles that would reveal reality not piecemeal or by fragments but as a whole.[1] True, he made the skeptical inquiry into the fundamental notions of philosophy a condition of success; but this was to be a therapy preliminary to the positive work of constructing a systematic metaphysics. And indeed, as if in response to his appeal the first decades of the twentieth century were remarkably productive of metaphysical systems: witness the idealist systems of Bosanquet and McTaggart and the realist metaphysics of Alexander and Whitehead. At mid-century, however, English philosophers no longer have confidence or interest in such ambitious ventures. The prevailing style of philosophy is analytical rather than speculative, the purpose of analysis being the clarification of language or thought rather than the discovery of new truths or facts. The scope of inquiry is correspondingly limited to what Russell calls "piece-meal investigations," in contrast to that of the metaphysicians who attempted to discover ultimate truths and to know the whole of reality. The notion of philosophical therapy is much in evidence since Wittgenstein began his work, but it is often practiced as a release from metaphysical questions rather than as a propaedeutic to their solution. The logical positivists, for their part, wish to eliminate metaphysics in principle.

The voluminous works of C. D. Broad manifest the trend toward critical and analytical philosophy that arose in England in reaction to the metaphysical speculation of the absolute idealists.[2] An avid reader of Bradley and McTaggart, Broad came under the influence of Moore and Russell at Cambridge and was won over to realism. Moore's *Refutation of Idealism*, he says, "knocked the bottom out of my youthful subjective idealism."[3] He was also persuaded that philosophy at its best is the critical analysis of the basic concepts of science and of everyday life, such as space, motion, and substance. For him, "the most fundamental task of Philosophy is to take the concepts that we daily use in common life and science, to analyse them, and thus to determine their precise meanings and their mutual relations."[4] The special sciences discuss the meaning of their concepts only incidentally and insofar as this is needed for their own particular purposes; it is the essence of philosophy to deal with these questions for their own sake.

Broad does not mean that philosophy consists entirely of discussions about the meanings of words, as though its task were purely verbal. The essential work of philosophy, according to him, is to find out exactly what properties are present in objects. Thus the method of analysis aims to answer questions not only about words but also about things and their properties.

After analyzing and defining concepts, "critical philosophy" has the task of clearly stating the basic beliefs of science and common sense, such as that nature as a whole always acts uniformly. It then subjects these beliefs to a resolute criticism by honestly exposing them to every possible objection.

Only on the foundation of such a critical philosophy can there be a valid "speculative philosophy." The object of this part of philosophy, according to Broad, "is to take over the results of the various sciences, to add to them the results of the religious and ethical experiences of mankind, and then to reflect upon the whole. The hope is that, by this means, we may be able to reach some general conclusions as to the nature of the Universe, and as to our position and prospects in it."[5] He shows sympathy with such a synoptic view of the world, especially as the idealists attempted to formulate it. Critical philosophy, in his opinion, is rigid and arid without speculation. By its nature, however, he thinks speculative philosophy incapable of rising to the level of demonstration. It consists of more or less happy guesses made on a very slender basis and usually prejudiced by the subjective bias of the philosopher who makes them. This does not prevent Broad himself from indulging in speculation, for instance regarding psychical phenomena, but he keeps his theory under the control of scientific findings and critical analysis.

Ludwig Wittgenstein

Far more original was the work of Wittgenstein, called the most powerful and pervasive influence on the practice of philosophy in England today.[6] An Austrian by birth, he studied engineering in Germany and England. In 1911 his interest in the philosophy of mathematics drew him to Cambridge to study under Russell. The impact of Russell and Frege is evident in his first book, the *Tractatus Logico-Philosophicus*, which he wrote during the First World War and published in German in 1921. After retiring from philosophy for about ten years, he returned to Cambridge in 1929 and studied and lectured there until 1936. In 1939 he succeeded G. E. Moore in the Chair of Philosophy—a position he held until his retirement in 1947. The main fruit of this second period at Cambridge was the *Philosophical Investigations*, published posthumously. This works corrects and revises some of the key notions in the *Tractatus*, while developing and deepening its over-all conception of philosophy.

For several reasons it is unusually difficult to summarize Wittgenstein's views. The first is the condition in which he left his works. He himself published little; we owe to his friends and disciples the printing of his unfinished *Philosophical Investigations* and of his classroom notes. He was highly doubtful that these writings would adequately convey his thoughts, and indeed his style of philosophizing lends itself better to oral than to written communication. The second cause of the difficulty of summarizing his thought is his way of "doing philosophy." To him philosophy is an activity with great therapeutic value in releasing one from his philosophical puzzles, but it does not result in a settled body of doctrine, in the sense that issues can be decided once and for all and embodied in definitive formulae. Consequently, Wittgenstein does not have a philosophy in the usual sense of the term. To fail to see this is to miss his originality as a philosopher and the meaning of the revolution he effected in contemporary English philosophy. Because of these inherent difficulties and the limits of space we will be concerned mainly with his conception of philosophy and its role in human thought, first as expressed in the *Tractatus* and then in the *Philosophical Investigations*.

philosophy according to the tractatus

In the *Tractatus* Wittgenstein draws a sharp distinction between the natural sciences and philosophy. Investigation in the sciences, he says, leads to true propositions but this is not the case in philosophy. Philosophizing does not result in a body of truths but in the clarification of thoughts arrived at by science. Consequently, there are no distinct philosophical questions and answers as there are scientific ones. Philosophy is not a theory alongside that of science, but an activity—the activity of elucidating ideas obtained through other means. The distinctive contribution of philosophy is not to discover new facts unknown to the sciences but to clear up muddles in our thinking and to make our ideas more precise. "Without philosophy," he writes, "thoughts are, as it were cloudy and indistinct: its task is to make them clear and to give them sharp boundaries."[7]

Why have so many philosophers been misled into believing that it is their business to formulate true propositions like the scientists? They have failed to understand the logic of our language and have tried to say what cannot be said. As a consequence most of their questions and statements are neither true nor false but meaningless.

> Most of the propositions and questions to be found in philosophical works are not false but nonsensical. Consequently we cannot give any answer to questions of this kind, but can only establish that they are nonsensical. Most of the propositions and questions of philosophers arise from our failure to understand the logic of our language.[8]

This misunderstanding arises from the confusion of the apparent logical form of a proposition with its real form—a distinction Wittgenstein owes to Russell but which he does not think Russell himself always observes. Wittgenstein illustrates this confusion by the word "is."[9] "Is" functions in a proposition as the copula, signifying the identity of subject and predicate; but it is also used as a predicate signifying existence, as in the proposition "John is." Because this proposition has the same logical form as "John goes," it may be thought that "to exist" is an intransitive verb like "to go," and that "exists" is really a predicate of the same kind as "goes." This has led philosophers to ask many puzzling metaphysical questions about existence, which, as we have seen in the last chapter, Russell easily handles by his logical theory of descriptions.

This is but a single example—though an important one—of the way philosophical problems result from the failure to understand the logic of language.

Because words make sense in certain propositions we are misled into using them in others in which they no longer make sense.

When exactly do words make sense in a proposition? What, in short, are the limits of language? This brings us to Wittgenstein's notion of a proposition, which dominates his whole *Tractatus*. A proposition (*Satz*), he tells us, is a picture of reality, a model of reality as we think of it. If it faithfully portrays a fact it is true, if it does not it is false.[10]

A proposition can be a picture of a fact because it itself is a physical, sensible fact. It consists of elements (say, written words), combined in a definite way, which correspond to, and stand for objects in reality. The arrangement of these elements shows the structure of the fact. Thus the propositional picture "is attached totality; it reaches right out to it. It is laid against reality like a ruler."[11]

According to Norman Malcolm, Wittgenstein's biographer and disciple, he hit upon the notion of a proposition as a picture of reality while reading a newspaper account of an automobile accident.[12] It occurred to him that the accompanying diagram or map served the same function as a written statement: it showed a fact. Does this not give us the clue to the nature of all propositions, that they are pictures of reality? It little matters whether words or other physical means are used to express a thought; as long as they portray a fact they can be viewed as a proposition. Tables, chairs, books, sound waves, musical notes—all of these can be arranged in a pattern that reveals the structure of a fact. They can have the same logical structure or form as the fact and consequently they can exhibit the pattern of reality. For Wittgenstein, however, no language can equal the purity and lucidity of mathematical logic; it mirrors most clearly the basic structure of facts.

While propositions of logic exhibit the structure of the world, they themselves do not *say* anything about reality, In Wittgenstein's view they are tautologies without a subject-matter.[13] If they treated of anything they would be pictures of facts and we could speak of them as either truly or falsely reporting facts. But the question of truth or falsity does not arise in their connection. The same is true of the propositions of mathematics. Wittgenstein contends that they are merely equations and hence pseudo propositions.[14] As we have seen, this is a point Russell learned from him and which caused the mathematician great disappointment. According to Wittgenstein, only propositions whose terms stand for things and their qualities can be either true or false. And since these propositions concern facts that can be verified by the senses, they all fall within the domain of the natural sciences. Consequently, "The totality of true propositions is the whole of natural science (or the whole corpus of the natural sciences)."[15]

This puts the philosopher in a paradoxical position, for there are no propositions distinctly his own. In the past, philosophers have acted as though they were scientists and have made pronouncements about facts; but these were unwarranted incursions into the field of science. For example, they have made assertions about the theory of evolution, which is a scientific and not a philosophical subject. They have proposed theories of the self, a matter reserved for the psychologist. But even though there are no distinctive philosophical assertions, the activity of the philosopher is still an important one. Philosophy can show clearly what can be said and what cannot be said; that is, it can set limits to language and consequently to thought. It can also settle controversies about the limits of natural science.[16] All of this comes within the competence of philosophy in its role as a critique of language.

In order to fulfill this role the philosopher has to furnish a theory of the proposition and its relation to reality. He has to make statements about language, as Wittgenstein himself does throughout the *Tractatus*. But Wittgenstein realizes that on his own theory this is impossible. If the *Tractatus* is correct, we can talk about the world, and our propositions will be meaningful. Our language will even reveal the basic, ontological structure of the world. But we cannot *say* what this structure is, for in trying to do so we would have to use the very language that shows its structure, and thus we would presume what we intend to say. Neither can we talk about the relation between language and the world, because to do this we would have to assert propositions about the world in a non-pictured form, in order to compare the world with the picture. But this is something Wittgenstein's theory does not allow.

The upshot of this is that the propositions of philosophy and metaphysics are nonsense (*Unsinn*). They go beyond the limits of language and attempt to say what is inexpressible. The philosopher cannot talk clearly about such matters as God, immortality, or ethics; the "riddle of life" lies beyond time and space and hence it is strictly inexpressible. "We feel that even when *all possible* scientific questions have been answered, the problems of life remain completely untouched. Of course there are then no questions left, and this itself is the answer. The solution of the problem of life is seen in the vanishing of the problem."[17] This, then, is the correct method in philosophy: "to say nothing except what can be said, i.e., propositions of natural science—i.e., something that has nothing to do with philosophy—and then, whenever someone else wanted to say something metaphysical, to demonstrate to him that he had failed to give a meaning to certain signs in his propositions."[18]

Wittgenstein does not deny the existence of the inexpressible. There are things, he says, that cannot be put into words but which nonetheless manifest themselves to us. Such, for example, is the existence of the world. The natural sciences can say *how* things are in the world; *that* the world exists simply shows itself. It belongs to the realm of the inexpressible, which Wittgenstein calls "the mystical." Another example of the mystical is the feeling of the world as a limited whole. We cannot think or speak about the limits of the world, for in order to do this we would have to get outside the world and consider the limits from the other side as well as from this side.[19] But we *feel* the world as a limited whole. So too, our language shows the structure of the world, though this structure cannot be expressed in words. In one of his few references to God in the *Tractatus*, Wittgenstein denies that he reveals himself in the world.[20]

The propositions in the *Tractatus* itself are meant to show what is clearly expressible in words and hence what the limits of language are. At the same time they are intended to reveal the structure of language and thought and thereby the structure of the world.[21] But in doing so these propositions attempt to say "what cannot be said," for they are concerned with language, its limits, and its relation to reality. In what is surely one of the most paradoxical statements in the history of philosophy Wittgenstein frankly admits at the end of the *Tractatus* that its propositions are nonsense; but he defends them as important nonsense. The philosopher does not read them in vain, for through them he comes to understand the function and limitation of language and even to have a clearer view of reality. Wittgenstein declares:

> My propositions serve as elucidations in the following way: anyone who understands me eventually recognizes them as nonsensical, when he has used them—as steps—to climb up beyond them. (He must, so to speak, throw away the ladder after he has climbed up it.)

> He must transcend these propositions, and then he will see the world aright.
>
> What we cannot speak about we must consign to silence.[22]

language games

After writing the *Tractatus* Wittgenstein withdrew from philosophy, convinced that his problems in all essentials were solved. He lived near Vienna for a while, keeping in contact with philosophy through his acquaintance with Schlick and Waismann of the Vienna Circle. About 1928 his interest in philosophy revived and the following year he returned to Cambridge. Thus began a new phase in his philosophy in which he rejected many of the views of the *Tractatus.* Language, however, continued to be his main concern. He was still convinced that metaphysical perplexities arise from a misuse of language and that they can be removed by linguistic therapy. Hence there is continuity between his early and later periods despite the radical change of views in his maturity.

The main source for his ideas during his later period is the *Philosophical Investigations*. Of lesser value are his lecture notes, called the *Blue and Brown Books*, which were mimeographed in his lifetime and circulated and discussed in England. The *Philosophical Investigations* is a large notebook of remarks, discussions, questions, and aphorisms, all loosely strung together, and even less systematic in form than the *Tractatus*. As Wittgenstein says in the preface, it is really only an album that travels "over a wide field of thought criss-cross in every direction." His philosophical remarks "are, as it were, a number of sketches of landscapes which were made in the course of these long and involved journeyings." But there is method in this apparently aimless wandering: a method imposed by his new notion of language. He now conceives of language as a group of varied games with only "family resemblances" between them. All the actual uses of language must be taken into account if we are not to get lost in the forest of words. The very nature of philosophical investigation requires that we travel over a wide area of linguistic uses, seeing language from every possible point of view. Only then do we command a wide view of the landscape and know our way about.

The *Tractatus* assumes that language has essentially one purpose: the stating of facts. Language is said to consist of sentences containing names, whose meaning is taken from objects for which they stand. The truth of sentences is their correctly picturing facts. Finally, it is assumed that there is a fixed, simple, and definite structure of language that can be expressed in the formulae of mathematical logic.

In his later period Wittgenstein rejects all these assumptions. His conception of language is now more flexible, complex, and pragmatic. Words are likened to tools, and their uses are said to be as various as those of tools. "Think of the tools in a tool-box," he asks us: "there is a hammer, pliers, a saw, a screw-driver, a rule, a glue-pot, glue, nails and screws. The functions of words are as diverse as the functions of these objects."[23] Words are used to assert, question, command, describe, report, speculate, joke, ask, thank, curse, greet, pray, and so on. There is nothing common to all these uses of language, no essential function to be discovered beneath them all. Each is part of an activity or "form of life," and it must be understood within the context of this behavorial pattern. Suppose, for instance, a builder teaches a laborer to bring him a slab every time he calls "Slab!" The laborer responds correctly to the order; he learns the "language-game," which Wittgenstein defines as "the whole, consisting of language and the actions into which it is woven."[24]

How many language-games are there? They are as countless as the uses of words. We are inclined to think that there is something common to all language, an "essence" of language lying beneath the multiplicity of linguistic phenomena. Wittgenstein confesses that at one time he and Russell held this over-simple view. They thought that words were essentially names that derive their meaning from objects. They were held captive by a picture, he says, the picture (which he illustrates from a passage of St. Augustine's *Confessions*, I, 8) of a man learning the meaning of words by being shown the things they name.[25] But now he insists that there is really no one way in which words get their meaning. Many words are not the names of anything; and even when a word does name something, the act of naming is only preparatory to the use of the word. We do not learn a language simply by knowing what labels are attached to things; we must learn how names are used in a specific language-game. To be more precise, then, language is not like *a* game but like a family of games; and the rules of these games, their purposes, and the ways they are played are endlessly diverse.

In order to discover the meaning of a word, then, we have to know how it is used in a particular language-game. Its meaning is not something "behind" or independent of its use; its meaning is its use. If someone asks, "What is a pawn?" we explain that it is a piece used in a game of chess and then we state the rules governing the moves of the pawn. Similarly, we learn the meaning of a word by finding out how it is used in various contexts. Its meaning is discovered by seeing how it is used in different language-games and by observing the rules that govern its use in them.

A common mistake of philosophers, according to Wittgenstein, is the supposition that there is a hidden process of thinking, remembering, or feeling "behind" language and expressed by it. These ghostly processes are thought to explain language and give it its meaning. But Wittgenstein contends that there are no such hidden events. "Thinking," he says, "is not an incorporeal process which lends life and sense to speaking, and which it would be possible to detach from speaking..."[26] Like reading, thinking necessarily involves the use of language. Thus Wittgenstein will not have us say that animals do not think and therefore they do not talk; we should simply say that they do not talk. As he acknowledges, this comes close to behaviorism; but he does not intend to make pronouncements in psychology, much less in metaphysics. He wants to describe the phenomena of language as we actually encounter it. From this point of view everything lies on the surface and is readily observable. Words are simply counters used in games, tools or materials employed in a certain work. They derive their meaning from their use in some actual or possible situation. Words have meaning because the speaker is prepared to apply them in a definite context. Thus speech anticipates and prognosticates an action, and this is precisely what gives it its meaning. This brings Wittgenstein close to the pragmatic theory of meaning of the American philosopher C. S. Peirce.

According to this notion of language the limits of what can be said are by no means as rigid as Wittgenstein describes them in the *Tractatus*. In that work the meaning of a proposition is defined univocally as the picturing of a fact. Words make sense only in function of the "picture" relation to reality. In the *Philosophical Investigations* there are still limits to language, but these are determined by the rules of a particular language-game. And there is no way to determine *a priori* how many language-games there are or what their rules are. All the philosopher can do is to observe and to describe the workings of language in actual use; for example, in everyday speech and in science and mathematics. "Philosophy," he declares, "may in no way interfere with the actual use of language; it can in the end only describe it."[27] It is not his task—contrary to

Russell's belief—to try to improve on ordinary speech by constructing an ideal language "to show what a correct sentence looks like." According to Wittgenstein, an ideal language, such as mathematical logic, has a certain value, but it is artificial and fictitious and in no way a substitute for ordinary language.

What, then, is the business of the philosopher? He seeks complete clarity by describing the rules of the various language-games and by removing puzzles that occur when language is misused. As long as the rules of language are followed no confusions arise. Language is then doing its work. Confusion does arise, however, when it is not functioning properly. Because an expression makes good sense within one language-game we may think that it makes equally good sense in another, whereas in fact it does not function in this context at all. For example, because it is meaningful to ask what the length of a piece of metal is, we may think that it makes sense to ask for the length of the standard meter in Paris. Of course this is nonsense because "length" means being measured against the standard meter. Again, because it makes sense to ask what the meaning of language is within a given language-game, we may be led to think that it is equally sensible to ask what the meaning of language itself is—as though there were an "essence" of language common to all language-games. But, as we have seen, there is no hidden "essence" of language; there are only various language-games with resemblances between them.

These are but a few examples of how we can lose our way in the intricacies of language and ask meaningless questions. And such precisely are the problems of philosophy according to Wittgenstein. They are not real problems that admit of real answers but puzzles that arise from a misuse of language. A philosopher in a muddle is like a man who does not know his way about; he has strayed off the path and is lost in the forest of words. "Philosophy," Wittgenstein declares in one of his best-known aphorisms, "is a battle against the bewitchment of our intelligence by means of language."[28] And again, "The results of philosophy are the uncovering of one or another piece of plain nonsense and of bumps that the understanding has got by running its head up against the limits of language."[29] Philosophy relieves us of our "mental cramp" by bringing the linguistic confusion into the open. Thus philosophy brings "words back from their metaphysical to their everyday usage."[30] It relieves us of our mental anxiety. It shows "the fly the way out of the fly-bottle."[31] This may give the impression that Wittgenstein considers philosophical perplexities a trivial matter.

The contrary is true: "The problems arising through a misinterpretation of our forms of language have the character of *depth.* They are deep disquietudes; their roots are as deep in us as the forms of our language and their significance is as great as the importance of our language."[32]

Accordingly, the *Philosophical Investigations* and *Tractatus* fundamentally agree that philosophy is not a doctrine or theory but an elucidating and therapeutic activity. It does not add to the sum total of our knowledge as science does, but it uncovers nonsense in our language and sets language straight. The main differences between the two works are their notions of language and the methods of analyzing language. When he wrote the *Tractatus* Wittgenstein was convinced that every proposition has a clear and definite meaning that can be elucidated by one and only one complete analysis. This process of analysis consists in reducing complex propositions to more simple ones and finally to elementary propositions consisting of names in immediate combination. These elementary propositions point directly to the world, and their meaning consists in the fact that they picture the structure of the simple entities in the world. In the *Philosophical Investigations* Wittgenstein abandons this notion of analysis and the logical atomism that underlies it. He now teaches a linguistic pluralism: there are many uses of language, each of which is governed by its own rules. Philosophy is said to consist in the description of the uses of language for the purpose of removing philosophical problems. These problems are removed by bringing words back from philosophical to actual usage in the language which is their original home.[33]

Wittgenstein's legacy to his followers, then, was primarily a method of linguistic analysis. He claimed to hold no philosophical opinions but only, according to G. E. Moore's report, "that a 'new method' had been discovered, as had happened when 'chemistry developed out of alchemy'; and that it was now possible for the first time that there should be 'skilful' philosophers, though of course there had in the past been 'great' philosophers." "As regards his own work," Moore continues, "he said it did not matter whether his results were true or not: what mattered was that 'a method had been found.'"[34]

The fecundity of Wittgenstein's ideas can be measured by the extent of their influence on two quite different movements in contemporary philosophy: logical positivism and the so-called analysis of ordinary language. Logical positivism did not originate with Wittgenstein, but its proponents used (and sometimes misused) his *Tractatus* in the development and defense of their own position. Since the founders of this movement were scientists or mathematicians, it is understandable that they were chiefly interested in the analysis of the language of science, and that their method of analysis involved the use of scientific, ideal techniques such as mathematical logic, which Wittgenstein himself had employed in the *Tractatus*. The analysts of ordinary language, on the other hand, were mainly influenced by the later Wittgenstein and used the analytical method of his *Philosophical Investigations*. These two types of philosophical analysis are often confused in the popular mind, and even some philosophers fail to distinguish them clearly,[35] much to the distress of the analysts of ordinary language, who rightly regard their way of doing philosophy as essentially different from that of the logical positivists.

Logical Positivism and the Vienna Circle[36]

The origin of twentieth-century logical positivism goes back to Moritz Schlick,[37] a Viennese scientist and philosopher who taught the philosophy of science at the University of Vienna from 1922 to 1936, occupying a chair formerly held by Ernst Mach.[38] Like Mach, Schlick had an empirical and positivist outlook and an antipathy to metaphysics.

He became the center of a group of philosophers, scientists, and mathematicians who at first formed a discussion club and then launched an organized movement for the propagation of their ideas. Among the best-known philosophers of the group, besides Schlick, were Friedrich Waismann, Rudolf Carnap, Otto Neurath, Gustav Bergmann, and Herbert Feigl, and among the scientists and mathematicians Philipp Frank, Karl Menget, Kurt Gödel, and Hans Hahn. In 1929 they published a manifesto entitled "The Scientific Outlook of the Vienna Circle." Thus was born the name "The Vienna Circle" by which they are known to history.

In 1929 the Vienna Circle also made its first attempt to extend its influence beyond Austria by holding an international congress in Prague. In the 1930s further international congresses were held in Königsberg, Prague, Copenhagen, Paris, and Cambridge. Through these meetings contact was made with positivist philosophers and logicians in the Scandinavian countries, Holland, Poland, England, and the United States. An early connection was established with the Society of Empirical Philosophy or so-called Berlin School, of which Hans Reichenbach, Richard von Mises, and later Carl Hempel were the leaders. Among sympathizers of the movement were the American logicians Ernest Nagel, Charles Morris, and Willard Van Quine, the Polish logician A. Tarski, and the Austrian logician Karl Popper. The Circle propagated its ideas through the journal *Erkenntnis*, later called *The Journal of Unified Science*, and through several series of monographs and books with the general titles *Einheit swissenschaft*, *Schriften zur wissenschaftliche Weltauffassung*, and *International Encyclopedia of Unified Science*.

As early as the 1930s the Vienna Circle began to break up through the death or dispersal of its members. It disappeared as a school with the rise of the Nazi party, which was inimical to its ideas, and with the outbreak of the World War. Carnap, Neurath, Feigl, Gödel, Frank, Hempel, Reichenbach, von Mises, and Tarski went to American universities, and Waismann and Popper to England. With the large migration of German and Austrian members of the Vienna Circle and Berlin School to the United States, this country has become the center for logical positivism. Through their teaching and writing they have had an important influence on American philosophy. "In the United States," writes A. J. Ayer, "a number of philosophers like Quine, Nagel and Nelson Goodman conduct logical analysis in a systematic scientific spirit that is probably closer to the original ideal of the Vienna Circle than anything that is now to be met with elsewhere."[39] The influence of logical positivism is less strong in England, where the Oxford philosophers conduct their analysis of ordinary language in a quite different spirit. Logical positivism is a living force in contemporary English philosophy mainly through the work of A. J. Ayer.

In its manifesto the Vienna Circle acknowledged the influence of Wittgenstein, but he had no formal relations with the group. He was not a member and he attended none of its meetings. His ideas were first reported to the Circle by Schlick and Waismann, who were close friends of his in Vienna. Later the members of the Circle read his *Tractatus*, which confirmed them in their anti-metaphysical and positivist views. To the Viennese positivists metaphysics attempts to demonstrate the existence of entities lying beyond experience—entities such as Kantian things-in-themselves or a transcendent God—and this, they contended, is impossible. Wittgenstein convinced them that metaphysics goes beyond the limits of language; that all significant statements can be analyzed into elementary statements about ultimate or "atomic" facts that are verifiable through sense experience, and consequently that the only meaningful propositions are those of natural science. Wittgenstein also showed the Vienna group how to reconcile logic and mathematics with this empiricist view of propositions. They learned from him that logical and mathematical propositions are not empirical generalizations, as Mill claimed, but tautologies and identities respectively—purely formal propositions that tell us nothing about the world.

The Vienna Circle found these notions of Wittgenstein valuable in elaborating its own positivist philosophy. It also accepted the general method of philosophy proposed by the *Tractatus*, namely the logical analysis of language, especially the language of science. This was the method of logical atomism, worked out by Russell and skillfully incorporated by Wittgenstein in his *Tractatus*. The Viennese positivists, however, rejected the metaphysical implications of logical atomism. They did not agree with Russell or the early Wittgenstein that the logical analysis of propositions reveals the basic structure of the world but only that of language.

As we have seen, Wittgenstein himself later abandoned the metaphysical side of logical atomism; and indeed even in his *Tractatus* he dismissed all of its propositions as nonsensical because they went beyond the limits of language in talking about the structure of the world and its relation to language. The logical positivists did not take this dismissal too seriously. As positivists, they wanted to establish a theory of meaning that would restrict meaningful statements about the world to those that are verifiable by sense experience. But how can such a theory be established without relating propositions to facts? Wittgenstein avoided this problem by simply refusing to theorize about meaning, or to subscribe dogmatically to the "verification principle" so dear to the logical positivists. In his view it is not the business of the philosopher to establish theories of any kind but simply to clarify the meaning of propositions. Because the logical positivists refused to follow this narrow path in philosophy and strayed into the thickets of dogmatic theory, he completely dissociated himself from their movement, as most of his contemporary followers also do.

These general remarks about logical positivism will become more meaningful if we study the movement in two of its leading representatives, Rudolf Carnap and A. J. Ayer.

Rudolf Carnap

Following Wittgenstein, Carnap wants to break completely with traditional schools of philosophy and perennial ways of raising and answering philosophical questions.[40] Speaking in the name of the Vienna Circle, he insists that "we are not a philosophical school and that we put forward no philosophical theses whatsoever."[41] Philosophy is an activity and not a theory or system—an activity that can be described as the logical analysis of scientific terms and statements, which include the factual statements of everyday life. All of these statements, in Carnap's view, are verifiable by sense experience, and their meaning lies in the method by which they are verified. Since he holds that the statements belonging to the traditional branches of philosophy, such as metaphysics, ethics, and epistemology, cannot be verified empirically, he concludes that they are meaningless. They are not statements at all but pseudo statements. What remains as valid in philosophy is general logic and the logic of science, that is to say the logical analysis of the language of science. Carnap's career has been devoted to the pursuit of logical analysis, following what he calls an exact, scientific method. By the application of this method he thinks that philosophy has finally become scientific, and that in the traditional sense of the term it has ceased to be philosophical.

We have seen how difficult, if not impossible, it was for Wittgenstein to make philosophy a pure method, avoiding philosophical commitments and theories. Carnap also wants to establish philosophy as a pure method, but he is less careful than Wittgenstein to eschew theorizing. In particular, he has a definite theory of language and its meaning; in other words, a theory of semantics, an essential element of which is the "principle of verifiability," which states that the meaning of a proposition consists in its method of verification.[42]

A language, according to Carnap, consists of a vocabulary and a syntax; that is to say, a group of words with meanings and rules for formulating sentences with them. What is the meaning of a word? What makes it significant? First of all its syntax must be fixed: it must occur in a definite way in an elementary sentence. For example, the word "stone" occurs as the predicate in the elementary sentence form "x is a stone," where "x" stands for a word designating a thing. Second, there must be a known method of verifying the sentence. This verification must be by means of empirical data. The sentence is either immediately verifiable by such data, in which ease it is a primary or "protocol" sentence, or it is deducible from one of more primary sentences.[43]

In his early work *Der logische Aufbau der Welt* (1928), Carnap describes the empirical data that verify protocol sentences and thereby give meaning to words as our immediate, private, subjective experiences. These experiences are said to be the primitive ingredients out of which we construct our concepts. This construction is made possible by the linking together of a number of experiences by the relation of "recognized-similarity." For example, remembering the similarity of a number of experiences, we link them together and form the concept "red." The primitive relation of "recognition of similarity," according to Carnap, is the basis for the whole structure of knowledge. What we call the world, including physical objects, other minds, and societies, is a logical construction which gives organization and structure to our experiences.

At the beginning this was the view of Moritz Schlick and most of the members of the Vienna Circle. They held that all meaningful statements about objects can be reduced to certain primary statements expressing one's private, immediate experiences. Under the influence of Neurath, however, Carnap soon realized that such private experiences can never account for the public world of scientific knowledge. The statements of science are verifiable by all scientists, whereas protocol sentences, which are supposed to be their foundation, can be verified only by the individual whose experiences they express. If every protocol sentence records a private experience, how can such sentences be the basis for the public knowledge of science? To avoid this difficulty, Carnap adopted a new view of protocol sentences. While still maintaining that they are records of direct experience, he thinks that they can be translated into statements about bodily states that can be verified by anyone. For example, the statement "At ten o'clock Mr. A was angry" can be translated "At ten o'clock Mr. A was in a certain bodily condition which is characterized by the acceleration of breathing and pulse, by the tension of certain muscles, by the tendency to certain violent behaviour, and so on."[44] In this way all statements about experiences are translatable into statements about human behavior and these can be verified by anyone. This doctrine, called "physicalism," makes it possible to express all empirical statements in the language of physics, by referring to processes occurring in space and time. In Carnap's view, this has the added advantage of bringing all sciences to the same level, thus making possible a unified scientific language.

At the same time this theory of semantics eliminates all metaphysical language as meaningless. Metaphysics, Carnap states, attempts to discover and formulate a kind of knowledge that is not accessible to empirical science; but this is enough to condemn it as meaningless, for if it lies outside the field of science its statements cannot be verified by sense experience. Carnap is not saying that metaphysics is mere speculation or the telling of fairy tales, for the former may be true and the latter, though in conflict with experience, may not be illogical. He is saying that metaphysical statements are not statements at all. "According to this view," he writes, "the sentences of metaphysics are pseudo sentences which on logical analysis are proved to be either empty phrases or phrases which violate the rules of syntax."[45]

But if the statements of metaphysics have no cognitive meaning, how can we account for the persistent efforts of eminent thinkers to formulate a metaphysics? Carnap attributes the perennial interest in metaphysics to man's effort to express his general attitude toward life. Like the religious thinker and artist, the metaphysician gives expression to his emotional and volitional reaction to the world about him, only he uses verbal expression and argumentation in place of, say, the purer media of poetry or music. Metaphysicians "have a strong inclination to work within the medium of the theoretical, to connect concepts and thoughts. Now, instead of activating, on the one hand, this inclination in the domain of science, and satisfying, on the other hand, the need for expression in art, the metaphysician confuses the two and produces a structure which achieves nothing for knowledge and something inadequate for the expression of attitude." In short, "Metaphysicians are musicians without musical ability."[46]

Carnap includes in metaphysics, as meaningless verbiage, epistemological theories such as realism, subjective idealism, solipsism, phenomenalism, and positivism (in the older, classical sense of the term). The judgments of value of normative ethics and aesthetics are likewise eliminated as meaningless statements on the ground that the objective validity of a value or norm cannot be empirically verified or deduced from empirical statements.

The only meaningful statements Carnap admits beside the factual assertions of the empirical sciences are those of mathematics and logic (and their contradictories, which are false but meaningful). Following Wittgenstein, he considers these necessary truths but devoid of content. They are tautologies that are necessary in terms of their formal structure. They are not verifiable in experience but are known *a priori*.

The most serious problems arose for Carnap, as they did for Wittgenstein, concerning the status of philosophical statements. Carnap does not consider them to be statements about facts or states of affairs, like the statements of science. This would make philosophy a rival of science, concerned with the same physical objects, though from a different point of view. But philosophy, according to Carnap, is not about reality at all; it is a branch of logic (the logic of science), and its sentences describe the logical form of sentences, especially the sentences of science.

But can the forms of language be described by language? As we have seen, Wittgenstein in his *Tractatus* thought they could not. Writing as a logical atomist, he says in this work that the form of language mirrors reality,[47] and consequently it refers to something beyond language. Accordingly, a statement about the form of a proposition would concern not only language but also the relation of language to reality, which is inexpressible. Because the propositions of the *Tractatus* do concern the form of language, Wittgenstein dismisses them as nonsensical.

In his *Logical Syntax of Language* Carnap finds a way to avoid this distressing conclusion. He maintains, contrary to Wittgenstein, that it is possible to construct meaningful sentences about the forms of language because these forms have no reference to reality: they are simply conventional rules determining within a language when a sentence is well formed or grammatical and describing the way in which one sentence can be derived from another. There is nothing to prevent such syntactical rules for the formation and transformation of sentences from being described by the language they govern. Consequently, it is entirely possible for the language of science to describe its own syntax. The sentences of the logic of science can be formulated within science itself; and since it belongs to philosophy to formulate these sentences, philosophy is safely lodged within the domain of science: it is the logic of science.[48]

According to Carnap, then, philosophical questions are not about physical objects (it is the business of science to ask questions of this sort); nor do they concern pseudo objects such as the Absolute, the ultimate cause of the world, values, or things-in-themselves. Rather, the philosopher asks logical questions, concerning the meaning and content of terms and sentences or their form. The propositions of philosophy are meaningful, therefore, not as empirical propositions concerning the physical world, but, like all logical propositions, as tautologies or verbal equivalences.

But is it possible to eliminate from philosophy all reference to things or objects outside of language, so that the statements of philosophy will concern language alone and not reality? Philosophers often talk about things. Indeed, even Carnap and the other logical positivists refer to bodily states and other data of experience when speaking of the verification of statements, as though they were concerned with something extra-linguistic that gives meaning and truth to language. But Carnap contends that the philosopher only seems to be talking about things; he never really gets outside of language.

Carnap explains this essential point of his theory of semantics by distinguishing between two ways in which we can talk about language: the formal mode and the material mode. In the formal mode we explicitly talk about language, as when we say "The word 'Babylon' occurred in yesterday's lecture." This sentence, however, can be rephrased in the material mode without an explicit sign that it concerns language; for example, "Babylon was treated of in yesterday's lecture." This looks like a sentence about a real object, like the sentence "Babylon was a big town," but in fact it is a sentence about a word: it tells us nothing about the city of Babylon but only about the appearance of a word in a group of sentences. According to Carnap, it is not wrong to use the material mode of speech, but it is dangerous. He considers the misuse of the material mode to be one of the main sources of metaphysics. For example, a philosopher may not realize that the sentence "Five is a number" is a statement in the material mode of the syntactical sentence "'Five' is a number-word," with the result that he speculates about the essence of number as though it were an extra-linguistic object.

But surely the scientist talks about real objects. How can the philosopher, in his role as logician of science, avoid taking these objects into account? Carnap meets this difficulty by distinguishing between two kinds of questions about existence. First, there are questions about the existence of certain entities within a given framework; and second, there are questions about the existence or reality of the framework itself. For instance, within the framework of everyday language—the spatio-temporally ordered system of observable things and events—it may be asked: Is there a white piece of paper on my desk? This question, which is internal to the framework, can be answered by empirical investigation. If the answer is in the affirmative, the paper is known to be a real thing, incorporated into the framework of things recognized as real, according to the rules of the framework. This concept of "reality" is empirical, scientific, and non-metaphysical. It is another question whether the whole world of things is real. This is a question raised by the philosopher, not by the scientist or man in the street. Realists answer in the affirmative, subjective idealists in the negative. But the question admits of no solution for it is framed in the wrong way. To be real in the scientific sense means to be an element in the framework of science. Hence this notion of reality cannot be applied to the framework itself. The question whether the whole world of things is real, Carnap suggests, is simply the practical question whether the *language* of things is acceptable. We may decide that this language is useful because of its high degree of efficiency in dealing with the practical problems of life; but this does not confirm the reality of the world of things.[49]

Accordingly, the philosopher can talk meaningfully of the reality of certain objects without committing himself to metaphysical theories of the reality or non-reality of the external world. This problem, like the metaphysical problem of the reality or non-reality of universals (realism or nominalism in the medieval sense), admits of no theoretical solution. All soluble problems in philosophy are problems of language and semantics. In this perspective there can hardly be a more serious philosophical error than Wittgenstein's statement that there *is* something that reveals itself to us but is inexpressible in words.[50]

A. J. Ayer

One of Carnap's pupils at the University of Vienna was the Englishman A. J. Ayer.[51] Ayer had already studied under Gilbert Ryle at Oxford and under Schlick in Vienna. On his return to England he published his widely read *Language, Truth and Logic* (1936), in which he popularized the continental logical positivism, while tempering it with traditional English empiricism. In the preface he expresses his indebtedness to the Viennese positivists. "The philosophers with whom I am in the closest agreement," he says, "are those who compose the 'Viennese Circle,' under the leadership of Moritz Schlick, and are commonly known as logical positivists. And of these I owe most to Rudolf Carnap."[52] Among others whom he names as having influenced him are Moore, Russell, Wittgenstein, and the classical empiricists Berkeley and Hume.

The impact of the early views of the Vienna Circle is most obvious in the first edition of *Language, Truth and Logic*. In the preface to the second edition

(1946), and in his more recent works, he considerably modifies his earlier positions. Even more than the later Carnap he has given up the strict form of logical positivism. Indeed, Carnap himself now comes under his criticism. Ayer's thought has become more flexible and subtle; his views about knowledge, for example, have so changed, one historian says, "as to be scarcely any longer regarded as a form of logical positivism."[53]

In *Language, Truth and Logic* Ayer contends that it is not the business of the philosopher to furnish speculative truths like the scientist but rather to analyze language. What language should he analyze? Not our everyday language, for that is already sufficiently analyzed. The philosopher's task is "to clarify the propositions of science by exhibiting their logical relationships, and by defining the symbols which occur in them."[54] Of course, the philosopher is in no position to evaluate scientific theories, for he is not concerned with matters of fact. But he can assist the scientist by defining the concepts used in these theories (as Einstein defined the concept of simultaneity, to the great benefit of modern science). The philosopher can also help the scientist to coordinate his inquiries and to emancipate himself from metaphysical notions. Ayer goes so far as to say that science is blind without philosophy, though he sets the balance straight by adding that philosophy is virtually empty without science. Indeed, science and philosophy are but two sides of the same endeavor: science is its speculative aspect and philosophy its logical aspect. The role of the philosopher is to develop the logic of science; and in order to do this he must become a scientist.[55]

Does this mean that there are no philosophical propositions distinct from those of science, as Wittgenstein and the Viennese positivists claimed? In the preface to the second edition of *Language, Truth and Logic,* Ayer says that this has the merit of emphasizing that philosophy is not a source of speculative truth, but he thinks it is incorrect to say that there are no philosophical propositions. His own book contains propositions that fall into a special category; they are the sort that are asserted or denied by philosophers. Why not, then, call them philosophical?[56] Unlike Wittgenstein, Ayer is by no means inclined to dismiss his propositions as nonsensical—not even as important nonsense.

What kind of propositions are philosophical? Ayer contends that they are linguistic propositions concerning the usage of words. But this does not distinguish philosophy from lexicography. Lexicographers also give information about the use of words, but about the use of particular expressions, whereas philosophers enlighten us about the use of classes of expressions. Moreover, the propositions of lexicography are empirical, telling us how words are actually used, while those of philosophy are usually analytic, embodying verbal definitions and unconcerned with matters of fact. The only empirical propositions Ayer admits into philosophy are those occurring in the history of philosophy. The value of these propositions, he says, is that they furnish examples that can be used for philosophical purposes.

All propositions, according to Ayer, are either empirical or analytic. A proposition is analytic "when its validity depends solely on the definitions of the symbols it contains."[57] An example is "All oculists are eye doctors." One only needs to know the definitions of the subject and predicate to know that the proposition is true. Such propositions are not factual; they are known *a priori* or independently of experience; and they are tautologous. But they are not meaningless. They may even give us new knowledge, not by telling us a new fact but by calling our attention to linguistic usage of which we might otherwise be ignorant; and they can even surprise us by disclosing unsuspected implications in our assertions and beliefs. According to Ayer, the propositions of formal logic and mathematics are analytic. A proposition of the form "Either *p* is true or *p* is not true" is known to be true independently of experience, through the definition of its symbols. So, too, the proposition "7 + 5 = 12" is an analytic truth whose validity depends solely on the fact that the symbolic expression "7 + 5" is synonymous with "12."

At one time Ayer described analytic propositions as linguistic rules, as though they simply express a verbal definition, or "record our determination to use symbols in a certain fashion."[58] Under criticism, however, he modified this position. As first stated, it seems to imply that analytic propositions simply describe the way certain symbols are used in a particular language, and hence that they are a subclass of empirical propositions; and if this is true they are not necessarily true but arbitrary. In order to safeguard the necessary truth of analytic propositions he now denies that they are themselves linguistic rules (that is to say, determinations as to how words are to be used in a certain language). They are, he says, statements *grounded in* the rules of language, and therefore necessarily true. For example, "it is a contingent, empirical fact that the word 'earlier' is used in English to mean earlier, and it is an arbitrary, though convenient, rule of language that words that stand for temporal relations are to be used transitively; but, given this rule, the proposition that, if A is earlier than B and B is earlier than C, A is earlier than C becomes a necessary truth."[59] Of course, this does not remove all arbitrariness from such propositions; they are not absolutely but hypothetically necessary, since their truth rests on linguistic rules which are themselves arbitrary.

A proposition is empirical, according to Ayer, "when its validity is determined by the facts of experience"; in other words, when it is empirically verifiable. But what is meant by "verifiable"? Ayer has written much on this subject without—by his own admission—dispelling all vagueness from it. He distinguishes between a strong and a weak sense of the term. In the strong sense a proposition is verifiable if its truth can be conclusively established by experience; it is verifiable in the weak sense if it is possible for experience to render it probable. The only class of empirical propositions that admit of strong verification are basic propositions, which refer solely to an immediate experience such as "this is green" or "I feel a headache." All other empirical propositions are only weakly verifiable; for example, general propositions such as "all men are mortal," and all statements about the past and future. These cannot be conclusively established; at best they are highly probable.[60]

Ayer does not mean that every significant empirical statement must actually be verified, but it must at least be able to be verified, either directly or indirectly, by some observations that would be "relevant to the demonstration of its truth or falsity."[61]

In Ayer's view this rules out metaphysical propositions as meaningless. They are not intended to express a tautology, like the propositions of mathematics or logic, but rather to assert something about reality transcending the limits of all possible sense experience. But this means that in principle they cannot be verified. Ayer asks us to consider F. H. Bradley's statement that "the Absolute enters into, but is itself incapable of, evolution and progress." We cannot conceive of an observation that would prove this true or false; it is in principle unverifiable. For the same reason Ayer argues that the propositions "God exists" and "human souls are immortal" are unverifiable. Such metaphysical utterances are neither true nor false; they are literally meaningless.[62]

Ayer also uses the verification principle to rule out normative ethical and aesthetic judgments as true or false. In saying that a certain type of action is right or wrong, or that a work of art is beautiful or hideous, I am not making a factual statement, not even one about my own state of mind. I am merely expressing my sentiments or feelings. No objective validity can be attributed to these statements.[63] Ayer does not abandon this view in his later writings, though he concedes that ethical statements are not purely emotive. A large number of such statements, he now asserts, contain factual elements, such as descriptions of actions or situations, and insofar as ethical statements involve such elements they can be the subject of reasonable debate.[64] In his essay "On the Analysis of Moral Judgments" Ayer grants that "ethical features in some way depend upon the natural." We can and do give reasons for our moral and aesthetic judgments—reasons that are used to influence other people by calling their attention to "certain natural features of the situation."[65] Ayer has here abandoned the purely "emotive theory" of ethics.

Since the criterion of meaningfulness in empirical statements is the verification principle, it is important to know what status the principle itself has as a proposition. Ayer does not consider it to be an empirical proposition, capable of being verified by sense experience, but an analytic, *a priori*, proposition, expressing a definition of "meaning." It is not, however, an arbitrary definition. He writes:

> It purports to lay down the conditions which actually govern our acceptance, or indeed our understanding, of common sense and scientific statements, the statements which we take as describing the world "in which we live and move and have our being." This leaves it open to the metaphysician to reply that there may be other worlds besides the world of science and common sense, and that he makes it his business to explore them. But then the onus is on him to show by what criterion his statements are to be tested: until he does this we do not know how to take them.[66]

In the preface to the second edition of *Language, Truth and Logic* Ayer grants a certain arbitrariness to the verification principle. While not "entirely arbitrary," he says, it is "open to anyone to adopt a different criterion of meaning and so to produce an alternative definition which may very well correspond to one of the ways in which the word 'meaning' is commonly used."[67] This is far from his early notion of the principle and from that of the Vienna Circle.

It leaves room for a metaphysical criterion of meaning, distinct from that of common sense and natural science. As John Wisdom remarks of the verification principle: "The poor thing is not what is was, and it is quite incapable of eliminating metaphysics or anything else."[68]

Although Ayer's views on the principle of verification have become more liberal with the years, he himself does not accept any other criterion of meaning for empirical statements than their verifiability in sense experience. On this point he has not budged from his early position. In saying that an empirical statement refers to experience, he does not mean that it always refers to one's own experience. It is meaningful as long as it can be verified (or falsified) through *some* experience, no matter whose this may be. Carnap believes that experience is private and incommunicable; but Ayer argues that, although we cannot literally share the experience of another person, we can understand what he says about them. Hence experiences are communicable; and once this is granted, there is no need to resort to Carnap's physicalism to explain the public language of science. For a language to be public it does not have to refer to public objects; it can refer to, and be verified by, communicable experiences. Ayer thinks that physicalism is not only unnecessary but that it rests on the erroneous principle that to say something about a person's thought, feelings, or sensations is always equivalent to saying something about his physical condition.[69]

Ayer also parts company with Carnap on the question of the data of experience that directly verify empirical propositions. Are these primitive data material things such as pencils and match boxes, or are they sense data such as particular sounds and feelings? In line with his belief that all philosophical problems are linguistic, Carnap holds that this is a verbal matter. It is equivalent to asking what kind of words occur in observation sentences, material object words or sense data words? And this, in his view, is merely a matter of choice and convention. Ayer, on the contrary, insists in his *Foundations of Empirical Knowledge* that the question of the primitive data of experience goes beyond language and involves matters of fact. It concerns the primary evidence for the truth of empirical statements, and this evidence is extra-linguistic: it is that to which statements must directly conform in order to be true. As for the nature of this primary evidence, Ayer concludes that it is sense data.[70]

Ayer sees clearly the implications of this position for the nature of philosophical statements. At one time, following the continental logical positivists, he thought that they were purely linguistic and analytic, unconcerned with matters of fact. Philosophy was a matter of analysis and clarification of propositions, without reaching out to the factual world. In his recent *The Concept of a Person* he doubts whether questions of analysis can be so neatly distinguished from questions of fact, and he concludes that "it appears that philosophy does after all intrude upon questions of empirical fact."[71] This is a clear indication that in recent years Ayer has abandoned classical logical positivism.

The Analysis of Ordinary Language

The most faithful followers of Wittgenstein today—at least of the later Wittgenstein—are not the logical positivists but the so-called analysts of ordinary language. Unlike the members of the Vienna Circle most of these men received their early intellectual formation in the classics and not in science or mathematics. Hence they are more interested than the Viennese positivists in language for its own sake and in the language of ordinary use rather than in an ideally constructed and artificial language such as mathematical logic. They do not agree with Ayer that our everyday language has been sufficiently analyzed; on the contrary, they regard the analysis of this "natural" language as sadly neglected by philosophers and the most fruitful approach to philosophy today.

After Wittgenstein's return to Cambridge, following his long retreat from philosophy in Austria, he took a teaching post and attracted a group of disciples who offered him a veritable cult and adopted his new method of philosophizing. As they listened to the master their excitement mounted. Men had been grappling with philosophical problems for several thousand years. Now at last, they believed, the true nature of these perplexities was being revealed, and techniques were being discovered whereby they could be released from them. The group around Wittgenstein can hardly be called a school, for its members did not profess a common doctrine. Wittgenstein claimed to hold no philosophical opinions and he discouraged his followers from regarding him as the creator of a philosophical system. What he offered to them was something more fundamental: a radically new conception of the nature of philosophical thinking and therapies for ridding themselves of philosophical doubts. It was the common acceptance of this new way of "doing philosophy" that gives unity to the movement that originated with him at Cambridge.

cambridge analysts

The Cambridge group of therapeutic analysts included Morris Lazerowitz and Norman Malcolm; but the outstanding pupil of Wittgenstein was John Wisdom, his successor in the Chair of Philosophy at Cambridge. Before coming under Wittgenstein's influence, Wisdom studied under Moore and Broad, and his first book, *Problems of Mind and Matter*, is heavily indebted to their methods of analysis.[72] The name of Wittgenstein does not appear in it. After his contact with Wittgenstein, however, Wisdom adopted his analytical method in place of Moore's. He became dissatisfied with Moore's cheerful reliance on common sense and his setting aside doubts without answering them. Does the external world exist? To this Moore replies by raising his hand and saying "Here's a hand," as though this settles the matter. Instead of resolving the problem of the existence of matter, he offers an analysis of matter in terms of sensations. But the philosopher who asks whether matter is real does not deny that he perceives a hand; what he wants to know is whether there is a material reality over and above his sensations. Wisdom did not think Moore settles this question by his appeal to common sense and ordinary language.

The Wittgensteinian method, in Wisdom's opinion, is more successful in resolving difficulties of this sort. When someone is in the grip of a philosophical problem, such as whether other minds exist beside his own or whether he can be certain of anything, it cannot be settled by pretending it does not exist. But he can be shown the causes of his perplexity, and once he understands these his puzzlement vanishes. Wittgenstein said that "the philosopher's treatment of a question is like the treatment of an illness."[73] In short, a man disturbed by a philosophical problem is intellectually sick. Wisdom suggests that the correct treatment of such a case is similar to that of psychoanalysis.[74] The philosopher is in a state of confused tension, with almost equal forces pulling him to each side of the question. Release does not come from an absolute and definitive solution of the problem, for it admits of none, but from the complete description of the causes that gave rise to it. The patient "is cured by having him describe himself (as in psychoanalysis)." An advantage of this therapeutic method is that it leaves the philosopher free from doctrinal commitments; his method is justified not by a theory but, like psychoanalysis, by its practical success.

Some of the Cambridge linguistic analysts—for example, Lazerowitz and Farrell—see no essential difference between philosophical and psychopathological doubt, or between their methods of treatment.[75] Wisdom thinks that the big difference between these states of mind "lies in the flow of justificatory talk, of rationalization, which the philosopher produces when asked why he takes the extraordinary line he does."[76]

The cause of all metaphysical problems, according to Wisdom, is the application of models of language and thought that are appropriate in some context to others in which they are inappropriate. Like Wittgenstein he thinks that the metaphysician is "held captive by a picture." For example, even after the philosopher has consciously rejected the image of the soul as a ghost in the body, he may still be dominated by its power and think of the mind or soul as something not only behind bodily events but even behind mental events, thus leading him to "a purely metaphysical dance."

Although to Wisdom and his colleagues philosophical problems do not admit of absolute answers, they find the conflicting proposals of philosophers valuable insofar as they help to clarify certain aspects of our language and thought, and even of reality itself. Thus metaphysical statements have a positive value for Wisdom unrecognized by Wittgenstein. "Wittgenstein," he says, "too much represents them [i.e., philosophical paradoxes] as merely symptoms of linguistic confusion. I wish to represent them as also symptoms of linguistic penetration."[77] For example, when a philosopher surprises us with the statement "We can never really know that other people have minds," he is saying something false but useful because he helps us to see that we do not verify statements about other people's minds in the same way that we verify statements about tables and chairs.

oxford analysts

In recent years the center of philosophical activity has passed from Cambridge to Oxford.[78] Wittgenstein's ideas have continued to be the dominant factor in English philosophy; but at Oxford they have developed in a different intellectual climate. Most of the Oxford analysts came to philosophy through a study of the classics. Consequently, they are more aware than Wittgenstein of the classical tradition of philosophy and the part that analysis plays in it. They are not as inclined as he was to see analysis as the whole of philosophy but rather as an introductory method—a necessary starting point for the philosopher but not his goal.

The Oxford form of linguistic philosophy, often described as "ordinary language philosophy," owes much to Moore and the later Wittgenstein. Its exponents do not form a school with common doctrines or even with exactly the same methods, but they clearly belong to the same movement, sharing the view that philosophy is primarily concerned with the ordinary use of language and its analysis. They have in common a dislike of the grandiose metaphysical systems and the high-flown and pedantic language that characterized the English idealists at Oxford at the turn of the century. In comparison their interests and aims in philosophy seem modest indeed. As Brand Blanshard says, "To anyone whose expectations had been set by the Oxford of a generation earlier, the Oxford of Caird and Bradley, the new philosophy was in a low key, and its almost ostentatiously casual language about 'doing philosophy' as studying 'the jobs' of 'a lot of words' was not always prepossessing."[79]

The analysts themselves claim to have returned to the old tradition of the English empiricists which had been interrupted in the nineteenth century by the importation of German idealism into England. And indeed they share with philosophers such as Hobbes, Locke, Berkeley, Bentham, and Mill the analytical and empirical spirit, and a concern for clarity and simplicity in their thinking and writing.

The influence of Wittgenstein is obvious in Gilbert Ryle's contention that the philosopher does not talk directly about facts but rather about one's talk about facts. If the philosopher took reality itself as his subject, Ryle claims, he would be setting himself up as a rival to the scientist, as though philosophy were a distinct way of knowing the actual world. Its business is quite different: it concerns language in its ordinary use and detects "the sources in linguistic idioms of recurrent misconstructions and absurd theories."[80]

If philosophy is a study of language, how does it differ from philology? The philologist studies words, but he fastens on their differences of form, sound, and origin. These do not concern the philosopher. What interests him is the kind of work a word does, our way of using it or operating with it. Ryle calls this "the logical behaviour of words." Adopting this point of view, the philosopher does not study the use of English words alone. What Hume discovered about the use of the word "cause" is equally true of its German counterpart "Ursache," for the logical behavior of these two words is the same.

How many uses of words are there? Ryle agrees with Wittgenstein that they are numerous indeed. P. F. Strawson limits their use to mentioning or referring to something.[81] But Ryle points out that beside referring, words describe, ask, exclaim, and so on. John Austin has drawn attention to a class of expressions which he calls "performative utterances."[82] These are not statements about something but expressions that do something; examples are "I baptize you" and "I take you for my lawful wedded wife." These utterances are neither true nor false, but they are meaningful. Like all words and expressions, their meaning is discovered by examining the use to which they are put.

Ryle is concerned with ordinary language because he believes that it systematically tends to mislead the philosopher. In his view, as in Wittgenstein's, it is the main source of philosophical puzzles. Not that the man in the street or the scientist or mathematician is confused by his language. When the reader of the *Pickwick Papers* says, "Mr. Pickwick is a fiction," he knows what he is talking about. But the metaphysician, with his concern for categories of being, is likely to be misled by the similarity of this sentence to "Mr. Menzies is a statesman" and considers it to be a description of a person, Mr. Pickwick, with the property of being fictitious.

Philosophers, Ryle contends, constantly make category mistakes. By this he means "the presentation of facts belonging to one category in the idioms appropriate to another." In short, it is the mistake of trying to make one category do the work of another. Thus, it makes sense to say, "John is in bed," but it would be a mistake to say, on the analogy of this sentence, that "Saturday is in bed."[83]

A prime example of a category mistake discussed by Ryle in his *Concept of Mind* is the bifurcation of man into two entities, mind and body.[84] The ordinary man uses words expressing mental conduct without great difficulty. He knows how to decide whether John is intelligent or thinking. But the philosopher puzzles over the category in which these concepts are to be placed. The "official" or Cartesian theory is that they refer to a strange sort of entity called "mind" or "soul," which is distinct from the body because it is non-spatial, spiritual, private, and known only by introspection. Ryle insists, however, that it is a category mistake to think that mental-conduct words like "thinking" name an entity at all. Like the word "running," they describe human behavior. Owing to Descartes' category mistake he conceived of man as composed of two different entities, mind and body—as "a ghost in a machine," and from this new puzzles arose: How can the mind act on the body? How can the mind peer through the body to the world around it?

Thus, according to Ryle, ordinary speech by its form deceives the philosopher regarding the structure of the fact it asserts. But he assures us that this can be rectified by "stating this fact in a new form of words which does exhibit what the other failed to exhibit." "And I am for the present inclined to believe," he adds, "that this is what philosophical analysis is, and that this is the sole and whole function of philosophy."[85] This is entirely in the spirit of Wittgenstein. Other philosophers at Oxford regard this attitude toward philosophy as too negative; in their opinion philosophy has more to do than resolve problems generated by language. Since the last world war a more positive notion of philosophical analysis has come to the fore at Oxford. Philosophers are making very detailed and minute analyses of ordinary language in the hope of uncovering its hidden riches. They describe the different functions of all sorts of linguistic expressions. One of the most accomplished Oxford analysts, John Austin, has given good examples of this kind of analysis in his study of "performative utterances" and in his discussion of the words "mistake," "accident," and "inadvertence" and their use in connection with judgments of responsibility.

To some these meticulous descriptions of ordinary language should not be dignified by the name "philosophical," but this criticism does not deter the analysts. They are convinced that their analyses are of value in uncovering the conceptual contents of language and even in deepening our knowledge of the world to which we apply these concepts. More modest than Wittgenstein, they do not equate their techniques with the method of philosophy, but they consider them to be an indispensable part of that method. They point out that most great philosophers of the past carefully examined their words and recognized that they could be led astray by misinterpreting them. As Austin puts it, analysis may not be the "end-all" of philosophy but it is at least its "begin-all."

A topic only slightly touched upon by Wittgenstein but extensively treated by his Oxford followers is ethical language. They point out that ordinary language contains not only descriptions but also prescriptions and evaluations. We say, for example, that a certain action is right or that it ought to be done. We also make value judgments, saying that such and such is good or bad. According to R. M. Hare, ethical words and statements fall under the class of prescriptive language, including both imperative sentences and value judgments.[86]

Like his colleagues S. E. Toulmin and P. H. Nowell-Smith, Hare's main concern is to describe correctly the language we use in making ethical statements. For these men ethics is primarily the logical study of the language of morals. They insist that this language is *sui generis* and irreducible to any other. Ethical prescriptions are not to be confused with statements of facts, and they cannot be deduced from them.

The Oxford analysts are critical of all ethical theories that fail to recognize this irreducible character of ethical language. Like G. E. Moore they criticize "naturalist" ethical systems, which equate the moral good with a natural quality such as pleasure. But they think Moore himself slipped into the fallacy of confusing prescriptions with descriptions by assuming that the word "good" designates a "non-natural" quality. In Hare's opinion, the value word "good" does not signify an objective quality or fact; it is not primarily a descriptive but rather a prescriptive and commendatory word. Hence he is also critical of the "emotive theory" of ethics, proposed by logical positivists such as A. J. Ayer, according to whom ethical propositions express our wishes and feelings and are intended to arouse similar feelings in others. This assumes that value words such as "good" are meaningful because they designate wishes and interior attitudes. But Hare insists that ethical language does not describe or report facts, either objective or subjective. It is meant to guide us in our actions by instructing, advising, commanding, exhorting, and so on, and it is meaningful because of these multiple uses to which it can be put.

Beyond the logical analysis of ethical expressions, the Oxford analysts do not think that ethics can teach us how we are to act. "Ethics, as a special branch of logic," says Hare, "owes its existence to the function of moral judgments as a guide in answering questions of the form 'What shall I do?' "[87] But he does not think that ethics itself can answer such questions. It is up to each person to make his own decision as to how he ought to live.[88] Nowell-Smith comes to the same disappointing conclusion:

> My purpose has been the less ambitious one of showing how the concepts that we use in practical discourse, in deciding, choosing, advising, appraising, praising and blaming, and selecting and rejecting moral rules, are related to each other. The question "What shall I do?" and "What moral principles should I adopt?" must be answered

> by each man for himself; that at least is part of the connotation of the word "moral."[89]

An unexpected development in post-Wittgenstein analytical philosophy is the revival of interest in metaphysics. Wittgenstein himself maintained a negative attitude toward metaphysics in both the *Tractatus* and *Philosophical Investigations*. The former rules out of bounds both metaphysical and theological language, and the latter does not explicitly recognize metaphysical or theological language games. But one of his disciples, Miss Anscombe, assures us that he had no "initial doctrine about the impossibility of metaphysics."[90] In this respect he differed from the logical positivists who, as we have seen, try to eliminate metaphysics by the principle that the only meaningful propositions are tautologies and empirically verifiable statements. Analysts such as Wisdom and Lazerowitz oppose this principle, pointing out that the restriction of "meaning" to what is supported by empirical evidence or to what is tautologous is purely arbitrary. Why should there not be metaphysical statements that are meaningful because they are supported by metaphysical evidence?

Since Wittgenstein proposed no theory of meaning, his followers are not committed in principle to a denial of metaphysics. Indeed, P. F. Strawson protests against Wittgenstein's negative attitude toward metaphysics and his concentration on therapeutical analysis. He does not see why analysts might not "make room for a purged kind of metaphysics, with more modest and less disputable claims than the old."[91] The metaphysics he proposes would not be an ontology. Without attempting to give causal explanations, it would simply "describe the actual structure of our thought about the world."[92] It would show how the fundamental categories of thought are interconnected and how these in turn are related to such general notions as existence, identity, and unity.

Another recent development in analytical philosophy is an interest in the analysis of religious language.[93] As we have seen, Wittgenstein in the *Tractatus* rules theological talk out of court. The mystical, he says, shows itself but we cannot conceive it or talk about it. The new approach to language in the *Philosophical Investigations* leaves room for religious language and linguistic analysts are now exploring this field.

Thus analytical philosophy has moved far since the days of Wittgenstein. There is a growing conviction among analytical philosophers that philosophy cannot be a pure method of clarification free from all theory; in short, that "clarity is not enough." H. H. Price voiced this complaint in 1945, and since then it has been echoed by an increasing number of English and American analytical philosophers.[94] While not denying the achievements of pre-war linguistic analysis, they are conscious of its limitations and of the need for a return to speculative metaphysics—not to the idealism of the early twentieth century, but to a "scrubbed and chastened" metaphysics.

❖ ❖ ❖

PART FOUR

AMERICAN PHILOSOPHY

by Armand A. Maurer

XXII.

The Beginnings

THE story of American philosophy begins with the Puritan settlers of the New England colonies in the seventeenth century.[1] These intrepid pioneers brought with them from England not only their material possessions but also their religious and philosophical convictions. Thus they implanted in the New World the ideas of the Old, so that from the very beginning philosophy in the colonies had strong ties with English thought. Despite the incredible hardships and dangers of colonizing the New World, the Puritan Fathers had time and interest to cultivate theology and philosophy. It was not long before they opened their first schools. As early as 1636 they founded Harvard College in Cambridge, Massachusetts; it reigned without a rival until 1681, when Yale College was opened in New Haven, Connecticut. These schools were the scenes of the first awakening of philosophical thought in New England.

The Puritans had broken away from the Established Church of England and had adopted Calvinism. Their philosophical leanings were toward Platonism, especially as taught in the works of Peter Ramus and the Cambridge Platonists. Although communication with the motherland was infrequent and difficult, the New England colonies remained sensitive to the changing philosophical scene in Europe during the seventeenth century. Large shipments of books arrived from England for both Harvard and Yale. One of the most important of these was the gift of Jeremiah Dummer, Connecticut's agent in London. In 1714 he shipped nearly a thousand volumes for the Yale library. Dummer's collection contained the main works of the New Learning then transforming philosophy and science in England, including Locke's *Essay concerning Human Understanding* and Newton's *Principia* and *Opticks*, the latter volumes a gift of the author himself. As we shall see, these works brought about an immediate change in the intellectual climate of the colonies. They eagerly embraced the new "Experimental Philosophy"—to use Cotton Mather's phrase[2]—and set

American thought along a path it was never to abandon. English writers for their part were happy to see their books read in the colonial wilderness, which appeared to the romantic imagination as the land of innocence and promise.[3]

Thus American philosophy began through the importation of ideas from England, and throughout its history it has reflected the changing philosophical scene across the Atlantic. Each new movement in European philosophy has had almost immediate repercussions in America. The winds of doctrine have constantly blown westward, wafting new seeds to take root in this continent. At first they came mainly from England; later France, Germany, Italy, and even Asia made their contributions. But even though the seeds came from other countries, the plants have grown from native American soil, so that we can truly speak of an American philosophy. As used here, the term simply means the ensemble of those philosophical doctrines taught within the borders of the United States.

This introductory chapter is devoted to the first awakening of philosophical speculation in America. It does not pretend to tell the whole story of American philosophy up to the nineteenth century; its aim is the more modest one of introducing the reader to the most important men and movements in the formative period of its history.

Philosophizing Divines

cotton mather

One of the most illustrious names in the ecclesiastical and educational circles in Massachusetts in early colonial days was Mather. For generations the Mather family was in the forefront of the intellectual life of Boston. Increase Mather, the foremost divine of New England in his day, was one of Harvard College's first presidents, and his son Cotton was one of its most distinguished graduates.[4]

Mather was one of the first colonials to appreciate the revolution in ideas taking place in England and Europe in the seventeenth century. He saw Europe casting off the shackles of Aristotelianism "with fierce and long Struggles" and replacing them with the "New Learning" championed by such men as Francis Bacon, John Locke, and Isaac Newton. The scholastic art of logic and the Aristotelian physics he called so much jargon. He was grieved to see universities still bowing the knee to Aristotle: "prodigious Cartloads of Stuff," he writes, have been written on him and he still remains unintelligible, "and forever in almost all things Unprofitable."[5]

By the standards of his day Cotton Mather was a competent scientist and a well-read philosopher, but his chief interests were theological. He was what Dryden called, echoing a medieval notion, a "philosophizing divine."[6] A Puritan minister, he was anxious to promote the cause of the Calvinist religion and to settle the many religious quarrels raging among his contemporaries. To him, the new physics of Newton and the English empirical philosophies were the most effective means of achieving these ends. Hence his zeal in using science and philosophy in the work of religion.

Mather's *The Christian Philosopher* is the best illustration of how he thought this should be done. The purpose of this book is as old as the Fathers of the Church and the medieval schoolmen: the use of secular learning for the understanding of Scripture. "The Essays now before us," he writes, "will demonstrate that Philosophy is no Enemy, but a mighty and wondrous Incentive to Religion; and they will exhibit that Philosophical Religion, which will carry with it a most sensible Character, and victorious Evidence of a reasonable Service."[7] Referring to a passage from St. Chrysostom, he points out that there is a twofold book of God: the book of creatures and the book of Scriptures. Mather intends to read the former: "…'twill help us in reading the Latter: they will admirably assist one another."[8]

The topics of the essays that make up *The Christian Philosopher* include light (Newton's laws of motion are expounded as "the Laws of the Great God, who formed all things"), stars, planets, the rainbow, snow, gravity, earth, minerals, vegetables, fishes, birds, quadrupeds, and finally men. Natural science is used to show that the world is well planned, well ordered, and beautiful, leading us to appreciate its creator; the study of physics, therefore, is an acceptable and profitable way to pay tribute to God. He writes: "Even a Pagan Plutarch will put the Christian Philosopher in mind of this, That the World is no other than the Temple of God; and all the Creatures are the Glasses, in which we may see the Skill of Him that is the Maker of all."[9] Cicero and St. Bernard are cited in agreement with this. It is only to be expected that philosophy ends in theology and even in forming an imperfect idea of the incomprehensible mystery of the Trinity.

Properly philosophical notions are conspicuously absent from *The Christian Philosopher* and those we do meet are shallow and undeveloped. On the union of soul and body, for example, Mather has only this to say: it consists, "as Monsieur Tauvry expresses it, in the Conformity of our Thoughts to our Corporeal Actions."[10] Mather's account of the origin of knowledge recalls the occasionalism of Malebranche. "Objects do affect our Senses," he writes, "and make Impressions on them; the Senses receiving such Impressions, the Modifications of the Organs produced by them terminate in the Brain; if they do not so, the Soul is unconcerned in them; but there is a law given to the Soul by the glorious God, who forms the Spirit of Man within him, that in their doing so there shall be such and such Thoughts produced in the Soul."[11]

Newton explained the universe by means of the laws of motion and gravity, but he could not explain gravity itself. Mather does not pretend to be wiser than Newton. "Gravity," he says, "is an Effect insolvable by any philosophical hypothesis; it must be religiously resolv'd into the immediate Will of our most wise Creator, who, by appointing this Law throughout the material World, keeps all Bodies in their proper Places and Stations, which without it would fall to pieces and be utterly destroy'd."[12]

Along with this religious orientation of science and philosophy, we find in Mather an ethics of benevolence that makes the Christian life consist in doing good. In his *Essays to Do Good* he tells us that we should do good "with a rapturous delight, as a most suitable business, as a most precious privilege."[13] In order to do good, a man must first be born again by grace; good works will follow, not as the cause or occasion but as the mark of his election by God. Mather promoted humanitarianism and social service as the proper aims of the elect. In his *Busybody Papers* Benjamin Franklin poked fun at Mather for his conscientious interfering in the affairs of others on the grounds of universal benevolence, but in later life he acknowledged that the *Essays* taught him to be a useful citizen.[14]

samuel johnson

Samuel Johnson (not to be confused with the English Dr. Johnson) was the son of a deacon of the Congregational Church at Guilford, Connecticut.[15] He studied at the newly founded College at New Haven, later called Yale, and obtained his Bachelor's degree in 1714. He became the first president of King's College in

New York, the ancestor of Columbia University. His literary remains, including an autobiography and college notebooks, give us a good picture of the state of education in the New England colonies in the early eighteenth century. He tells us that the condition of learning in his student days was deplorable; indeed, it had sunk beneath the level of the early settlers who had been educated in England. Their sons had little time for education, and they had nothing on which to feed their minds except "the scholastic cobwebs of a few little English and Dutch systems" and some of Ramus' and Alsted's works.[16] However, about 1714, when Johnson was eighteen years old, Dummer's shipment of books from England arrived in New England and revolutionized education. Among other books, this library included the works of Bacon, Locke, Wollaston, Norris, Boyle, and Newton. Johnson's later writings reflect the impact of this New Learning. Another decisive influence in his life was his meeting with Berkeley, who lived in Rhode Island from 1728 to 1731. Johnson corresponded with Berkeley and was won over to his idealist philosophy.

Johnson's main purpose was, in his own words, "to make the study of nature subservient to religion." Like the other Puritan divines, he had no use for science or philosophy as ends in themselves, but only insofar as they were of use to religion. He inherited from the Cambridge Platonists and Peter Ramus a dislike for Aristotle (although his scholastic philosophy contains many Aristotelian notions) and for secular science apart from theology. He condemned the Peripatetics because they "learn their philosophy not from the sacred pages [of the Bible], but from the heathen Aristotle...."[17]

Johnson's main work is the *Elementa Philosophica*, the first textbook in philosophy published in America. It was printed in Philadelphia by Benjamin Franklin in 1752. It contains two parts: *Noetica*, or things pertaining to the mind, and *Ethica*, or things pertaining to moral behavior. All learning is divided into two main parts: philology or the study of words and other signs, and philosophy or the study of the things signified by words. Young persons of the age of fifteen or sixteen should study philology and its branches: the languages, rhetoric, the classics, ancient historians, and poetry. They should then proceed to philosophy at the age of sixteen or seventeen. First to be learned should be logic and its foundation; then metaphysics or ontology, "the noblest and most elevated part of science."[18] Starting from the sensible world, it rises to the purely intellectual level and treats of being, abstracted from every particular nature, whether body or spirit. It also deals with the general distinctions and relations of things, laying the groundwork for clear and correct reasoning. After the student has learned general metaphysics and logic, he should apply himself to a study of mathematics, physics or natural philosophy, and science. After this he can rise to ethics or moral philosophy, applying himself first to its speculative foundation in the study of man and God (theology).

The *Noetica* contains Johnson's basic metaphysical and epistemological ideas. Mind or spirit he defines as any intelligent active being. We are immediately aware that we have within us a mind which is the principle of our conscious perception and intellectual activity. At present our minds are joined to gross, tangible bodies, but this union of mind and body is not natural; it is only due to "an arbitrary establishment" of God.[19]

Following Locke, Johnson calls the immediate objects of sense perception "ideas." The objects of pure intellect he prefers to call "notions" or "conceptions." At creation our mind was a *tabula rasa* devoid of both ideas and notions. These, together with the light by which we see and know, are impressed upon the mind by God. The objects of sense, or ideas, are generally thought to be pictures of things existing outside our mind, and even outside the divine mind, but Johnson argues that this is incorrect. We cannot perceive what is external to our own minds; what we call reality, therefore, is nothing but our ideas. "I am therefore apt to think," Johnson writes, "that these ideas, or immediate objects of sense, are the real things, at least all that we are concerned with, I mean, of the sensible kind; and that the reality of them consists in their stability and consistence, or their being, in a stable manner, exhibited to our minds, or produced in them, and in a steady connection with each other, conformable to certain fixed laws of nature."[20] In short, sensible reality is nothing but a system of ideas communicated to our minds as faint copies of the archetypal ideas in God's mind.

Besides the senses and imagination we have a "pure intellect," which is the power of conceiving abstract and spiritual ideas and the relations between them. These ideas or notions are entirely different in kind from the objects of sense and they are directly communicated to us by God by means of a light analogous to sensible light. This intellectual light is one and common to all intelligent beings; it is, in fact, the light that "enlighteneth alike every man that cometh into the world."[21] Through this light a man has an intuitive knowledge of first principles in both thought and action; from it he also derives his taste for the beautiful and his moral sense or conscience. Since we are passive and receptive with regard to this light, we are sure that we are not its author. Johnson writes, "I do humbly conceive that God does as truly and immediately enlighten my mind internally to know these intellectual objects, as He does by the light of the sun (His sensible representative) enable me to perceive sensible objects."[22]

The first truth revealed by this light is the existence of our own mind, deduced from the existence of its perceptions and their objects. The mind, Johnson writes, "immediately infers, I perceive and act, therefore I am: I perceive such an object, therefore it is, etc."[23] From this arises our general notion of being as "what really is and exists," and the primary distinction of being into spirit and body. Spirit is that which perceives and acts; body is that which is perceived and acted upon. Johnson defended the pure passivity of matter against Cadwallader Colden, who taught that not only spiritual beings but also bodies are active causes. Johnson argued that only minds are active; bodies (that is, the ideas of sensible things impressed on our minds by God) are completely inactive. When Colden appealed to the Newtonian conception of inertia as an active force in matter, Johnson countered by asserting that inertia is simply resistance, and this is nothing else than the direct action of God upon our mind.[24]

Johnson uses several arguments to prove the existence of an Eternal Mind or God. We are aware of eternal truths, he says, such as that the whole is equal to all its parts. These truths do not depend on our minds or on the actual existence of things, but on a mind that, like them, exists eternally and necessarily. This Eternal Mind communicates truths to us by its light so that we behold them in it.[25]

Since this Mind is eternal, it always existed; hence it is independent in its being, while all other things must depend on its will and power. Johnson concludes from its independence that it is infinite and consequently that it contains all reality and the fulness of being. Following Descartes and a late medieval conception, Johnson explains that grammatically the word "infinite" is negative but "what it expressed! is truly positive, as implying all that absolutely is."[26] Moreover, there can be only one such infinite being, since it is plainly impossible for two or more beings each to consist of all possible reality.

God is, therefore, perfect unity (το ἓν); He is also, as the ancients called him, Being (το ὂν) and the Really Real (ὁ ὀντως ὢν). And this, Johnson goes on to explain, is the true meaning of the sacred names of God, Jah, and Jehovah.[27] In God alone essence implies existence. Essence Johnson defines as "whatsoever goes to the definition of a thing," and existence as "a thing's being actually in fact and nature as well as in idea or conception." Now, "Essence doth not necessarily imply existence, except in that of the necessarily existent being, in whom necessity of existence is implied in His very essence, and accordingly His original name Jehovah, given by Himself does literally signify, *The Essence existing*, as Mr. Hutchinson shows in *Mos. Sine Princip.*, ch. 2."[28] By an improbable turn of events, the medieval scholastic conception of God as the sole Being whose essence is identical with its existence entered American philosophy through the writings of John Hutchinson![29]

In 1722 Johnson gave up Calvinism and joined the Church of England. In his polemic against the Calvinist doctrine of predestination he stressed the activity and freedom of man's will. If all our actions are predestined, he argues, moral laws are useless and moral sanctions unjust. The Calvinists deny our highest moral perfection, which consists in freedom or liberty, "a power to act, or not to act, as we please, and consequently to suspend judging or action." "Our highest moral perfection," he continues, "consists in freely doing what we know tends to make us entirely happy in the whole of our nature and duration."[30] Johnson's ethics does not deny the moral corruption of man and his imperfection in his fallen state, but unlike the Puritans, who maintained man's utter moral depravity and helplessness, he insists on man's natural desire for happiness and he outlines the means man has in his power to achieve it. "Our true happiness," he writes, "consists in being secure from all pain or uneasiness, which is called natural evil, and in being possessed of such pleasures and satisfactions as are suitable to our nature in the whole of it, which are called natural good."[31] By pleasures, he does not mean sensual enjoyments but the perfections and pleasures of mind, which are the true end of man as an incorruptible spirit.[32]

jonathan edwards

One of Johnson's pupils at Yale was a boy of extraordinary intelligence and philosophical acumen named Jonathan Edwards.[33] At twelve he wrote an essay on spiders remarkable for its keen observations. Another early essay on colors shows his acquaintance with Newton's *Opticks*. At the age of fourteen he read

Locke's *Essay concerning Human Understanding* and found more enjoyment in it, he says, "than the most greedy miser finds, when gathering up handfuls of silver and gold, from some newly discovered treasure."[34]

While at Yale, Edwards began the custom, which he continued all his life, of jotting down reflections and meditations in notebooks. These notes were the first draft of a proposed systematic work entitled *A Rational Account of the Main Doctrines of the Christian Religion Attempted.* Unfortunately he did not live to complete this monumental project, but he wrote enough of it to give us a good idea of its purpose and essential themes. It was to be a vast *summa* explaining and defending Calvinism by means of the New Learning recently introduced into the American colonies from England. It proposed "to show that all the arts and sciences, the more they are perfected, the more they issue in divinity, and coincide with it, and appear to be as parts of it"[35]—a Puritan counterpart of St. Bonaventure's "reduction of the arts to theology"!

The notes "Of Being," written by Edwards as a student at Yale, show his precocity in metaphysics. Taking up the Parmenidean thesis of the necessity of being, he proves the impossibility that there be nothing at all. This he does by showing that "perfect nothing" is contradictory and therefore inconceivable. "It contradicts the very nature of the soul," he writes, "to think that it [i.e., nothing] should be."[36] We cannot even talk about nothing without contradicting ourselves, for in speaking of it we assume that it is something. Since we cannot think pure nothingness, "it is necessary that some being should eternally be." Moreover, being must be everywhere, for it is just as great a shock to the mind to think of pure nothing in any one place as to think of it in all places. Hence the conclusion: "this necessary, eternal being must be infinite and omnipresent." Furthermore, being cannot be solid, because solidity is nothing but resistance to other solids and there is no being outside Being.

What is this non-solid, necessary, infinite, omnipresent being except space? Edwards accepts this as self-evident. We can remove from our minds, he says, and conceive as non-being everything except space; space is the one thing that we can never remove and conceive as not being. If we imagine space to be divided so that there is nothing between the divided parts, the space between remains. Once we get rid of our gross conceptions of space, therefore, we see that it has divine attributes, indeed that it is God Himself.[37] Obviously Edwards meditated deeply the Cambridge Platonists and the *General Scholium* of Newton's *Principia*: he united Parmenides' reflections on the necessity of being with the Newtonian notion of absolute space as the divine *sensorium*.

In his "Notes on the Mind" Edwards presses further his inquiry into the nature of being. He examines the notions of excellence and beauty and finds that they consist in harmony, symmetry, or proportion. What is excellent or beautiful has proportion; what is evil or deformed lacks proportion. Proportion itself is the equality or likeness of ratios. Hence excellence or beauty consists in equality. Edwards says by way of example, "Thus if there be two perfect *equal* circles, or globes, together, there is something more of beauty than if they were of unequal, disproportionate magnitudes."[38] Now being is identical with excellence or beauty; consequently it is nothing else than proportion or equality. All being is excellent and beautiful in the measure of its intensity of being. As one thing has more being than another, so it has more equality, proportion, and beauty. Bodies, for example, are only the "shadows of being"; hence their proportions are only the shadows of proportion. The senses delight in the harmony and proportion in the visible world, but spiritual harmonies are more perfect than material ones, with the result that they give far greater delight to the mind.

Minds alone are beings in the proper sense of the term. And the excellence of minds is love, or the consent of being to being. All virtue, therefore, which is the excellence and beauty of minds, consists in love of being, and primarily in the love of God, who is Being itself. Edwards will return to this theme in his later treatise on *The Nature of True Virtue*.

The influence of Locke is apparent in Edwards' "Notes on the Mind." Following Locke he distinguishes between two faculties of the mind: understanding and will. Understanding is the faculty by which the soul perceives, speculates, and judges. Its operations include sensation, imagination, memory, and judgment.

Sensation is the first activity of the mind and all the others depend on it. Edwards planned to show that without the senses the mind would be without ideas. As for the objects of the senses, he insists that they are not real qualities of bodies but impressions and ideas. Color, for example, is not real but a mental impression. Every knowing philosopher, he says, now grants that colors are not really in things any more than pain is in a needle.[39] This was Locke's view of secondary qualities (colors, sounds, smells, tastes, etc.), though he regarded as real the primary qualities (solidity, extension, figure, motion, etc.).[40] In

Edwards' view Locke's arguments against the reality of secondary qualities are equally valid for primary qualities, and these he likewise describes as ideas. All the primary qualities can be reduced to resistance. Solidity, he argues, is nothing but resistance; figure is the termination of resistance; extension is an aspect of figure; motion is the communication of resistance from place to place. Consequently, a visible body or substance is made up of a number of ideas, including color, resistance, and modes of resistance. Resistance itself is immaterial: it is "nothing else but the actual exertion of God's power." Hence Edwards concludes that the world has only a mental existence; it exists in God's mind as "his determination, his care, and his design," and it is communicated to our minds in a series of united and regularly successive ideas.[41]

It is not certain whether at this early period (about 1718) Edwards had read Berkeley. Historians are still debating whether he owes his idealism directly to Berkeley, to discussions of his views at Yale, or to his own precocious philosophical genius.[42] Although he did not take up these youthful idealistic themes in his later writings, he never retracted them and they remain implicit in much that he wrote.

In Edwards' universe spirits or minds alone are properly real. Of these, God is the only efficient cause or agent. He determines the existence and structure of the universe by an "arbitrary constitution" of his will. "All dependent existence whatsoever," Edwards writes, "is in a constant flux, ever passing and returning; renewed every moment, as the colours of bodies are every moment renewed by the light that shines upon them; and all is constantly proceeding from God, as light from the sun. "*In him we live, and move and have our being*" (Acts 17:28).[43] Thus the universe is a constant revelation of God to created minds, a panorama of shadows and images exhibiting the divine will and wisdom. In his notes entitled *The Images or Shadows of Divine Things* he pictures nature as a symbol of God. God reveals himself in the Bible, and also in visible creation (the sun, green fields, pleasant flowers) and in "the soul of man that is made in the image of God." A mind needs to be purified by divine illumination to interpret rightly these natural "types" of God, but to such a mind there is no more sublime or delightful activity.

By the second faculty of mind, called will, the soul is in "some way inclined with respect to the things it views or considers."[44] Liking and disliking, approving and disapproving, being pleased or displeased, are activities of will. The chief among these passions or affections is love; all the others originate in it and exist for its sake.

That Edwards' interest in the affections was not primarily philosophical but religious is evident from his *Treatise concerning Religious Affections*. The thesis of this work is that all human actions, and especially those of religion spring from affection. For Edwards, the affections are the very life and soul of all true religion. Since love is pre-eminent among the affections, the essence of all true religion lies in holy love, and especially in the love of God.[45] In the 1740s a wave of religious enthusiasm, known as "The Great Awakening," swept through the colonies. Often marked by extravagant emotion and sensationalism, Edwards insisted that religious feeling be centered around the "gracious affections" springing from the awareness of God and divine things.

In order to explain this religious experience, Edwards postulated a "sense" different in kind from the five bodily senses, by which the elect are aware of God and of the effects of God's Spirit within them. This is a supernatural sense acquired by divine grace; it gives man, regenerated by grace, a new kind of sensation or perception by which he passively receives simple ideas of God and divine truths.[46]

The essential passivity of the intellect as the recipient of ideas from God is paralleled in Edwards' system by the passivity of the will. The will, he says, is not an active, self-determining power; it is a purely passive faculty by which we are inclined to what we find agreeable and repelled by what we find disagreeable. Thus the will is moved by motives presented to it by the understanding. It was inconceivable to Edwards, as it was to Newton and Locke, that anything should happen without a cause. To the question, "what cause determines the will to act?" he replies, "it is that motive, which, as it stands in the view of the mind, is the strongest, that determines the will."[47] In short, the will is determined by the strongest motive presented to it by the understanding.

From this Edwards concludes that the will is not free in its activity; a man cannot help but will as he does. But he is free *to do* as he chooses, and in this sense a man enjoys liberty. This is in the tradition of Hobbes, Locke, and Collins, who regarded liberty as the absence of impediments to action rather than as the self-determining power of the will. To Edwards this is the only definition of freedom in harmony with his Calvinist beliefs in the total depravity of man and predestination.

Edwards' ethical notions, especially as expounded in *The Nature of True Virtue*, are a blend of these Calvinist convictions and the ethics of disinterested benevolence of Shaftesbury and Hutcheson.[48] With these moralists he argues that true virtue does not consist in the selfish pursuit of pleasure or the utility of human actions, but in the intrinsic beauty of the dispositions of man's heart. To know if an action is good, we should not ask what advantage it is to ourselves or to others, but solely whether it springs from a beautiful disposition or will. In short, virtue is a kind of beauty or excellence that commends itself to us for its own sake. Any other motive in acting is based upon self-love and consequently falls short of true virtue. Accordingly, Edwards makes virtue wholly a matter of disinterested benevolence or affection. He insists that we owe affection to all beings, but especially to God, who has the most being or the greatest share of existence, and who shows the greatest benevolence to others.

While thus emphasizing with Hutcheson the objective and disinterested character of true virtue, Edwards parts company with him in denying any natural impulse in man to such virtue. His Calvinism convinced him that man is totally depraved and entirely given over to self-love. This is man's "dreadful condition" as a result of original sin; he can rise above it and become truly good only by the election of God and the gift of efficacious grace. Without this supernatural help, seemingly disinterested affections, like the natural love of parents for their children, are accompanied by self-love, and consequently they are not truly virtuous: at most they are secondary virtues or the shadows of true virtue.

Cadwallader Colden and the Beginnings of the Philosophy of Nature

The beginnings of the philosophy of nature in the American colonies were not as impressive as those of metaphysics or ethics, no doubt owing to the low level of the natural sciences themselves. There were a few reputable scientists in New England at this period, such as Thomas Brattle of Harvard, whose observations on the comet in 1680 were used by Newton, and the younger John Winthrop, who first taught Newton's *Principia* at Harvard. But these men can hardly be called original scientists; their main effort was to absorb and to teach the new scientific methods and views recently developed in England and Europe. Even this was often beyond them. Thus Samuel Johnson tried to teach Newton's physics at Yale in place of the antiquated Aristotelian and Ptolemaic systems, but his efforts to master calculus met with small success.

One of the foremost Newtonians in America in the early eighteenth century was Cadwallader Colden.[49] Born in Ireland of Scottish parents, he emigrated to America in 1710, and there he had a successful career as the Lieutenant-Governor of the Province of New York. He wrote several works in natural philosophy in which he gave a philosophical explanation of gravitation and physical action in general. Unfortunately these treatises have not been printed since the eighteenth century. More readily accessible are his correspondence with Samuel Johnson and his *Introduction to the Study of Philosophy Wrote in America for the Use of a Young Gentleman.*

Colden's *Introduction* begins with a brief and highly inaccurate sketch of the history of philosophy, then turns to a criticism of scholasticism, which is described as a hodgepodge of abstract notions, perplexed definitions, and useless distinctions, invented by "popish priests" to divert inquisitive minds from acquiring real knowledge and thus freeing themselves from ecclesiastical tyranny.[50] Colden's criticism is directed mainly against "School Logic" or the scholastic method of disputation and what he calls the schoolmen's notion of substance. He curtly dismisses the method of the schoolmen as the art of continuing an argument without bringing it to an end or convincing anyone by it. As for substance, he continues, the schoolmen define it as "something we conceive to subsist of itself, independently of any created being, or any particular mode or accident."[51] Consider, for example, a candle that is round, white, and lighted. Roundness is its mode of being, the school-men say, whiteness is its quality, and being lighted is accidental to it. The substance of the candle can exist without these additions: it can be square, yellow, and unlighted and still be a candle. Consequently, if we want to know what the candle really is, that is, its substance, we must remove all its qualities, modes, and accidents. But then, Colden protests with Locke, we have no conception of the candle left. Material and immaterial beings have an underlying substance distinct from their actions, but, following Locke, Colden denies that we have any idea of this substance. "We have only ideas of their actions," he writes in a letter to Johnson; or to put it more exactly "the ideas are the effects of their actions on our minds."[52]

Colden praises Descartes as the man who liberated philosophy from authority but he has little liking for his thought. His physics, Colden says, is "an amusing philosophic romance," though it stimulated others to make new discoveries, and was the first in modern times to use geometry.[53] As for Descartes' philosophy, it carries doubt too far: I am as sure of your existence, Colden insists, as I am of my own. His criticism of the Cartesian identification of matter with extension derives from one of his most cherished themes: the activity of matter. Extension alone, he says, cannot explain the dynamism we observe in nature. For the same reason he criticizes Jonathan Edwards' view of matter. According to Edwards, matter is an absolutely passive substance incapable of doing anything by itself: all its activity is imparted to it by minds which alone are active substances. But Colden protests that he cannot conceive of a being that does nothing. We have no idea or perception of anything external to us unless it impresses itself upon our senses. Consequently, if something has no power, force, or action, we would have no way of knowing that it exists.

Colden points out that Berkeley avoided this difficulty by denying the existence of matter; what we call matter Berkeley claimed exists only in the mind. Was Berkeley serious in making such a shocking statement? "Yes he was," writes Colden, "he wrote a large and learned treatise in proof of this doctrine: and he has obtained disciples, who have formed a sect in philosophy called *Idealists*, which has extended to America, where you will find men of sense advocates of it."[54] In Colden's eyes, Berkeley's arguments lose all their force once we see that bodies are really active.

The remainder of Colden's *Introduction* deals with the Newtonian laws of motion, which, he insists, presuppose the dynamism of matter. Newton, he says, established that bodies attract each other at a distance reciprocally to the squares of their distances. While acknowledging that this must be done through some power, Newton did not pretend to know what this power is; he was only sure that it was not in matter. This Colden denies. He attempts to show that gravitation is due to the union of three forces in matter: light, the original moving power; inertia, or the power of resistance; and ether, the elastic power that transmits movement and resistance, thereby making possible action at a distance.

Colden's *Introduction* is hardly a first-rate piece of physics or philosophy. It abounds with bigotry, errors, and prejudices, but it does have perceptive moments and shrewd argumentation. It is a precious document for the understanding of early American philosophy.

Colden's ethics, contained in the unpublished *First Principles of Morality*, are hedonistic and utilitarian. The purpose of man's life is happiness, and man's actions are good insofar as they conduce to it. A man is happy to the extent that he enjoys pleasure and is free from pain. Not even religion is exempt from this rule: religion is cultivated with a view to obtaining the divine favor. Observing the results of the current revivalism, he warns his reader not to cultivate religion to the neglect of all other pleasures lest he fall into the "most dangerous sin of enthusiasm."

Beginnings of Social and Political Philosophy

puritan theocracy

The Puritan immigrants who settled in New England brought from the Old World a theocratic conception of the state. Like the Jews, they considered themselves the elect of God, exiled from their homeland to people a Promised Land, and ruled by God through his ministers. The theocratic ideal is clearly expressed in the English Puritan Richard Baxter's *A Holy Conmonwealth*, published in England in 1659. In a remarkable adaptation of St. Augustine's *City of God*,[55] Baxter identifies the state with the church, the visible City of God. He proclaims the world a kingdom in which God is the absolute monarch and all men are his subjects. Accordingly, the commonwealth should be holy and divine, subject to God's laws and existing for his good pleasure. This leaves little room for a distinction between civil and religious rule. Baxter writes, "...in a true Theocracy, or Divine Common-wealth, the matter of the Church and the Common-wealth should be altogether or almost the same, though the form of them and administrations are different..."[56] From this, Baxter draws the conclusion that theocracy is the best form of government and that democracy is usually the worst.

Unable to establish their ideal theocracy in England, the Puritans tried to do so in America. One of their most eloquent spokesmen, John Eliot, a minister of Roxbury, Massachusetts, advocated a unified administration of church and state under the rule of God, the supreme king. The elect of God, he says, should take from Scripture their laws and the essential platform of their civil government. God, and not the people, is the true ruler of the state.[57] John Winthrop held that the people have the right to select their magistrates, but once elected their power is absolute and cannot be resisted without resisting the ordinances of God. Hence he declared revolution or rebellion a religious as well as a civil crime. The Puritans also denied social equality. They likened civil society to the human body, whose order demands inequality of its parts. To abolish the inequality of the parts of society is to destroy its order.

The Puritan theocratic views were undermined by the New Learning introduced into the colonies from England and the Continent during the eighteenth century. Under the influence of Hobbes, Locke, and Montesquieu, a secularization of social and political theory took place. God's existence was not denied, but he came to be regarded as remote from the world and little concerned with its affairs. The state was viewed as a work of men, formed by a voluntary contract among them, and existing for their own good. The way was being prepared for the democratic conception of government as an institution established *by* the people and *for* the people.

In the early eighteenth century John Wise, a Puritan minister in Massachusetts, contended that because civil society is founded upon a social contract the people have the right to decide their own form of government. Wise himself preferred monarchy to democracy, but his political thought was broader than that of most Puritan divines: he took into account the natural law, the "natural immunities" or rights of man, and the light of reason. Another Puritan clergyman, Jonathan Mayhew, published a sermon in 1750, which John Adams called the opening gun of the American Revolution. In it Mayhew claimed that society is the work of man and that the people themselves give to their government the authority to rule and to maintain peace. Hence they have the right to resist it and even to overthrow it if it fails to do its work. Men do not owe unquestioning obedience to their rulers; sometimes they are justified in disobeying and resisting them. Mayhew went so far as to make love of liberty and country, and hatred of tyranny and oppression, the essence of true religion.

This was a far cry from the early Puritans' doctrine of the utter depravity and passivity of man and his total subjection to authority. Americans were learning to see man as the master of his own destiny and the creator of his own history. In this regard the Scottish philosopher Adam Ferguson's *Essay on the History of Civil Society* was influential. Published in Edinburgh in 1767, it was reprinted in Boston in 1809 and in Philadelphia in 1819. Chiefly influenced by

Montesquieu, it presents a secular conception of history and social progress. The development of the secular notion of the state brought with it a clearer awareness of the basic difference between civil and religious society. As early as 1644 Roger Williams maintained the essential distinction between state and church, and argued that because of this distinction a state can harbor different and even contrary religious bodies, such as Christians and Jews. But Williams was considered a heretic by the Puritans; expelled from Massachusetts, he founded the colony of Rhode Island, where he put into effect his liberal views on state and religion.[58]

By the end of the eighteenth century the distinction between church and state and the ideal of religious freedom were more widely accepted. James Madison's *Memorial and Remonstrance on the Religions Rights of Man* (1785) and Thomas Jefferson's *Act Establishing Religions Freedom in Virginia* (1786) proclaimed the inalienable right of every man to follow his own conscience in religious matters. They taught that man has civil rights that flow from his very nature. Similarly, man has duties owing to the fact that he is a man. One of these duties is the worship of God, his creator, but the manner of this worship cannot be dictated by civil society. Man's primary allegiance is to his universal sovereign, God; only secondarily does he owe allegiance to the state. Hence the state cannot legislate concerning man's relations to God.

thomas jefferson

No one had more to do with laying down the basic principles of American democracy than Thomas Jefferson, the author of the *Declaration of Independence* (1776).[59] Its words are known to all: "We hold these truths to be self-evident: that all men are created equal, that they are endowed by their Creator with certain unalienable rights, that among these are life, liberty, and the pursuit of happiness. That to secure these rights, governments are instituted among men, deriving their just powers from the consent of the governed..."

In calling these truths self-evident, Jefferson did not mean that they are known to be true as soon as their terms are understood. They are not known *per se*, like the proposition "A whole is greater than its part." He meant only that the truths of the *Declaration of Independence* commend themselves to the common sense or reason of men, and consequently they are generally accepted by men of experience.

Jefferson maintained the equality of all men, but he did not intend to deny differences among them in talent, knowledge, and virtue. He recognized the superior endowments of some, who form a natural aristocracy, and these he thought would inevitably be elected to office in a democracy. His ideal was not a classless society; on the contrary he had a strong conviction of the need for classes—at least insofar as they are based on occupations—and of their fundamental inequality. He himself was a gentleman farmer, and he rated his own class above all others. To him, farmers were the chosen people of God; the great mobs of the city were the diseased parts of the state. The aristocracy he opposed was one based on wealth or heredity. In his own State of Virginia he campaigned for the abolition of the laws making the eldest son sole heir of his father's property because these laws inevitably led to a moneyed or "tinsel aristocracy." In his view, every man should have an equal opportunity to develop his God-given talents and to gain the happiness for which he was created.

While laying down absolute and necessary truths in the *Declaration of Independence* as the basis of democracy, Jefferson admitted an area of relativism in ethical theory. The purpose of Government, as he saw it, is the happiness of the people. Happiness, therefore, is the yardstick by which we can judge what is morally good and what is morally bad. Utility thus becomes the test of moral goodness, and utility itself depends upon the circumstances in which we live. Hence Jefferson concluded, "The same act may be useful, and consequently virtuous in one country, which is injurious and vicious in another differently circumstanced." This relativism extends even to the form of government: democracy is the best government for America, but in other circumstances another form of government may be preferable.

Although not a systematic philosopher, Jefferson was the most articulate exponent of the social and political ideas that were ripening in America at the end of the eighteenth century. Well read in the current rationalist literature of Europe, he was confident in the natural goodness of man and in the power of human reason to solve the problems confronting him. He urged the abolition of every form of tyranny, the chief of which, in his eyes, were those of kings, merchants, priests, and lawyers. His ideal was a free mind; to this end he advocated political freedom, the separation of church and state, and universal education. He was convinced that once a man was freed from oppression and given the opportunity to learn he would naturally tread the path of goodness and achieve the happiness for which he was created.

XXIII.

New England Transcendentalism

THE transcendentalist movement began to take shape in Boston in 1836 at an informal meeting of Ralph Waldo Emerson and some friends on the occasion of the second centennial of Harvard College.[1] The group was dissatisfied with the state of theology and philosophy in America and they were determined to set it right. New England Unitarianism appeared to them cold and out of touch with life. It had begun as a reaction against the rigidity of Puritan Calvinism, and it had exercised a deeply liberalizing effect on the religious thought of New England. Under the influence of rationalism it had denied the Trinity (hence its name "Unitarianism"), the divinity of Christ, and salvation by grace. By the beginning of the nineteenth century the "pale negations of Boston Unitarianism"—to use Emerson's phrase—no longer satisfied the best minds of the time. One of the foremost Unitarian leaders, William Ellery Channing, expressed his dissatisfaction in these words: "I have before told you how much I think Unitarianism has suffered from a too partial culture of the mind. I fear we must look to other schools for the thoughts that thrill us, which touch the most inward springs, and disclose to us the depths of our own soul."[2]

Thus the Transcendentalists keenly felt the need to rethink religious and philosophical issues. The old catechisms, creeds, and systems no longer satisfied them. Unitarianism failed to give them truths "instinct with life and feeling." The favorite philosopher of the Unitarians, John Locke, would limit them to an empiricism barring access to the spiritual worlds of God and the soul. It was becoming clear that Locke's philosophy led to the skepticism of Hume, which casts doubt on the existence of spiritual beings and undermines religion and morals. Hence there was need of a new approach that would do justice to all aspects of human nature, give a more solid ground for belief in God and spiritual reality, and more firmly establish social and political thought.[3]

Although all the Transcendentalists agreed on what to oppose, they differed widely on how to oppose it. Orestes Brownson, a Transcendentalist in the early days of the movement, summed up the differences in their ranks in these words: "Some of them embrace the Transcendental philosophy, some of them reject it, some of them *ignore* all philosophy, plant themselves on their instincts, and wait for the huge world to come round to them. Some of them read Cousin, some Goethe and Carlyle, others none at all. Some of them reason, others merely dream."[4] From this it is clear that the group did not form a school or party holding the same opinions. Like the Existentialists of today, they were in revolt against the emptiness of their culture, but they could not agree on what to substitute for it. They even disliked being grouped together under a single name, and when they accepted the title "Transcendentalists" it was with misgivings and qualifications.

This name was given to Emerson and his circle almost from the start. It expresses their conviction that human reason has the power to rise above sense data and experience supra-sensible reality. Emerson wrote half-humorously in his Journals (October 6, 1836), "Transcendentalism means, says our accomplished Mrs. B., with a wave of her hand, *a little beyond*." In his essay "The Transcendentalist" he explains that the name comes from Immanuel Kant. The sage of Königsberg opposed the skeptical philosophy of Locke, which insisted that there was nothing in the intellect that was not previously experienced by the sense, by showing that there were ideas or imperative forms, which did not arise from experience but through which experience was acquired. He showed further that these forms, which he called transcendental, were intuitions of the mind. "The extraordinary profoundness and precision of that man's thinking," Emerson writes, "have given vogue to his nomenclature, in Europe and America, to that extent that whatever belongs to the class of intuitive thought is popularly called at the present day *Transcendental*."[5] Brownson similarly connects the name "Transcendentalism" with the intuition of spiritual reality: "So far as Transcendentalism is understood to be the recognition in man of the capacity of knowing truth intuitively, or of attaining to a scientific knowledge of an order of existence transcending the reaches of the sense, and of which we can have no sensible experience, we are Transcendentalists."[6]

Although the title of Transcendentalists connects the New England group with Kant, few of them had an exact knowledge of his critical philosophy and no one of them wholeheartedly accepted it. The only one who mastered Kant in the original language in the early days of the movement was Frederic Hedge (1805–1890). Hedge spent several years as a student in Germany, learned to real German well, and returned to Harvard in 1822 to introduce Bostonians to German idealism. He was one of the original members of the Transcendental Club, and so important was his contribution to it that Emerson always called it "Hedge's Club." Orestes Brownson, like others in the group, knew the Kantian philosophy through Victor Cousin, Coleridge, Carlyle, and others, but later in life he acquired a first-hand knowledge of Kant's works and subjected them to a penetrating criticism. Emerson had only a vague knowledge of Kant's philosophy, chiefly through Coleridge and Carlyle.[7]

In their enthusiasm for German idealism, the Transcendentalists were little concerned with Kant's distinction between speculative and practical reason and the limitation of the former to phenomena. Linking Kant, Fichte, and Schelling together, they saw in the idealism issuing from them a method with which to oppose the empiricism of Locke and Hume and the sensism of Condillac and the other French *philosophes*. It opened up for them the possibility of an intuition of spiritual reality transcending the reach of the senses. Later, when the philosophies of Rosmini and Gioberti came to be known, German and Italian idealism joined forces to storm the ramparts of Lockean empiricism.

It would be impossible here to treat of all the Transcendentalists. We have chosen two for more detailed consideration: Emerson, because he was their acknowledged leader and the main figure in the group; and Brownson, because, despite his short adherence to the movement, he was by far the most accomplished philosopher among them.

Ralph Waldo Emerson

transcendentalism

Although Transcendentalism owes its name to Kant, as Emerson uses the term it does not specifically mean the Kantian philosophy.[8] Transcendentalism, he says, is nothing but idealism in modern dress, and idealism is "the very oldest of thoughts," going as far back as Buddhism.[9] Emerson's Transcendentalism is an amalgam of Neoplatonic idealism, Kantianism as interpreted by Coleridge and Carlyle, and oriental mysticism. In all these forms of idealism he thought he discovered the most ancient and venerable wisdom of the human race. In adopting idealism, moreover, he was returning to the oldest philosophy in New England. The empiricism of Bacon and Locke was a novelty to the Puritan divines and one that Emerson, like all the Transcendentalists, deplored.

Materialism and idealism, in Emerson's view, are the basic philosophies proposed by the thinkers of mankind. The materialists are empiricists; they begin with the data of sense experience and see everything in the light of the senses. They concern themselves with facts and history, and they look upon man himself as a product of them. Idealists have an entirely different outlook. They begin with consciousness, and they are chiefly interested in spiritual or mental facts. While not denying the use and beauty of the senses, idealists rise above them and appeal to the power of thought and will, inspiration and miracle. To them, the senses report only the illusory representations of things and not their reality. Tables and chairs are but sensible appearances; they are the reverse side of the tapestry of reality whose true nature is of a higher, spiritual order.

Thus the idealist sees that "Mind is the only reality," and that men and all other natures are nothing but appearances reflecting Mind in different degrees of perfection. The mind or consciousness is the center to which the idealist refers everything in his experience. "His thought—that is the Universe," Emerson writes. "His experience inclines him to behold the procession of facts you call the world, as flowing perpetually outward from an invisible, unsounded centre in himself, centre alike of him and of them, and necessitating him to regard all things as having a subjective or relative existence, relative to that aforesaid Unknown Centre of him."[10]

Far from being a product of the external world, then, Emerson regards himself as a thought, into whose mold the world is poured and to whose shape it conforms. He writes, "I—this thought which is called I—is the mould into which the world is poured like melted wax. The mould is invisible, but the world betrays the shape of the mould." Again, "All that you call the world is the shadow of that substance which you are, the perpetual creation of the powers of thought..."[11]

This idealist view of man and the world entails ethical consequences. Since I am not dependent upon the external world, and since indeed I partake of the deity, I should be self-reliant and self-dependent: "The height, the deity of man is to be self-sustained, to need no gift, no foreign force."[12] Emerson has the Law-giver within himself; he is in need of no external commandment; he imposes no rule upon his spirit other than its own. The rule of the idealist is openness and freedom of spirit; he is opposed to anything positive, dogmatic, or personal.

Solitary and fastidious in manners, the idealist withdraws from the conversation and labors of the world. Emerson confesses that Transcendentalists are not good citizens. They do not bear their share of labor in the community; but for all that they are not useless members of society. Far from it. They are the beacon-lights pointing the way to a higher life. Surely, he pleads, society will "tolerate one or two solitary voices in the land, speaking for thoughts and principles not marketable or perishable."[13]

To preserve his independence and spontaneity of thought, Emerson kept clear of all organizations, lay or religious. He even denied that he belonged to the Transcendentalist Club. He was friendly with the Transcendentalists and with the group that founded Brook Farm, and he frequently visited it, but he never became one of them. The Farm was an experiment in communal living established in 1841 in West Roxbury, Massachusetts, by George Ripley. Charles A. Dana and Nathaniel Hawthorne were among its first members. It was organized according to the ideas of the French philosopher Charles Fourier (1772–1837), whose socialist ideas were popularized in America by Albert Brisbane (1809–1890). Fourier wanted to create a utopia by dividing men into groups of about one thousand eight hundred persons called phalanxes, each phalanx occupying six hundred acres of land and containing all the workers necessary to maintain a good life, working together in peace and harmony. The plan was a failure in France, but in America as many as forty-one "phalansteries" were formed, from New England to Texas.[14]

Although Emerson found some value in Fourier's ideas, he was repelled by the artificiality of his system. It is, he says, the height of "mechanical philosophy." Fourier has skipped nothing in his systematic arrangement of human living except life itself: "He treats man as a plastic thing, something that may be put up or down, ripened or retarded, molded, polished, made into solid or fluid or gas, at the will of the leader…but [he] skips the faculty of life, which spawns and scorns system and system-makers; which eludes all conditions; which makes or supplants a thousand phalanxes and New Harmonics with each pulsation."[15] While admitting that men of sound mind spontaneously adopt an order in their life, and that Fourier's system is one such order, Emerson did not want that particular system "imposed, by force or preaching or votes, on all men, and carried into rigid execution." This is an excellent illustration of Emerson's conviction that all human systems and social orders are but external expressions of an inner force or Soul in man that builds various systems for itself while remaining transcendent to all of them.

nature and the over-soul

One of the marks of the Transcendentalist is to be a lover and worshiper of beauty. Of the triad Truth, Goodness, and Beauty, each of which includes the others, he makes Beauty the chief. The special haunt of beauty is nature. "In the wilderness," he says, "I find something more dear and connate than in streets or villages."[16] The landscape offers him a beauty akin to that of his own nature; in the fields and woods he finds beings in hidden sympathy with himself: they nod to him and he to them.

What is nature? Emerson distinguishes between the common-sense and philosophical meanings of the term. To common sense, nature is the sum of essences unchanged by man; for example, space, air, rivers, leaves. In distinction to nature, works of art are essences changed by man's will; for example, houses, statues, pictures. The philosopher, however, defines nature as what is NOT ME; it is everything that is separate from me. This includes nature in the common-sense meaning of the term, art, other men, and even my own body.[17] What, then, am I? Following the Platonists, whom he rated the greatest of the philosophers,[18] Emerson identifies himself with his soul, and his soul in turn he describes as a living spark of a greater Soul, called "the soul of the whole," or "Over-Soul." Although he sometimes calls this Soul God, he prefers the impersonal name "Soul" to designate the universal eternal force active within each man and all nature. What common sense thinks nature to be is but the outward appearance of this Soul. The Soul is the whole reality appearing in the various aspects of nature. It is the One or Unity containing all particular beings and reconciling within itself all their differences and contradictions. "We see the world piece by piece," Emerson writes, "as the sun, the moon, the animal, the tree; but the whole, of which these are the shining parts, is the soul."[19]

In view of Emerson's Platonism we are not surprised to see him take sides with the realists in their dispute with the nominalists. In his essay "Nominalist and Realist" he finds that the realists have the better of the argument. The nominalist places greater emphasis on the details of reality: the individual, the particular, the personal. The realist, on the contrary, stresses the whole of reality: he is concerned with universals, general ideas, and essences.[20] In brief, the nominalist is an empiricist and materialist; the realist is a spiritual thinker and idealist.

The most profound experience in life is the awareness of one's identity with the Over-Soul or God. Emerson speaks of this experience in his first essay, "Nature." "Standing on the bare ground," he writes, "—my head bathed by the blithe air, and uplifted into infinite space—all mean egotism vanishes. I become a transparent eyeball; I am nothing; I see all; the currents of the Universal Being circulate through me; I am part or parcel of God."[21]

The most important function of nature is to be the means of this intoxicating experience. Emerson does not think we can test the accuracy of the senses and know whether there are real objects corresponding to the impressions made upon them; in the absence of proof to the contrary, he considers the world ideal. But whether nature is real or has only a mental existence, it is equally useful and venerable because it elevates us to a sense of our identity with the divine. Then we feel an influx of the divine mind into our own: it reveals truths to us, instills in us wisdom, purity, and virtue, and arouses enthusiasm in us. The trances of Socrates, the ecstasies of Plotinus, the conversion of St. Paul, the convulsions of George Fox and his Quakers, the illumination of Swedenborg, the revivalism of the Calvinist churches, are all instances of this "shudder of awe and delight with which the individual soul always mingles with the universal soul."[22]

Teachers can help us to achieve this sense of oneness with the divine, but only those who speak from inner experience, not those who are merely spectators and see nature from without. "Jesus," Emerson says, "speaks always from within, and in a degree that transcends all others." The idealist philosophers Spinoza, Kant, and Coleridge are also sacred teachers who talk "from within the veil." Not so the English empiricists Locke and Paley, or the Scottish common-sense philosophers Mackintosh and Stewart: they speak from without, as spectators of facts or as reporting them on hearsay.[23]

We should not be overly disturbed by Emerson's eclecticism, which holds together in precarious balance such widely different systems as Buddhism, Christianity, Confucianism, Neoplatonism, and German idealism. It is clear from his *Essays* that he thought of himself as above all such systems, and as speaking to mankind as a sacred teacher "from within the veil." From a philosophical point of view the *Essays* are consistent in favoring idealism, of no matter what source, rather than empiricism. What he abhorred above all was eighteenth-century English and Scottish philosophy, which in his day made up the core of the philosophical curriculum at Harvard.[24] In place of its empiricism, materialism, and common-sense realism he wanted to substitute the ancient idealism which joined East with West, and which found its best expression in contemporary German thought.

Although Emerson looked to Europe and Asia for religious and philosophical inspiration, there was a profound continuity between his romantic idealism and the native American idealism of Jonathan Edwards.[25] Both looked upon nature as an outward appearance of God, leading to a quasi-mystical experience of the divinity. Both sought the wilderness to be elevated to oneness with God. Emerson's idealism, however, is secularized, stripped of the Calvinist overtones of Jonathan Edwards. For Edwards the experience of oneness with God is possible only to the elect, who have been regenerated from sin by grace and raised to friendship with a personal God. Emerson, on the contrary, sees man as fundamentally good, and seeks the exhilarating sense of communion with nature and the impersonal, universal Over-Soul through purely natural means.

Orestes Brownson

Brownson was a member of the Transcendentalist group that met in Boston in 1836, and for a while he took a vigorous part in the movement.[26] He was to be seen among the guests of Brook Farm, truculently pounding on the table as he made his point, or walking in the grove with his friend Isaac Hecker.[27] But he was too restless to remain long with any party. Disillusioned by the loose thinking of the Transcendentalists, he went his own way, which led him into the Catholic Church.

In 1836 Brownson already had a stormy intellectual and religious life behind him. He had tried a number of Protestant sects but they failed to satisfy him. There ensued a period of religious skepticism, followed by a reconversion of Christianity recorded in his autobiographical "Charles Elwood, or the Infidel Converted," written in 1834. About the same time he was introduced to philosophy by the works of Victor Cousin. Up to then he had been contemptuous of philosophy; now he began to realize what a powerful force it can be in resolving religious questions. Cousin was Brownson's guide in philosophy for ten years, and even after he surmounted the French philosopher's eclecticism and psychologism, he remained strongly under his influence. He took from Cousin what he always maintained was the starting point of philosophy, namely the analysis of thought. Later he criticized the deficiencies of Cousin's analysis and turned to that of Gioberti, but this was a correction of Cousin rather than a supplanting of him. Brownson also owed to Cousin his interpretation of Kant's philosophy and many of his views (with all their shortcomings) on the history of medieval philosophy.[28] Although he is often neglected by historians, Brownson stands out as the most competent philosopher among the Transcendentalists and as one of the most profound metaphysicians and political thinkers in American history. For all his borrowings from French, German, and Italian philosophers, he quite rightly claimed that his philosophy was truly his own. Defending himself against the charge of importing foreign philosophies, he writes with nativist pride: "We are inquiring for ourselves, and following out the direction of our own minds, but willing to receive aid, let it come from what quarter it may. These distinguished foreigners are not our masters, but our fellow disciples, and we feel under no special obligation to defend their opinions. We have nothing to do with Hegel, or Schelling, or Kant, or Cousin, any further than our own inquiries lead us to approve their speculations. We are aiming at truth, and believe that here, where thought is free, and the philosopher may tell his whole thought without any circumlocution or reticence, we may attain to a purer philosophy than can be found in either France or Germany."[29]

philosophy and faith

The freedom of the philosopher from the restraint of external authority was a principle for Brownson. Without such freedom, he was convinced, there is no authentic development of reason. "The principal cause of the present deplorable state of philosophy," he writes, "is in the lack of free, independent thinkers—in the fact that we philosophize not for the sake of truth, but for the sake of some philosophical theory, ancient or modern, and always more or less under the weight of authority."[30] Neither Plato nor Aristotle, St. Augustine nor St. Thomas, nor any modern philosopher can be quoted in philosophy as an unquestionable authority. No true philosopher will neglect the profound and assiduous study of St. Thomas, but he will never agree that his opinions, or those of any other philosopher, are beyond dispute. In religion, authority plays the fundamental role; we believe Christian doctrine because God has revealed it, and we believe he revealed it on the testimony of the Church, which is his divinely constituted witness on earth. But the philosopher knows no other authority than human reason, which is the same in each and every man, Christian and non-Christian.

Brownson wishes to preserve the distinction between the domains of philosophy and religion. Philosophy is "the science of principles in the natural order, cognizable by natural reason, or the reason common to all men."[31] It is solidly based upon reason, unlike the Christian religion, which is founded upon authority. Even after this distinction has been recognized, it is easy to forget it. The human mind, Brownson astutely observes, loves unity and naturally tends to reduce everything to the same level. The Protestant, because of his insistence on private interpretation, inclines toward rationalism: he is apt to turn supernatural belief into reason. The Catholic has the contrary tendency toward supernaturalism: he is prone to carry the principle of authority from the supernatural to the natural order and to deny reason its legitimate functions within its own order.

This tendency of Catholics, Brownson claims, is behind the notion of Christian philosophy proposed by the *Annales de Philosophie Chrétienne.* M. Bonnetty, the editor of this review, advocated a traditionalism that denied to philosophy its distinctive rational order and placed it on the same level as supernatural theology, as a discipline to be received on authority. In Brownson's view, Bonnetty's notion of a *traditional* philosophy contradicts the nature of philosophy, for it makes its basis to be authority rather than reason. For the same reason, Brownson rejects the concept of Christian philosophy. It has a pious ring, he says, like Christian coats and pantaloons, but it fails to respect the rational character of philosophy. "There is a Christian *use* of philosophy," he observes, "but, correctly speaking, there is and can be no *Christian* philosophy. The Christian order, we take it, is the supernatural order, and in all that is peculiar to it included in the new creation, whose principle is grace; but philosophy belongs to the natural order, and is restricted to natural reason...."[32] If Christian philosophy means anything, it is Christian theology or the sacred science of which St. Thomas speaks; a science constructed not by reason from its own data, but by the use of reason from data furnished by faith of revelation. Moreover, there is no Christian philosophy in the sense of one thoroughly in agreement with faith; such an agreement is ideally possible, but in fact no one has yet achieved it.

To set the record straight in the case of St. Thomas, whose popularity was growing in Catholic circles in the mid-nineteenth century, Brownson adds that there is no such thing as a Thomistic philosophy, properly so called. St. Thomas never intended to found a philosophy; from first to last he was a Catholic theologian. So we can speak of a Thomistic theology, and of a Thomistic use of Aristotelian philosophy in theology, but we should not talk as though St. Thomas was a pure philosopher.

It will be noticed that Brownson does not object to a Christian use of philosophy in theology. Quite the contrary. All the great theologians, he writes, applied pagan philosophical notions to the mysteries of faith; and, what is more striking, in so doing they philosophized more correctly than when they philosophized for purely rational purposes. "There is in all the great theologians," Brownson claims, "a double philosophy, the philosophy they use as theologians, and the philosophy they set forth as philosophers."[33] For example, there is the philosophy contained in St. Thomas' theology, and there is the peripatetic philosophy of his commentaries on Aristotle; the former is superior to the latter. Undoubtedly, then, revelation is of help to philosophy; it "throws light on reason, or so employs reason that we better understand its use, and the problems really within its reach." More precisely, it does not furnish philosophy with its data, but it places natural reason in a position to understand and use better her own data.

From this it is clear that Brownson does not advocate Descartes' separation of philosophy from faith, as though philosophy can be an independent science, complete in itself and embracing the whole natural order. Brownson stresses the insufficiency of natural reason and its need to seek help from the light of faith.[34] It is also clear that he would not be opposed to the statement of Pope Leo XIII's encyclical *Aeterni Patris* (1879), that the best possible way of philosophizing is to combine religious obedience to faith with the exercise of philosophical reason. What he objects to is the application of the term "Christian philosophy" to the great theological syntheses of the Middle Ages. He grants that they contain much excellent philosophizing, but he will not admit that they are really philosophies, not even Christian philosophies, because their starting point is not data of reason but of revelation.

For the philosopher, therefore, it is all-important to choose the right starting point. The success of his whole enterprise depends upon it. The starting point must be one of reason and not of authority or faith, and it must contain in principle or implicitly all the truths reached by philosophy. In Brownson's view, the only starting point with these characteristics is the analysis of thought.

the ideal intuition

Since the time of Descartes, Brownson says, most philosophers agree that they must begin with an analysis of thought, but like him they analyze the subject of knowledge before considering its object. This is the error of psychologism. Psychologues, like Descartes, assume that thought is a purely subjective or psychological fact—"the fact of consciousness," to use the phrase of Victor Cousin—and that ontological truths can be inferred from it. In fact, there is a prior and more important feature of thought, namely the object that acts upon the subject and makes thought possible.[35]

A correct analysis of thought reveals three distinct but inseparable elements: the subject, the object, and the relation between them. Every thought is a synthesis of the three. Of these, the object is prior in nature and importance. Without an object the subject cannot think. For there to be thought, the object must stand over against the soul and act upon the soul by presenting itself. Unless there is an object, the soul cannot even think about itself or become aware of its own existence; it knows itself only in conjunction with the object intuitively presented. Similarly, the soul knows the relation between the object and the subject only through the knowledge of the object. "The object with the relation, or the correlation of subject and object, then, is presented to the soul or given to it, not created or furnished by it."[36] Hence the philosopher must give prior attention to the analysis of the object of thought.

Like the analysis of thought, the analysis of the object reveals three constitutive elements: the ideal, the empirical, and the relation between them. The ideal is the *a priori* and apodictic element that is absolutely required for an object to be intelligible. The empirical is the fact of experience, whether it belongs to the sensible or intelligible order. The relation between them is the bond uniting the ideal to the empirical. For example, if a man breaks a glass, he is known to stand in relation to the breakage as cause to effect. The empirical feature is the experienced fact; the ideal is the necessary law of causality revealed in this fact; the relation is the link joining the empirical fact with the necessary law.[37]

In Brownson's view, Kant adequately proved that an empirical fact is unintelligible without an *a priori*, ideal element. Kant was in error, however, in thinking that the ideal constituents of knowledge are *a priori* forms or categories of the human understanding; in thinking, in short, that they are subjective and not objective. Brownson's analysis of thought, on the contrary, shows that the ideal or *a priori* feature is on the side of the object rather than on the side of the subject. "Kant's doctrine, that the categories are forms of the subject," he writes, "is refuted in our analysis of thought. It implies that the subject can exist and operate without the object, and that we see the object as we do, not because it is such as we see it, but because such is the constitution or law of the human mind—which denies the objective validity of our knowledge already established."[38] For Brownson, all three elements of the object (the ideal, the empirical, and the relation between them) are equally real and objective. The ideal is as real as the empirical fact; indeed, it is prior in nature to that fact because without it the fact is impossible and unintelligible.

After analyzing thought and its object, Brownson turns to the most significant item in the object, namely its ideal content, and finds that this also can be analyzed into a triad: the necessary, the contingent, and the relation between them. This is established as follows: The object of knowledge must be real, or it could not function as an object by presenting itself to the intellect. Now whatever really exists is either necessary or contingent, that is to say, either it must be, or it can be or not be. Kant already showed that the categories of necessity and contingency are not empirical but *a priori* forms under which we necessarily apprehend every object. The only correction Brownson makes is that these ideal forms are real; they are on the side of the object and not, as Kant thought, on the side of the subject. Consequently, the ideal content in every object of thought must be either necessary or contingent being, or the relation between them.

This analysis leads to an important truth: necessary and contingent being are both real. The next step is to show the relation between them. The necessary can be thought by itself because it is self-sufficient and independent. Hence it can be expressed by the word "being," which can be asserted without asserting anything beside itself. For being means nothing but being *is*. The contingent, on the contrary, does not stand alone; it depends upon being. This dependence can be expressed by the word "existence" (from the Latin *ex stare*, to stand outside): what exists stands outside its cause. So we have found that the necessary is identical with real and necessary being (*ens necessarium et reale*), and that the contingent is identical with contingent existence. Being is thus seen to be different from existences. Being is uncaused and independent, consequently eternal and self-existence; existences are caused by being and dependent upon it.[39]

In what way does being cause existences? It must either evolve them from itself or create them from nothing by an act of will. The first supposition is impossible, for then existences would not be distinct from being. Being, then, must create existences. So the analysis of the ideal gives us being, existences, and the creative act of being as the nexus or copula uniting existences to being.[40]

Since the ideal is present to the mind in every experience, and the ideal contains these three elements, all thought presupposes the presence to the mind of creative being (*ens creans*). Brownson calls the act by which the ideal presents itself to thought "ideal intuition," and the formula in which it is expressed (following Gioberti) the "ideal formula": "Being creates existences (*Ens creat existentias*)."[41] The meaning of intuition should be carefully noted. Brownson stresses that it is not an act of the knowing subject, but the act of the object presenting itself to the mind. Intuition should not be confused with apprehension or cognition, which are activities of the knowing subject.

According to Brownson, the distinction between cognition and intuition is important for an understanding of the starting point of philosophy. Some philosophers think that philosophy begins with the abstract concept of being. Thus Rosmini claims that it starts with being-in-general (*ens in genere*), and Hegel that it begins with pure being (*das reine Seyn*). But, as Hegel clearly saw, being in this sense is not a reality; it is a nonentity, or at most a possible being. It is an abstraction formed by cognition, an empty concept incapable of functioning as the foundation of philosophy. The true starting point of philosophy is the being given to the mind in ideal intuition: real, necessary, creative being, which a little further analysis will show is God himself.[42]

the existence of god

In an idealist philosophy like Brownson's, the existence of God raises little difficulty. Indeed, the case with which it enables him to refute atheism was no small inducement for him to adopt it. He was from first to last a religious philosopher, and the firm establishment of God's existence was one of his primary concerns.

Once we are furnished with the ideal intuition, "the refutation of atheism is possible without any very long or intricate process of metaphysical reasoning."[43] We do not have to begin with principles distinct from God in order to establish his existence; all we have to do is to show that the human mind has an immediate intuition of that which is God, and that it could not operate or know anything at all if it had not.

Modern philosophers, Brownson points out, have assumed that a proof for the existence of God must begin from principles or premises more immediately known to the mind than God himself. Some propose *a posteriori* proofs, which start from effects and argue to God's existence as their cause. But this presupposes the necessary relation between cause and effect and the reality of a first cause. In short, it presupposes the reality of God. Others offer *a priori* proofs, which proceed from cause to effect, but with no better success. For these proofs assume that there are principles at least logically more ultimate than God, from which his existence can be deduced. But either God is contained in these principles or he is not. If he is not, he cannot be concluded from them, for nothing can be in the conclusion that is not contained in the premises. If he is contained in the principles, then he is apprehended along with them and he is not concluded from them. To sum up: "In what we know, God is either apprehended or he is not. If not, he cannot be concluded; if he is, then he is apprehended prior to the logical process, and not obtained by it, and all it can do is to clear up and establish the fact that what we do really apprehend is God."[44]

The correct approach to the existence of God, for Brownson, is much simpler and surer. The previous analysis of thought and its object established that in every act of knowing there is an intuition of real being, and that being is necessary, eternal, and creative; consequently, that being is God. Thus a little reflection on the content of ideal intuition suffices to show the reality of God. He is not so far from us that we have to reach him by a long process of reasoning. He is intimately present as the light by which we know and the object that makes everything intelligible: "Malebranche rightly maintained, after St. Augustine, that we see all things in God, in whom we live, and move, and are."[45] Brownson's identification of the ideal with the real also enables him to accept St. Anselm's argument for God's existence. What is not real cannot be thought; but we do think of the most perfect being, a greater than which cannot be thought; therefore such being is real. "If the most perfect being," Brownson writes, "a greater than which and the contrary of which cannot be thought, be only in our thought, then we are ourselves greater than the most perfect being, and our thought becomes the criterion of perfection, and we are greater than God, and can judge him."[46]

The contention that we have an immediate intuition of being, which is identical with God, leaves Brownson open—as it did Gioberti—to the charge of ontologism. In 1861 the Holy See condemned the proposition of the ontologists, that an immediate knowledge, at least habitual, of God is essential to the human intellect.[47] Does not the teaching of Gioberti and Brownson fall under this condemnation? Do they not make the mistake of attributing to man in the present life the vision of God, which in fact is reserved for him in the next?

Brownson strenuously defends himself and his Italian master against this charge. He points out that intuition, as they understand it, is not perception, cognition, or vision. These latter are acts of the intellect, whereas intuition is an act of the object presenting itself to the intellect. It is true that God offers himself to the mind in every act of knowing; without him the mind is not intelligent nor is any object intelligible. But we do not immediately perceive or know the divine presence. Reflection and analysis are needed before we grasp the stupendous fact that the being involved in every object of knowledge is creative being, and that this is God himself.[48] Brownson insists that the ideal formula, which is the beginning of philosophy, is "Being creates existences," not "*God* creates existences," because at this stage of the analysis being is not yet seen to be identical with God. Further reflective analysis is needed before this identity is grasped. In short: "We know by intuition that which is God, but not that it is God."[49]

However difficult it may be to maintain this distinction, there can be no doubt that Brownson wants to do so. He stresses that in this life we have no vision of God's essence in itself. The intuition of real being of which he speaks is indistinct and indefinite. Furthermore, it is not given to us alone, but in conjunction with some sensible experience. To know the identity of the object of intuition and God, we must reflect on it as it is represented to us in sensible signs and language.[50] It is here that the traditional arguments for God's existence find their place. Brownson especially approves of the Augustinian argument based on truth, and the Anselmian argument based on the being than which none greater can be thought, for these are closest to his own. Like his, they do not start from a being distinct from God and end with him; they begin with the same being with which they conclude. The proof is nothing but a reflective analysis enabling us to see more clearly the nature of the being with which we began.[51]

social and political ideas

Brownson's ideal philosopher is not a hermit or solitary thinker; he is a social man, living among his fellows, availing himself of the knowledge of all ages and nations, and applying his wisdom to the practical problems of his own day.[52] This accurately describes the kind of philosopher Brownson himself wanted to be. He tried to master the wisdom of the philosophers of antiquity, the Middle Ages, and modern times, and he passionately devoted himself to the economic, social, political, and religious problems of the young American republic.

New England in the early nineteenth century felt the effects of the Industrial Revolution. Commercialism and industry were expanding, and so too was the unpropertied, laboring class. The severe economic depression of 1837 aroused Brownson to speak out on the problem of capital and labor. He was an avid reader of the socialists Fourier and Saint-Simon, and he learned from them to analyze the current situation in terms of a class struggle between wage earners without property and the capitalists who own the means of production. To Brownson this situation condemned at least half the population to economic slavery. After the elimination of the nobility and the emancipation of the slaves, he called upon the world to turn its attention to the poverty and depression of the working man. "All over the world," he writes, "this fact stares us in the face, the workingman is poor and depressed, while a large portion of the non-workingmen…are wealthy."[53] Brownson prophetically saw the great work of the coming age as the raising up of the laborer to a social status befitting his dignity as a creature of God.

To achieve this end Brownson in his early days called for extreme measures: the abolishing of the capitalist system with its inherent inequality among men; the recall of men to the teaching of Christ with the elimination of the priesthood (which, before his conversion to Catholicism, he thought did not represent the teachings of Christ); the destruction of banks, monopolies, and all forms of privilege. Among the latter the most serious was hereditary wealth, and consequently Brownson advocated its abolition. Although deploring violence, he did not think these measures would be taken without applying physical force.

Brownson was attacked for these revolutionary ideas not only by the Whigs but also by members of his own Democratic party. Friends like William Channing and Theodore Parker, while agreeing that reforms were needed, were shocked by his proposals.[54] He himself later regretted the "horrible doctrines" he advanced in these early years, but he always defended the soundness of his views regarding the relation of capital and labor and the wage system.

Although a lifelong champion of the people, Brownson's estimate of the common man's sagacity underwent a change with increased political experience. In later years he recalled his optimistic views on the people in his early career. Then, like the French *philosophes*, he believed in the "divinity of humanity," and he looked upon the will of the people as the most direct and authentic expression of the divine will. "The people," he says, "held with me then, in some respects, the place the church now holds with me."[55] The people were endowed with "divine instincts," so that all that was needed for wise and just government was the removal of all restrictions on the free and full expression of the popular will.

The first presidential campaign in which he took an active part (that of 1840) dispelled his "democratic illusions" and shook to its foundations his belief in the divinity of the people and in their will as the expression of eternal justice. He saw that they could be easily duped and carried away by an irresistible passion in the wrong as easily as in the right.

This experience prompted him to review his political principles. If the people cannot be trusted to make just decisions or laws, the popular will is not divine or supreme; it is subject to a higher authority and bound by a higher law. Absolutely speaking, God alone is sovereign; the people are sovereign only in a limited sense, dependent upon the authority of God.

If this is true, we cannot say absolutely that "governments derive their just powers from the assent of the governed." Thus understood, the democratic principle means that governments originate solely through the will of the people by convention or social contract, and that laws derive all their force from the will of the people. In short, it "asserts the purely human origin of government, and rejects all law enjoined by any authority above the people."[56] This is political atheism: the denial that all power comes from God, or that there is a law of nations (*jus gentium*) which the nation itself is bound to obey.

Brownson's study of the American Constitution convinced him that it is not based upon political atheism, however much popular journalism tried to make him believe it is. The Constitution recognizes the rights of man, and consequently the rights of God. It establishes that every man has inalienable rights that the government must acknowledge and protect. "The peculiarity of the American Constitution," he says, "under the point of view we are now considering it, is not merely in asserting the equality of all men before the law, but in asserting their equal rights as held not from the law, but from the Creator, anterior to civil society, and therefore rights which government is bound by its very constitution to recognize and protect to the full extent of its power."[57] In this, American democracy differs from European. Democracy, in the true American sense, holds that the people under God are the source of all political power, but that they cannot originate or rightfully exercise any power incompatible with the rights of individuals. European democracy substitutes the people for God and makes the popular will the rule and measure of right.[58]

Herein lies the excellence of the American Constitution and its superiority over other political systems. In recognizing the existence of God-given rights, which the state has the duty to protect, it acknowledges the primacy of the moral or spiritual order over the temporal. By the same token it recognizes the subordination of the State, the supreme representative of the temporal order, to the Church, the representative of the spiritual order.

Although Brownson distinguishes between the spiritual and temporal orders and their respective guardians, the Church and the State, he insists that they are not separate. Each is supreme and independent in its own sphere, but they are not on the same level. The Church is above the State, and the State is subordinate to the Church. This is clear from their respective ends. The end or purpose of government is the maintenance of justice in all political, social, and domestic relations. The purpose of the Church is man's supernatural happiness in heaven. This is "the end, and the sole end, of man." Strictly speaking, man has no temporal end, and therefore no absolute temporal good. The temporal, therefore, does not exist for itself but only for the spiritual. "Man's end is spiritual," Brownson writes, "and therefore there is for him, strictly speaking, only spiritual good, and the temporal is, and can in the nature of things, be good for him only as it aids him to gain his spiritual end, his heavenly end, for which alone in the decrees of God he exists."[59]

Hence the temporal exists for the spiritual and the State for the Church. While distinct from the Church, therefore, the State is not absolutely independent of the Church's spiritual authority. "It depends on the Church in the sense that the Church is its superior, and defines its powers, and interprets for it the law under which it holds, and to which it is amenable in its acts." Brownson is quick to assure his reader that he is not proposing a theocracy. The State, like the individual, is free within its own domain. "We recognize in the state the same liberty and independence of action that we do in the individual in matters of private and domestic economy."[60] But because temporal affairs have a relation to man's spiritual end, which is eternal beatitude, from this point of view they fall under the jurisdiction of the Church and the pope, who is its head. Consequently, the pope has an indirect power over the temporal inasmuch as it has a bearing upon the spiritual.[61]

The great merit of the American Constitution, in Brownson's eyes, is that it acknowledges its incompetency in spiritual matters. It is not indifferent to religion; on the contrary, it recognizes its importance and respects and protects the religion of its citizens. Since it is not competent in spiritual affairs, it does not presume to judge which is the true religion; each citizen has freedom of conscience (as far as the State is concerned) to make this judgment by himself. Hence the Catholic Church is given no special recognition by the State, but it enjoys equal freedom with other religions. It is free to carry out its divine mission without hindrance from the State. True, the Church is not given aid in her mission by the State, but Brownson did not think this a serious loss. Indeed, the Church gains in the end, for it is freed from the burdens that State support inevitably entails.[62] In the long run, therefore, among political systems, the American Constitution is the best adapted to the nature and mission of the Church.

XXIV.

Idealism of the Schools

THE Transcendentalists played a major role in introducing German idealism into the United States, but their knowledge of it often lacked precision and depth. An exception was Frederic Hedge, who read Kant, Fichte, and Hegel in the original language and delved deeply into the intricacies of their philosophies. For the most part, however, the Transcendentalists were acquainted with the great German idealists through Coleridge, Carlyle, and Victor Cousin. Moreover, most of them did not teach idealism in the schools but in private groups, public lecture halls, and journals. Until the last quarter of the nineteenth century the colleges and universities remained attached to English empiricism and Scottish common-sense realism.[1]

During the last half of the century the situation of idealism in the United States was considerably changed. Americans went abroad in larger numbers, studied philosophy in the German universities, and acquired an exact knowledge of the German systems of philosophy. On their return they propagated the idealism of their German professors in the American colleges. A surprisingly large number of the teachers of philosophy in the United States at this period had studied philosophy in Germany. Another channel by which idealism came to America was the large German immigration, especially after the Revolution of 1848. Well-educated German immigrants took their part in the intellectual life of the cities and fostered a knowledge of the idealism of their native country. Thus in the last decades of the nineteenth century idealism came to maturity in the United States and occupied the dominant position in the colleges and universities.

Outside academic circles German idealism continued to flourish in small groups, both in the Middle West and New England. The first of these was the St. Louis School, founded by a young German immigrant, Henry Brokmeyer, who fled his country during the Revolution of 1848 and settled in New England. After studying Hegel at Brown University under Fledge, he traveled to St. Louis, where he inspired a group of professional men to translate and study Hegel, and to apply his principles to American education and history. Brokmeyer himself proposed the following Hegelian interpretation of the American Civil War: The thesis is abstract right, represented by the secessionists of the South; the antithesis is abstract morality, represented by the abolitionists of the North; the synthesis is the ethical State, which is the new Union. The St. Louis group included William T. Harris, United States Commissioner of Education from 1889 to 1906, who applied Hegel's dialectics to American education; Denton J. Snider, who applied it to American economics; and George Holmes Howison, later an influential professor of philosophy at the University of California. To Harris the United States owes its first exclusively philosophical journal, *The Journal of Speculative Philosophy*, which was published from 1867 to 1892.[2]

The Transcendentalist Bronson Alcott met the St. Louis group while on a lecture tour and became so enthusiastic over their Hegelian studies that, on his return to Massachusetts, he sponsored the Concord Summer School of Philosophy to propagate Hegelianism.[3] This School, which ran from 1879 to 1887, had many illustrious teachers, including Emerson, H. K. Jones, W. T. Harris, G. S. Morris (the Hegelian teacher of Josiah Royce and John Dewey at Johns Hopkins University), Theodore Palmer, and William James.

Influential as these groups were in fostering idealism in the United States, their importance is overshadowed by that of idealist college professors of philosophy in the late nineteenth and early twentieth centuries. We shall consider two of these academic idealists in some detail, Borden Parker Bowne as representative of personal idealism, and Josiah Royce as representative of absolute idealism. Each was the founder of a school of idealism that kept his name and ideas alive for more than a generation and left a permanent stamp on American philosophy.

Borden Parker Bowne

As early as his student days in New York University, Bowne expressed the central idea of his philosophy, that the person or "self" is the fundamental fact in experience.[4] In an essay against Herbert Spencer he argued that knowledge does not begin with particular sensations impressed upon a passive mind. This tenet, inherited by Spencer from John Locke, appeared to Bowne as incompatible with the notion of the person as a "substantial self." While continuing his studies in Germany from 1871 to 1873, he came under the influence of Hermann Lotze (1817–1881), who taught that the self or person is the ultimate, empirical reality, basic to both experience and nature. Lotze's idealism and emphasis on the person played a major role in arming Bowne against English empiricism and in shaping his own personalist philosophy. On his return to America, he taught at Boston University, where he enjoyed great success, especially among Methodist ministers. Among his notable disciples were E. S. Brightman (1884–1953), A. C. Knudson (1873–1954), and R. T. Flewelling (1871–1960).

"Philosophy," Bowne writes, "aims at a rational and systematic comprehension of reality."[5] This aim, he continues, is an ideal which can be very imperfectly realized. Philosophy begins with logic, or the theory of thought, which treats of the laws of normal thinking. Next comes epistemology, or the theory of knowledge, which analyzes the idea of knowledge, its general conditions and implications. Philosophy culminates in metaphysics, or the theory of being, inquiring into ultimate conceptions about real existence, or, more specifically, about man, nature, and fundamental reality. We shall limit our exposition to some of Bowne's most significant ideas in epistemology and metaphysics.

idealism versus realism

The main business of the epistemologist, in Bowne's opinion, is to settle as far as possible the debate between idealists and realists. There are various forms of idealism, he says, but they agree in holding that what we call material things exist only for, and in relation to, mind and consciousness. Realists, on the other hand, contend that things exist by themselves as material bodies, outside of and apart from mind, and in opposition to it.[6]

At first sight the realists seem to have the better of the argument. They appeal to our spontaneous conviction that there is a material world standing over against our mind and causing our perception of it. But this uncritical attitude, Bowne asserts, while invaluable for practical life, is shaken by a little reflection. How can we prove that there is a real world corresponding to our perceptions? Perception is a mental event that places certain "objective presentations before consciousness." But, given the appropriate stimuli, these presentations would be there even if there were no corresponding facts in reality. "To have perceptions, all that is needed is the appropriate stimulus; and there is no way of necessarily connecting this stimulus with the independent existence of the object. Often the perception takes place when there is nothing really objective, as in dreams, delirium, and insanity."[7]

It is equally futile to appeal to the law of causation. Realists argue that we experience objects acting upon us and coercing us, and therefore there must be an objectively real world. But this only proves that mental events have a cause; it does not tell us what this cause is. It may be the soul itself as Leibniz thought, or God as Berkeley claimed. Realists also appeal to the divine veracity, claiming that God would not deceive us in our natural belief in the independent existence of the material world. But it would be a sorry sort of veracity that would leave us in the hopeless contradiction of naïve realism. We spontaneously think that the material world exists independent of thought with all the qualities we perceive in it. Yet reflection shows that sense qualities such as sights, sounds, heat, and cold have only a subjective existence. It also reveals that the immediate cause of perception is not the object or anything like it; it is some sort of nervous change in the brain, which is totally unlike the object or mental event.

In order to avoid this objection some realists abandon naïve realism in favor of "transfigured realism." They affirm that the world of sights and sounds, of heat and cold—in short, the world of unsophisticated consciousness—has only a subjective existence, while the truly real world lies altogether beyond the reach of sense. But, Bowne argues, the existence of such an unperceived world cannot be demonstrated. To explain perception, all that is necessary is an orderly excitation of sensations; we cannot prove that they are caused by an independently existing material world. Besides, as Berkeley points out, this "transfigured realism" is foreign to spontaneous thought and is the parent of all kinds of skepticism and unbelief.[8]

Realism, therefore, cannot be demonstrated. Is it possible to demonstrate idealism? No, according to Bowne, if by this is meant proving that no reality lies behind our mental states or impressions. The objects of our knowledge are "primarily a projection of our own conceptions," but these conceptions may truly reproduce a reality existing apart from them. To deny this is to land in the absurdity of solipsism. If we could prove that we know only our own mental states, we could never transcend them and be certain that other persons and thoughts exist. Properly speaking, we cannot demonstrate the existence of other persons and thoughts, but solipsism is entirely incompatible with our experience of life. It is strictly impossible for anyone to hold to solipsism. "No one could ever persuade himself that all past history has occurred only in his own consciousness; that his neighbors exist only as his mental states; that a blizzard is only a tumult among his states of consciousness; that a city with its busy life is only a complex mental state of his own, which vanishes when he goes to sleep."[9]

There is a substantial area, then, in which Bowne agrees with the realists. Consciousness, he claims, grasps realities independent of itself, although he does not pretend to know how this is done or how to demonstrate the fact. He holds it on "natural faith."[10] The precise point on which he differs from the realists is on the nature of these realities. The realists claim that they are true ontological realities, existing in real space. Bowne, on the contrary, maintains that the spatial world has only a phenomenal existence. There is no noumenon lying beyond it; there is only the cause of phenomena, and since phenomena are ideal in nature their cause must be an intelligence: not our finite intelligence, but a cosmic one, or God. The world of things is completely a world of ideas, without any meaning except in relation to mind and consciousness. This world exists only in and for a supreme mind. It is not just a passive conception of that mind—not just an idea—but an act of will, projecting itself outward. The world "is essentially a going forth of divine causality under the forms of space and time, and in accordance with a rational plan."[11]

Bowne sums up his position in the following five points: (1) To the question, Does anything exist except myself? he replies, Yes, at least other persons; otherwise we land in the absurdity of solipsism. (2) The world of apparent objects does not exist only for me but for other minds as well; in short, we live in a common world. (3) The theory that this common world is nothing more than a similarity of impressions in finite minds cannot be disproved, but it is practically impossible: it does not fit our total experience. (4) Hence the world of things is a continuous existence independent of finite thought and consciousness. This cannot be demonstrated, but it alone presents no insuperable difficulties. (5) As to the nature of this world, it is completely a world of ideas, existing in and for a cosmic intelligence.[12]

Thus Bowne settles the great epistemological debate in favor of idealism. The idealism he adopts is not a subjective but an objective one, for it stresses the objectivity of the knowing process: every act of knowing is said to point outward to an object grasped by the knowing subject. This object is a projection of one's own conception, but it does not originate entirely within one's own self. Its primal source is a cosmic intelligence, or God, who, by an act of will, projects a world of appearances for all finite minds to perceive. The problem still remains as to the nature of this common world and of minds that know it. This is a problem not for epistemology but for metaphysics.

the nature of things

The first task of the metaphysician is to examine the notion of being. The words "being," "reality," "existence," have many meanings. They are commonly applied to thoughts, feelings, laws, and relations, as well as to things, but not in the same sense. For example, we say that a thought is real if it can be thought; that is to say, if it is not contradictory. Existing laws and relations are real in distinction to those that are imaginary; but they are not real in the sense that things are real. So there are different kinds of reality or being. In a wide sense, being is applied to every object of thought, but in its metaphysical sense it is used only of substantial things. The question the metaphysician proposes is, "In what does the reality or being of things consist?"[13]

Bowne warns against determining the content of the notion of being by a process of logical abstraction. We can form the notion of pure being by abstracting the factor common to all things and excluding all other elements. But this notion cannot really exist; like all abstract notions it has only ideal existence. There is no real "pure being," any more than there is a real "pure humanity." Bowne agrees with Hegel that pure being is equivalent to nothing. It is nothing real; what is real is definite and specific, never indefinite and indeterminate.[14] This applies to God as well as to creatures. He is not pure being; like all realities he is definite and determined. When we say that he is infinite, we mean that his activity is unlimited, both in intensity and range. By his activity he determines what he is. Thus God is always determined to some state, though this takes place by self-determination.[15]

Parmenides, in Bowne's opinion, made the mistake of reifying the abstract notion of being. He thought of being as something unitary, motionless, and unchanging; but in fact the real world is one of plurality, motions, changes, and interactions. In modern times, the infinite substance of Spinoza, the absolute being of Schelling, and the absolute idea of some Hegelians result from the same fallacy. These philosophers view being as unconditioned, unlimited, and undetermined; but this is "the old abstraction in a new form." Spencer's evolutionary philosophy makes the same mistake of considering the indefinite as prior to, and the basis of, the definite; but "the indefinite" is itself nothing, and consequently it founds and leads to nothing.[16]

Some philosophers, Bowne says, define being as substance or substratum, claiming that being is that which has or supports qualities. But Bowne regards this as a purely formal definition that fails to tell us how substance fulfills this function. Others maintain that being is what can be seen or touched; but common sense holds that things exist when unseen or untouched. Still others say that being is the permanent or regular possibility of perception; but common sense insists that perception recognizes, but does not make, things, so that their being is more than their being perceived.

What, then, is the specific content of the notion of being? After much casting about in his mind, Bowne concludes that the distinctive mark of being consists in some power of action. "Whatever is to be considered as existing must be capable of action in some form."[17] There is no reason to posit purely passive being. We cannot perceive such being because it cannot act upon us, and it cannot be the cause or ground of the phenomena we experience; hence it explains nothing and is nothing.

Matter appears to be inactive, but physics assures us that rest and inaction in matter are only the phenomenal resultants of incessant basal activities. Materiality is but the phenomenal product of an underlying dynamism; the under-realm of matter is incessant activity.

Thus being and action are identical. "To be is to act; the inactive is the non-existent."[18] Similarly, being and the power of acting are identical; we should not think of reality as divided into being and its inherent power, as though being in some way supports power. Being, as we have seen, is nothing, and hence it cannot support anything. There is only a logical distinction between being and power or cause. To think of a being as really distinct from its power is to be the dupe of language. We speak of man as possessing a soul, and of the soul as possessing various powers; but in reality man *is* a soul, and his soul *is* his power of acting. Every reality, in short, is an agent, and its reality consists in activity.

But a reality is not only an activity: what is real not only acts, it remains self-identical while acting. According to Bowne, the only type of being with both these characteristics is a person or self. The phenomenal world is one of perpetual process and change. "Things as they appear are only stages of the eternal flow, or transient eddies in the flood."[19] Heraclitus was right in describing the world as perpetual flux. But Parmenides was also correct: there is permanence in the world as well as change, identity as well as diversity. The union of change and permanence is found in personality, or in the self-conscious spirit, which through memory gathers up the past into the present and holds them in unity. "Each new experience leaves the soul other than it was; but, as it advances from stage to stage, it is able to gather up its past and carry it with it, so that, at any point, it possesses all that it has been. It is this fact alone that constitutes the permanence and identity of self."[20] As a result, we are the authors of our self-identity or personality: through our conscious activity we make ourselves to be what we are.

The only true realities, then, are persons or selves. Their reality does not consist in a permanent substance underlying the faculties and the changing accidental properties, but in conscious experience. Bowne calls his doctrine of the self an empiricism because it makes the self consist of experience; and he adds that it is a "transcendental" empiricism because the self lies beyond the categories and gives meaning to them. Categories such as being, cause, action, space, and time are universal ideas without a real and independent existence; they depend for their meaning upon the experience of persons. Hence the self or person is the fundamental fact that explains everything else; there is no idea or category that can explain it.[21]

It is natural for us to believe that there are other persons besides ourselves. We observe our fellow men acting with order and purpose and we conclude that they too are centers of conscious activity. Reality is ultimately spiritual and personal, but it appears to us as a plurality of persons. Is this plurality fundamental, or is it grounded in some deeper unity? Bowne is convinced that the plurality of finite persons is not ultimate; that it is but the created manifestation of an infinite, absolute Person or Intelligence. In short, there is a God who is the origin of both finite persons and of the phenomenal world of our experience.

Bowne's conviction of the existence of God is based primarily upon the intelligibility of the universe. There are more signs of order and purpose in the universe than in human actions. It is reasonable, therefore, to suppose the existence of a cosmic Mind as it is to assume the existence of human minds.

Moreover, the universe presents itself to us as a system of mutually related ideas which no finite mind can decipher in its limited experience. Accordingly, there must be an infinite Mind that constitutes this system. Thus God is the ultimate ground of ideas and truth; but, more than this, he is ultimate goodness and beauty. Bowne did not think this could be demonstrated beyond question, but he thought it reasonable to assume that because our minds strive for goodness and beauty, these values must be fully embodied in the ultimate ground of the universe, or God.

Josiah Royce

The title of Royce's first major work, *The Religions Aspect of Philosophy*, is indicative of the central role that religion played in his thought.[22] In the Preface he writes that he was driven to philosophy by religious problems, and that the interests of religion merit our best efforts and utmost loyalty. Royce's thought both in its idealism and in its deeply religious inspiration is in the main current of American philosophy flowing from the Puritan Fathers.

Royce contrasts religious with purely theoretical philosophy. The latter dispassionately investigates the real world; the former seeks, over and above this, to estimate its value. While not indifferent to the truth about reality, religious philosophy is mainly concerned with judgments of value about it. It asks, for example, What in this world is worth most? Above all, is there anywhere in the universe a reality of Infinite Worth?[23] So the main task of the philosophy of religion is to seek the ideal among realities. And since we are above all interested in the ideal in relation to human life, it must first discuss ethical problems and seek the ethical ideal.

quest of the ethical ideal

Ethics distinguishes between right and wrong conduct. It tells us what we ought to do. This requires, in Royce's opinion, the setting up of an ideal or good that we ought to realize in our lives. The main task of *The Religious Aspect of Philosophy* is to establish this ethical ideal.

The realist, he says, tries to set up his ideal differently from the idealist. The realist insists that our ethical ideals and code of conduct should be based on a knowledge of the real world. Morality should be solidly founded on the facts of nature. The idealist more correctly, in Royce's opinion, looks upon morality as an ideal to be striven for, not simply a reality to be discovered in the world of nature. By the ethical ideal we judge reality; hence it is possessed prior to physics or metaphysics and is independent of them. The idealist distinguishes between the judgments, *this is*, and *this is good* or *this ought to be*. The former judgment is made through an investigation of nature; the latter by a different type of investigation called ethical.

The realist wants us to take our moral code from the facts of social life. But since these facts differ in different social groups, there would be no absolute moral law; the moral code would be relative to the group. Morality would be "the body of rules governing successful adjustment to the social environment."[24] The realist may then appeal to a higher form of adjustment to one's surroundings. The world, he may argue, is constantly evolving to higher forms of life and society, and the ideal morality "is that form of adjustment of the social man to his environment towards which society in its progress forever tends."[25] So we should define our moral code by the facts, but the fact of evolution must be taken into account. Man is progressing toward a goal, and this goal gives us our ethical ideal.

While admitting the superiority of this realist view of evolutionary ethics over other realist ethics, Royce finds it also inadequate. Granted that the world is evolving, how can we be sure that it is progressing toward a better state? "Why is the last state in an evolution better than the former states? Surely not because it is the last stage, surely not because it is physically more complex, more definite, or even more permanent; but solely because it corresponds to some ideal that we independently form."[26] In other words, we can judge the moral value of anything physical only by a yardstick that is not physical but moral. And for this we need a moral ideal based not upon physics or even metaphysics but upon an ethical doctrine.

Looking over the history of moral theory, Royce finds much to praise in the Stoic ethical ideal. The Stoics hit upon the new idea that all men share in universal Reason and are perfectly equal in its presence. So all men ought to conform to Reason; they should be rational, striving to realize the rational not only in themselves but in everyone else. This is the origin of the Stoic maxim, "Do good to all men."[27] Even more perfect, however, was Jesus' moral principle, which Royce formulates as follows: "Act as one receiving and trying to return an

Infinite Love."[28] But in his view this ethical ideal is not purely idealistic because it is ultimately based upon the metaphysical truth of the Fatherhood of God. We are told that we stand in relation to God as sons to an all-loving Father, and therefore we should always act so as to return his love. But why should we return the Father's love? "Granting the fact of this love, how does it establish the ideal?" Once again, Royce reminds us that no physical or metaphysical fact will firmly establish our ethical ideal; for this, an ethical doctrine is needed.

How is this ethical doctrine to be gained? The world of dead facts, Royce assures us, will not give it to us.[29] We must look rather to the "world of ends," that is to say, to the specifically moral order, and gain our moral insight from it.

Considering the moral aims we pursue, we see that they are often in conflict with those of our neighbor. What I will is not always what he wills. How can this warfare of wills be ended? Only by desiring to realize all of them at once. I must desire the harmony of all wills. This gives us an insight into a Higher Good, an Ideal World, where all possible aims are pursued in absolute harmony. And this should become our goal in life—the ideal for which we should aim. It is not only a matter of loving our neighbor, of feeling pity or sympathy for him, but of reproducing in ourselves his opposing will. The ideal of Harmony commands us, "Act as a being would act who included thy will and thy neighbor's will in the unity of one life, and who had therefore to suffer the consequences for the aims of both that will follow from the act of either." Or more simply, "In so far as in thee lies, act as if thou wert at once thy neighbor and thyself"; or again, "Treat these two lives as one life."[30]

This moral insight is the foundation of Royce's ethics. It impels us to consider our neighbor's will and our own as different aspects of a Universal Will, and to act as this Will would in order to achieve its purpose. Individualism is seen to be an illusion. The individual has no rights in this world; he is only an instrument of the Universal Life or Will. He must bend all his efforts to serve this Will. His ultimate aim should not be his own individual happiness or that of his neighbor, but the harmony and unity of all men on a higher universal plane.[31]

This theory of Royce recalls the Hegelian conception of an Absolute moral person, of which individual persons are but fragments—a conception that will emerge more clearly in his later works. However, as early as the *Religious Aspect of Philosophy* he realized its implications for the moral life of man. If the individual has no value in himself, ethics is bound to be social rather than individual. The purpose of the moral life is to serve well the community in which we live; to submerge our own interests into those of the group; to work always for unification and harmonization. In one of his last works, *The Problem of Christianity*, Royce crowns this ethical ideal with his notion of the Spirit of Community, or Absolute Community. This is nothing else than God, conceived as a Community or Church—a perfect society which demands our utmost loyalty and love, and in whose supra-personal life we find the satisfaction of all our desires.

quest of truth

Royce long pondered the problem of knowledge and certitude He sought help from Kant's *Critique of Pure Reason*, which taught him that experience itself can give no certainty about general principles: we must bring to bear upon experience our own *a priori* principles (for example, causation), in order to have universal and necessary knowledge. But Royce asks how we can be sure that our present *a priori* principles will always remain the same. Granted that we must now think that every event has a cause, may not this some day become unnecessary and even nonsensical? Kant's failure lies in leaving; our fundamental principles unexplained and uncertain.[32]

The upshot of Royce's reading of Kant was that he began to doubt if there was any solid truth. He concluded that at best a judgment is true for the moment in which it is made, but not necessarily true for other moments. But he soon escaped this skepticism by reflecting on the implications of his state of doubt. Doubt implies the possibility that the statement doubted may be false. So it seems that there is at least one universal and necessary truth; namely, "All but the immediate content of the present moment's judgment, being doubtful, we may be in error about it."[33] Thus like Descartes, Royce finds doubt self-defeating: the possibility of doubt assures us of the existence of truth.

Reflection on the implications of error carries Royce further in his quest of truth, establishing the existence of an Absolute Truth or Mind. His examination of the problem of error unexpectedly turns into a demonstration of the existence of God, conceived in the idealist fashion as absolute experience.

Royce points out that error is certainly possible. How is it possible? What are the logical conditions that make it possible?

Error is generally defined as a judgment that does not agree with its object. I judge, "John is here." The judgment is thought to be erroneous if John is not here; that is to say, if the elements corresponding to the subject and predicate (John, here) are not combined as are the subject and predicate. The only difficulty Royce sees in this explanation of error is the assumed relation between the judgment and its object. What is meant by saying the judgment has *its* object? There is an infinity of possible or real objects. How does a judgment get its own object? Somehow, Royce says, it must pick it out; it must intend to conform to a given object. When it fails to conform to it, it is said to be false. But in order to intend to do something, that something must be known. If the common-sense notion of error is true, therefore, judgments can err only intentionally. A judgment can be in error only if it is knowingly in error.[34]

Perhaps an object has various aspects, one of which is known and the other not, and error concerns the unknown aspect. Royce argues that this does not solve the difficulty, for the unknown feature of the object is outside thought, so that we can make no judgment about it at all, not even one that is mistaken. How can we err about the unknown?

Another difficulty in the common-sense notion of error is its assumption that we can err about a neighbor's thought while remaining really distinct from him. Common sense, as expressed by the Scottish school, supposes that when I make judgments about my neighbor he himself does not enter my thoughts; I think of him by means of ideas that represent him. But how can I err about my neighbor if he is not even partly in my thought, but my only objects are my representative ideas of him?

Royce illustrates his point by the remark of a humorist, that when John and Thomas converse about each other six persons take part in the conversation. There is the real John and the real Thomas, John's image of himself and his image of Thomas, and Thomas' image of himself and his image of John. When John judges, it is plainly *his* Thomas who is the object of his thought. About whom can he err? Not about his own conception of Thomas for he knows this all too well, but only about the real Thomas. But this seems to be impossible, for according to common sense the real Thomas stands outside John's thought and never becomes a part of it.

And yet the fact remains that John can err about Thomas. How is this possible? Perhaps a third person must enter the picture, someone who knows both the real Thomas and John's idea of Thomas and compares the two. But if John and Thomas are really independent of each other, so that one cannot enter the other's thought, neither can they enter into the thought of a third person. Just as John's knowledge is limited to his own conceptions, so would this third person's knowledge be restricted to his: he could not know the real Thomas any more than John could, and therefore he could not make the desired comparison.[35]

The same difficulty arises concerning errors about the future. I can err in predicting a future event. But this presupposes, in the commonsense view, a comparison of my present experience with my past expectation, which are two thoughts widely separate in time. A present thought and a past thought are as separate as John and Thomas. How can they coincide in time and in object so that they can be compared with each other?[36]

The only solution of this difficulty, in Royce's opinion, is to abandon the common-sense, realistic notion that John and Thomas, or two moments of time, are really separate and independent. They must be seen as actually present to, and included in, a higher thought. This thought is universal and all-inclusive, a total consciousness embracing all truths and consequently the possibility of all errors. It is Absolute Truth and Absolute Knowledge. In it the real John and his conception of Thomas, the real Thomas and his conception of John, are contained as integral parts. It contains the finite thoughts one has of the other: both those that are adequate to their object (and hence are true) and those that are inadequate (and hence are false). Error, then, is possible as one moment or element in a higher truth; that is to say, in a consciousness that makes the error a part of itself, while recognizing it as error.[37]

Royce's reasoning leads him to the conclusion that no judgment by itself is erroneous; there is error only if a judgment is included in a higher thought which compares it with its intended object and sees that it misses the mark.[38] So we must abandon the common-sense notion that a judgment is true or false simply in relation to its object. Truth or falsity involves three terms: a judgment, an object, and a higher thought which, by embracing them both, knows whether or not they are in agreement.

Is this all-embracing thought or consciousness finite or infinite? Royce argues forcefully that it must be infinite. For there is an infinite number of possible errors. And not only are they possible; they actually exist. Even before a false judgment is made, it must have been false. "An error is possible only when the judgment in which the error is to be expressed always was false."[39] Hence if error is possible, it is eternally actual. And if there is an infinity of actual errors, there must be an infinite Mind to know them.

The conclusion of this remarkable reasoning is that an infinite Thought or Mind exists, containing in a rational unity not only all objects but also all the relations between them.

In *The Spirit of Modern Philosophy* Royce goes further, arguing that the Infinite Thought contains within itself all finite selves or persons. There is only one Self or Person—the Infinite Being or God, of whom all human persons and all natural objects are but parts. "You are part of one larger self," Royce writes, "along with the most mysterious or most remote fact of nature, along with the moon, and all the hosts of heaven, along with all truth and all beauty."[40] In justification of this position he appeals once more to the triadic nature of knowledge. Our thought is so related to its object that it cannot be true, false, or doubtful unless it is set in the context of a larger and deeper thought which gives it meaning. In short, all finite thought is meaningful only as a fragment of an Infinite Thought, and this is God.

Similarly, in *The Conception of God* Royce insists that our partial and fragmentary experiences are intelligible only in the light of an all-inclusive Absolute Experience or God. We have experiences and we undertake to interpret them. Since each of these experiences is limited and partial, it can be understood only by seeing how it fits into a larger and more complete experience. Proceeding in this way we must be able to reach a final experience which, including all other experiences, is determined by nothing other than itself. This is the Absolute Experience or God.[41]

At this point it will be well to pause to consider some of the idealist presuppositions that give cogency to these demonstrations of God's existence. It will be noted that Royce speaks of a judgment as picking out and intending its object. As we have seen, it is this characteristic of a judgment which, according to Royce, forces the realist to hold that all error is intentional, for in order to pick out an object, the object must be known in advance. This conception of a judgment implies that it has a volitional as well as a cognitive aspect, for picking and choosing are acts of the will. And indeed, this is Royce's teaching. Ideas, he tells us, are not only cognitive; they are primarily and essentially acts of the will, determining their own objects. He writes, "Moreover my idea is a cognitive process only in so far as it is, at the same time, a voluntary process, an act, the partial fulfilment, so far as the idea consciously extends, of a purpose. The object meant by the idea is the object because it is willed to be such, and the will in question is the will that the idea embodies."[42] In short, "The idea is a will seeking its own determination. It is nothing else."[43] If it succeeds in fulfilling its purpose, it is a true idea; if it fails to do so, it is a false idea. Error, then, is a failure on the part of my idea to achieve its purpose.

Thus Royce reduces error to a failure to understand our own aims. We have vague and ill-defined longings, and we want to make them more definite. We do this by expressing our will in a particular idea. The idea has an object or meaning but this object is simply the definite realization of our conscious purpose.

Realism, therefore, in all its forms is a delusion. We are not passive in knowledge, merely accepting the world as our object. There are no beings independent of thought, determining ideas; we construct our ideas as embodiments of our will. Royce thought that realism mainly originates in social convenience. For practical purposes it is advantageous to think of reality as divided into individual beings, independent of our knowledge of them. This helps the conservative-minded person to maintain "good order," and it enables the man of action to get things done, for we have "to think narrowly in order to act vigorously."[44] Idealism, on the other hand, is the only philosophy that satisfies our religious aspirations; it alone is a truly religious philosophy.

So the quest of truth leads Royce to the same goal as did the quest of the moral idea. Searching for this ideal, he discovered a Universal or Absolute Will, in which were reconciled all conflicts of individual wills and all good and evil. Now his quest of truth has led him to an Infinite Thought containing all judgments, true as well as false. And these two Absolutes are one: the Infinite Thought is identical with the Universal Will, for it realizes within itself the moral ideal that we imperfectly strive to attain. "In the Divine Thought is perfectly and finally realized the Moral Insight and the Universal Will of our ethical discussion."[45] Knowing all truth, the Infinite Thought must include a knowledge of all wills and of their conflicts; it must also know the outcome of this conflict and thus perfectly possess the moral insight Royce strove to attain in his quest of the moral ideal.

In short, the Truth is also the Good, and these together are the Infinite Spirit we call God. And lest we think this to be a barren abstraction, Royce, at the end of *The Religious Aspect of Philosophy*, points out the transformation this insight should make in our every act. "'What art thou, O man?' our ideal says to us. 'Art thou not in God? To Whom dost thou speak? With whom dost thou walk? What life is this in whose midst thou livest? What are all these things that thou seemest to touch? Whose is all this beauty that thou enjoyest in art, this unity that thou seekest to produce in thy state, this truth that thou pursuest in thy thought? All this is in God and of God. Thou hast never seen, or heard, or touched, or handled, or loved anything but God. Know this truth, and thy life must be transformed to thee in all its significance. Serve the whole God, not the irrationally separate part that thy delusions have made thee suppose to be an independent thing. Live out thy life in its full meaning; for behold, it is God's life.'"[46]

Sage School of Idealism

In concluding this sketch of American idealism in the nineteenth century, a word should be said of the Sage school of idealism at Cornell. Its first head, Jacob Gould Schurman (1854–1942), studied philosophy in England, Scotland, and Germany, and became an enthusiastic Kantian. After teaching philosophy at Dalhousie College in Nova Scotia, he went to Cornell in 1886, and became president of the university in 1892. James Edwin Creighton (1861–1924), a former pupil of his at Dalhousie, succeeded him as head of the Sage school.[47] Associated with Creighton at Cornell was Frank Thilly. Through the initiative of the Sage school, *The Philosophical Review* was founded and the American Philosophical Association was formed in 1902. Creighton was the association's first president. He was also the American director of *Kantstudien* from 1896 until his death.

The Sage school opposed English empiricism and also the idealism of Berkeley. The latter, in Creighton's opinion, reduced the universe to mental elements—either mental substances (God and human souls), or passive ideas, to the neglect of the external or objective order of nature. Creighton's own philosophy is an objective idealism, which stresses the objectivity of nature, while maintaining that the object is of the same kind of being as the subject which produces or "objectifies" it.

The Sage school was also critical of the personal idealism of Howison and Bowne for giving too much importance to the individual mind or self. Against Bowne's pluralism of persons, Creighton taught a monistic idealism inspired by Bosanquet. Since the mind is a whole, the thinker is not a solitary being. Thinking is the outcome of the functioning of a society of minds; it must be social and historical, a continuous process and a group achievement. Truth is the product of many minds working together. With this notion in mind the Sage school began *The Philosophical Review* and founded the American Philosophical Association.

With the growth of realism and pragmatism in the first decades of the twentieth century, idealism lost ground in America as it did in England. The clear-cut lines between the schools of idealism tended to be blurred. Idealism was often mingled with realist and pragmatic tendencies, and efforts were even made to transcend the dichotomy between realism and idealism. Nevertheless Royce's influence remained strong in the United States and it is still active today. Among his notable disciples were John Elof Boodin (1869–1950), who combined a pragmatic realism with a cosmic idealism, William Ernest Hocking (1873–1966), who proposed an empirical idealism, DeWitt H. Parker (1895–1949) and Wilbur Marshall Urban (1873–1952), both of whom taught value-centered philosophies influenced by Royce.[48] The leading idealist in the United States today is Brand Blanshard (b. 1892). In his *Nature of Thought* Blanshard adopts an idealism akin to that of Royce, his former professor at Harvard. He argues that coherence is not only the test of truth but its very nature. On this basis he develops the theme that reality is a coherent, all-inclusive system, whose parts are internally related. The defense of these idealist theses makes Blanshard a lonely figure in contemporary American philosophy; but he is a witness to the enduring appeal of Hegelianism to the philosophic mind.[49]

XXV.

Resurgence of Realism

THE opening decade of the twentieth century was a time of change and revolt in American philosophy. Writing about 1904, William James noted "a curious unrest in the philosophic atmosphere of the time, a loosening of old landmarks, a softening of oppositions, a mutual borrowing from one another on the part of systems anciently closed, and an interest in new suggestions, however vague, as if the one thing sure were the inadequacy of the extant school-solutions."[1] The new generation found the current idealism too abstract and academic and craved a philosophy more in tune with the vagaries and caprices of life, even if this meant some loss of logical rigor.

As James remarks, his observations undoubtedly reflect his own discontent with the state of American philosophy, but the revolution he forecast did in fact take place, with himself as one of its principal authors. The idealism that had breathed new life into philosophy less than a hundred years before had now lost much of its vigor and vitality; it suffered from the dryness and inflexibility of all philosophies in long use in the schools. Philosophers, always ready for fresh experiments, were forming new alliances with the physical sciences, biology, mathematics, psychology, and the social sciences. There was a stirring of interest in empiricism. Even before the turn of the century, C. S. Peirce and William James were proclaiming the pragmatic approach to philosophy and John Dewey was developing the form of pragmatism called "instrumentalism." But as James viewed his own time, the strangest appearance on the philosophic scene was realism. The nineteenth century had seen the triumph of idealism. Now, as James says, "natural realism, so long decently buried, raises its head above the turf, and finds glad hands outstretched from the most unlikely quarters to help it to its feet again."[2]

This revival of realism in the United States was not an isolated phenomenon in the Western world. The spirit of the times was turning against idealism, and everywhere there were signs of a return to realism. In England this return was heralded by G. E. Moore, Bertrand Russell, Samuel Alexander, and Alfred North Whitehead. Whitehead came to the United States and spent the last part of his academic career at Harvard, introducing many to a basically realistic philosophy. In Germany the tendency toward realism found expression in phenomenology, which was promoted by Husserl at the turn of the century. In Italy the reaction against the idealism of Rosmini and Gioberti began in the second half of the nineteenth century with the revival of the realism of St. Thomas Aquinas. From Italy this revival spread to France and from there to the United States. However, Thomistic realism had little influence in America in the early twentieth century and none in secular circles. As the early American realist William Pepperell Montague says, "The great Thomistic realism of the Catholics was unfortunately regarded by the non-Catholics as too closely bound up with theological dogmas to be of any significance for secular thought."[3] Montague is here describing the state of affairs at the end of the nineteenth century, but with some exceptions his words apply equally well today. Within Catholic circles, however, Thomism is now flourishing, and it is one of the most significant realistic philosophies in America. We are here concerned with the realism of the early decades of the twentieth century, which took two forms called "New Realism" and "Critical Realism."

The New Realism

In the spring of 1910 six American teachers of philosophy formed a group to expound and defend what they considered to be a new kind of realistic philosophy. The group consisted of Ralph Barton Perry and Edwin B. Holt of Harvard, Walter T. Marvin of Rutgers College, Edward G. Spaulding of Princeton, and William P. Montague and Walter B. Pitkin of Columbia. After several meetings they agreed on a basic program for a realistic philosophy which was published under the title "A Program and First Platform of Six Realists." This was followed a year and a half later by a volume entitled *The New Realism* to which all contributed essays on various aspects of the new philosophy.[4]

All of these authors had defended realism before engaging in this co-operative program. As early as 1902 Perry and Montague had replied to Josiah Royce's scathing attack on realism in his Gifford Lectures of 1899 (published in *The World and the Individual*).[5] Now, in the spirit of co-operative inquiry enjoined by the idealists themselves, they banded together with their four colleagues to launch a concerted attack on idealism in all its forms.

Although the members of the new group held widely different views in metaphysics, they agreed on two methodological rules and a few fundamental epistemological principles. In their original Program they lamented "the lack of deliberate co-operation in research" in philosophy, in contrast to the procedure of science. They also regretted the failure of philosophers to agree on a common terminology or working agreement on fundamental presuppositions, with the result that genuine philosophical problems are obscured and real philosophical progress is seriously hindered. This gives the impression that philosophical problems and their solutions are essentially personal. The New Realists hoped to give to the world an example of philosophical teamwork that would dispel the illusion that philosophy is a matter of personal opinion and taste. However, the disagreements that soon divided them showed plainly the limited advantage of such co-operative programs in philosophy.

The second methodological rule on which they agreed was also taken from science. They proposed to isolate their problems and tackle them one by one. In the case under consideration they tried to center their attention on the relation between the knower and the object known, without prejudging or even raising the question of the ultimate nature of the knowing subject or of the known object. This was opposed to the method of the idealists, who aimed at establishing a universal system of ideas in which no one would be meaningful unrelated to the others. In carrying out their plan, the realists admitted at least partial failure. As Montague conceded, it was impossible to eliminate all metaphysics and cosmology from their epistemology; the best they could do was to keep them as much as possible in the background.[6]

The epistemological postulates the New Realists shared in common can be reduced to three: (1) At least some of the particular things of which we are conscious exist when we are not conscious of them. (2) At least some of the essences or universals of which we are conscious subsist when we are not conscious of them. (3) At least some real particular things and universals are apprehended directly, rather than indirectly through copies or mental images. We shall examine each of these in turn.

The first postulate, which Montague calls the "existential realism of common use" asserts that particular things in space and time do not seem to depend for their existence on the fact that they are perceived by the senses or conceived by the mind. The world seems to exist independent of our knowledge of it. This is opposed to the idealism of Berkeley, which denies to material things a status independent of our knowledge and equates their existence with our consciousness of them. The New Realists insist that their own view of the matter is the natural, instinctive belief of all men, so that the burden of proof lies with those who would discredit it. And this cannot be done simply by appealing to the fact that when objects are observed, consciousness is always present. The idealist argues that in order to prove the independence of things we would have to observe them both as they are related to consciousness and as they are unrelated to it; only then could we be sure that knowledge makes no difference to things. But, the realist rejoins, this is an unfair and absurd demand. We cannot look at a thing before we see it or after we have seen it and note whether our seeing it has changed its appearance. We are in the predicament of being unable to eliminate the cognitive factor from the situation, as Ralph Barton Perry makes abundantly clear in his famous article "The Egocentric Predicament."[7] But, as he also shows, this predicament does not settle the question in favor of idealism. The bare fact of having to be conscious of something in order to observe it does not prove its dependence on consciousness. The issue between idealism and realism must be decided by the behavior of objects under observation. The result of this test is to show that consciousness has no constant or significant effect upon the behavior of objects. There is no law of physical nature that depends for its reality upon the mere fact that it is or can be experienced.[8]

Since the debate between realists and idealists is over the independence or dependence of objects with regard to consciousness, a primary need is to clarify the meaning of these terms. In Perry's view, the first and most general meaning of the term "independence" is negative; it simply denies dependence. The dependence denied in the statement of realism is not that of relation: obviously when an object is known it is related to a knower. It is not so related, however, that it owes its existence or nature to the circumstance of being known. Moreover, if realism is to be thoroughgoing, it must assert the object's independence not only of finite knowledge but of all knowledge. Absolute or objective idealism claims that reality is independent of our finite knowledge but not of the Absolute Mind. But this is a "half-realism" that ultimately makes things dependent on experience—at least on absolute experience—and this is fatal to realism.[9]

While maintaining that things are independent of experience, the New Realism asserts that when they are known they are ideas in the mind. "They may enter *directly into* the mind," Perry writes, "and when they do, they become what are called 'ideas.'"[10] In short, they are not only independent of consciousness but also immanent in it. How is this possible? It is tempting to explain these two aspects of things by a dualism of mind and body, and of thought and things; but once these have been separated by definition in the Cartesian manner, how are we to account for the fact of their union? In order to avoid the perplexing difficulties of the Cartesian dualism, the New Realism proposes that the difference between mind and body, as well as that between knowledge and things, is only a relational and functional difference and not one of substances or natures. Referring with approval to a statement of Ernst Mach, Perry asserts that the elements of the physical and mental worlds are the same. For example, color in itself is neither physical nor mental, but it can enter into different relationships and thus become either physical or mental, or both at the same time. It is an everyday experience that one and the same thing can belong to different groups or can be the subject of several different relations: a man, for example, can be simultaneously a citizen of the United States, a Democrat, and a proletarian. Similarly, an element that is neutral in itself with respect to being physical or mental can be invested with a relationship that renders it physical, and with another relationship that renders it mental. In short, it can belong at one and the same time to the group of physical and psychical things. Thought and thing, mind and body, therefore, are not separate entities, but two different sets of relationships whose constitutive elements are neutral to both. In the context of one relationship a thing is a body, in the context of another the same thing is a thought or idea. Perry calls this "epistemological monism."[11]

The second postulate of the New Realism is that at least some universals or essences have a reality independent of thought. These universal realities are said *to subsist*, whereas particular things or events are said *to exist*, but they are equally real in the sense that they are equally unaffected by consciousness. The New Realist is therefore a Platonic realist: "He accords full ontological status to the things of thought as well as to the things of sense, to logical entities as well as physical entities, or to subsistents as well as to existents."[12] His reason for wanting independent reality to universals is identical with that for granting independent reality to individual things: they appear to be completely indifferent to our consciousness of them. For example, the mathematical equation 7 + 5 = 12 is entirely explained by the natures of seven, of five, and of twelve, and not at all by our awareness of it. Numbers, universal qualities like blue and yellow, and their relations and configurations show a complete indifference to the fact that we are conscious of them. Everything indicates that they are real whether or not we are conscious of them, and that we discover rather than create them by knowing them.[13]

We should carefully note the kind of reality the New Realist ascribes to universals. Like the reality individual things have in themselves, that belonging to universals in themselves is neither physical nor mental; it is simply the reality of their own nature or meaning. Like individuals in themselves, universals are neutral with respect to being physical or mental, and because of this neutrality they can become physical or mental, or both at the same time, by entering into the organization of bodies or minds.

It is not difficult to recognize in this a new form of an old doctrine in Western philosophical tradition. Since the Middle Ages philosophers of Platonic tendencies, such as Avicenna, Duns Scotus, and Suarez, conceived essences or natures as possessing a reality of their own distinct from the existence they have in the physical or mental world. The reality essences have in themselves, according to this tradition, is not that of an existent but of a nature capable of existing in various ways: in the real world and in the mind.[14] As this doctrine appears in American New Realism, the modes of being that essences can have are reduced to different organizations or relational contexts in which entities can function.

The third and final postulate of the New Realists is that at least some realities are perceived directly and not through mental copies or images. In this they agreed with the older realism of the Scottish philosopher Thomas Reid (1710–1796), who taught that the direct objects of knowledge are not ideas, as Locke and Descartes held, but external realities. For example, Reid maintained the common-sense view that we directly perceive color and extension, both of which are real qualities of bodies. So we do not have to begin with ideas, as Descartes thought, and infer the existence of a real world corresponding to them. Our first knowledge carries us to a real world existing independent of our knowledge of it.

The New Realists gave enthusiastic assent to this latter point, but they could not accept Reid's claim that substances underlie the qualities wo directly perceive. In short, Reid's realism, in their view, was compromised by its doctrine of substance. He did not think that qualities constitute a body, or that mental states constitute a mind, but that bodily and mental substances underlie these qualities and states. But if this were true, the New Realists argue, only the attributes and qualities of substances would be known; substances would remain unknown in themselves. The New Realists saw no reason to postulate an unknown substratum for qualities or activities: the substratum, in their view, is not made up of qualities or activities, and without them it "is reduced to a nullity," so it can easily be ignored as a non-entity.[15] Accordingly, the New Realists do not grant the existence of substances underlying the objects we directly perceive in the world; theirs is an empirical realism, in close affinity to that of Flume.

The New Realists call their theory of knowledge "Presentative Realism" in order to contrast it to the representative realism of Locke and Descartes. Representative realism holds that the mind directly perceives only its own ideas or states and from these infers the reality of the external world. The ideas represent external objects and lead us to a knowledge of them. But the New Realists protest that the objects we perceive at least appear to be external, so the presumption is on their side. The burden of proof lies with those who deny the externality of the immediate objects of perception. The New Realists also insist that the representative theory of knowledge leads to the subjectivism of Berkeley, for it offers no guarantee that our ideas truly represent an external world. The main effort of the New Realists was to eliminate subjectivism, and to them this entailed the defense of presentative realism rather than the representative or "copy theory" of knowdedge.[16]

One of the main objections to presentative realism urged by its opponents is that it cannot account for illusions, hallucinations, and in general erroneous experiences. If we perceive the real world directly, and not through images or ideas, how can this world become distorted in our view? Do not all our experiences present the world to us as it truly is, with the result that error is impossible?

One way out of this difficulty is to maintain the objective existence of errors, illusions, and hallucinations. Railroad tracks are parallel to each other when seen from directly above, but they appear to converge in the distance. Perhaps the convergent rails exist just as objectively in space as the parallel rails. This was the position of Edwin B. Holt and Ralph Barton Perry. In their view, errors and illusions are not distortions caused by the mind or the organs and media of perception; they have their own objective existence which causes our experience of them. "It seems to me," Holt writes, "that the extra-mental world is teeming with contradictions and unrealities, and that these can come to consciousness by virtue of a psychical process, which presents no elements of 'distortion.'"[17] He does not claim that extra-mental errors or illusions are *real*. Reality should not be confused with mere being or existence. Some beings are real; others are unreal or illusory, but even these latter exist or subsist as objects of experience. The main point Holt wants to make, against idealism, is that even such unreal objects are independent of consciousness and that they sufficiently account for our erroneous and illusory experiences.[18]

On the latter point Montague disagreed with his colleagues. In his essay in *The New Realist* he was willing to grant that unrealities and contradictions objectively exist or subsist. A "subsistent," he says, is any actual or possible object of thought, and this even includes negations. But he could not see how an unreal object or mere negation could exercise any causality and thus contribute to our knowledge of it.[19] Error, therefore, cannot be explained simply by the perception of erroneous or illusory unrealities. It results from a distortion of the real object when it produces its effect upon the brain. The distortion may be either (1) physical or peripherally physiological, in which case a sensory illusion results (for example, a straight stick appears bent in water); or (2) cerebral, in which case there is an error of inference, or, when the error is persistent, the delusions of insanity.[20]

In a later essay Montague accuses his colleagues of teaching an "objective relativism," according to which "every object that *appears* to be in space *is* in space." For example, when different observers see the same railroad tracks as convergent and parallel, both of these contradictory objects exist objectively in space. An object at one moment has no single position and shape in its own right, but many positions and shapes, each of which is relative to an observer. But in Montague's view this theory does not take into account the radical inequality between true and false perceptions. True perceptions can explain illusory perceptions but not vice versa. "If we assume that the rails *are* parallel, we can easily explain why and how and when an *appearance* of their being convergent will arise. But if we reverse this procedure and assume that they are in fact convergent, we cannot explain why the appearance of their parallelism should occur under the circumstances in which it does occur."[21] For this and other reasons Montague refuses to give a physical locus to the unreal objects of illusion, though he still treats them as subsistent objects which under certain circumstances can appear in consciousness.

Critical Realism

The difficulties inherent in the New Realists' theories of error pointed to the need for a re-examination of realism. This re-examination was made a few years later by a second group of philosophers who called themselves "Critical Realists" in order to contrast their own more sophisticated brand of realism to the naïve realism of their predecessors. There were seven members of this group of realists: Durant Drake of Vassar, Arthur O. Lovejoy of Johns Hopkins, James Bissett Pratt of Williams, Arthur K. Rogers of Yale, Roy Wood Sellars of Michigan, George Santayana of Harvard, and C. A. Strong of Columbia. The last two had retired from teaching by the time they joined the group. Like the New Realists these men published a co-operative book, which they called *Essays in Critical Realism* (1920).[22] Again like their realist predecessors, while frankly admitting differences of opinion in metaphysics, they tried to isolate the problem of knowledge and come to a general agreement on its solution.

The Critical Realists begin by examining the two historical types of realism most familiar to them: the naïve realism of their immediate predecessors and the inferential realism of philosophers such as Descartes. The former "objectively minded" philosophers suppose that we directly apprehend the physical world, whereas the latter "subjectively minded" philosophers suppose, on the contrary, that we are immediately aware of psychological entities or ideas, which are mental substitutes for objects in the outer world. Both of these theories of knowledge are realistic because they assert that the mind can know a real world independent of knowledge, either by direct perception or by deducing its existence from ideas in the mind. The object of the Critical Realists is to show the errors in each of these theories and to establish a more satisfactory form of realism which, while incorporating their valid insights, avoids their objectionable aspects.

A little reflection on naïve realism, according to Durant Drake, reveals the difficulties in the way of this too simple solution of the problem of knowledge. Realists such as Holt claim that all the qualities we seem to see in objects are really present in them. But if this were true, the same object would be red to a man with normal vision and gray to one who is color-blind. Moreover, it would contain the infinitely different shades of red seen by men with "normal" eyes. Drake insists on the absurdity of such an incoherent, indefinite, and contradictory world. Neither common sense nor science pictures it this way: they "view physical existents as having a definite shape, size, color, etc., and not as consisting of a chaos of mutually exclusive qualities simultaneously occupying the same points."[23] Naïve realism, he charges, fails to use Ockham's Razor; it "multiplies the qualities of the outer existent *praeter necessitatem*." It also makes errors impossible; for if all the qualities we see in objects exist "out there" in space, how can anyone's verdict as to the nature of the physical existent be any truer than anyone else's?

The basic mistake of naïve realism, in the opinion of the Critical Realists, is to suppose that we directly perceive things existing in the external world. Since different observers perceive the same existent as clothed with different and even contradictory qualities, it is natural for the Naïve Realists to ascribe all these qualities to the thing itself. Rejecting this absurdity, the subjectively minded realist concludes that we do not directly perceive the physical world at all, but our own mental states, which in some way represent the real world. The Critical Realists were equally unwilling to accept this kind of realism. In their view it not only plays into the hands of the idealists by closing the mind in upon its own states and ideas, but it is contrary to the facts. What is given in perception, Drake insists, is not a mental state but the essence of a physical object. Suppose I dream of a bear chasing me. My datum is the "character-complex" or essence "a bear chasing me." The dream-state exists; but the bear I am dreaming of does not. The bear in my dream, therefore, is not the mental state of dreaming.[24]

Similarly, Critical Realists distinguish in a true perception between the mental state in which the datum is given and the datum itself. Suppose there appears to me "a black, oblong desk over there." This datum is a particular group of qualities or character complex; it is not a mental state, though the perception of it implies such a state. The difference between a dream or illusion and a true perception is that in the latter we instinctively attribute the datum to the external world. We feel the appearances to be the characteristics of real objects, though we cannot conclusively prove that they are. As we shall see, the Critical Realists could not agree on what data, if any, really belong to the physical world. They were in accord, however, in holding that the data of perception have an outward reference to objects independent of knowledge, and that these data are the means by which we perceive objects and think about them. This belief, in their view, is the only one that works, for it alone explains why our sense data appear, disappear, and change as they do. "Everything is *as if* realism were true; and the *as if* is so strong that we may consider our instinctive and actually unescapable belief justified."[25]

When the Critical Realists began to elucidate and defend their key notion of "datum," it became clear that their ranks were not as solid as they thought. At first they claimed that the differences between them were only verbal, but as the discussion advanced fundamental divergences in doctrine began to appear.

The basic issue between them was the nature of a datum. While agreeing, in opposition to the New Realists, that we do not perceive a physical object directly but only by means of data or "characters," they differed on the nature of these data and their relation to the perceiver and the thing perceived. One group held that data are pure essences without any existential status in themselves, timeless universal natures of a logical character. This was the opinion of Drake, Strong, Santayana, and Rogers. The first two philosophers give the clearest exposition of it in their contributions to *Essays in Critical Realism*. The second group, comprising Sellars, Pratt, and Lovejoy, was repelled by the Platonic overtones of their colleagues' conception of a datum. Their conception of a datum was more conceptualistic and mentalistic. If we are to do justice to the Critical Realists, we must distinguish between these two notions of a datum and consider them separately.

According to Strong, expressing the doctrine of the first group, a datum is "what we are immediately conscious of"; for example, in a sense perception, red or gray. He carefully distinguishes a datum from (1) something actually existing in the external world, and from (2) something existing internally in the mind. In other words, a datum is not an existent: it is neither the existing object of knowledge nor the knowing subject. It does not belong to the class of existents at all, but to the class of concrete natures or essences.[26] The red I perceive is a datum in the sense that it is "given" to me in sensation as an essence or "character" of the thing perceived, but in itself it has no existential status. It is not given to me as something existing in the real world or in the mind. Drake writes that "the datum that appears, the character-complex remembered or thought of, is not, *qua* datum, an existent, but is simply a character-complex *now* 'given' ('imagined'), but which (if memory or conception is accurate) was or is the actual character of the object remembered or thought of."[27]

The difficulty with this notion of a datum is that it is completely de-existentialized: a datum is not an existent but a "mere essence." And yet the Critical Realists call it an "entity," even a "logical entity," and they describe it as "hovering" between the knower and the thing known, as though it actually existed. We must keep in mind, however, that the entity it enjoys is not that of an existing thing but only that of an essence or group of qualities.

A great advantage is gained by recognizing the datum as a mere essence and not as an existent. If it were an existent, the datum and the object known by the datum would be two existing things, and our awareness of the datum would not be at the same time an awareness of the object. The datum would be like a picture representing something distinct from itself. But when you see a person's portrait, you do not see the person; you see a different embodiment of his essence in the picture, and you do not know its original embodiment in the person. But if the datum is not an existent but only an essence, it can be truly the essence of the object. Straightness, for example, can truly be a character of the perceived object. Then the essence or character presented to us in perception, and the essence embodied in the object are not two but one, and our awareness of the datum is also the awareness of the object. By means of the datum we truly perceive the object. This is what happens in every true perception. An illusion, on the contrary, is the consciousness of a datum and the assigning of it to a physical object to which it does not belong. This is how Rogers distinguishes between truth and error: "The definition which critical realism gives of error is briefly this: When we 'know' an object, we are assigning a certain 'essence'—a character or group of characters—to some reality existing independently of the knowledge-process. And as truth is the identity of this essence with the actual character of the reality referred to, so error stands for the lack of such agreement, and the ascribing of an ideal character to what we are mistaken in supposing to be real, or the ascribing to a reality of a wrong character instead of a right one."[28]

This does not mean that in a true perception every trait or character in the datum is to be found literally in the physical object. According to Drake, "our perceptual data are at best only in part genuine aspects of outer reality. So that what appears, *as a whole*, is never quite what exists."[29] The datum is usually a complex structure made up of parts deriving from various sources. Thus Drake held the generally accepted view that only primary qualities (for example, size) are literal characteristics of physical objects; secondary qualities (for example, color) are contributed by the perceiver. Thus "in the case of the black-oblong-desk-over-there, there really is a 'desk' in existence, it really is 'over there' (i.e., at a certain distance from the perceiver), it really is 'oblong,' and of such and such a size. But it is not, in itself, 'black,' except in the sense that it has definite characteristics which cause the character-trait 'black' to appear to us."[30]

While applauding the general line taken by these Critical Realists, the second group, made up of Sellars, Lovejoy, and Pratt, adopt a more subjectivist attitude toward a datum. They maintain that although a datum is a mere complex of characters or qualities which does not include existence, in reality all these characters exist only in the consciousness of the knower. As Sellars puts it, "the existential locus of these characters and meanings is the psycho-physical organism. They are intrinsic characters in the structure involved in interpreting objects…they are features of the field of consciousness."[31] Knowledge is defined as the interpretation of an object in terms of characters and meanings which are present in the consciousness of the knower. These characters and meanings have an outer reference to external things, but they exist only within the mental framework of the knower. Hence Sellars does not object to anyone calling his philosophy "mentalistic."

The publication of *Essays in Critical Realism* in 1920 was followed by a long series of articles in philosophical journals criticizing the doctrines of the Critical Realists. The latter replied, clarifying their positions and attempting to answer the criticisms of their opponents. One of the main difficulties in Critical Realism, according to its critics, is the passage from the experienced datum to the physical object. The Critical Realists deny the possibility of inferring the existence of the external world from the immediate data of consciousness. They insist that we pass to the external world "instinctively." But it is not at all clear how the datum, which has no existential content, leads the mind to the existence of the external world. In short, the Critical Realists place a gulf between data and the physical world that reason cannot bridge. They themselves are not absolutely certain of the existence of such a world; they rest their claim to its existence on simple belief or "animal faith."[32]

The critics also asked how perception of a datum accounts for the perception of a physical object. According to the Critical Realists, the latter is not directly perceived or literally grasped by the mind. But if this is so, in what sense are objects perceived at all? Are they not unknown in themselves, like the discredited substance of Locke?[33]

Under the pressure of these and similar attacks Critical Realism began to disintegrate as a distinctive theory of knowledge. Moreover, its defendants drew farther and farther apart from each other as they clarified their positions and placed them in their metaphysical settings. One of the main lessons to be learned from their experiment, as from that of the New Realists, is the impossibility of separating the epistemological problem from metaphysics. In discussing the nature of knowledge, they could not avoid speaking of being, entity, existence and essence, all of which are metaphysical notions. But as soon as they defined their meaning, it was evident that there was no one theory of knowledge called "Critical Realism," but a host of theories, some incompatible with others. We shall examine the theory of George Santayana in more detail because of his importance in American philosophy and literature.

George Santayana

Or all the Critical Realists, Santayana has attained the greatest stature as a philosopher and man of letters.[34] A superb stylist and literary artist, he has expressed himself on almost every major philosophical subject; besides this he has written books and articles of literary criticism, poetry, and a best-selling novel.

Santayana himself points to the oscillation in his thought between materialism and transcendentalism.[35] He frankly espouses a materialistic philosophy, proclaiming Democritus as his hero. The realm of the spirit, including intelligence, poetry, and religion, is to him but an expression or function of matter, which alone is real. And yet his interests and sympathies lie chiefly with the spiritual side of man's nature—which for him is the fanciful, epiphenomenal concomitant of matter as it is organized in human beings. He does not take transcendentalism lightly, but rather attempts to ground it in materialism and naturalism.

The circumstances of Santayana's birth and education help to explain this paradoxical position. Born of Spanish and nominally Catholic parents, he never lost the taste for their Latin Catholic culture. Although he spent half his life in New England, studying and teaching at Harvard, he was not at home in its genteel, Puritanical atmosphere, and he preferred to end his days in the more congenial surroundings of Rome. This return to Rome, however, was not a conversion to the Catholic faith. He made no pretense to be a practicing Catholic. His deistic mother and agnostic father taught him to regard all religion as a work of the imagination; he differed from them only in considering the fancies of the imagination as something good. On the subject of religion—which he called "the head and front of everything"—from his youth he saw the choice as one between Catholicism and complete disillusion, and he fearlessly chose disillusion.[36]

At Harvard his principal teachers were Royce and James, the former a representative of nineteenth-century idealism and transcendentalism, the latter a pioneer in the newer realism and empiricism. Both influenced him, James more than Royce. He liked Royce for his dialectical prowess and James for his naturalism and empiricism, although he could not accept the pragmatism and pure empiricism of James' later works. During his years of philosophical development in Germany and England, he read deeply in German idealism, Hinduism, and Platonism, all of which contributed to the transcendental temper of his philosophy. Thus, like C. S. Peirce and others at the turn of the century, his mind was formed by both naturalism and transcendentalism, and his philosophy holds both in precarious balance.

skepticism and animal faith

Like Descartes, Santayana uses doubt and skepticism as a methodological discipline to purify his mind of illusion and error, thus clearing the way for his positive philosophy. However, he pushes skepticism much farther than Descartes.

Santayana distinguishes between two stages or levels of skepticism. The first and more superficial level, which he calls the "empirical criticism of knowledge," consists in separating facts from the interpretation of facts. By facts he means existing things or events; by their interpretation he means opinions or beliefs about them. On this level the skeptic comes to realize that all opinions are open to argument and discussion, but he considers facts safe from criticism. Facts are thought to be indubitable: they are the sure ground on which he strives to ground his beliefs.[37]

The radical skeptic, however, goes farther in distinguishing what he knows from what he thinks he knows. A "transcendental criticism of knowledge" brings him at last to ultimate skepticism. At this second stage the philosopher turns his attention to facts themselves and discovers that they too are questionable: all alleged knowledge of matters of fact is seen to be nothing but opinion or faith, which can always be doubted.

This level of radical skepticism is reached by recognizing that a fact (that is, an existing thing or event) is not an immediate object of awareness or an irreducible datum of experience. What we are immediately aware of, and therefore absolutely certain of, is an essence or datum, such as redness, hotness, or pain. The existence of these data is not given along with them, and therefore it is questionable. For example, my awareness of yellow in no way involves an awareness of its existence. As proof of this Santayana points out that we experience the same yellow whether our eyes are open or closed, whether we are suffering an hallucination or enjoying normal perception. Hence the essence or datum "yellow" does not contain the characteristic of existence, nor by itself does it prompt us to attribute existence to it. "Each essence that appears appears just as it is, because its appearance defines it, and determines the whole being that it is or has."[38] Existence is added to essence from outside as an "unintelligible accident," or as "a conjunction of natures in adventitious and variable relations."[39] But these relations are external to the natures or essences which they bind together, and hence they are not given in the intuition of the essences themselves.

If this is true, at the extreme limit of skepticism we can doubt whether the yellow we perceive is really the yellow of an existing object; whether the pain or the thought we are aware of belongs to an existing self or mind; whether the world itself has a substantial existence; whether it existed a moment ago or will exist in the next moment. In short, skepticism can be carried to the point of denying the reality of all facts. What is left as absolutely indubitable are the essences directly given to us in experience.

Thus ultimate skepticism introduces the philosopher to a strange world: a realm of pure essences detached from space and time and the substantiality and flux of existence. He sees with the greatest force and clarity objects which are nothing but images or appearances, behind which there may be nothing that appears. A "solipsist of the present moment," the skeptic by an heroic effort refrains from asserting or implying anything about the existence of what he experiences, concentrating solely on the essences hovering before his gaze.[40]

Satisfying as this luminous intuition of essences may be to the philosopher, it is hardly enough for him when he enters the work-a-day world. Skepticism, Santayana says, is an exercise, not a life; it is a discipline for purifying the mind of prejudice and for rendering it more apt, when the time comes, to believe and to act wisely.[41] And the time comes when we have to act. We live an animal life, and animals "being by nature hounded and hungry creatures, spy out and take alarm at any datum of sense or fancy, supposing that there is something substantial there, something that will count and work in the world."[42] They treat the data of experience as signals or images of things to be used or avoided, thereby instinctively ascribing existence and reality to them.

The sense of existence or reality, accordingly, comes from our engagement and involvement in action, not from intuition or immediate experience. The latter gives us nothing but essences, and from its point of view the reality of the world is doubtful. But we are assured of its reality by "animal faith." By this Santayana means the instinctive conviction of the reality of the world around us springing from our practical attitudes toward it, such as action, expectation, fear, hope, and want. By moving, devouring, or transforming things, we assure ourselves of their existence.[43]

Hence skepticism does not have the final word in Santayana's philosophy. In the end he agrees with common sense that the external world exists, though he does not think we are immediately aware of its existence. In all this he is in accord with Descartes. He differs from the French philosopher, however, in denying that we can demonstrate the existence of the sensible world beginning with the immediate data of consciousness. The pure essences with which Santayana begins are completely void of existence, unlike the thinking self of Descartes, and no logical reasoning can deduce existence from them. Only the irrational impulse of animal life convinces us of the existence of the external world.[44]

the realms of being

In examining the role of skepticism and animal faith in Santayana's philosophy we have made some acquaintance with his notions of essence and existence. We will now take a closer look at them in the context of what he calls the "Realms of Being." These realms are four in number: essence, matter, truth, and spirit.

1. *The Realm of Essence.* Skepticism is not the only approach to the realm of essence recommended by Santayana. Other avenues opening upon this world are logic, aesthetic contemplation, and moral experience. The logician is not concerned with knowledge through animal faith; he is content to analyze ideal forms with their patterns or logical relations. Thus he is thoroughly at home in a world of essences. In aesthetic experience we delight in an essence to which our nature is attuned, so that the intuition of it is a delightful exercise to the senses and the soul. Indeed, the beautiful itself is an essence.[45] Through our moral triumphs we become aware of virtues, each of which is an essence.[46]

No matter which experience introduces us to the realm of essence, it is found to be a world without time, change, or existence. It consists of ideals or types, each of which is identical with itself and different from all others.[47] Each essence has its own being which is strictly determined by its definition. And since the definition of an essence does not include existence (we can know *what* a thing is without knowing *that* it is), existence is not contained in essence. We should not imagine, therefore, that essences exist somewhere, either in the perceiving mind, or in matter, or in a divine mind. In short, "essences do not exist." For all that, they are not non-entities; they enjoy an ideal or phenomenal being peculiar to themselves which is more truly "being" than the being of physical things.

Nothing prevents an essence, while remaining unchanged and perfectly itself, from being copied or embodied an indefinite number of times in nature. Physical obstacles may prevent its exact reproduction, but this does not affect its essential universality. Essences, accordingly, are universal, but not in the sense of being mental abstractions or linguistic terms. The latter exist, whereas essences do not. "An essence is, then, not at all a mental state, a sensation, perception, or living thought; it is not an 'idea,' as this word is understood in British philosophy. It is an 'idea' only in the Platonic or graphic sense of being a theme open to consideration."[48] Neither is an essence a constituent part of things; it is not, for example, their inherent form. By perceiving material objects we project essences upon them, so that essences seem to inhabit them. Thus when we look at the sky it appears to be blue and round. But blueness and roundness are not intrinsic characteristics or forms of the sky; they are adventitious qualities which the sky acquires through perception, and they are real only in relation to the perceiver.[49]

2. *The Realm of Matter.* Santayana uses the terms "matter," "substance," and "existence" as practically synonymous. Matter is the basic substance or stuff of the universe; it is "the matrix and the source of everything; it is nature, the sphere of genesis, the universal mother."[50] It is also the realm of existence, which, as we have seen, animal faith posits as independent of thought.[51] We do not intuit or observe substance or matter, but only the essences with which it is clothed. We assume for practical reasons that these essences are signs of an independent, substantial world.

Since we encounter matter through our actions, we posit it as something dynamic and creative. Matter, according to Santayana, "is a primeval plastic substance of unknown potentiality, perpetually taking on new forms; the gist of materialism being that these forms are all passive and precarious, while the plastic stress of matter is alone creative and, as far as we can surmise, indestructive."[52] Essence is inert and incapable of acting: it must be chosen, if it is chosen, by some agent. This agent is matter, which blindly and irrationally selects, assumes, and exchanges essences. These essences in turn give concreteness and character to matter, making it, for example, in the observed sky, to be blue and round. Thus, for Santayana, "the lovely cloak nature wears is but essence playing over the flux of existence."[53]

Santayana agrees with Heraclitus' description of matter as a constant flux. However, he does not think that this flux is purely chaotic and lawless. The laws of nature, as we formulate them, are eternal essences more or less descriptive of nature but never adequate to express it. In matter itself there are not laws but only certain recurring habits or "tensions" which make measurement and prediction possible. The flux of matter in the universe has been somewhat canalized or habituated, so that we observe regularities in it, which we can symbolize in mathematical laws. Basically, however, matter remains inscrutable to us; not at all because it is unknowable in itself as Spencer thought, but because we are blind to its depths.[54] Our mind is geared to the intuition of essences, which is a world of appearances whose whole value lies on the surface.

3. *The Realm of Truth.* The flux of matter picks up and reflects only a portion of the infinite number of essences inhabiting the Realm of Essence. There are other essences, equally real and equally waiting selection, that in fact never have been or ever will be realized in nature. Still other essences cannot be manifested in nature at all, but are discovered only in the mind; such are the fancies of the imagination and the ideal constructions of logic and mathematics. For Santayana, truth is found only in the realm of essences that happen to be caught up by nature. When an event occurs, it has definite characteristics, each of which "illustrates" an eternal essence. The event itself is temporal and contingent; but once it has occurred it is eternally true that it has occurred at a particular point in space and time.[55] The truth of any fact or event, accordingly, is the complete and comprehensive description of it, including not only the immediate factors determining it but also the infinite relations it bears to other events and ideas. In Santayana's dramatic words, truth is "the splash any fact makes, or the penumbra it spreads, by dropping through the realm of essence."[56]

Essences themselves are neither true nor false; they are simply data to be experienced. If there were no existing facts or events, there would be no truth. But as soon as anything exists, truth appears, for "this existence must have one character rather than another, so that only one description of it in terms of essence will be complete; and this complete description, covering all its relations, will be the truth about it."[57] Hence truth finds a place among essences, not as they are in themselves, but as they are manifested in nature. The Realm of Truth is a part of the Realm of Essence; namely, the segment that is reflected in existence.

Truth, then, is an absolute and eternal essence which we can discover though never grasp in all its ramifications. It remains an ideal standard which our opinions should measure up to, and in relation to which they are correct or incorrect. Santayana sometimes speaks of opinions and judgments as true or false, but he prefers to call them correct or incorrect, lest a true opinion be thought to be truth itself. An opinion, judgment, or idea, he insists, is not the truth, for they are contingent facts whereas the truth is an eternal essence. Opinions may reproduce the truth in part, but "the truth in its wholeness outruns and completes their several deliverances, and is the standard which these deliverances conform to, in so far as they are true."[58] He rejects the pragmatic test of usefulness and the idealist criterion of coherence as irrelevant to truth.

An idea may be useful, beautiful, or comforting without being true; and even illusory ideas may be harmonious with each other. Truth is something different from utility, or coherence, or even conformity of opinion with fact; and it is also something more noble. It is the whole Realm of Essence, or the whole ideal system of qualities and relations, which the world has exemplified or will exemplify; or, to borrow Spinoza's phrase, it is all things seen under the form of eternity (*sub specie aeternitatis*).[59]

4. *The Realm of Spirit.* The intellect, seeking enlightenment, is interested only in the truth, but, for Santayana, this is not man's sole or most important interest. Truth is the good of the intellect, but it is not our ultimate good. The man who clings to the truth and nothing but the truth has a cold and prosaic mind. "Happiness in the truth," writes Santayana, "is like happiness in marriage, fruitful, lasting, and ironical. You could not have chosen better, yet this is not what you dreamt of."[60] Especially in his later writings the romantic tendency of his thought comes to the fore, and he strives to mount above truth to "the region of the imagined or the desired or the beautiful." It is here that he finds the highest ideals of the Realm of the Spirit.

In the Preface to the final part of the *Realms of Being*, entitled *The Realm of Spirit*, Santayana reiterates that he is a convinced materialist and naturalist, lest the title of his book mislead the reader. By the Realm of Spirit he does not mean a creative God, or a world of disembodied substances, or immaterial souls animating bodies. All substances, in his view, are material. Spirit is the inner light by which man becomes aware of the world and of his own self. It can also be called consciousness, attention, feeling, thought, "or any word that marks the total *inner* difference between being awake or asleep, alive or dead."[61] Spirit, then, is not something substantial like matter; it is an epiphenomenon—an evanescent, flickering flame—produced by a body that has developed a certain degree of organization and responsiveness to its environment.[62] Neither is Spirit a phenomenon or datum like an essence, though it has an affinity to essences because, like them, it is immaterial and unsubstantial. In short, spirit is neither the matter that generates it nor the essences that it beholds. It belongs neither to the Realm of Matter nor to the Realm of Essence but forms a new realm of being peculiar to itself.[63]

At first the spirit in man was formed for practical purposes: to look, to remember, to understand, so that it might guard the animal organism. But once awakened it could not help becoming reflective and contemplative. It became a spectator of the horrors and absurdities in the world and of its own tragic situation. Finding itself tied to the blind forces of matter, man's spirit, fascinated and tortured, asks to be saved. The primary concern of the philosopher, accordingly, is the problem of human freedom.[64]

Santayana pursued this problem throughout his life, from the early work *The Life of Reason* to the more mature *Realms of Being*. In the former he stresses that man's salvation consists in the development of intelligence and imagination for practical adjustment to his environment and for the harmonious organization of personal and social life. While granting with Aristotle that contemplation is the reward of action, he insists that "there is nothing stable or interesting to contemplate except objects relevant to action—the natural world and the mind's ideals."[65] In his later writings, while not repudiating the essential role of reason in the moral life, the emphasis shifts to disinterested contemplation, to detachment from worldly interests, and to disintoxication from human values. Happiness is now sought more resolutely in aesthetic experience and in "the pure spiritual life," which he describes with Plato as a turning from the temporal to the eternal Realm of Essences, without, however, subscribing to the Platonic enthusiasm for, and love of these essences, as though they were objects of urgent need or adoration.[66] The spiritual life, as Santayana advocated it and lived it in his later years, is well described by M. K. Munitz as "the free play of fancy that can roam undisturbed and joyful among strangely novel, distant, and different worlds, the varied imaginative excursions into which are to be enjoyed in their immediacy as subjective impressions, significant as indications neither of natural conditions nor of possible moral ideals."[67]

XXVI.

Pragmatism

SAILING home to America in 1900 after a successful lecture tour that took him to Aberdeen, Edinburgh, Glasgow, and Oxford, Josiah Royce wrote to his friend William James, "Everywhere they ask about you, and regard me only as the advance agent of the true American Theory. *That* they await from you."[1] The "true American Theory" which Royce's Scottish and English audiences were eagerly waiting to hear from James was pragmatism. The absolute idealism of Royce was familiar enough to them in its original Hegelian source and in the forms given it by the Cairds, Green, Bradley, and Bosanquet. But pragmatism was a new name in philosophy, a new way of philosophizing originating in America and expressing the practical—even, it was said, the commercial—spirit of its people. And James soon arrived to satisfy British curiosity. In 1901–1902 he gave, at Edinburgh, the Gifford Lectures entitled *The Varieties of Religious Experience*, and in 1908, at Oxford, the Hibbert Lectures, later published under the title *A Pluralistic Universe*. By this time the pragmatic movement was well known both in America and abroad through John Dewey's *Studies in Logical Theory* (1903), James' *Pragmatism* (1907), and F. C. S. Schiller's *Studies in Humanism* (1907).

The origins of pragmatism go back to the Metaphysical Club, an informal group that met for philosophical discussions at Cambridge, Massachusetts, in the early 1870s.[2] The meetings were generally held in the studies of either Charles Sanders Peirce or William James. Among others, the Club included Chauncey Wright, a competent mathematician, disciple of J. S. Mill, and defender of Darwinian evolution; Nicholas St. John Green, a skillful lawyer and follower of Jeremy Bentham; Oliver Wendell Holmes, Jr., later Associate Justice of the Supreme Court; and John Fiske, a philosophical historian and admirer of Darwin and Spencer. Although widely different in their interests and training, these men shared an empirical and positivistic approach to philosophy. In the main they were men of science, or at least they were vitally concerned with its new findings, especially Darwin's theory of evolution by natural selection, and they were eager to extend them to philosophy.[3] The title "The Metaphysical Club" expressed their defiance of the current antipathy to metaphysics. They did not want to exclude metaphysics from their discussions, at least insofar as it presented "a scientific side."[4]

It was at the meetings of this Club in 1871 that C. S. Peirce first propounded pragmatism as a logical method of handling philosophical problems.[5] At first it attracted little attention; not until it was taken up and considerably modified years later by William James did it receive wide notice. James considered Peirce to be the founder of pragmatism, and Peirce himself seems to have accepted this title. But he acknowledged his indebtedness to Nicholas St. John Green. In their meetings, he says, Green often stressed the importance of Alexander Bain's definition of belief as "that upon which a man is prepared to act."[6] "From this definition," Peirce continues, "pragmatism is scarce more than a corollary; so that I am disposed to think of him as the grandfather of pragmatism."[7] Whether "him" refers to Bain or, as appears more likely, to Green,[8] this clearly connects pragmatism with the nineteenth-century British positivist school of psychology, of which Bain was an outstanding exponent. In American pragmatism we find the meeting of the two main lines of nineteenth-century philosophy: British empiricism and utilitarianism with their insistence that ideas are to be tested and evaluated through their experienced effects or results, and German idealism with its exaltation of practical reason and will above the speculative intellect. The Americans, however, thoroughly reappraised and transformed these philosophies, so that pragmatism can truly be called an original creation.

It is impossible to give a simple account of pragmatism or to enclose it in a neat formula that all members of the movement would accept and interpret in the same way. Like contemporary existentialism, it defies definition. The founders themselves could not agree on its meaning. Thus, when Peirce saw the direction in which James was turning the movement, he gave up the name "pragmatism" in favor of "pragmaticism." The best way to grasp the American movement in all its complexity is to study it in the form it takes in its three chief exponents: C. S. Peirce, William James, and John Dewey. In Chapter XIX we have already considered the humanistic pragmatism of F. C. S. Schiller.

Charles Sanders Peirce

Ever since the collapse of Aristotelianism at the end of the Middle Ages there have been men who aspired to reconstruct philosophy on a new basis and to achieve for the modern world what Aristotle did for his. Peirce's aims as a philosopher were no less ambitious than this.[9] Convinced that the structure of Aristotle's philosophy was outmoded, and that the system of German idealism, then in vogue, was unbearable, he proposed to erect a new philosophical edifice that would last for generations. Like Aristotle, he wanted "to outline a theory so comprehensive that, for a long time to come, the entire work of human reason, in philosophy of every school and kind, in mathematics, in psychology, in physical science, in history, in sociology, and in whatever other department there may be, shall appear as the filling up of its details."[10]

The philosophical work Peirce actually accomplished fell far short of this goal. He wanted to be a system-builder on the grand scale, but he was unequipped for it both by temperament and ability. Instead of a comprehensive philosophical synthesis, he left to posterity a large number of printed articles and unpublished manuscripts, many of them in bits and pieces, containing at best a fragmentary philosophy. Filled with brilliant reflections, some of great moment for the development of American philosophy, his works are also replete with obscure, partially worked out, and even inconsistent ideas. It is no wonder that historians, making their way through the eight printed volumes of his posthumous *Collected Papers*, disagree on the final interpretation of his thought. No one of them, however, would think of questioning his philosophical acumen or his importance for twentieth-century philosophy.

search for a method

The philosopher who has ambitions to supplant Aristotle must begin by establishing a new logic and method of inquiry to take the place of Aristotle's. This is what Francis Bacon and René Descartes did at the beginning of modern philosophy, and it was also the procedure of C. S. Peirce. In his maturity, when he tried to put his writings into some order, he collected twelve or fourteen essays under the title *Search for a Method*. These essays concern the fundamentals of his new logic and pragmatic approach to philosophy. Space does not allow an exposition of the technicalities of his logic. All that can be done here is to explain the main points in his pragmatic method of inquiry.

All inquiry, according to Peirce, begins with doubt and, if successful, ends in belief. What is the difference between these two states of mind? There is, of course, a difference in the sensation of doubting and believing, but more important than this is the practical difference between them. Doubt irritates us and stimulates us to action until we get rid of it; it makes us struggle to reach a state of belief. Belief, on the other hand, is accompanied by calmness and satisfaction; we have no desire to avoid or change it. And once we are established in it, it shapes our actions by creating a habit prompting us to behave in a certain way when the occasion arises. Indeed, Peirce sometimes identifies a belief or an opinion with a habit of acting in a certain way. Thus he writes, "a genuine belief, or opinion, is something on which a man is prepared to act, and is therefore, in a general sense, a habit." Again, belief is "a habit of which we are conscious."[11]

Peirce stresses that inquiry must begin with "a real and living doubt," not with a "make-believe" doubt such as Descartes proposed. It is impossible to rid ourselves of all our opinions and convictions and begin in a state of universal doubt. We have to start our inquiry in the state in which we find ourselves at the moment, with all our prejudices and beliefs. The inquiry is set in motion by some new experience that challenges one of these beliefs.[12]

Another illusion of Descartes, inherited from Aristotle, is that inquiry must begin with certain self-evident principles. In Peirce's view there are no such principles or truths. If there were, he argues, philosophers should agree on their number and content, but in fact they do not. Their supposed primary principles are simply beliefs, which vary from person to person. Going to the heart of the matter, Peirce denies any intuitive knowledge that would give rise to self-evident principles. All knowledge, according to him, including knowledge of the self, of mental states, and even of sense data, involves a comparison or reference to other known objects, and hence it is not a direct intuition but a belief or hypothesis.[13] Moreover, he points out that an intuition would have to occur immediately, in a moment of time; but all knowledge requires a certain length of time in which to take place. An inquiry, therefore, does not begin with some ultimate and absolutely indubitable data, either first principles or first sensations, but only with propositions at the moment perfectly free from all actual doubt.[14]

Although its principles need not be self-evident, a properly conducted inquiry must use clear ideas. What is the best method of clarifying the meaning of our ideas? If we believe Descartes, an idea is clear when it is so familiar that it is never mistaken for another. But, Peirce argues, this does not enable us to distinguish between an idea that seems to be clear and one that really is. A familiar notion may well be very hazy. Leibniz, trying to improve on Descartes, placed the clarity and distinctness of ideas in the analysis of their abstract definitions. But this is also insufficient for Peirce; the analysis of definitions helps to put order into our concepts but it does not enable us to learn anything new.[15]

Peirce's own answer to this problem brings us to his new, pragmatic method of clarifying the meaning of ideas. According to this method, the only way of forming a clear idea of an object is to conceive its practical effects. The whole conception of the object will consist in its conceivable results. For example, what do we mean by calling a thing hard? Simply that it will not be scratched by many other substances. Similarly, a clear idea of weight consists simply in this, that a heavy body, in the absence of opposing force, will fall. In brief, "consider what effects, that might conceivably have practical bearings, we conceive the object of our conception to have. Then, our conception of these effects is the whole of our conception of the object."[16]

The most striking feature of this new theory of a concept is its recognition of an inseparable connection between rational cognition and rational purpose. The theory holds that "a *conception*, that is, the rational purport of a word or other expression, lies exclusively in its conceivable bearing upon the conduct of life." In order to express this practical bearing of knowledge upon life, Peirce calls his theory *pragviatism*.[17]

The newly coined term soon became popular, and it was adopted by Peirce's friend William James and the English philosopher F. C. S. Schiller. The meaning these men gave it, however, was not exactly Peirce's; so he coined the term "pragmaticism" to express his own theory—a term "ugly enough to be safe from kidnappers."[18] Unfortunately, but understandably, the new term never gained recognition, with the result that the name "pragmatism" covers several different, though allied, doctrines.

What is peculiar to the pragmatism of Peirce? First of all, he presents it as a method of clarifying ideas, and not precisely as a theory of truth, as William James does in *The Meaning of Truth*. The pragmatic method, for Peirce, aims at clarifying the meaning of our ideas as a necessary step in the inquiry for truth. Second, Peirce clarifies the meaning of ideas through the general consequences of experimenting with objects and not through their particular, sensible effects. In this respect, too, Peirce's pragmatism differs from that of James. James, the psychologist, was concerned with the individual, sensible effects of things upon human conduct. Peirce, the scientist and philosopher, was mainly interested in the universal or general aspects of observable objects, and he defined their meaning not by the private experience of the individual, but by the public or common experimental phenomena to which things give rise. He admits that pragmatism cannot account for the meaning of a proper name, like "George Washington"; such a word simply points out or denotes an individual. Pragmatism is concerned with the rational meaning of general words or ideas; and it defines their meaning not in terms of the sense data or phenomena to which they correspond, but by the phenomena to which things give rise when we act upon them by our experiments. For a pragmatist, rational meaning does not consist simply in an experiment (that is, some event that took place in the past), but in experimental phenomena, or "what *surely will* happen to everybody in the living future who shall fulfill certain conditions."[19]

A third feature of Peirce's pragmatism is that it posits as real the general objects whose meaning it establishes. These general objects, as we shall see, are primarily the laws of nature. Hence, even though pragmatism rejects almost all the statements of "ontological metaphysics" as meaningless gibberish, it does not eliminate metaphysics completely; it aims at purifying metaphysics by making it as far as possible "scientific." In so doing it retains the doctrine of scholastic realism (though re-interpreted), according to which universals are real.[20]

Having determined the nature of inquiry and having laid down the method of clarifying our ideas, Peirce next considers the correct way of establishing or "fixing" belief. Many men, he points out, use the method of tenacity. This consists in holding a fancied opinion, repeating it to oneself, and avoiding everything that might disturb it. This leads to great peace of mind, but it fails in practice because a man is bound to be shaken in his belief when he finds other men thinking differently. A man cannot suppress his impulse to question his beliefs if he finds them opposed to those of other men.

A more successful method, used by institutions, is authority. The state fixes political doctrines and the churches theological doctrines in this way. The results are "majestic" but the means do not respect freedom of inquiry. And yet,

"For the mass of mankind…there is perhaps no better method than this. If it is their highest impulse to be intellectual slaves, then slaves they ought to remain."[21]

A far more intellectual and respectable way to fix belief than the former two is the *a priori* method used by the founders of the systems of metaphysics. These systems usually do not rest upon observed facts, but upon fundamental principles that seem to be in agreement with reason. This is just another way of saying that they appeal to the taste of the philosophers who founded the systems; so that, for them, inquiry was a matter of developing their taste. The difficulty with this method is that taste loses fashion, with the result that metaphysicians have never come to any fixed agreement.[22]

The trouble with all these methods is that they rely upon some human factor or agency to establish belief. What is needed is a method of settling opinions by something permanent, external to man, and independent of our thinking. This, according to Peirce, is the method of science. The fundamental hypothesis of this method is: "There are real things, whose characters are entirely independent of our opinions about them; those realities affect our senses according to regular laws, and, though our sensations are as different as are our relations to the objects, yet, by taking advantage of the laws of perception, we can ascertain by reasoning how things really are and truly are; and any man, if he have sufficient experience and he reason enough about it, will be led to the one True conclusion."[23] The method of tenacity has strength, simplicity, and directness; the method of authority is the path of peace; the *a priori* method affords comfortable conclusions; but the scientific method alone enables us to form opinions that are in harmony with the facts. Faced with contradictory propositions, we have a feeling of dissatisfaction; we vaguely feel that there is some one thing to which a proposition should conform, and science alone offers a method of fixing our belief in harmony with it.

The scientific method extolled by Peirce was not something he learned from books but from long experience as a practicing scientist. Briefly stated, this method consists in the formulation of an hypothesis from data of observation, the derivation of consequences from the hypothesis, and the verification of these consequences by observation or experiment. In all cases, the conclusions of science are provisional and capable of further correction; they continually approach closer to reality but never completely coincide with it.

If an opinion or belief never absolutely corresponds to reality, what is meant by saying it is true? The application of the scientific method leads to stable or satisfactory beliefs, and their ultimate stability or satisfaction is a mark of their truth. But may not a man hold a false belief firmly and with perfect satisfaction? How can stability or satisfaction define truth without making it depend on the individual? In the opinion of Peirce, James and Schiller do not avoid this disastrous consequence, for they interpret the satisfaction in which truth consists to be that of the individual. In later life, when Peirce saw the individualistic trend that pragmatism was taking, he clarified his own view by stressing that the satisfaction in which truth consists is not the actual satisfaction of any individual, but "the satisfaction which *would* ultimately be found if the inquiry were pushed to its ultimate and indefeasible issue…a very different position from that of Mr. Schiller and the pragmatists of today."[24]

Peirce is here defining truth as an ideal to be sought, not by an individual, but by a community of minds working in concert. The quest for truth is the quest for the ideally satisfactory beliefs reached by a co-operative scientific inquiry. In short, truth may be described as "that concordance of an abstract statement with the ideal limit towards which endless investigation would tend to bring scientific belief."[25]

scientific metaphysics

Peirce classifies metaphysics among the theoretical sciences and divides it into ontology, or the study of the most general features of reality; religious metaphysics, or the study of God, human freedom, and immortality; and physical metaphysics, or the study of the real nature of space, time, matter, causation, and the like.

The importance Peirce gives to metaphysics can be seen from his statement that "the more abstract sciences should be developed earlier than the more concrete ones. For the more concrete sciences require as fundamental principles the results of the more abstract sciences…."[26] Now metaphysics, like logic, is a highly abstract science. Its healthy condition, therefore, is a requisite for progress in the other sciences. But at present it is "a puny, rickety, and scrofulous science," a "mere arena of ceaseless and trivial disputation."[27]

The reason for the deplorable condition of metaphysics is not its intrinsic difficulty. Its highly abstract character should make it the simplest and easiest of the sciences. True, not all its objects are open to direct observation, but neither are all the objects of physics. Metaphysics, like all the other sciences, rests upon observation: not upon special observations but upon the kinds "with which every man's experience is so saturated that he usually pays no particular attention to them."[28] Peirce thinks the main reason for the backward condition of metaphysics is the fact that it is cultivated by theologians and not by men of science. Theologians, he asserts, do not have the scientific spirit. Using the method of tenacity to fix their beliefs, they strive to confirm themselves in the beliefs of their childhood and to silence any suggestion in their hearts that they abandon their beliefs. The man of science, on the contrary, tries to see the errors of his beliefs—if he can be said to have any.[29]

Far from wishing to abandon metaphysics, therefore, Peirce wants to reform it and to establish it as an essential part of scientific inquiry. It is worth trying, he says, "whether by proceeding modestly, recognizing in metaphysics an observational science, and applying to it the universal methods of such science, without caring one straw what kind of conclusions we reach or what their tendencies may be, but just honestly applying induction and hypothesis, we cannot gain some ground for hoping that the disputes and obscurities of the subject may at last disappear."[30]

As Peirce pursues metaphysics, it is largely a quest for the ultimate categories in terms of which we can interpret the real world. The establishment of these categories results in hypotheses that admit of verification through their observable consequences. In this way Peirce feels that his metaphysics is truly scientific and that its method of inquiry conforms to that outlined in the preceding section. His metaphysics is not intended as a final or infallible statement, but tentative and subject to modification in the light of further evidence.

Peirce clearly distinguishes between metaphysics and phenomenology. The latter science (which he came to recognize only in later life through Hegel's *Phenomenology of Mind*), is the observation and analysis of experience and of all the features common to the objects of experience; in short, of "the collective total of all that is in any way or in any sense present to the mind, quite regardless of whether it corresponds to any real thing or not."[31] Hence phenomenology is not concerned with the reality or unreality of its objects, but attempts to formulate the essence of whatever appears to the mind. Metaphysics, on the other hand, is devoted to the study of phenomena insofar as they are real. Hence the importance, at the outset, for the metaphysician to have a clear grasp of the meaning of reality.

1. *Metaphysical terms.* The basic terms a metaphysician must elucidate, according to Peirce, are "being," "existence," and "reality." By being, Peirce means the sum total of possible objects of thought or speech. In short, being is the possible or the knowable.[32] How do we arrive at this notion? Not by observing that all possible objects of thought have in common some property called "being," for there is no such thing to be observed. We obtain the notion of being chiefly from the copula of propositions. We observe that in statements such as, "A man *is* a rational animal," and, "A griffin *is* a winged quadruped," the copula "is" has the same function of joining the predicate to the subject, and from this observation we form the conception of being. Accordingly, when we say that something possesses being, we do not mean that it has some property over and above the predicate attributed to it by the copula; we only mean that the predicate may be asserted of it.[33] From this, Peirce concludes that the notion of being has no content. It is completely indeterminate. Yet it is infinitely determinable; just as the copula "is" has no determination in itself, but an infinite variety of predicates can be added to it, thereby determining it and the subject to which it is joined.

Since being is completely indeterminate and lacking in content, Peirce, like Hegel, practically equates it with nothing. In a dialogue entitled "Truth, Being, and Nothing" Peirce's interlocutor objects to this depreciation of the notion of being. Remembering Parmenides, he exclaims, "Why, Pure Being is the very foundation of all wisdom." To which Peirce drily replies, "Say rather of that love which winds itself up in needless and senseless paradoxes."[34] One of these paradoxes is that "nothing" is also a being because it is a meaningful word.[35]

Existence comprises everything that actually is. It is the realm of the actual, in distinction to being, which is the realm of the possible. In the epistemological sense, an existent is that which is truly experienced; that is to say, an appearance that is due to the normal action of the senses, as distinguished from an illusion or hallucination, which is an appearance due to some organic fault. An existent impresses us with a strength and compulsion lacking in the experience of a nonexistent. Hence it can be described as a brute, irrational insistency—the notion, Peirce adds, that Duns Scotus likely wanted to convey by the term *haecceitas* (thisness).[36] Every existent is an individual; for "experience only informs us that single objects exist, and that each of these at each single date exists only in a single place." In the metaphysical sense, an existent is an individual in dynamic interaction with all the other individuals in the same universe.[37]

Although Peirce sometimes uses the words "reality and existence synonymously, speaking more exactly he distinguishes between them. Existents are individual facts, realities are the enduring laws or regularities that govern facts, the persistent patterns things follow in their interactions. Accordingly, a reality is general or universal, whereas an existent is individual. In the debate between nominalists and realists Peirce sides with the latter, insisting that universals are real. Nominalism in all its forms comes under his severe criticism. He sees nominalism everywhere: not only in William of Ockham but in most of the English philosophers, Descartes, Leibniz, Kant, and Hegel.[38] Duns Scotus receives warm praise for his realism, but Peirce thinks that even he was too nominalistic because he claimed that universal natures like *man* or *horse* are contracted to the mode of individuality in individual existents.[39] Scotus' views on universals "were only separated from nominalism by a hair."[40] Peirce says that he himself goes further than Scotus in the direction of scholastic realism. Not only are universals, in the sense of general laws of nature, real, but they are more real than the individual, contingent facts governed by the laws.[41] For Peirce, "Metaphysics is the science of Reality." By this he means that it deals with all phenomena insofar as they are governed by laws of nature, abstracting from their qualities and existential aspects.[42]

The exact meaning of reality is somewhat ambiguous in Peirce's philosophy. "Reality," he says, "is persistence, is regularity," for it is equivalent to universal law.[43] Sometimes he defines reality as independent of all human thought, not only individual but collective.[44] At other times, however, he asserts that reality, though independent of what any one individual thinks, is not independent of the co-operative thinking of men. He writes, "What anything really is, is what it may finally come to be known to be in the ideal state of complete information, so that reality depends on the ultimate decision of the community."[45] Thus, in the eyes of the New Realists, Peirce would not measure up to true realism, for he defines reality in terms of thought; he does not escape the egocentric predicament described in the preceding chapter. And indeed, he could hardly avoid this predicament, given his pragmatic method of clarifying ideas. As we have seen, this method consists in eliminating from the meaning of a concept everything except its practical effects. Applying this method to the concept of reality, he points out that the only effect real things have is to cause belief. Now, those who use the scientific method to establish belief may at first form different opinions, but "as each perfects his method and his processes, the results are found to move steadily together toward a destined centre. . . ." Truth is the opinion that is destined to be ultimately agreed upon by all scientists, and reality is the object represented in this opinion.[46]

2. *The reality of God.* The central point in Peirce's metaphysics is his doctrine of God. He frankly expresses his belief in the existence of God, or rather, as he prefers to say, the reality of God. The reason for this preference is that in the strict philosophical sense "to exist" means "to react with other like things in the environment." Since God obviously does not stand in this relation to the universe, it is better to speak of his reality.

Although Peirce does not hesitate to acknowledge God's reality, he makes it clear that our knowledge of God is slight indeed. It suffers from the fallibilism endemic to all our knowledge, and even more so than our knowledge of physics or psychology, for "man has no such genius for discoveries about God, Freedom, and Immortality, as he has for physical and psychical science."[47] No terms apply to God in the same sense in which they apply to creatures; they do not designate him literally but by analogy.

What is the meaning of the term "God"? Using his pragmatic maxim, Peirce looks to the effects God has on our actions. He suggests the following comparison. Suppose someone is well acquainted with a man of great character, who so influences his whole conduct that a mere glance at his portrait is enough to change his way of acting. Our situation is similar if we contemplate and study the physico-psychical universe: it can imbue us with principles of conduct just as a great man's works or conversations can. Thus we are led to form the notion of a cosmic mind or "vast consciousness" analogous to the human mind, and this is what we mean by God.[48]

That meditation on the universe can make a difference in one's conduct is abundantly clear from the examples of Buddha, Confucius, and Socrates, all of whom "from any point of view have had their ways of conduct determined by meditation upon the physico-psychical universe. . . ."[49] It is also evident from the superhuman courage such contemplation has given to priests who spend their lives helping those inflicted with leprosy. Is their strength derived from the power of truth or is it silly fanaticism? In short, is there really a God, or is he a figment of the mind?

Peirce does not think the reality of God can be proved by either deductive or inductive reasoning. It cannot be proved by pure deduction, which is the method of mathematics, because the conclusions of such deduction are as ideal as its hypothetical premises. Moreover, deduction does not lead to new knowledge; it only unfolds what the premises contain. Induction must also be ruled out, because God is not a theory to be tested by experiment. Nevertheless, we have an irresistible belief in God's reality; and if this is not the result of reasoning, it must arise from direct experience. This experience of God, according to Peirce, is not through reason but through instinct and love. These latter, Peirce assures us, are true means of knowing God: we have only to open our eyes and our heart, "which is also a perceptive organ," and we shall see him.[50]

In Peirce's view, belief in God's reality is not weakened but immeasurably strengthened by basing it upon instinct and sentiment and not upon reason. For, in his opinion, instinct is far more reliable than reason in practical questions and "matters of vital importance," though the opposite is true in theoretical matters. The scientist in the laboratory cannot rely upon instinct; he can only try its suggestions. But in regard to the greatest affairs of life, "the wise man follows his heart and does not trust his head."[51] This romantic exaltation of feeling and sentiment Peirce owes to the New England Transcendentalists, among whom he was born and raised. It is a side of his philosophy that is difficult, if not impossible to reconcile with his hard-headed, scientific approach to reality; and vet it is essential for understanding him completely.[52]

While rating rational argument below instinct as a means of knowing God, Peirce does not entirely dismiss it. He proposes what he calls a neglected argument for the reality of God, a "humble argument" that appeals to every honest man and produces a truly religious belief in God's reality and nearness. The method of this argument, which Peirce calls "musement," does not follow a rigidly logical pattern, but allows the mind to drift freely over its object, somewhat as in reverie or in pure play, but with a lively exercise of its powers. It is the method the scientist uses as he ponders observed facts and casts about for an hypothesis to explain them. Now, if the "muser" contemplates the vast extent and order of the universe, the unspeakable variety of its parts with their similarities and mutual connections, "the idea of God's Reality will be sure sooner or later to be found an attractive fancy.... The more he ponders it, the more it will find response in every part of his mind, for its beauty, for its supplying an ideal of life, and for its thoroughly satisfactory explanation of his whole...environment."[53] Although this hypothesis cannot be verified by experiment, it has a much greater initial plausibility than others, and it has a commanding influence over the whole conduct of life of those who accept it.[54]

William James

William James' acquaintance with Peirce dates from 1861, when they studied chemistry together at the Lawrence Scientific School at Harvard.[55] In the late 1860s James attended Peirce's lectures in the philosophy of science at Harvard, read his articles, and often talked privately with him about philosophical matters. As a member of the Metaphysical Club in the early 1870s, he had the opportunity of hearing Peirce debate, and he himself took an active part in the discussions that gave birth to pragmatism. Although only three years his junior, James was far behind Peirce in philosophical development, and he listened with fascination to the words of this gifted man who proposed a pragmatic way of philosophizing in close harmony with the scientific spirit of the time.

Both men were scientists, but the cast of their scientific thinking was very different. Peirce was attracted to mathematics and logic—subjects whose abstractness and universality repelled James. His own bent was rather toward biology, physiology, and psychology—sciences of life, suffused with warmth and color and marked by concreteness and individuality. He was soon to devote himself passionately to psychology and to become a pioneer in making it a true science. Later he worked out his own version of pragmatism, which reveals the deep influence of Peirce but which differs from Peirce's pragmatism precisely in its psychologism and individualism.[56]

Pragmatism appealed to James as the only solution of the dilemma of philosophy in his day. At the beginning of the twentieth century, he tells us, aspirants to philosophy were offered a choice between two kinds. The first, represented by men such as Haeckel and Spencer, was materialistic, empiricist, and irreligious. It appealed to those whom James calls "tough-minded" thinkers, who wanted scientific evidence and facts and were willing to bow religion politely out of the front door. The second proposed by transcendentalists such as

Green, the Cairds, Bosanquet, and James' own confrere Royce, was idealistic, rationalistic, and religious. It found favor with "tender-minded" philosophers, who by temperament incline to religion and intellectualism and not to science and the concrete facts of life. In short, the choice was between an empirical philosophy that was not religious enough, and a religious philosophy that was not empirical enough.

The merit of pragmatism, in James' view, is to offer a way out of this dilemma. At no time in history, he says, have there been as many men with a decidedly empiricist bent; the men of his generation are almost born scientific. But not only do they want facts and science; they also want religion. In other words, they are not simply "tough-minded" or "tender-minded"; they have a mingling of these two temperaments. James thought that pragmatism would appeal to both sides of the contemporary mind. It is an empiricism, and therefore grounded on concrete facts; but it also takes into account man's religious aspirations. Unlike Spencer's philosophy, it does not dismiss the positive religious constructions of mankind but respects them and reveals their basis in religious experience. Thus pragmatism is an apt mediator between materialism and idealism, and it plays this mediating role while remaining within the limits of strict empiricism.[57]

radical empiricism

The philosophy of William James, considered in its generality, is best described as a radical empiricism. This embraces not only a theory of knowledge, of which pragmatism is a part, but it also aspires to be a metaphysics of experience. It is an empiricism because it demands that ideas be tested by particular experiences and that the meaning of ideas be limited to such experiences. In James' view, the only subjects of philosophical debate are those that are definable in terms drawn from experience. His thought is also empirical because it lays stress on the individual and the part, in opposition to rationalism which tends to emphasize universals and to make wholes prior to parts both in the logical and real orders.[58]

James' empiricism flows from the main stream of English philosophy and particularly from Hume. However, he is critical of Hume's empiricism for failing to be radical enough. A radical empiricism, he insists, must not admit any element not directly experienced, but neither must it exclude any feature of direct experience. Hume erred on the second score; he failed to see that the facts of experience are not "loose and separate" but mutually connected, and that their relations are also items of direct experience. For an empiricism that is radical, "the relations between things, conjunctive as well as disjunctive, are just as much matters of direct experience, neither more so nor less so, than the things themselves."[59] For example, we experience the relations of similarity, difference, causality, and change. The advantage of recognizing relations as items of experience is that it forestalls the rationalist objection to empiricism that there must be something beyond experience—substances, intellectual categories, or selves—to account for the continuity and connection of experienced facts.

The picture of the world drawn by James is that of a flux or stream of discrete but interconnected experiences. Like all phenomenalists, he is opposed to a reality lying beyond experience. There is no "trans-empirical reality"; the world is pure experience, which James defines (in a manner reminiscent of Bergson) as "the immediate flux of life which furnishes the material to our later reflection with its conceptual categories."[60]

What is the experience that makes up the universe? There is no general stuff of which experience is made, no undifferentiated or neutral element underlying all experiences. James rejects all forms of monism, which would reduce the plurality in the universe to a basic unity. He feels no attraction to the pantheism of Spinoza with its reduction of all things to the unity of one substance, or to the idealism of Royce with its assumption of the manifold of experience in the unity of an Absolute Mind. The universe, in James' view, is irreducibly pluralistic. Experience is made of "just what appears, of space, of intensity, of flatness, brownness, heaviness, or what not.... Experience is only a collective name for all these sensible natures, and save for time and space (and, if you like, for 'being') there appears no universal element of which all things are made."[61] This may give the impression that James identifies experience with spatio-temporal phenomena, but he makes it clear that it includes other experiences as well, such as the ideal worlds of logic and mathematics, and the mystical world of religious experience.

It will be noted that here James uses the word "experience" to designate the *objects* of experience. However, he does not limit the word to these data; pure experience also includes mind or consciousness. In other words, experience embraces both the knowing subject and the known object. Thus James does not deny the duality of subject and object, familiar to all theories of knowledge, but he gives it a thoroughly empirical interpretation. Philosophers, he says, have generally treated the knower and the thing known as two completely separate entities and then they have tried to connect them in some artificial way; for example, by placing a representative image between them or by appealing to an Absolute Mind to bridge these finite entities. James prefers to embrace both subject and object within experience.

Knowledge, according to James, is of two types: immediate or intuitive, and conceptual or representative.[62] The first type he calls "knowledge of acquaintance," the second "knowledge about."[63] Knowledge of acquaintance is the first and most basic kind. It is the direct perception of something; for example, the sight of a piece of white paper. Knowledge about something is mediate knowledge through an image or concept; for example, the knowledge most of us have of tigers in India. We know most things with mediate knowledge, but in every case our knowledge about anything derives from direct knowledge and it is never more than a provisional substitute for it. Knowledge is at its best when it is intuitive and direct.

When we know something intuitively or immediately, the object known and the content of our experience are identical. Thus when we see a piece of paper, it enters into our experience, so that "the paper seen and the seeing of it are only two names for one indivisible fact which, properly named, is *the datum*, *the phenomenon*, or *the experience*."[64]

"Paper" and "mind" are not two separate entities but two names given to one experience. We call it paper insofar as it stands in relation to a pen, a desk, and so on; in short, insofar as it is part of the spatiotemporal world. We call it mind insofar as it enters the stream of our internal thinking. Hence the paper plays two different roles; one as the object thought of, the other as the thought of the object. In its first role the paper is objective, in the second it is subjective.[65]

In this view, mind or consciousness is not an entity but a function; it is nothing but the function of knowing. By this function we do not passively mirror the external world, nor do we create it. We select or choose those items in it that interest us for our survival and for our well-being. Strictly speaking, consciousness does not exist, for it is not a substance or a being. It is only the special activity of an organism, selecting and grouping elements of experience for its own use. An individual consciousness or mind is the experience of a special grouping or arrangement of items of experience. This relational or functional view of consciousness was elaborated by James as early as his *Principles of Psychology*.

The second type of knowledge described by James is conceptual or representative. We know some things even though they are not present to us, such as tigers in India. But in what sense do we "know" them? We have no immediate acquaintance with them, so that the function of knowing does not directly introduce them into our thought. In this case there is no identity between the object known and the content of our experience. Rather, an image or idea substitutes for the object. The problem, then, is to know how the image or idea can perform this function. How does it render something absent present to the knower?

James has no liking for the answer of scholastic philosophy, "which is only common sense grown pedantic," that the object has a special kind of existence, called "intentional inexistence," within the knower. This is hardly the empirical answer James is looking for. More satisfactory is the reply that an idea *points* toward the absent object. If we ask what an empiricist means by *pointing*, James replies that it is nothing mysterious; it is only some operation consequent upon the idea, such as rejecting a jaguar if that beast were shown to us as a tiger, or assenting to a genuine tiger if one is brought into our presence, or traveling to India to see a tiger. In brief, when I have an idea of tigers in India, my mind is so connected with the actual tigers in that country that if I were to follow up the idea I should be brought face to face with them. The pointing of our thought to the tigers, then, "is known simply and solely as a procession of mental associates and motor consequences that follow on the thought, and that would lead harmoniously, if followed out, into some ideal or real context, or even into the immediate presence, of the tigers."[66]

This not only solves the problem of the relation between an idea and its object in a thoroughly empirical way; it also gives James a pragmatic criterion for distinguishing between true and false ideas. A true idea is one that leads to successful operations such as were described above; a false idea is one that fails to lead to successful operations. Thus James' radical empiricism leads naturally to his pragmatism.

pragmatism

In all likelihood it was C. S. Peirce who coined the term "pragmatism" while presenting his revolutionary approach to philosophy in the discussions of the Metaphysical Club in the 1870s. For twenty years little notice was taken of his revolutionary approach to philosophy, until James took it up in 1898 in a lecture entitled "Philosophical Conceptions and Practical Results." With the publication of his *Pragmatism* in 1907 and *The Meaning of Truth* in 1909 he launched the pragmatic movement in American philosophy, and ever since he has been popularly identified with it. His pragmatism, however, is not exactly the same as that of Peirce. While Peirce acknowledged a basic agreement between his own philosophy and James' radical empiricism, he protested that James did not always interpret the pragmatic maxim in the same way as he did.[67]

James speaks of pragmatism both as a method of settling disputes and also as a theory of truth. We shall consider each of these aspects of his pragmatic theory, noting the divergences between himself and Peirce.

The pragmatic method, in James' view, is "primarily a method of settling metaphysical disputes that otherwise might be interminable."[68] For example, is the world one or many, determined or free in its activities, material or spiritual? The pragmatist asks what practical difference it would make which of these alternatives is true. If they come to the same thing, as far as their consequences are concerned, the dispute is idle. "There can *be* no difference anywhere," James writes, "that doesn't *wake* a difference elsewhere—no difference in abstract truth that doesn't express itself in a difference in concrete fact and in conduct consequent upon that fact, imposed on somebody, somehow, somewhere and somewhen."[69] James thinks that many philosophical controversies fade into insignificance the moment this test is applied.

If a philosopher accepts this criterion, James continues, it will affect the whole temper of his thought. He will adopt the empiricist rather than the rationalist attitude toward the world. He will turn away from bad *a priori* reasoning, fixed principles, closed systems, pretended absolutes, and finality in truth, toward concrete facts and the practical consequences of theories. Theories will not be considered to be final answers to enigmas but instruments by which to change reality. The pragmatist, in brief, adopts the "attitude of looking away from first things, principles, 'categories,' supposed necessities; and of looking towards last things, fruits, consequences, facts."[70] He agrees with the nominalist in always appealing to particulars, with the utilitarian in stressing the practical aspects of ideas, and with the positivist in disdaining verbal solutions, useless questions, and metaphysical abstractions.

This description of the pragmatic attitude is faithful to the spirit of Peirce insofar as it stresses the turning toward the consequences of theories for the determination of their truth, but he thought that it betrayed pragmatism in making it nominalistic. For Peirce, the greatest need of philosophy in his day was to abandon nominalism. Nor did Peirce agree with James that pragmatism could solve any real problems. In Peirce's view, all that it can do is to show that some problems are not real ones, and to open our minds to the reception of evidence that appertains to those real problems but not to furnish the evidence for their solution.[71]

Besides defining a certain philosophical method and attitude, James conceives pragmatism as a theory of truth. In developing it in this direction he once more departs from Peirce's original conception of it, which was primarily that of a method of clarifying ideas and fixing beliefs. Peirce left only scattered suggestions as to the nature of truth; James worked out in detail a pragmatic theory of truth, but one that was not entirely to Peirce's liking.

When describing James' radical empiricism, we noted that ideas function as substitutes for objects when the latter are not present to us; by means of ideas we can have "knowledge about" things, failing an immediate acquaintance with them. Truth is a property of some of these ideas. Ideas are true when they point to, or agree with objects; they are false when they fail to do so. The crux of the problem of truth is the nature of this agreement or "pointing."

We should notice at the outset that James conceives this agreement as a relation between two parts of our experience: the idea or subjective side, and reality or the objective side. We have already seen that James' radical empiricism places both of these within experience. It is true that a reality is independent of the idea we have of it. But there are no realities independent of experience: all being, like all thought, falls within experience. Hence the relation by which an idea agrees with reality, or points to it, must also fall under experience. The relation begins in one part of experience (the idea) and terminates in another (the reality). Accordingly, truth is the satisfactory accommodation of one item of our experience to another, not the agreement of experience with a reality independent of it.

But what precisely is the relation of agreement or "pointing" in which truth consists? An idea is not simply a mirror or passive reflection of reality; it is a habit of acting in a certain way, and therefore it is a plan or guide for our action. If we follow out this plan, we will have a series of experiences that either lead up to the reality or do not. For example, our idea of tigers prompts us to perform certain actions that either lead us into the presence of tigers or do not. If these experiences carry us to the reality, the idea that prompted them is true, if they fail to do so it is false. In short, an idea is true if it leads us to its object. The series of experiences linking the idea with the reality is the concrete relation of agreement or pointing.[72]

Accordingly, truth is not an unchanging or inherent property of an idea; it is something that happens to an idea when it is verified by experience. "The truth of an idea is not a stagnant property inherent in it. Truth *happens* to an idea. It becomes true, is *made* true by events. Its verity *is* in fact an event, a process, the process namely of its verifying itself, its verifications."[73] Neither is truth something we discover in reality, as though it existed there before we thought about it. We make truth by formulating ideas and acting upon them; the process of verification (as the word indicates) is indeed one of "truth-making." Bergson puts his finger on the essential nature of truth in James' philosophy when he writes: "We invent truth in order to use reality, as we create mechanical devices to use natural forces. It seems to me that we can sum up the whole essence of the pragmatic conception of truth in a formula such as this: *while in other doctrines a new truth is a discovery for pragmatism it is an invention.*"[74]

Although James insists that it is one of man's primary duties to pursue true ideas, he does not regard their possession as an end in itself but only as "a preliminary means towards other vital satisfactions."[75] This is understandable against the background of his voluntaristic psychology, which claims that perception and thinking are only for the sake of action, and action is for the satisfaction of some human need.[76] Hence James sees little value in a purely objective knowledge divorced from human desires and human reasons for knowing. True ideas are always useful ones; they enable us to use reality in order to satisfy some need. Thus truth is a species of good: "The true is the name of whatever proves itself to be good in the way of belief, and good, too, for definite, assignable reasons."[77]

There are, accordingly, two aspects to a true idea: its verification by the facts, and its usefulness for life. These can be distinguished but not separated; unless we have some need or desire for an object, we will not be led to verify our idea of it. If we have no interest in tigers, we will not be prompted to set in motion the actions that will lead us into their presence. An idea is nothing but an instrument for satisfying some desire or need, and its verification in experience is not an end in itself but a process that is fulfilled only in its actual use.

This twofold aspect of truth introduces a certain ambiguity into James' pragmatism. When he speaks of a true idea as one that works, or is successful, this can have two meanings. It can mean that a true idea is verified by reality, that it fits the facts; or it can mean that a true idea serves our interest or need. James sometimes speaks of truth in the first sense, protesting that his notion of truth is identical with that of science; but sometimes he speaks another language, as when he says that "an idea is 'true' so long as to believe it is profitable to our lives."[78] He sees no real difference in these two ways of speaking of truth; it means exactly the same thing, in his view, to say that something is useful because it is true, and to say that it is true because it is useful.[79]

James' critics were quick to exploit the ambiguity in his language. When he said that the true is the expedient in our ways of thinking, Josiah Royce protested that to reduce truth to expediency is to be disloyal to the demands of objective scientific inquiry. He imagined a pragmatist taking the witness stand and swearing: "I promise to tell whatever is expedient and nothing but what is expedient, so help me future experience!"[80] When James spoke of the truth of an idea as its "cash value in experience," Bertrand Russell objected that this is the typical American attitude of seeing everything in terms of money. When James used the term "satisfactory" as a criterion of truth, his critics protested that the mere fact of finding it satisfying to think one is Napoleon does not make it true that one is Napoleon.

In reply to his critics James insists that he does not mean to identify truth with the expedient or the practical in the narrow sense of these terms. An idea is said to "work" or to be practical (and consequently to be true) in the broad sense of fitting in with the rest of our experience. "Any idea upon which we can ride, so to speak; any idea that will carry us prosperously from any one part of our experience to any other part, linking things satisfactorily, working securely, simplifying, saving labor; is true for just so much, true in so far forth, true *in-*

strumentally."[81] James does not think this is different from the scientific notion of truth. He protests that he never claimed that just anything we find satisfactory can be treated as true; no matter how satisfactory a belief may be, it would have to be called false if it were unsatisfactory because it contradicted what we know of physical reality.

In justice to James, this objective side of his theory of truth must be given full recognition; but its subjective side must also be taken into account. He holds that there are objective realities, independent of our ideas, and that our beliefs start from them and terminate in them. But reality is not something fixed and eternal, as the rationalists claim; nor is truth a static relation between our ideas and reality. Both are interacting parts of our experience: truths emerge from facts, and then mingle with them and add to them. Thus truth, like reality, is ever on the move; it is faced toward the future, toward growth and progress. A truth is a verification process, and as such it is made by us for the purpose of satisfying some desire or need. The truth of the process consists in its success in putting us in contact with reality, thereby satisfying our desires.

Since individuals differ in their needs and desires, it is understandable that James' pragmatism should stress the role of the individual in determining the truth. An idea is true insofar as it is satisfactory, but what satisfies one person does not always satisfy another. Hence truth is to a certain degree plastic and relative to the individual.[82] James is here moving in the opposite direction to that of Peirce. As we have seen, Peirce stresses truth as a communal aim, and he denies that the meaning of ideas is in any way determined by the individual. James, on the contrary, has the temperament of an individualist and nominalist. With Peirce, he sometimes speaks of an absolute truth ("that ideal vanishing-point towards which we imagine that all our temporary truths will some day converge"),[83] but in his view the temporary truth we have to live by must be in accord with the vital interests and beliefs of the individual person who holds them.

belief and religion

The pragmatic method enables the philosopher to arrive at some truths; not absolute truths, to be sure, but beliefs supported by adequate reasons. These beliefs are grounded on intellectual evidence, and they are true as far as the evidence goes. Other propositions or hypotheses are supported by insufficient evidence to call forth our assent. For James, the main religious beliefs held by men fall within this category. Although these beliefs play a most important role in the lives of individuals and of societies, they make no more than a probable appeal to the intellect.

Faced with this situation, James asks if it is ever right to believe beyond the evidence. Is it ever justified to decide an issue on other than intellectual grounds; to let our will or emotional nature tip the scales when reason fails to do so?

To these questions the English mathematician and philosopher W. K. Clifford (1845–1879) replied with a resounding NO! Like his contemporary Thomas Huxley (1825–1895), Clifford considered it immoral to believe anything on insufficient evidence. In his essay "The Ethics of Belief" he argued that we have a duty to mankind to guard ourselves from all beliefs that are unproved or questionable. Even if a belief is true, if it is accepted on insufficient evidence the pleasure taken in it is stolen and sinful. Clifford did not want to restrict our beliefs to those based on our own experience; he admitted the validity of inferring truths from our experience on the assumption of the uniformity of nature, and even of relying upon the statements of other persons as long as they were reputable and knowledgeable. But in his opinion great religious leaders, such as Mohammed and Buddha, were not trustworthy witnesses to the supernatural truths they taught, and consequently it would be presumptuous to believe them. Clifford did not mention the name of Christ, but one feels that this was to avoid directly offending his Christian readers. The burden of his essay is that we are morally obliged to limit our judgments to those supported directly or indirectly by scientific evidence, and this excludes religious belief.[84]

James' essay on "The Will to Believe" is a forceful reply to Clifford. In his opinion, Clifford looks upon human nature with the narrow eyes of an intellectualist, unappreciative of the volitional and "passional nature" of man. James urges that our will and emotions play a large part—indeed the major part—in producing our beliefs, and it is only fair to recognize the fact. Men of Clifford's type are unconsciously swayed by their emotions and feelings. "When the Cliffords tell us how sinful it is to be Christians on such 'insufficient evidence,'" James writes, "insufficiency is really the last thing they have in mind. For them the evidence is absolutely sufficient, only it makes the other way. They believe so completely in an anti-Christian order of the universe that there is no living option: Christianity is a dead hypothesis from the start."[85]

James was not a credulous person; in fact, at one period he suffered from incredulity, and only after undergoing a personal moral crisis did he appreciate the vital importance of faith. In 1870 he acutely felt the lack of a philosophy to live by and the ebbing of his desire to live. How could one live and act effectively without adopting a moral attitude toward the world; that is to say, without striving for the *good*, whether this takes the form of a hope of overcoming evil or a resolve to die bravely in the face of an unconquerable evil? In either case a man needs a vigorous will, and this is possible only if we believe in its freedom. But how can we be sure the will is free? The answer to this question and the solution of James' crisis came with his reading of Charles Renouvier's *Deuxième Essai*. Renouvier, who has been called the greatest single influence upon the development of James' philosophy,[86] defined free will as "the sustaining of a thought *because I choose to*, when I might have other thoughts."[87] For Renouvier, the best argument for the freedom of the will is our ability to think freely: we are faced with a choice of positions in many theoretical matters, and we can freely adopt the one we prefer. The freedom of the will is a case in point. Is the will free or determined? The only way we can finally settle the matter is by an exercise of free choice affirming our liberty. Renouvier says in a passage quoted by James: "I prefer to affirm my liberty and to affirm it by means of my liberty."[88]

This vigorous affirmation of the freedom of the will was balm to James' flagging spirit. It was just what he needed to cure his soul-sickness. He records in his diary on April 30, 1870: "I think that yesterday was a crisis in my life. I finished the first part of Renouvier's second *Essai* and see no reason why his definition of free will—'the sustaining of a thought *because I choose to* when I might have other thoughts'—need be the definition of an illusion. At any rate, I will assume for the present—until next year—that it is no illusion. My first act of free will shall be to believe in free will."[89]

This experience confirmed in James' mind the right to believe in what is desirable or salutary for life, even though the intellect does not have sufficient evidence for the belief. But is there no danger in thus allowing the will and emotions to determine our beliefs? Is not Clifford right in warning that we become dupes if we allow our desires and fears to sway our judgments? Is it not better to go without belief forever rather than take the chance of believing a lie?

James is willing to agree that matters of fact should ordinarily be investigated as fully as possible before judgment is passed on them. As long as there is no urgent need to act and no grave loss in missing the truth, we should not make up our minds until the objective evidence is at hand. This is the case with almost all scientific questions. There is no hurry in deciding them, so it is better not to risk making a mistake by a premature judgment. But sometimes we are forced to make up our mind. A judge in a law court, for example, has to decide on the best evidence attainable at the moment. Forced judgments are often necessary in such practical matters; but even in speculative questions we cannot always wait with impunity until coercive evidence has arrived. Chief among these are moral and religious questions. By their very nature they cannot be settled by appealing to sensible or logical proofs, and yet we have to act on them, and our action implies that we have adopted a position in their regard.

Consider moral problems first. A moral question does not concern what sensibly exists but what is good, or would be good if it did exist. For example, is the world morally good? Is truth possible for man? Is man's supreme good the unlimited discovery of facts and correction of false beliefs? Science cannot settle these questions; it can tell us what exists but not the value or worth of what exists or does not exist. For this we must not consult science but what Pascal calls our "heart." Even the scientist consults his heart and not his science when he lays it down that man's supreme good lies in the unlimited discovery of facts or in some other good resulting from their discovery. The skeptic who casts doubt on the moral character of the world does so not with irrefutable logic but with his whole nature, including his emotions and will. In short, moral beliefs are ultimately decided by our will and not by our head.[90]

Does this mean that they are completely arbitrary and incapable of verification? Not at all, according to James. Like all hypotheses they are verified by their results or consequences. If we adopt a moral attitude toward the world and act upon it, we bring moral values into existence; we help to make the world better. In this case, "belief creates its own verification." "This world *is* good, we must say, since it is what we make it,—and we shall make it good."[91] The pessimist or moral skeptic, on the other hand, by refusing to commit himself to the good, fails to contribute to the world's betterment and loses any chance of gaining the goods he might win by getting on the winning side. It does no good to advise prudent skepticism in morality; in moral matters doubt is often practically the same as outright denial. If I refuse to stop a murder because I am doubtful whether it be justifiable homicide, I am virtually abetting the crime. "Skepticism in moral matters is an active ally of immorality. Who is not for is against. The universe will have no neutrals in these questions. In theory as in practice, dodge or hedge, or talk as we like about a wise scepticism, we are really doing volunteer military service for one side or the other."[92] Consequently, in moral matters faith is necessary, both because proof comes only after we have made an active choice of one side of a question, and because our act of belief is a necessary factor in promoting moral goodness.

Since religion, for James, is largely an assertion of values, this justification of faith applies to it as well. Stripped of their accidental differences, he says, religions make two basic claims: (1) There is an eternal perfection or good, which religions represent in the personal form of a God, or gods; (2) We are better off even now if we believe in this eternal good. These affirmations of religion cannot be proved scientifically, and yet James does not think we should on this account suspend judgment on them. For this is tantamount to denying them, and to deny them is to lose the good religion brings to us if it be true. Like Pascal, James is willing to wager on the truth of religion, because it is his only chance to reap its harvest. Clifford and his fellow scientists may rail against him for risking error, but is not their fear of error also an expression of passion and of will? Has he not an equal right to hope, to follow the inclination of his "passional nature" in this case where no less than his salvation is at stake?[93]

James feels he has the more right to religious belief as it is the most rational in the broad sense of satisfying "those powers of our nature which we hold in highest esteem." "Not an energy of our active nature to which it does not authoritatively appeal, not an emotion of which it does not normally and naturally release the springs. At a single stroke, it changes the dead blank *it* of the world into a living *thou*, with whom the whole man may have dealings."[94] Hence belief in God satisfies "every mental need in strictly normal measure"; He is "the normal object of the mind's belief," so that we can never feel at home with materialism or agnosticism even if they were true.[95]

These broad assertions receive colorful documentation in James' *The Varieties of Religious Experience*. This great study in religious psychology, which draws upon religious phenomena from various ages, places, and religions, concludes that religious experience increases the spiritual strength of the believer; it opens up a new life for him and puts him in contact with a new saving force outside himself. The believer "becomes conscious that [his] higher part is conterminous and continuous with a MORE of the same quality, which is operative in the universe outside of him, and which he can keep in working touch with, and in a fashion get on board of and save himself when all his lower being has gone to pieces in the wreck."[96]

Is this experience only a psychological phenomenon or is the religious man in contact with a reality distinct from, and superior to himself? The evidence of religious experience leads James to believe that the higher reaches of our being plunge into "an altogether other dimension of existence from the sensible and merely 'understandable' world." This mystical or supernatural region is the source of our moral ideals and impulses. When we commune with it, changes take place in our personality: "We are turned into new men, and consequences in the way of conduct follow in the natural world upon our regenerative change."[97] Pragmatically, therefore, this unseen or mystical world makes a difference in our lives; it produces effects in our world, so there is no philosophical reason for calling it unreal. This supreme reality, whom Christians call God, is real because he produces real effects.

James' pragmatic approach to religion permits him to hazard little more than this about God. He denies any significance to the metaphysical, as distinct from the moral attributes of God, such as his aseity, necessity, immateriality, simplicity, infinity, and so on. These call for no distinctive adjustment in our conduct, and hence their truth or falsity makes no vital difference to religion. It is ordinarily assumed that there is only one God and that he is infinite, but James' study of religious experience does not necessarily lead to these conclusions. "The only thing that it unequivocally testifies to is that we can experience union with *something* larger than ourselves and in that union find our greatest peace."[98]

As for the immortality of the soul, at least in his later years James considered it probable. In *The Varieties of Religions Experience* he does not commit himself on the subject, though he shows respect for the results of psychical research pointing to the possibility of "spirit-return."[99] His essay on *Human Immortality* attempts to remove objections to immortality and to show its compatibility with the findings of psychology. To the objection that since thought is a function of the brain it must perish with this organ, he suggests that the brain does not produce thought but simply transmits it, somewhat as a prism transmits light. Consciousness may stream into us from a world beyond, our brain being an instrument that at once particularizes and distorts it. On this hypothesis, destruction of the brain does not entail the elimination of thought itself but only of "the particular determination which the brain imposes."[100] Immortal life would then be a possibility, though not personal immortality.

conclusion

The pragmatisms of Peirce and James were ingenious attempts to bring together in one consistent doctrine two widely different aspects of the intellectual life in America at the turn of the century: (1) Transcendentalism, which had its beginning in Jonathan Edwards' religion of the "heart" and came to full flower in Emerson, and (2) the scientific movement, which was gaining momentum and would soon carry the day. Scientists in their own right, Peirce and James wanted to formulate a philosophy in accord with the new scientific spirit; but they were unwilling to abandon completely the metaphysical and religious heritage of the past two centuries of American thought. As a consequence, they elaborated a pragmatic theory broad enough to include meaningful statements and truths not only about objects capable of scientific verification, but also about objects of belief, such as God and human freedom, that cannot be verified in such a rigorous fashion.

The consistency of this broad theory was quickly challenged by the critics of pragmatism. In an article of 1908, Arthur Lovejoy found that pragmatism, far from being a single coherent doctrine, broke down into thirteen divergent pragmatisms![101] Pragmatism, he says, is primarily a theory of the meaning of propositions, but it is so ambiguously conceived that it divides at once into two different doctrines. The first holds that the meaning of a proposition consists in the future consequences in experience which it directly or indirectly predicts will occur, whether it be believed or not. The second places the meaning of a proposition in the future consequences of *believing* it. The difference between these two variants of pragmatism distinguished by Lovejoy is the role belief plays in the second. In the first, a statement is meaningful because it has experiential consequences; in the second, a statement is meaningful because *belief* in it has experiential consequences; for example, the statement "God exists" has meaning because I experience a difference in my life as a result of believing it.

Although Lovejoy and other critics of James stress the distinction between these two criteria of meaning, James himself sees no fundamental difference between them, and he embraces both within the same pragmatic theory. In his view, in the actual work of determining the meaning of propositions and of verifying them by their experiential consequences, belief is always necessary. Even the scientist must have faith in his hypothesis if he is effectively to put it to the test.[102] The difference between a scientist and a religious thinker is not that the latter has faith and the former does not, but that the religious thinker cannot verify his beliefs as rigorously or as technically as the scientist. For all that, both Peirce and James agree that the most significant and vital beliefs of man are those of religion. To James especially, the problems of God, freedom, and immortality are the most absorbing of all, and he does not hesitate to call himself a supernaturalist, though a "piecemeal" one.[103]

Not all pragmatists, however, employed the pragmatic method with the interests and spirit of William James. John Dewey, for one, did not think that it could be fruitfully applied to problems touching the supernatural. Interpreting pragmatism in a much narrower sense than James, he abandoned the metaphysical and religious heritage of the nineteenth century and pointed American philosophy toward naturalism.

John Dewey

There was little in Dewey's early philosophical development to suggest the commanding position he would one day hold in pragmatism, or the enormous influence he would wield on the broader educational, social, and cultural scenes in America.[104] His first acquaintance with philosophy was as an undergraduate at the University of Vermont under H. A. P. Torrey. Torrey's lectures were based on Scottish common-sense realism, the philosophy that still predominated in the colleges of New England but was moribund in Dewey's time. Since the American Revolution it had been used by the clergy (who almost exclusively occupied the chairs of philosophy) as a bulwark against the sensism and materialism of eighteenth-century philosophy. Dewey was unimpressed by its alliance with religion or by its appeal to intuition as a source of truth. More significant, in his view, were the teachings of James Marsh, a former professor at Vermont. Marsh was one of the first Americans to study and teach German philosophy, and his ideas were still alive on the campus when Dewey was a student.

New vistas opened up for Dewey in the graduate school of the newly founded Johns Hopkins University, which he attended from 1882 to 1884. There he followed two courses in logic given by C. S. Peirce, and he was a member of the Metaphysical Club begun by Peirce in imitation of the Cambridge Club. At this time, however, Dewey seems to have learned little from the founder of pragmatism. He knew him chiefly as a teacher of formal logic—a subject that had little appeal to him. He does not even mention the name of Peirce in his autobiographical sketch "From Absolutism to Experimentalism."

The most important figure in the development of Dewey's thought at Johns Hopkins was George Sylvester Morris, his professor of philosophy. Morris had studied philosophy in Germany under Adolf Trendelenburg, and on his return to the States he taught a form of Hegelianism mingled with elements of Aristotelianism. Morris tried to reconcile idealism with the nineteenth-century movements in the experimental and natural sciences, which were being championed at Johns Hopkins. In particular, he attempted to integrate with his idealism the view that mental powers are natural energies whose development and functions can be studied experimentally. His pupil, John Dewey, both at Johns Hopkins and later as a teacher of philosophy under him at the University of Michigan, continued this line of thought. During this early period Dewey was a firm adherent of idealism. Hegelianism appealed to him as a means of unifying his emotional and intellectual life, which he sought unsuccessfully to do in the Congregational Church in which he was raised. He also looked upon the philosophy of Hegel as the best philosophical framework into which the current discoveries in biology and psychology could be integrated. Even at this early date he was convinced that these findings, especially Darwin's theory of evolution, demanded a radical change in the conception of nature and philosophical thinking, but he thought that this was possible within the broad structure of idealism.[105]

During the next fifteen years Dewey drifted away from Hegelianism, though he acknowledges that it left a permanent deposit in his thinking. He abandoned Hegel's notion of an objective mind that is manifested in social institutions, but he kept the idea of the power of the individual's cultural environment to shape his beliefs and intellectual attitudes. He also retained an emphasis on continuity and on the role of conflict in nature and experience, though he held these on empirical grounds rather than on a theory of dialectic. These were years in which he was vainly striving to accommodate his growing naturalism to an idealistic interpretation of nature; when, for example, he attempted to integrate the discoveries of Wundt in psychology and Darwin in biology within the view that the bodily organism and nature as a whole have a mind or spirit which predetermines man's ideals and values.

Dewey's reading of James' *Principles of Psychology* (1890) was the most important single influence in turning him away from idealism toward a behavioristic and naturalistic view of man. James taught him that intelligence has a biological foundation, having evolved in nature as the result of the interaction of organisms and their environment. In this view, intelligence itself is a mode of behavior; it is the specific way in which a living organism interacts with its environment, pursuing ends and choosing means to attain them. Values and purposes are not predetermined by an Absolute Mind but are either discovered in reality or created by man himself as he struggles to adapt himself to the world in which he lives. As the full import of James' notion of intelligence came home to Dewey, he became convinced that no mere revision of idealism was needed, but a radical reconstruction of philosophy.[106]

reconstruction of philosophy

The reconstruction of philosophy Dewey proposes cannot be understood without an appreciation of his theory of the origin of philosophy. Only if we grasp his notion that philosophy originated in the emotional and social life of man, and not in the search for the answers to purely intellectual problems, can we see the role he conceives for it in the modern world.

Dewey pictures primitive man as a creature of emotion, moved primarily by his desires, hopes, fears, loves, and hates. It was foreign to his primitive nature to check his fancies by facts and to organize his ideas logically. Out of his emotional experiences he wove dramatic tales which, when repeated, were generalized in the traditions of a social group. These traditions were the social heritage and possession of the group, establishing its beliefs and norms of moral conduct, and tending to be consolidated in order to establish wider social unity, as in Judea, Greece, and Rome. The rulers accelerated the centralization of traditions and beliefs in order to extend and strengthen their political authority and power.[107]

Philosophy had its beginning with the organization and generalization of ideas and beliefs, but it did not truly emerge until they were incorporated into a logical system and bolstered by intellectual proofs. The impetus to base them upon such proofs came from the growing body of factual knowledge in the community. Factual knowledge was amassed chiefly in the pursuit of technology, that is, in the construction of tools to be used in controlling nature for the benefit of man. The knowledge of facts originated among the lower class, and hence lacked the prestige and authority of the ancient beliefs guarded by the ruling classes. On one side, then, were the religious and poetical beliefs with their definite social and political value and function, kept by the ruling classes; on the other, was the prosaic, factual knowledge in the keeping of the common people. Clash between them was inevitable, as in Greece at the time of Socrates. He tried to reconcile the two, while giving preference to the method of matter of fact. The result was his condemnation for contemning the gods and corrupting the youth.

As positive knowledge and the critical, inquiring spirit grew, they tended to undermine the traditional beliefs and the society they held together. So a solution was sought by basing the essentials of the traditional beliefs on reason. "To put it in a word, that which had rested upon custom was to be restored, resting no longer upon the habits of the past, but upon the very metaphysics of Being and the Universe. Metaphysics is a substitute for custom as the source and guarantor of higher moral and social values—that is the leading theme of the classic philosophe of Europe, as evolved by Plato and Aristotle—a philosophy, let us always recall, renewed and restated by the Christian philosophers of Medieval Europe."[108]

Thus the classical philosophies of the Western world grew up with a social mission to perform; they aimed "to justify on rational grounds the spirit, though not the form, of accepted beliefs and traditional customs."[109] For example, Plato and Aristotle gave a reasoned defense of the deepest ideals and aspiration of Greek civilization; medieval Christianity used classical philosophy, especially that of Aristotle, to justify itself to reason; Hegelian idealism defended the ideas and institutions that were menaced by the new spirit of science and popular government.

The emotional and social origins of philosophy, in Dewey's view, account for still other traits of philosophy of the classical type. It displays a great devotion to logical system and to the apparatus of reason and proof in order to compensate for the fact that it does not deal with matters of fact that can be empirically verified. Its over-pretentious claim to certainty can be traced to the same source. The traditional customs, from which philosophy grew, claimed to give certain and immutable laws of conduct, and philosophy itself very early in its history likewise pretended to be conclusive and final. The classic philosophers have kept something of this temper; they have insisted that, unlike the special sciences, philosophy reaches final and complete truth. They also arrogated to themselves the universality and comprehensiveness of traditional customs and beliefs. As tradition influenced all the details of community life, so philosophy claimed to be universal and all-embracing. Classic philosophy supported this pretension to universality by distinguishing between two realms of being: the realm of ultimate and absolute reality, and the empirical, phenomenal world of everyday life. The first realm (the special domain of philosophy) corresponds to the religious and supernatural world of popular tradition, and like this world it is held to be the final source of truth about the empirical world and the ultimate sanction of moral conduct. Over against this realm is the imperfect and perishing world of practical affairs and positive science. Philosophy claimed to demonstrate the existence of a transcendent and absolute reality or God, and to reveal his nature and attributes; correspondingly it boasted possession of a higher means of knowledge than that used by positive science and ordinary practical experience. This characteristic of classic philosophy, in Dewey's opinion, affects its nature most deeply, and it is the characteristic that he repudiates most vigorously.

Dewey's purpose in presenting this theory of the genesis of philosophy is both critical and constructive. By showing its origin in the emotional and social experiences of man, he thinks he has undermined the classic type of philosophy more effectively than if he tried to refute it logically. At the same time he hopes to give his reader a new, positive view of what philosophy should be in the future. Philosophers have believed that they were dealing with ultimate reality, while in fact they were occupied with "the precious values embedded in social traditions." In other words, they thought that their subject matter was intellectual, but in reality it was social and emotional. Philosophers of the future should openly and deliberately do what their predecessors did unconsciously; they should "clarify men's ideas as to the social and moral strifes of their own day."[110] They should give up their barren metaphysics of Being, with its distinction between two realms of existence, its claim to a higher mode of knowing than that of the positive sciences, and its pretension to reach absolute certainty. To compensate for this, they will throw light on the moral forces that move mankind and lead it to a more ordered and intelligent happiness. Philosophy will still be a vision, but not an intuition of a supreme reality. Its chief function will be "to free men's minds from bias and prejudice and to enlarge their perceptions of the world about them."[111]

This is the aim Dewey himself relentlessly pursues in numerous books and articles written over the period of more than half a century. A glance through their titles suffices to reveal his broad interest in the social, educational, scientific, economical and political issues of his day. One finds few of the usual philosophical titles among them, with the exception of logic and ethics. This is only to be expected in the light of his conception of the nature and purpose of philosophy. Philosophy, he says, is not outside of and above all other pursuits, with a preserve of its own; it is one among other human activities, different in its scope and function, but not isolated from them. Its subject matter is not some reality apart from the changing world in which we live; it is "a continuously interconnected field of experience." In this field the philosopher analyzes and interrelates the typical modes of human experience, such as the practical or utilitarian, the ethical, the aesthetic, scientific, and religious. He also deals with society in its organized and institutional form—the sociocultural world that generates social questions, such as "the value of research for social progress; the bearing of psychology upon educational procedure; the mutual relations of fine and industrial art," to mention but a few.[112]

Such is the material that Dewey finds grist for his mill. He regards inquiry into the problems of the existence of God, creation, or the final end of the universe as futile and unrewarding. Philosophy is rather a method "of locating and interpreting the more serious of the conflicts that occur in life, and a method of projecting ways for dealing with them: a method of moral and political diagnosis and prognosis."[113] The main task of American philosophy at the present time is to resolve the pressing problems of democracy.

If this is the appropriate subject matter of philosophy, what is the method of inquiry best suited to deal with it? Dewey's logic of inquiry brings us to the very heart of his projected reconstruction of philosophy.

theory of inquiry

As we have seen, philosophy, in Dewey's opinion, is an intellectual expression of the ideals and aspirations of a particular culture. This is true of logic as well. The logic of Aristotle, for example, was fitted to the conditions of Greek science and culture in the fourth century B.C. Greek culture was characterized by a highly developed aesthetic sense, and the Greek philosopher-scientists transferred the qualities of a work of art to nature: as a Greek urn or temple was a qualitative whole with measure, proportion, and fixed limits, so they looked upon a natural object as something having design and form. In the technical language of the Greeks, it had an *eidos*; that is to say, a species or fixed form, which was thought to be the central principle of intelligibility in nature. Change, as such, was considered to be unintelligible; it could be known only as it was enclosed within fixed limits which mark its beginning and end. Change began and ended with substances whose essences or forms were unchanging. The purpose of science was to uncover, within the flux of change, the permanent essential forms of substances. In the logic of Aristotle, these substances became logical subjects, and rules were laid down for defining and classifying their essential forms.[114]

Although it was adequate for its day, Aristotle's logic is ill-fitted to serve the needs of modern man. The revolution in modern science, especially since the appearance of Darwin's *Origin of Species*, has banished fixed forms or species from nature and forced attention upon the importance of change. Today scientists no longer try to define substances or to discover their essential attributes; for the most part they seek laws of nature. They want to know the conditions under which changes take place and the most general laws exemplified in them. This implies a radically new attitude toward change. Whereas the Greeks regarded it as unintelligible and even as something evil, modern science makes it the center of attention: it seeks to correlate one change with another in order to control future events and use them for the benefit of mankind. In short, its object is to gain power over nature.[115] Never in history has Francis Bacon's aphorism been truer: Knowledge is power. Dewey regards Bacon as the great forerunner of the modern spirit and the prophet of the pragmatic conception of knowledge because he stressed that the true aim of knowledge is control over natural forces.[116]

Dewey's logic is entirely geared to this practical end. He defines thinking as the intelligent way of dealing with predicaments in which a man finds himself. Faced with a doubtful or problematic situation, he will, if he is wise, begin a chain of inquiry to find a satisfactory solution of his problems. As Peirce already noted, in the beginning of inquiry there is doubt, but this doubt is not only "subjective"; the existential situation itself that sets the inquiry going is problematic or indeterminate. The purpose of inquiry is to make the situation determinate, and therefore controllable. More exactly, "Inquiry is the controlled or directed transformation of an indeterminate situation into one that is so determinate in its constituent distinctions and relations as to convert the elements of the original situation into a unified whole."[117]

Thinking is thus an indirect way of reacting to a problematic situation. A man may use direct action to solve a problem, as when he kicks a stone to remove it from his path. But in most situations direct action is not successful; thinking is necessary, and by this is meant that we reconstruct a problematic situation in our imagination so as to suggest activity that will bring about a new situation in which the problem is solved. Thought is not a passive reflecting on an already existing situation, or a mere copying of an antecedent reality. Rather it has the active role of reconstructing situations and of selecting and organizing means to achieve desired ends.

It will be noticed that for Dewey knowledge is essentially a way of dealing with situations[118]; it is not the direct or immediate grasping of reality. Dewey has the Kantian aversion to the notion of an intellectual insight into reality. In scholastic terminology, thinking is *ratio* rather than *intellectus*: rational procedure or inquiry rather than intellectual insight.[119] Not that he denies a direct knowledge or apprehension of the meaning of words or objects. Do we not know at once and without questioning what a centaur or book is? Do we not see directly that *this* is a typewriter and *that* is a book? What Dewey does deny, however, is that this knowledge is truly original and immediate, in the sense of unmediated by previous experience: "it is a product, mediated through certain organic mechanisms of retention and habit, and it presupposes prior experiences and mediated conclusions drawn from them."[120]

There is, then, no primary intellectual apprehension of reality; there are no self-evident first principles at the beginning of knowledge. There is only the experience of objects—for example, the perception of the stone blocking my path—that raises the problem the mind attempts to resolve. But is not this experience a kind of knowledge? Not at all, according to Dewey. Experiences are undergone, enjoyed or suffered, but they are not known or understood prior to some intelligent action. A scientist and a clodhopper have the same sense perceptions of objects in a laboratory, but only the scientist *knows* them, because only he has experimented with them. As Dewey uses the term, knowledge is not the passive experience of objects; it is the result of the active processes of thinking, the end product of intelligent acting.[121]

Just as there is no intellectual insight into reality at the beginning of an inquiry, so there is none at the end. Dewey vigorously attacks the view that the object of inquiry is the conformity of the mind to some previously existing reality, or the knowledge of the real properties of things. He traces this classic notion to what he calls the "spectator theory of knowledge," according to which knowledge has a fixed and timeless object to which human knowing makes no difference. This presupposes that the object of knowing is antecedent to our mental acts and is totally unaffected by them. In fact, Dewey claims, the object of inquiry or knowledge is *the solution of a problem*, and this solution is *made* by our thinking. The object known, then, is a construction, or better a reconstruction, of our own; it is the original problematic situation refashioned by our activity so as to solve the problem.[122]

Dewey finds this theory of inquiry best exemplified in modern science. The scientist today, he says, has abandoned the notion—current even in Newton's time—that science reveals the inner structure of things. Instead he is content to observe, to experiment, and to measure objects in order to control them for man's use. It is important to notice that he does not simply observe nature; he operates upon it, often with elaborate laboratory techniques, varying the conditions under which objects are observed and making new arrangements among them. In order to handle objects more effectively, he translates them into quantitative terms; red, for example, becomes a certain number and green another number. He knows, of course, that the object in its ultimate reality is not a number, any more than an article for sale is so many dollars and cents. The price is the effective way to think of the article for the purpose of exchange; and so, too, the most efficient way to think of nature for the purpose of control and use is to resolve it into mathematical terms.[123]

Thus the trend in modern science is toward operational concepts or ideas, concepts that designate "operations to be performed or already performed."[124] Using the illustration of the physicist P. W. Bridgman, Dewey points out that the scientific concept of length includes nothing but the set of operations by which length is determined; for example, the laying of one physical object alongside another a number of times. When this is done, new relations are set up between the two objects, owing to the operation performed upon them; and it is these relationships, which are deliberately superadded to our original experience of things, that is disclosed by the concept of length.[125] This is an example of a physical concept, because it designates operations performed upon reality. Mathematical or logical concepts are also operational, but the operations they designate are performed upon symbols; the concept of two, for example, designates the adding of one and one.[126] According to this view, "In general, we mean by any concept nothing more than a set of operations; the *concept is synonymous with the corresponding set of operations*."[127]

If this is true, ideas are plans of operations to be performed. Their role in inquiry is the practical one of being instruments for reaching the solution of a problem. Ideas are essentially instruments of action, whether the action is exercised upon the physical world or upon mathematical or logical symbols. For this reason, Dewey's version of pragmatism is aptly called "instrumentalism."

As plans of future operations, the truth-value of ideas will be determined by the outcome of these operations. If the operations they direct give us the results we require, they will be sound ideas; if they fail to yield these results, they will be unsound. Hence the test of the validity of an idea is not its conformity to an independent reality, but its success in reconstructing a problematic situation so as to bring about its solution.[128]

A true idea, then, is one that is satisfactory; but Dewey explains that the satisfaction referred to is not just a personal one, but the "satisfaction of the conditions prescribed by the problem."[129] He protests that he does not believe that just *anything* that satisfies him is true: "I have never identified any satisfaction with the truth of an idea, save *that* satisfaction which arises when the idea as working hypothesis or tentative method is applied to prior existences in such a way as to fulfill what it intends."[130]

This instrumental theory of ideas does away with the classic distinction between knowing and doing. Knowing is no longer an operation distinct from action and superior to it; it is intelligently directed action. The experimental method puts action at the center of ideas and makes doing "the very heart of knowing."[131] We shall have occasion to see later the influence of this notion on Dewey's philosophy of education.

Dewey does not claim that the operational way of forming ideas is the only valid one. But he does maintain that it is the most effective way of thinking and that it is the ideal to be reached in every department of thought. It has already been successfully applied to the physical sciences since the time of Galileo, and to the biological sciences since the time of Darwin. In his own day, Dewey was most anxious to extend it to the political and social sciences. Of what value are ideas that merely reduplicate the already existing world? They may afford the satisfaction of a photograph, but they make no difference in our lives. Science and philosophy should improve the world in which we live; they should heighten its value, or else they miss their main goal. Ideas are of value only if they pass into actions that rearrange and reconstruct the world.[132]

theory of values

The upshot of Dewey's theory of inquiry is that knowledge should not be occupied with the contemplation of eternal Being; rather, it should be thoroughly domesticated and naturalized within the life of society and put to the service of human ends and purposes. Knowledge is not an end in itself; it is a means or instrument for directing human actions to appropriate goals. We have still to know, however, what these goals are. What is the good life for man that knowledge should help him to achieve? How are we to judge whether or not something is good for man? In short, what is of value for human life? These questions bring us to Dewey's theory of values, which complements and completes his theory of inquiry.

Looking over the history of philosophy, Dewey finds theories of value divided into two kinds.[133] The first holds that there are eternal values transcending concrete experience, and that these are the standards or models by which we should judge the goods and evils of human life. Loyalty to a Supreme Being and to the values that derive from it is the hallmark of this notion of value. The mass of people, under the influence of institutional religion, believe that eternal values are divinely revealed as norms for their conduct; rationalist philosophers, formulating this belief in philosophical terms, claim that these values can be known by reason. As examples of such philosophers Dewey cites contemporary idealists, such as Josiah Royce.

The second theory of value is that of traditional empiricism. According to this view, the very fact that an object is liked or enjoyed confers value upon it, so that values can be discovered empirically by observing the actual preferences and enjoyments of men.

Dewey prefers the empirical view of values to the rationalist because it associates values with the concrete experiences of desire and satisfaction; but he objects to it for the same reason that he criticizes the traditional empirical theory of knowledge. Traditional empiricism, of the type of Locke and Mill, derives conceptual knowledge from the sense perception of actually existing objects. Dewey, on the contrary, insists that such knowledge, while empirically based, refers to the future consequences of activity. Pragmatic or operational thinking locates the objects of knowledge in constructs of human acts rather than in antecedently existing beings; in short, it is *prospective* and not *retrospective*. Similarly, Dewey argues that when values are seen from a pragmatic or operational point of view, they are not based simply on desires or satisfactions but on desires and satisfactions that are consequences of intelligent action.[134]

If this is true, there is a distinction between judgments of fact and judgments of value. It was a fact that the first man to taste roast pig, in Charles Lamb's story, liked it. But this is not the same as to judge that roast pork is good for man. To say that something is liked or enjoyed is to report an existing fact; it is not to express a value. Roast pork might have turned out to be harmful, and then, while tasting good, it would not have been valuable. It would have been desired, but not desirable. In order to discover whether roast pork is good for man, further inquiry was needed. More factual information had to be obtained: that roast pork can be easily digested, that it contains nutritious elements, that it contributes to bodily growth, and so on. After this the value judgment could be made that roast pork is good for man.

This example shows that judgments of fact and of value are not identical, but it also reveals that value judgments are ultimately reducible to factual judgments. Dewey vigorously opposes the separation of value and fact, such as we found, for example in the ethics of Royce. For Royce, no amassing of factual data about man and the world will yield a value judgment; physics and metaphysics can tell us *what is*, but not *what ought to be*. Only a distinctly moral insight enables us to make the latter judgment. Dewey retorts that "The 'desirable,' or the object which *should* be desired, does not descend out of the a priori blue or as an imperative from a moral Mount Sinai."[135] We learn what ought to be desired, or what is valuable, as a result of intelligent inquiry. In other words, we come to know the good exactly in the same way that we arrive at a knowledge of the truth: by investigation, experimentation, and observation of the consequences of our actions. This means that in order to make intelligent judgments of value we should call upon the help of the scientific method and of scientific knowledge. Our moral theory, then, will be based upon the realities of human nature and upon a scientific study of the connection of these realities with the physical world. The result will be an ethics that is not idealistic, but realistic and naturalistic. It will not automatically solve all the moral problems of man; but it will enable us to approach these problems with a fund of growing knowledge that will add significant values to our lives.[136]

When Dewey speaks of adding values to our lives he is to be taken quite literally. From his pragmatic point of view, values are not discovered ready-made in the world; they must be constructed by us through intelligent action. There is an analogy, then, between knowledge and value. As we have seen, a reality is only a possible object of knowledge; it becomes an object only when it has been reconstructed by us in the process of solving a problem. Similarly, our initial experience of enjoying or liking is only the possibility of a value. The enjoyment becomes a value when we bring our mind to bear upon it, so that it is the result of intelligent action. In Dewey's example of the eating of roast pork, the original enjoyment is only the possibility of a value; it becomes a secure and significant good after an investigation has established the beneficial effects of roast pork on man.

As we construct truth, then, so we construct the good. We do not *discover* goods or ends to pursue; we have to create them for ourselves by our thinking. Nor is there a fixed and final end that we should strive to reach, the attainment of which brings happiness. Each end that we intelligently create for ourselves, when attained, becomes a means toward a further end. Just as each problem solved raises a further problem for the human mind, so each good attained opens up new possibilities of enriching human life. What was an end thus becomes a means to the creation of new values. "Moral good, like every good," Dewey writes, "consists in a satisfaction of the forces of human nature, in welfare, happiness."[137] But this satisfaction or happiness is not reached once for all by attaining perfection, or by the contemplation of supreme Being; it is gained by vital activity, which for man means process and growth. In Dewey's reconstruction of morals, "The end is no longer a terminus or limit to be reached. It is the active process of transforming the existent situation. Not perfection as a final goal, but the ever-enduring process of perfecting, maturing, refining is the aim in living.... Growth itself is the only moral 'end.' "[138] Thus, Dewey's moral theory is thoroughly in accord with his view of life as creative activity and evolutionary growth. It has the "forward look" typical of all pragmatic thinking; prospective rather than retrospective, it makes the best life for man the one that assures him the greatest future expansion of his creative powers.

Dewey's theory of value culminates in his doctrine of religion. For him, God is not a living reality. The notion of God—or, as he prefers to say, of the divine—refers to the unity of the ideal ends or values that we project in our imagination and strive to realize by our action. These ideal possibilities are not actually present in a supernatural deity, nor are they pure fantasies. They are realized embryonically in the natural order (for example, love in human society, beauty in art, truth in knowledge). The imagination seizes upon these most precious natural goods, idealizes and unites them, and situates them in a supernatural Being. According to Dewey, this localization of ideal values in a supernatural God has obscured their real nature and has weakened their force. But he thinks that the unifying work itself of the imagination is useful and indeed urgently needed. It introduces perspective into the piecemeal and fluctuating experiences of life. "It can unify interests and energies now dispersed; it can direct action and generate the heat of emotion and the light of intelligence."[139] Whatever does this is, so far forth, religious. In short, the religious sense gives us a comprehensive attitude toward moral ideals to be striven for, and at the same time unifies the self and integrates it with the universe.

democracy and education

Dewey's political views are dominated by his ethical ideal. The supreme test of any social institution is the contribution it makes to "the all-around growth of every member of society."[140] If this test is applied to political systems, the democratic is found to be the most desirable. No other political arrangement enables all the members of society to share so extensively the interests of the group, or allows its members to interact so freely and fully. Internally and externally, it removes the barriers that would keep the members of society from free intercourse and communication of experience.[141] Thus democracy opens the way for a man to participate most completely in the good life of society; it affords him the fullest measure of "shared experience," which for Dewey is the greatest of human goods.[142]

The democracy that Dewey praises is not merely a political system. Democratic government, with its universal suffrage, recurring elections, responsibility of those in political power to the voters, and so on, is only a means of bringing about democracy "as the truly human way of living." This is democracy in the moral sense of the term. "The keynote of democracy as a way of life," writes Dewey, "may be expressed, it seems to me, as the necessity for participation of every mature human being in formation of the values that regulate the living of men together: which is necessary from the standpoint of both the general social welfare and the full development of human beings as individuals."[143] The social welfare demands that everyone help to create the values of the social body because each person has a distinctive contribution to make, without which society is the poorer. The social body must draw upon all its potential resources, and these extend even to the masses. It is the democratic faith that intelligence, though distributed unequally among men, is sufficiently general that each individual has something to contribute to the wisdom of the group. The full development of the individual also demands that we share in producing and managing the social institutions by which he lives. All men are not equally endowed by nature, but they are equal before the law, and they are entitled to equal opportunity of developing their own capacities, whether they be large or small. They cannot do so under an autocratic and authoritarian regime, which assumes that the intelligence needed for social action is limited to a superior few.

Dewey's writings on democracy have won for him the title "The Philosopher of American Democracy." He is even better known, however, for his philosophy of education. Not content with formulating a theory of education, he founded the Laboratory School of Education at Chicago in order to put it to the test. His name is usually—and quite rightly—associated with progressive education, although he would not agree with some of the extreme forms it has taken.

Dewey's philosophy of education follows naturally from his ethical and epistemological views. The traditional conception of education, he says, is that it is a preparation children have to undergo in order to get ready for adulthood: it is the process whereby they acquire knowledge for future use and form habits required in later life. But this implies that adulthood is the end of human life, whereas Dewey has assured us that it has no fixed end: the only goal it has is growth and the continuous reconstruction of experience. It is not the future, then, but the present that is most significant in education. No matter what stage a person is in, he is still in process of growth, and he is still in need of education. Education, accordingly, "is not, save as a by-product, a preparation for something coming later. Getting from the present the degree and kind of growth there is in it is education. This is a constant function, independent of age. The best thing that can be said about any special process of education, like that of the formal school period, is that it renders its subject capable of further education: more sensitive to conditions of growth and more able to take advantage of them. Acquisition of skill, possession of knowledge, attainment of culture are not ends: they are marks of growth and means to its continuing."[144]

If this is true, the education of children should follow the same pattern as that whereby adults grow and develop in experience. Now this, as we have seen, is the method of experimental inquiry. Knowing is intelligently directed activity; it is experimenting with things, reconstructing problematic situations in order to find their solutions. This, then, is the most effective way for a child to learn. He should take an active part in investigating some problem until he has reached its final resolution. Education should proceed not by inculcating fixed conclusions but by developing intelligence as a method of action.

Under these conditions, activity will be normal in the classroom. Children will not be made to assume a rigid posture, as though their minds alone are to be educated while their bodies are disciplined to inactivity. Desks and chairs will be designed not just for listening but for working.[145] Subjects will be chosen by the teacher that interest the student and pose a problem for him. The student will then be supplied with the materials necessary to solve his problem and directed to work out the solution in such a way that the solution is his own. Thus the student will learn how to think problems through and will experience the actual process of learning. This educational procedure—Dewey assures us—requires discipline and order in the classroom; not a discipline that is applied externally as in traditional education, but one that is imposed by the nature of the students' activity. Dewey contrasts previous theories with the new "progressive" education as follows: "To imposition from above is opposed expression and cultivation of individuality; to learning from texts and teachers, learning through experience; to acquisition of isolated skills and techniques by drill is opposed acquisition of them as means of attaining ends which make direct vital appeal; to preparation for a more or less remote future is opposed making the most of the opportunities of present life; to static aims and materials is opposed acquaintance with a changing world."[146]

Since education, according to Dewey, is a process of living, and since human life is social in character, the school must be organized as a social unit. The school should aim at developing a spirit of social co-operation and community life. "The school itself shall be made a genuine form of active community life, instead of a place set apart in which to learn lessons."[147] Students should be stimulated to act as members of a group, sharing common interests and sympathetically communicating with each other as they work out their problems together. This social type of education is the only one in harmony with the democratic ideal, and it is the only one that will develop citizens who can advance society through intelligent activity within a social context.

EPILOGUE

NINETEENTH-CENTURY philosophical speculation was dominated by the Kantian revolution. Inasmuch as metaphysics had set out to ask questions for which no empirically verifiable answers could be found, it had been pronounced dead. This destructive part of the work of Kant was to become the charter of the many minds that find in scientific knowledge the complete answer to their intellectual needs. The legitimate posterity of Kant's critical examination of the limitations of speculative knowledge have been, in all countries, those to whom philosophy is essentially a reflection on the methods and conclusions of scientific knowledge. Theirs has been an ametaphysical philosophy and it is of its very essence that it should stay so. All the philosophies of science are, directly or indirectly, the upshot of the *Critique of Pure Reason*. A large number of neo-Kantians have kept that tradition alive. Their place in the history of philosophy is a limited one, not because they are scarce, but rather because no distinct positive contribution to philosophy can be attributed to them.

But Kant himself was not that kind of a Kantian. In order to show the limitations of pure reason he had submitted its structure to a searching investigation. Possessing a great philosophical mind, he had pushed his analysis of knowledge up to the point where it springs from a twofold source, composed of sense experience and reason. The great German school of metaphysicians whose names dominate the early history of nineteenth-century philosophy (Fichte and Hegel, for instance) attempted to look beyond that twofold source in order to discover its origin. In looking for it, they found the source of nature itself, so that with them the methodological realism of Kant became a straight metaphysical idealism of the ego. Besides, the *Critique of Pure Reason* and the *Critique of Judgment* had left open other doors through which metaphysical speculation could effect its reappearance. Kant had, not indeed admitted, but proclaimed that there is in reason an ineradicable need to ask questions transcending the domain in which empirical verification is possible. So, of course, men continued to ask them. Nor could they content themselves with positing the great metaphysical notions as mere "postulates" required for the possibility of morality. God may be necessary for making the notion of moral duty a legitimate assertion of the mind, but if we are sure there is a God, the whole structure of reality and of metaphysical knowledge is bound to be altered by that certitude. The ground for its certitude does not matter. After the *Critique of Practical Reason* men could no longer pretend they were following in the wake of Kant unless they could find either a justification or at least a substitute for the metaphysical notion of God.

The country that kept metaphysics alive in the nineteenth century, and up to our own day, was Italy. For some time, the Italians indulged in the kind of philosophical reflection they called "ideology." Its father was Locke, who had begotten Condillac and, through him, the French school of the ideologists. Ideology was essentially a systematic decomposing and recomposing of the human mind. Starting from sensation, the problem was to reconstruct the mind, as a kind of puzzle, on the basis of that initial fact. French philosophers struggled to overcome that method from within. The reflexive method of Maine de Biran was an effort to find metaphysics within ideology or, at least, at its end. Quite recently, Bergson was still trying to achieve a metaphysical interpretation of the world founded on the data of inner experience. But the method was a slow and embarrassed one, for it is not certain that experience can transcend itself so as to become a metaphysics.

The Italian thinkers of the *Risorgimento* simply followed the great metaphysical tradition. In fact, they promoted it. Malebranche had never been forgotten in Italy. Cardinal Gerdil had kept the Christian metaphysics of Malebranche before the eyes of those of his own contemporaries who could find in that philosophy a satisfactory answer to their own problems. Rosmini and Gioberti achieved entirely personal reinterpretations of what had been, at the core, an Augustinianism revisited and reassessed. Through these two great Italians metaphysics firmly stood its ground against the empiricism of Locke as well as against the criticism of Kant: firmly, and successfully, for the Rosminian tradition is far from dead in Italy. Its French counterpart, "ontologism," brought about an unexpected result, in that it motivated the official reaction of the Church of Rome and the revival of the Thomist tradition, still represented in several countries by a philosophical criticism of contemporary culture in the light of Christian philosophy.

Philosophy of English expression has remained open to the suggestions coming from continental Europe but, by and large, it has kept faith with its own solidly empirical tradition. The spirit of Francis Bacon is still with it. Its more original expression and contribution to the common treasure of Western philosophy probably is American "pragmatism," especially under the form it was given by Peirce. As a critical examination of the crucial notion of *praxis*, the tradition initiated by Peirce and James is far from having said its last word.

Under its present form, however, philosophy bears the mark of heterogeneous influences whose factual convergence has created a situation that is not only complex but somewhat confused, and yet, in the last analysis, of an undeniable philosophical fecundity. In this respect, an event of decisive importance was the decision of Franz Brentano to turn away from the idealist worship of systems, and to revive the Aristotelian conception of philosophy as "science," the word being understood by him in its Greek rather than in its Kantian sense. Through the influence of Husserl and his "phenomenology," the modest suggestion of Brentano has become one of the leading themes of today's philosophical reflection.

For reasons still obscure to us because we are too near the events, the Protestant religious reaction of Kierkegaard and the passionate personal experience of Nietzsche finally combined, and even joined forces with Brentano's descendants to promote the present school of thought that goes by the name of "existentialism." When all is said and done, existentialism is a one-man show. Its name is Martin Heidegger. Not unlike Socrates, Heidegger is less a philosopher than philosophy itself. Except, unlike Socrates, he writes; so instead of imitating what he does, many imitate what he says. However, it is noteworthy that this latest reincarnation of metaphysical research takes it back to the very problem from which it started twenty-five centuries ago: What is being?

Like time, history never concludes. For historians its only conclusion is the fleeting present, itself the seed of the future. Its distinctive trait, which the history of the present has a duty to note, is the philosophical inflation observable in our time.[1] The chief cause of this inflation is the multiplication of colleges and universities, in each of which one or more professors of philosophy are charged with teaching it. To write and to publish theses, books and articles or memoirs of all sizes has become the natural thing for them to do and in some cases a sort of professional obligation. Philosophical journals and reviews have had to be created in order to provide an outlet for this continually increasing literature. Philosophical societies have been established in all civilized countries; philosophical world fairs, called international congresses of philosophy, are periodically meeting and publishing their Acts. Who finds time to read this enormous philosophical production is another problem. At any rate, the inflation is there and its presence is typical of the present-day condition of philosophy in the Western world.

In viewing this situation a historian of philosophy cannot help wondering how long it will remain possible to present a general conspectus of philosophical speculation, especially in modern times. For centuries the philosophies of the Far East and those of the West have pursued separate courses. Fifty Upanishads were translated from Persian into Latin in the very first years of the nineteenth century. Schopenhauer was the first European to assimilate important aspects of their message, but his example has not been followed, and the present trend of the European mind does not seem to be in that direction. The symbolic mode of thought prevailing in the Vedantas is not easily assimilated by readers used to the clear-cut categories of Greek logic. Our only chance to communicate with the wisdom of the East is to be informed of it by its modern representatives, for they at least show themselves perfectly capable of mastering our Western ways of thinking. The progressive universalization of Western science, itself an offspring of Greek thought, is likely to bring about a corresponding universalization of the philosophical techniques of the West.

Despite the foreseeable multiplication of its material beyond all conceivable limits, there remains one solid ground of hope for the future possibility of a history of philosophy. The recent controversies about matter, energy, causality, and predictability have not been initiated by philosophers but rather by scientists anxious to ascertain for themselves the meaning of their own conclusions. While the scientists were thus rediscovering philosophy, the philosophers were rediscovering the unavoidability of metaphysical problems by a criticism of the very critique that had pronounced it dead. And this is the best reason for believing that it will always remain possible to write the history of philosophy, however big its object may happen to grow in the future. The visibly cyclical character of philosophy will always provide it with a certain organic unity. As far as can be judged from its past history (which, of course, is far from being a perfectly safe ground but still the safest one at our disposal), future historians will always be able to order its material around its effort to find answers to ultimate questions. What the answers will be, history does not know, but it knows that the questions have always been alive in many minds, and that they still are. As of today, there is no valid reason to suppose that they are not there to stay. The day is not yet in sight when men will cease to ask themselves: What is man? What is existence? What is being?

É. G.

NOTES

PART THREE: ENGLISH PHILOSOPHY

XVI. Utilitarianism

1. É. Gilson and T. Langan, *Modern Philosophy: Descartes to Kant* (New York: Random House, 1963), pp. 289–308.

2. For the history of Utilitarianism, see L. Stephen, *The English Utilitarians* (3 vols., London: Duckworth, 1900): Vol. I, *Jeremy Bentham*; Vol. II, *James Mill*; Vol. III, *John S. Mill*. E. Albee, *A History of English Utilitarianism* (New York: Macmillan, 1902). E. Halévy, *The Growth of Philosophical Radicalism*, trans. M. Morris (London: Faber & Faber, 1928). J. Plamenatz, *The English Utilitarians* (Oxford: Blackwell, 1958).

3. William Hamilton, b. Glasgow, 1788; d. Edinburgh, 1856. Taught logic and metaphysics at the University of Edinburgh from 1836 to 1856. Published one work of collected essays: *Discussions on Philosophy and Literature, Education and University Reform* (London and Edinburgh, 1852; 2nd ed., 1853). Four posthumous volumes, *Lectures on Metaphysics and Logic* (Edinburgh and Boston, 1859–1860), were published by his pupils H. L. Mansel and J. Veitch.
Studies: D. S. Robinson, *The Story of Scottish Philosophy* (New York: Exposition Press, 1961), pp. 214–238 (biographical and selections); S. A. Grave, *The Scottish Philosophy of Common Sense* (Oxford: Clarendon Press, 1960). For Hamilton's interpretation of Kant, see René Welleck, *Immanuel Kant in England 1793–1838* (Princeton: Princeton University Press, 1931), pp. 51–62.

4. Inspired by Newton's use of the principle of gravitation to explain the harmonious unity of all physical bodies, Hartley (1705–1757) employed the principle of the association of ideas to explain the mechanism of our mental processes and the development of our moral sense. See his *Observations on Man, His Frame, His Duty, and His Expectations* (2 vols.; London, 1749). For Hartley's thought and its influence, see E. Albee, *A History of English Utilitarianism* (New York, 1902), pp. 113–129; B. Willey,

The Eighteenth Century Background (New York: Columbia University Press, 1940), pp. 136–154.

5. Jeremy Bentham, b. London, 1748; d. London, 1832. After studying at Oxford and Lincoln's Inn, ho practiced law for a short time, then devoted himself to the reform of law and government. In 1785 he visited his brother Samuel in Russia; there he wrote his *Defense of Usury*, a treatise in political economy following Adam Smith's *laissez-faire* principle. He worked for the codification of English law and the reform of prisons. His insistent questioning of the established order of Church and state, law and government, and his anti-dogmatism in all departments, won for him the title of philosophical radical.
Works: *The Works of Jeremy Bentham*, ed. J. Bowring (11 vols.; Edinburgh: William Tait, 1843; New York: Russell & Russell, 1962). *Deontology*, ed. J. Bowring (2 vols.; London: Longmans, 1834); edited after Bentham's death, it should be used with caution for it appears that Bowring took liberties with Bentham's manuscripts.
Studies: C. W. Everett, *The Education of Jeremy Bentham* (New York: Columbia University Press, 1931). D. Baumgardt, *Bentham and the Ethics of Today* (Princeton: Princeton University Press, 1952). L. Stephens, *The English Utilitarians*, vol. I, *Jeremy Bentham* (London: Duckworth, 1900). Mary P. Mack, *Jeremy Bentham: An Odyssey of Ideas, 1748–1792* (London: Heinemann, 1962). J. Plamenatz, *Man and Society*, Vol. II, *Bentham through Marx* (New York: McGraw-Hill, 1963).

6. *General View of a Complete Code of Laws*, 2nd ed. J. Bowring, III, 159.

7. *The Limits of Jurisprudence Defined*, ed. C. W. Everett (New York: Columbia University Press, 1945), p. 88.

8. See M. Mack, *Jeremy Bentham*, pp. 187–188.

9. Ibid., pp. 164–165.

10. Quoted ibid., p. 152.

11. See ibid., Appendix A, p. 445.

12. Quoted ibid., p. 103.

13. *Principles of Morals and Legislation*, 1, n. 1; ed. J. Bowring, I, 1, note. Bentham took the term "utility" from Hume's essay "Why Utility Pleases," in *An Enquiry concerning the Principles of Morals*, V. Later he realized that he was using the term in a somewhat different sense from Hume. On this point, see M. Mack, *Jeremy Bentham*, p. 102.

14. Francis Hutcheson was the first to state exactly the utilitarian formula: "That action is best which procures the greatest happiness for the greatest numbers; and that worst

which, in like manner, occasions misery" (*An Inquiry into the Original of Our Ideas of Beauty and Virtue*, II, treatise: "An inquiry concerning moral good and evil," sect. 3, no. 8, 1729, p. 180).

According to Bentham's friend and editor J. Bowring, the "first embers" of the principle of utility were kindled in Bentham by his reading Fénélon's *Télémaque* at the age of six or seven. (*Works*, XIX, pp. 10b, 79b). Bentham reports that he first became acquainted with the principle in Joseph Priestley's *An Essay on the First Principles of Government and on the Nature of Political, Civil and Religious Liberty* (1768). Priestley writes, p. 17: "The good and happiness of the members, that is of the majority of the members of any state is the great standard by which everything relating to that state must finally be determined." (See *Deontology*, ed. J. Bowring, Vol. I, Appendix, pp. 298–300). In his "Commonplace Book" Bentham is not so sure of his first acquaintance with the principle: "Priestley was the first (unless it was Beccaria) who taught my lips to pronounce the sacred truth: that the greatest happiness of the greatest number is the foundation of morals and legislation" (*Works*, ed. J. Bowring, XIX, p. 142b). For the principle of utility and Bentham's place in its history, see D. Baumgardt, *Bentham and the Ethics of Today*, pp. 33–63.

15. *The Limits of Jurisprudence Defined*, ed. C. W. Everett (New York: Columbia University Press, 1945), p. 115. Bentham attempts to prove the principle indirectly by showing that it is assumed even by those who deny it. See *Principles of Morals and Legislation*, I, 13; ed. J. Bowring, I, 2–3.

16. *Bentham's Conversations*, ed. J. Bowring, X, 585.

17. *Principles of Morals and Legislation*, I, 1; ed. J. Bowring, I, 1. This passage is taken almost literally from Helvétius, *De l'esprit*, III, 9; *Oeuvres complètes* (Paris, 1818), vol. I, 293f.

18. Ibid., X, 34, p. 56.

19. Bentham defines the common good in a nominalistic fashion: "The community is a fictitious *body*, composed of the individual persons who are considered as constituting as it were its *members*. The interest of the community then is, what?—the sum of the interests of the several members who compose it" (ibid., I, 4, p. 2).

20. *The Rationale of Reward*, III, 1; ed. J. Bowring, II, 253.

21. *Principles of Morals and Legislation*, V; ed. J. Bowring, I, 15–17.

22. Ibid., IV, 5, pp. 16–17.

23. *Deontology*, ed. J. Bowring (London, 1834), I, 130–131.

24. Quoted in C. W. Everett, *The Education of Jeremy Bentham*, pp. 35–36. "Pleasure itself not being ponderable or measurable, to form an estimate...take the general source, and thence representative, of pleasure, *viz.* money" (*Codification Proposal*, 3; ed. J. Bowring, IV, p. 540).

25. J. S. Mill, *Mill on Bentham and Coleridge*, ed. F. R. Leavis (London: Chatto & Windus, 1950), p. 63.

26. James Mill, b. Northwater Bridge, 1773; d. London, 1830. Studied at Edinburgh, distinguishing himself as a Greek scholar. In 1802 he went to London to follow journalism. As a result of writing his *History of India* he was made an official of the India House, whose head he became in 1830. Wrote on education, freedom of the press, and economics. He was the leader of the liberal politicians and the center of the group called Political Radicals. They combined Benthamism with the new political economy of Adam Smith, the metaphysics of Hartley, and the Malthusian theory on population. In politics (J. S. Mill writes of his father) he had an almost unbounded confidence in the power of representative government and complete freedom of discussion. "In psychology, his fundamental doctrine was the formation of all human character by circumstances, through the universal Principle of Association, and the consequent unlimited possibility of improving the moral and intellectual condition of mankind by education" (J. S. Mill, *Autobiography*, 4 [Oxford: University Press, The World Classics, 1924], p. 91).

Main philosophical work: *Analysis of the Phenomena of the Human Mind* (London, 1829); re-edited by J. S. Mill, 1869.

Study: L. Stephen, *The English Utilitarians* (London: Duckworth, 1900), Vol. II, *James Mill.*

27. John Stuart Mill, b. Pentonville, 1806; d. Avignon, 1873. Educated by his father, James Mill. At the age of three he was introduced to Greek and at eight he had read some Greek classics and English history. He then began to study Latin, Euclid, and algebra. By thirteen he had read extensively in the Greek and Latin classics; he had also learned Aristotelian logic and political economy. Through his father he met Jeremy Bentham and his brother Samuel, with whom he spent a year in France. He became a convert to Benthamism, which he considered to be a creed and religion. In 1822 he established the Utilitarian Society, which met at Bentham's house. The same year he became a clerk in the India House under his father; remained with the East India Company until its dissolution in 1858. At the age of twenty he passed through a severe crisis; revolted against the arid and stern creed of his father which gave small place to the feelings and emotions, and none to poetry. He recovered from the despair of the value of life, cultivated the feelings, poetry (particularly Wordsworth), and music. In 1858 he retired to a villa at St. Veran, near Avignon, but returned to England in 1865 when elected to Parliament.

Biographical: *Autobiography*, World Classics edition, ed. H. J. Laski (Oxford: University Press, 1924). Michael St. John Packe, *The Life of John Stuart Mill* (London: Seeker and Warburg, 1954).

Main philosophical works: *System of Logic* (2 vols.; London, 1843; 8th ed. [People's edition], London, 1884). *Examination of Sir William Hamilton's Philosophy* (London: Longmans, 1865). *Auguste Comte and Positivism* (London: Routledge & Sons, 1908). *Three Essays on Religion* (London, 1874; Third Essay, "Theism," ed. R. Taylor [New York: The Liberal Arts Press, 1957]). *Dissertations and Discussions* (London, 1867). *On Liberty and Considerations on Representative Government*, ed. R. B. McCallum (Oxford: Basil Blackwell, 1948). *Mill on Bentham and Coleridge*, ed. F. R. Leavis (London: Chatto & Windus, 1950). The publication of the *Collected Works of John Stuart Mill* is in progress at the University of Toronto Press. Volumes XII, XIII, *The Earlier Letters, 1812–1848*, appeared in 1963.

Studies: Alexander Bain, *John Stuart Mill: A Criticism, with Personal Recollections* (London: Longmans, 1882). L. Stephen, *The English Utilitarians*, Vol. III (London: Duckworth, 1900). R. P. Anschutz, *The Philosophy of J. S. Mill* (Oxford: Clarendon Press, 1953). I. W. Mueller, *John Stuart Mill and French Thought* (Urbana: University of Illinois Press, 1956).

28. *Autobiography*, 3, p. 56.

29. *Utilitarianism*, 2; ed. P. Wheelwright (New York: Doubleday, Doran, 1935), p. 404.

30. "Bentham," in *Dissertations and Discussions*, I, 318. To Bentham, "All poetry is misrepresentation." Mill points out, however, that Bentham's philistinism was confined to poetry. Music was his favorite amusement, and he recognized at least some social value in painting, sculpture "and the other arts addressed to the eye." Nevertheless, "his ignorance of the deeper springs of human character prevented him (as it prevents most Englishmen) from suspecting how profoundly such things enter into the moral nature of man, and into the education both of the individual and of the race" (ibid., p. 318).

31. *Autobiography*, 5, p. 125.

32. *Utilitarianism*, 2, p. 406.

33. Ibid., p. 408.

34. "Bentham," in *Dissertations and Discussions*, I, 293.

35. *Logic*, VI, XII, 7; pp. 021–622.

36. *Utilitarianism*, 2, p. 415.

37. "Coleridge," in *Dissertations and Discussions*, I, 330. For Coleridge's role in nineteenth-century English thought, see Basil Willey, *Nineteenth Century Studies* (London: Chatto & Windus, 1949), pp. 1–50.

38. "Bentham," op. cit., p. 271.

39. *Autobiography*, 7, p. 191. Mill tells us that he wrote his *Logic* to supply a pressing need for a textbook opposed to the German or intuitionist point of view. His work "derives all knowledge from experience, and all moral and intellectual qualities principally from the direction given to the associations" (ibid., p. 190). Hence the theory of inductive reasoning occupies the central part of Mill's logic, contrary to the logic manuals of the day, which stressed deduction and syllogistic reasoning; for example, the *Elements of Logic* of Richard Whately (Boston and Cambridge, 1856). Mill acknowledges his indebtedness to William Whewell's *History of the Inductive Sciences* (1837) and *Philosophy of the Inductive Sciences* (1840). Whewell gathered up vast material on induction, which was used by Mill; but Mill opposes his Kantian view that there is an *a priori* element in knowledge.

For a summary account of Mill's logic, see W. and M. Kneale, *The Development of Logic* (Oxford: Clarendon Press, 1902), pp. 371–377. See also *John Stuart Mill's Philosophy of Scientific Method*, ed. with an introduction by E. Nagel (New York: Hafner, 1950).

40. *Logic*, III, X, 8; p. 298a.

41. *Logic*, VI, VIII, 1; pp. 578ff.

42. Hence a science of individual morality (ethology), as well as one of social morality is possible. Human actions, like other natural events, are subject to invariable laws: "the law of causality applies in the same strict sense to human actions as to other phenomena..." (*Logic*, VI, II, 1; p. 547a). Mill denies, however, that this leads to the necessity of human actions or to fatalism. He wants to retain the doctrine of free will, at least in the sense that "we have real power over the formation of our own character" (*Autobiography*, 5, p. 144). This he does by maintaining that, while our actions are determined by circumstances, our will can influence them, and hence the will co-operates in forming our character. Mill opposes the notion of free will as an ontological or efficient cause of our actions; like all causes our volitions are related to their effects simply as antecedents to consequents. There is no "peculiar tie or mysterious constraint exercised by the antecedent over the consequent." *Logic*, VI, II, 2; p. 548. This leaves room for freedom from necessity not only in the order of mind but also in the order of matter. It is against the background of this phenomenalist doctrine of freedom that Mill's *Essay on Liberty* should be read.

43. *Logic*, VI, IX, 2; p. 585b.

44. Ibid., III, XIII, 7; p. 317.

45. Ibid., III, II, 1; p. 188a.

46. Ibid., III, 5, 2; p. 213b. "I make no research into the ultimate or ontological cause of anything. To adopt a distinction familiar in the writings of the Scotch metaphysicians, and especially of Reid, the causes with which I concern myself are not *efficient*, but *physical* causes. They are causes in that sense alone in which one physical fact is said to be the cause of another. Of the efficient causes of phenomena, or whether any such causes exist at all, I am not called upon to give an opinion" (ibid., p. 213a). Mill adds that invariable sequence is not synonymous with causation; day invariably follows night, but we do not call night the cause of day because the union of the two is in a way accidental. "Invariable sequence, therefore, is not synonymous with causation, unless the sequence, besides being invariable is unconditional." This leads Mill to say that causal laws do not assert "actual results" but "underlying tendencies" (*Logic*, III, 5, 6; III, 10, 5). Accordingly, Mill's doctrine of causality makes room at least for underlying tendencies in nature though not for known essences.

47. Ibid., III, XXI, 2; p. 372b.

48. Ibid., III, XXI, 3; p. 373a.

49. Ibid., p. 376b. For Mill's attempt to make induction a method of establishing true causal laws of nature, see R. P. Anschutz, *The Philosophy of J. S. Mill*, pp. 97–114.

50. *Autobiography*, 2, p. 36.

51. *Theism*, ed. R. Taylor, p. 5.

52. Ibid., p. 19.

53. *Logic*, III, V, 2; p. 213b. See above, note 46.

54. *Theism*, p. 29. Mill classifies this true induction as an example of "the method of agreement," which is the least cogent type of induction. It is, however, a strong argument of this type (ibid., p. 30).

55. Mill calls God the *demiourgos* (ibid., p. 36).

56. Ibid., p. 50.

57. See *The Letters of John Stuart Mill*, ed. H. S. R. Elliot, I, 183.

58. *Auguste Comte and Positivism*. For Mill's relations with Comte and other French philosophers, see I. W. Mueller, *John Stuart Mill and French Thought* (Urbana: University of Illinois Press, 1956).

59. *Theism*, p. 86. For Mill's notion of God, see J. Collins, *God in Modern Philosophy* (London: Routledge & Kegan Paul, 1960), pp. 287–298.

60. Alexander Bain, b. Aberdeen, 1818; d. Aberdeen, 1903.
Main works: *The Senses and the Intellect* (London: Parker and Son, 1885). *The Emotions and the Will* (London: Parker and Son, 1859). These two works were published together in 1868 under the title: *Mental and Moral Science* (London: Longmans, Green). *Logic Deductive and Inductive as a Science* (London: Longmans, Green, 1870). *Mind and Body* (New York: Appleton, 1873). *John Stuart Mill: A Criticism* (London: Longmans, Green, 1882). *Autobiography* (London: Longmans, Green, 1904).
Study: G. S. Brett, *History of Psychology*, ed. R. S. Peters (London: Allen & Unwin, 1953), pp. 441–450.

61. Henry Sidgwick, b. Yorkshire 1838; d. Cambridge, 1900.
Main work: *The Methods of Ethics* (London: Macmillan, 1874).
Studies: W. C. Havard, *Henry Sidgwick and Later Utilitarian Political Philosophy* (Gainesville: University of Florida Press, 1959). C. D. Broad, *Five Types of Ethical Theory* (London: Kegan Paul, 1930).

62. *The Methods of Ethics* (7th ed.; London, 1907), p. 388.

XVII. Philosophy of Evolution

1. J. Royce, *The Spirit of Modern Philosophy*, reprint ed. (New York: Braziller, 1955), p. 286.

2. See J. C. Greene, *The Death of Adam* (Ames: Iowa State University Press, 1959), p. 307.

3. Quoted ibid., p. 128. Among the works of John Ray are *The Wisdom of God Manifested in the Works of the Creation* (4th ed.; London, 1704); *Three Physico-Theological Discourses* (3rd ed.; London, 1718). R. W. T. Gunther has edited *Further Correspondence of John Ray* (London: The Ray Society Publications, 1928). On Ray's views on the fixity of species, see C. E. Raven, *John Ray, Naturalist, His Life and Works* (Cambridge: University Press, 1942). Ray's friend, William Derham, shared these views. See his Boylean Lectures entitled *Physico-Theology* (1711–1712).

4. Quoted by G. Himmelfarb, *Darwin and the Darwinian Revolution* (New York: Doubleday, 1959), p. 167.

5. C. Darwin, *The Origin of Species* (Everyman Library, 1956), p. 7.

6. Quoted J. C. Greene, ibid., p. 139.

7. Charles Robert Darwin, b. 1809 in Shrewsbury, England, grandson of the biologist Erasmus Darwin (1731–1802); d. in the village of Down, 1882. Studied medicine at Edinburgh and ecclesiastical subjects at Cambridge. From 1831 to 1836 he traveled on the *Beagle* on a surveying expedition to the coasts of South America and the South Seas. During this voyage he observed animals and fossil remains, preparing himself for his life work. On his return to England he lived in Cambridge and London until 1842, then settled in the village of Down, where he did research and wrote scientific treatises.

   Main writings: *On the Origin of Species by Means of Natural Selection, or the Preservation of Favoured Races in the Struggle for Life* (London, 1859; 6th ed., 1882). *The Descent of Man and Selection in Relation to Sex* (London, 1871; 2nd ed., 1874). *Autobiography and Selected Letters*, ed. Francis Darwin (his son) (3 vols.; London, 1887; New York: Dover Publications, 1958). *The Life and Letters of Charles Darwin, Including an Autobiographical Chapter*, ed. F. Darwin (2 vols.; New York: Appleton, 1898). *More Letters of Charles Darwin*, ed. F. Darwin (2 vols.; New York: Appleton, 1903).

   Studies: Julian Huxley, *Evolution, The Modern Synthesis* (London: Allen & Unwin, 1942). L. Eiseley, *Darwin's Century, Evolution and the Men Who Discovered It* (New York: Doubleday, 1958). G. Himmelfarb, *Darwin and the Darwinian Revolution* (New York: Doubleday, 1959). *Darwin's Vision and Christian Perspectives*, ed. W. J. Ong (New York: Macmillan, 1900). *Evolution after Darwin*, ed. Sol Tax (3 vols.; Chicago: University of Chicago Press, 1960). T. A. Goudge, *The Ascent of Life, a Philosophical Study of the Theory of Evolution* (Toronto: University of Toronto Press, 1961). J. C. Greene, *The Death of Adam* (Ames: Iowa State University Press, 1959; Mentor Book, 1961); *Darwin and the Modern View* (Baton Rouge: Louisiana State University Press, 1961; Mentor Book, 1963). R. J. Nogar, *The Wisdom of Evolution* (New York: Doubleday, 1963). S. Toulmin and J. Goodfield, *The Discovery of Time* (London: Hutchinson, 1965).

8. *The Life and Letters of Charles Darwin*, I, 384.

9. For a recent critical estimate of Darwinism, see W. R. Thompson's Introduction to *The Origin of Species* (Everyman Library; New York: Dutton, 1956), pp. vii-xxiv.

10. *The Life and Letters of Charles Darwin*, I, 282.

11. *More Letters of Charles Darwin*, I, 194.

12. William Paley, b. Peterborough, England, 1743; d. Lincoln, 1805. Educated at Christ's College, Cambridge, and lectured there on philosophy. Later he was rector of Bishop-Wearmouth. For his argument for God's existence from design, see *Natural Theology, or Evidences of the Existence and Attributes of the Deity collected from the Appearances of Nature*, in *Works* (London, 1844), pp. 255–355. Among his other writings are: *A View of the Evidences of Christianity* (2 vols.; London, 1794), and *The Principles of Moral and Political Philosophy* (London, 1875).

The "physico-theological argument" for God's existence, based on design in nature, was criticized from different points of view. According to Kant (1724–1804), it implies the ontological argument, which he rejected. See his *Critique of Pure Reason*, trans. N. K. Smith (London: Macmillan, 1950), pp. 518–524.

John Henry Newman (1801–1890) considered Paley's argument both philosophically inaccurate and ineffective in converting man to religion. In his *Grammar of Assent*, published in 1870, he admits that "order implies a purpose" (New York: Image Books, 1955, p. 75), but later the same year he wrote to a friend: "I have not insisted on the argument from *design*, because I am writing in the 19th Century, by which, as represented by its philosophers, design is not admitted as proved. And to tell the truth, though I should not wish to preach on the subject, for 40 years I have been unable to see the logical force of the argument myself. I believe in design because I believe in God; not in a God because I see design." In Newman's eyes what makes the argument ineffective from a religious point of view is that, even though design may teach us the power, skill, and goodness of God, it tells us nothing of his sanctity, mercy, or future judgment, which are of the essence of religion. See Newman's letter to W. R. Brownlow, in *Philosophical Readings in Cardinal Newman*, ed. J. Collins (Chicago: Regnery, 1961), p. 189. Newman's favorite proof of the existence of God is based on conscience. According to him the "feeling" of conscience implies the recognition of an obligation involving the notion of an external being obliging us. See A. J. Boekraad, *The Argument from Conscience to the Existence of God according to J. H. Newman* (Louvain: Nauwelaerts, 1961), p. 117.

While a Fellow at Oriel College, Oxford, Newman was the favorite pupil of Richard Whately (1787–1863), who had been a pupil of Paley and was in Newman's day the leader of the Noetics, a group of theologians at Oxford who cultivated logical thought and sought a rational, and even a formally logical basis for Christianity. Newman says of Whately: "He, emphatically, opened my mind, and taught me to think and to use my reason" (*Apologia pro Vita Sua*, 3; New York: Modern Library, 1950, p. 41). In the Preface to his influential *Elements of Logic* (London, 1826), Whately acknowledges the considerable help of Newman. For Newman's part in the writing of this Logic, see *The Letters and Diaries of John Henry Newman*, ed. C. S. Dessain and V. F. Biehl (London: Nelson, 1964, XV, 175–179). But Newman thought Whately's views on reason too narrow; besides formal, syllogistic reasoning, which Whately stressed, Newman accepted concrete and non-formal types of thinking. See J. Collins, op. cit., pp. 6–7.

In his *Essay on the Development of Christian Doctrine*, published in 1845, fourteen years before Darwin's *Origin of Species*, Newman proposed a theory of the evolution of doctrine. This theory recognizes the importance of time and history for the development of ideas, but it has no immediate connection with the biological theory of evolution. For Newman's sympathy with the theory of evolution, see J. Collins, op. cit., p. 424, 11.2. For Newman's theory of the development of doctrine, see J. Guitton, *La philosophie de Newman, Essai sur l'idée de développement* (Paris: Boivin, 1933).

13. *The Life and Letters of Charles Darwin*, I, 278–279.

14. See L. Eiseley, *Darwin's Century*, p. 197.

15. T. Huxley, "On the Reception of the Origin of Species," *The Life and Letters of Charles Darwin*, I, 554–555.

16. *The Life and Letters of Charles Darwin*, p. 282.

17. *The Descent of Man*, p. 66. See p. 126.

18. Ibid., p. 132.

19. Ibid., p. 126.

20. Ibid., p. 121.

21. Herbert Spencer, b. Derby, England, 1820; d. Brighton, 1903. Educated privately, he was attracted especially to mathematics and natural science. From 1837 to 1841, he was employed as an engineer in constructing the London and Gloucester railway. In 1843 he came to London to follow a literary career. From 1848 to 1853 he was subeditor of the *Economist*.

Autobiography, 2 vols., published posthumously in 1904.

Works: *Social Statics* (London, 1808). *Synthetic Philosophy* (10 vols.; New York: Appleton, 1860–1896): Vol. I: *First Principles*; Vols. II, III: *The Principles of Biology*; Vols. IV, V: *The Principles of Psychology*; Vols. VI, VII, VIII: *The Principles of Sociology*; Vols. IX, X: *The Principles of Ethics*. *Education* (New York: Appleton, 1880). *Illustrations of Universal Progress* (New York: Appleton, 1889).

Study: H. Elliot, *Herbert Spencer* (London: Constable, 1917).

22. *First Principles* (6th ed.; New York: Appleton, 1903), p. 119.

23. *Social Statics*, p. 80.

24. *Illustrations of Universal Progress*, p. 3.

25. *First Principles*, p. 307.

26. Ibid., p. 369. Spencer's extension of the notion of energy to the philosophical concept of force opens his system to Bergson's criticism. Bergson argues that "force" either has the meaning scientists give to the word "energy" and then Spencer cannot draw his general philosophical conclusions from it, or it has a broader meaning than the scientific one, in which case the Spencerian philosophy is not based on positive science. See H. Bergson, *Ecrits et paroles*, t. 1 (Paris: Presses Universitaires, 1957), p. 234.

27. For a convenient summary of these points, see *First Principles*, pp. 494–506. Spencer is not certain whether evolution will finally bring the universe to a state of total equilibrium and cessation of change, or whether there will be an endless cycle of evolution and dissolution. Like all ultimate questions, this must remain unknown. But Spencer concludes, "If, however, we lean to the belief that what happens to the parts will eventually happen to the whole, we are led to entertain the conception of Evolutions that have filled an immeasurable past and Evolutions that will fill an immeasurable future" ibid., p. 506).

28. Ibid., p. 89.

29. "In the very assertion that all knowledge, properly so called, is Relative, there is involved the assertion that there exists a Non-relative.... From the necessity of thinking in relations, it follows that the Relative is itself inconceivable, except as related to a real Non-relative" ibid., p. 82).

30. Ibid., pp. 84–106, 506–507.

31. *The Principles of Ethics* (2 vols.; New York: Appleton, 1903), I, 15.

32. Ibid., p. 19.

33. Ibid., pp. 25–26.

34. Ibid., p. 45. There are degrees of pleasure depending on degrees of emotion. Pleasure accompanying the higher emotions is a better guide to right conduct than that which accompanies the lower ones. See H. Elliot, *Herbert Spencer*, p. 186.

35. *Illustrations of Universal Progress*, p. 58.

36. Quoted in J. C. Greene, *Darwin and the Modern World View* (Mentor Book), p. 85.

37. T. H. Huxley, *Evolution and Ethics and other Essays* (New York, 1898), pp. 81, 83.

38. Quoted in J. C. Greene, ibid.

39. For bibliography on the pragmatists and evolution, see below, Chapter XXVI, notes 2, 3.

40. C. S. Peirce, *Chance, Love, and Logic* (New York: Harcourt, Brace, 1923), p. 162.

41. H. Bergson, *Creative Evolution* (London: Macmillan), p. xiv.

42. Conwy Lloyd Morgan, b. London, 1852; d. 1936. Studied at the Royal School of Mines in London, then under Huxley in biology. From 1884 he was professor of zoology and geology at University College, Bristol.

Main philosophical works: *Herbert Spencer's Philosophy of Science* (London: Williams and Norgate, 1913). *Emergent Evolution* (London: Williams and Norgate, 1923). *Life, Mind, and Spirit* (London: Williams and Norgate, 1926). *The Emergence of Novelty* (London: Williams and Norgate, 1933). "A Philosophy of Evolution," in *Contemporary British Philosophy* (First Series), ed. J. H. Muirhead (New York: Macmillan, 1924), pp. 275–306.

Study: R. Metz, *A Hundred Years of British Philosophy* (New York: Macmillan, 1938), pp. 651–662.

43. The term "emergent" Morgan owes to G. H. Lewes, who first used it in his *Problems of Life and Mind* (1875). See L. Morgan, "A Philosophy of Evolution," p. 296.

44. Samuel Alexander, b. Sydney, Australia, 1859; d. Manchester, 1938. After studying at Melbourne he came to England in 1878 and entered Balliol College, Oxford. Later he taught at Oxford and at Manchester. He retired in 1924 and received the Order of Merit in 1930.

Main works: *Moral Order and Progress: An Analysis of Ethical Conceptions* (London: Trübner, 1889; 3rd ed., 1899). *Space, Time, and Deity* (2 vols.; London: Macmillan, 1920; reprinted New York: The Humanities Press, 1950). *Spinoza and Time* (London: Allen & Unwin, 1921). *Art and Instinct* (Oxford: Clarendon Press, 1927). *Beauty and Other Forms of Value* (London: Macmillan, 1933).

Studies: P. Devaux, *Le système d'Alexander; exposé critique d'une théorie néo-réaliste du changement* (Paris: Vrin, 1929). G. Van Hall, *The Theory of Knowledge of Samuel Alexander* (Rome, 1936). M. R. Konvitz, *On the Nature of Value: The Philosophy of Samuel Alexander* (New York: King's Crown Press, 1946). J. W. McCarthy, *The Naturalism of Samuel Alexander* (New York: King's Crown Press, 1948). A. P. Stiernotte, *God and Space-Time: Deity in the Philosophy of Samuel Alexander* (New York: Philosophical Library, 1954).

45. A. Einstein, "Space-Time," in *Encyclopaedia Britannica*, 14th ed., XXI, 105. See S. Alexander, *Space, Time, and Deity*, I, 58–60.

46. S. Alexander, "Artistic Creation and Cosmic Creation," in *Philosophical and Literary Pieces* (London: Macmillan, 1939), p. 272.

47. S. Alexander, "The Historicity of Things," in *Philosophy and History*, ed. R. Klibansky and H. J. Paton (Harper Torchbooks, 1963), p. II.

48. *Space, Time, and Deity*, II, 347.

XVIII. Idealism

1. *Mill on Bentham and Coleridge*, ed. F. R. Leavis (London: Chatto & Windus, 1950), pp. 103, 108. The expression "seminal minds," applied to Bentham and Coleridge, is in the essay on Bentham, p. 40. On Coleridge's role in bringing German philosophy to England, see R. Wellek, *Immanuel Kant in England 1793–1838* (Princeton: University of Princeton Press, 1931), pp. 65–85.

2. Samuel Taylor Coleridge, b. Ottery Saint Mary, Devonshire, 1772; d. Highgate, 1834. Studied at Jesus College, Cambridge, but left without taking a degree in 1794. Lectured in Bristol on politics and religion. In 1795 he met Wordsworth, with whom he wrote *Lyrical Ballads*. Went to Germany for a year (1798–1799); learned the German language and attended lectures at Göttingen. In 1809 he started the magazine *The Friend*, which ran for eight months. He died in communion with the Church of England.
   Complete Works, ed. W. G. T. Shedd (7 vols.; New York: Harper, 1884). Of main interest for his philosophy: Vol. I: *Aids to Reflection*; Vol. II: *The Friend*; Vol. III: *Biographie Literaria*; Vol. V: *Confessions of an Inquiring Spirit*. His *Philosophical Lectures* (on the history of philosophy) have been edited by K. Coburn (New York: Philosophical Library, 1949). Same editor: *The Notebooks of Samuel Taylor Coleridge* (2 vols.; New York: Pantheon Books, 1957–1961).
   Studies: A. D. Snyder, *Coleridge on Logic and Learning* (New Haven: Yale University Press, 1929). J. H. Muirhead, *Coleridge as Philosopher* (London: Allen & Unwin, 1930; new edition, 1954). K. Coburn, *Inquiring Spirit* (London: Routledge & K. Paul, 1951). J. Pucelle, *L'Idéalisme en Angleterre, de Coleridge à Bradley* (Neuchâtel: Editions de la Baconnière, 1955), pp. 17–39. J. D. Boulger, *Coleridge as Religious Thinker* (New Haven: Yale University Press, 1961). P. Deschamps, *La formation de la pensée de Coleridge, 1772–1804* (Paris: Didier, 1965).

3. *Letters*, Vol. I, ed. E. H. Coleridge (London: Heinemann, 1895), p. 113.

4. *Biographie Literaria*, VII (New York: Dutton, 1906), p. 63.

5. Ibid.

6. *Table Talk*, in *Works*, VI, 351. The underlying fallacy of the whole Newtonian philosophy, according to Coleridge, is to conceive the mind as a mere spectator of nature. Ibid.

7. *Biographie Literaria*, IX, p. 72. For the influence of the German mystic Jacob Boehme, see p. 73. For Coleridge's account of Erigena, see *Philosophical Lectures*, pp. 270–272; 433, n. 17. Thomas Taylor translated the works of Plato and parts of the works of Plotinus and Proclus during Coleridge's lifetime. For the revival of Platonism in England during this period and its influence on William Blake, see G. M. Harper, *The Neoplatonism of William Blake* (Chapel Hill: University of North Carolina Press, 1961).

8. *Biographie Literarie*, IX, p. 76.

9. J. H. Muirhead regards Coleridge's thought as essentially native in hue. He quotes Coleridge's statement: "I can not only honestly assert but I can satisfactorily prove by reference to writings...that all the elements, the differentials, as the algebraists say, of my present opinion, existed for me before I had ever seen a book of German Metaphysics later than Wolf and Leibnitz or could have read it, if I had." *Letters*, II, 735. See J. H. Muirhead, *Coleridge as Philosopher*, p. 54, n. 1. According to R. Wellek, however, Kantian thought determined the essentials of Coleridge's philosophy and colored even the minutiae of his terminology. R. Wellek, *Immanuel Kant in England 1793–1838*, p. 102. Wellek's statement on p. 67 is better balanced: "By temperament and education, Coleridge is a traditional idealist. The whole bent of his mind led him to Plato and Plotinus, to the English Platonic tradition and to the new German idealism which he felt to be deeply akin with the older thought."

10. *Biographie Literaria*, IX, p. 72.

11. Quoted in J. H. Muirhead, *Coleridge as Philosopher*, p. 281.

12. *Biographie Literaria*, XII, p. 144. See Exodus 3:14. For the historical background of this interpretation of the divine name, see É. Gilson, *Elements of Christian Philosophy* (New York: Doubleday, 1960), pp. 113–114, 124–133.

13. *Biographie Literaria*, XII, p. 146.

14. For the first diffusion of Kant's influence in England, see R. Wellek, op. cit.

15. For the introduction of Hegel into England, see J. H. Muirhead, *The Platonic Tradition in Anglo-Saxon Philosophy* (London: Allen & Unwin, 1931), chap. ii.

16. *Prolegomena to Ethics* (2nd ed.; Oxford: Clarendon Press, 1884), p. 15, n. 11; p. 40, n. 38. See W. D. Lamont, *Introduction to Green's Moral Philosophy* (London: Allen & Unwin, 1934).

17. *Prolegomena to Ethics*, p. 192, n. 183.

18. Francis Herbert Bradley, b. Clapham, England, 1846; d. Oxford, 1924. Educated at University College, Oxford, 1865–1870; became a Fellow of Merton College, 1870. He lived much of his life at Oxford, in poor health and seclusion. He received the Order of Merit the year of his death.

Main works: *Ethical Studies* (London, 1876; 2nd ed., Oxford: Clarendon Press, 1927). *The Principles of Logic* (London, 1883; 2nd ed., 2 vols., with *Commentary and Terminal Essays*, London: Oxford University Press, 1922). *Appearance and Reality* (London, 1893; 2nd ed., 9th impression, Oxford: Clarendon Press, 1930). *Essays on Truth and*

Reality (Oxford: Clarendon Press, 1914). *Collected Essays* (2 vols.; Oxford: Clarendon Press, 1935).

Studies: J. H. Muirhead, *The Platonic Tradition in Anglo-Saxon Philosophy* (New York: Macmillan, 1931), pp. 219–304. G. Watts Cunningham, *The Idealistic Argument in Recent British and American Philosophy* (New York: Century, 1933), pp. 78–113. T. T. Segerstedt, *Value and Reality in Bradley's Philosophy* (Lund, 1934). W. F. Lofthouse, *F. H. Bradley* (London: Epworth, 1949). M. T. Antonelli, *La Metafisica di F. H. Bradley* (Milan: Fratelli Bocca, 1952). J. Pucelie, *L'Idéalisme en Angleterre, de Coleridge à Bradley* (Neuchâtel: Editions de la Baconnière, 1955), pp. 191–253. R. Wollheim, *F. H. Bradley* (Harmondsworth, Middlesex: Penguin Books, 1960; good bibliography). T. S. Eliot, *Knowledge and Experience in the Philosophy of F. H. Bradley* (New York: Farrar, Straus and Co., 1964). A. C. Ewing, *Idealism: A Critical Survey*, 3rd ed. (London: Methuen, 1961).

19. *Ethical Studies*, p. 62.

20. Ibid., p. 73.

21. Ibid., p. 88.

22. Ibid., p. 128, n.

23. Ibid., p. 147.

24. Ibid., p. 178.

25. Ibid., p. 206.

26. Ibid., p. 279.

27. *Appearance and Reality*, p. x.

28. Ibid., p. 9.

29. Ibid., p. 18.

30. Ibid., p. 144. "It is the real, which there appears, which is the subject of all predicates" (ibid., p. 223). See *The Principles of Logic*, p. 10: "Judgment proper is the act which refers an ideal content (recognized as such) to a reality beyond the act."

31. *The Principles of Logic*, p. 456.

32. *Essays on Truth and Reality*, p. 190.

33. *Appearance and Reality*, p. 127.

34. *The Principles of Logic*, 2nd ed., II, 515–516. See J. H. Muirhead, *The Platonic Tradition in Anglo-Saxon Philosophy*, p. 257.

35. *Appearance and Reality*, p. 223.

36. Ibid., p. 482.

37. Ibid., p. 471. For Bradley's notion of God, see C. Fabro, *Introduzione all' Ateism o Moderno* (Rome: Editrice Studium, 1964), pp. 719–752.

38. Ibid., p. 489.

39. Bernard Bosanquet, b. Rock Hall, Northumberland, 1848; d. London, 1923. Studied under T. H. Green and R. L. Nettleship at Balliol College, Oxford, which he entered in 1867. In 1871, he obtained a fellowship at University College and taught Greek history and philosophy there for ten years. In 1881, he gave up his teaching career and went to London to write and to devote himself to the Charity Organisation Society. He was professor at the University of St. Andrews from 1903 to 1908. His wife, Helen, wrote *Bernard Bosanquet: A Short Account of His Life* (London: Macmillan, 1924). See *B. Bosanquet and His Friends, Letters Illustrating the Sources and Development of his Philosophical Opinions*, ed. J. H. Muirhead (London: Allen & Unwin, 1935).

Main works: His Gifford Lectures, *Individuality and Destiny*, were published in two volumes: *The Principle of Individuality and Value* and *The Value and Destiny of the Individual* (London: Macmillan, 1912, 1913). *Knowledge and Reality* (London: Swan Sonnenschein, 1885). *Logic, or the Morphology of Knowledge* (2 vols.; Oxford, 1888; 2nd ed., 1911). *A History of Aesthetics* (London: Allen & Unwin, 1892; 2nd ed., 1904). *A Civilization of Christendom and Other Studies* (London: Sonnenschein, 1893). *The Philosophical Theory of the State* (London: Macmillan, 1899; 4th ed., 1923). *Three Lectures on Aesthetic* (London: Macmillan, 1915). *Social and International Ideals* (London: Macmillan, 1917). *What Religion Is* (London: Macmillan, 1920). *The Meeting of Extremes in Contemporary Philosophy* (London: Macmillan, 1921). *Three Chapters on the Nature of the Mind* (London: Macmillan, 1923).

Studies: G. Watts Cunningham, *The Idealistic Argument in Recent British and American Philosophy* (New York: Century, 1933), pp. 114–148. F. Houang, *Le Néo-Hegelianisme en Angleterre. La philosophie de Bernard Bosanquet* (Paris: Vrin, 1954); *De l'Humanisme à l'Absolutisme. L'Evolution de la pensée religieuse du Néo-Hegelian anglais Bernard Bosanquet* (Paris: Vrin, 1954). J. Pucelle, *L'Idéalisme en Angleterre* (Neuchâtel: Editions de la Baconnicrc, 1955), pp. 254–281. A. C. Ewing, *Idealism: A Critical Survey*, 3rd ed. (London: Methuen, 1961).

40. *The Principle of Individuality and Value*, pp. 10–13.

41. Ibid., p. 29.

42. Ibid., p. 21.

43. Ibid., p. 268.

44. *The Value and Destiny of the Individual*, p. 15.

45. *The Philosophical Theory of the State*, p. 79. See *The Principle of Individuality and Value*, pp. 68–69.

46. *The Principle of Individuality and Value*, p. 37.

47. Ibid., p. 60.

48. Ibid., pp. 45–46. Contradiction disappears in the Absolute, but not negativity. Following Hegel, Bosanquet claims that negativity is fundamental to reality. By negativity he means the "otherness" of elements in a system once the contradiction between them is resolved. It is "a successful or frictionless contradiction." Bosanquet conceives negativity, not in a static sense as a mere "difference," but, like contradiction, as a dynamic "tendency of every datum to transcend itself as a fragment and complete itself as a whole." Hence it is "diversity or distinctness as regarded from the point of view of an attempted union (Ibid., p. 233).

49. Ibid., p. 46.

50. *The Philosophical Theory of the State*, pp. 159–162.

51. Ibid., p. 165.

52. Ibid., p. 306, n. See *Social and International Ideals.*

53. *The Philosophical Theory of the State*, p. 172.

54. Bosanquet praises Rousseau for distinguishing between the general will (in the sense of the totality of particular wills) and the will of all (the sum of all wills). But he criticizes his method of deriving the general will from the common element of the particular interests of individual wills (Ibid., pp. 110-in).

55. Ibid., p. 109.

56. Ibid., p. 107.

57. *Three Lectures on Aesthetic*, p. 7.

58. Ibid., p. 108.

59. Ibid., pp. 32, 35.

60. Bosanquet, "Croce's Aesthetic," *Proceedings of the British Academy*, IX, 1919–1920, p. 261.

61. *Three Lectures on Aesthetic*, p. 19.

62. Ibid., p. 73.

63. "Croce's Aesthetic," pp. 270–271. Bosanquet refers to Croce's *Estetica*, p. 113.

64. *Three Lectures on Aesthetic*, p. 62.

65. "Croce's Aesthetic," p. 273.

66. *Three Lectures on Aesthetic*, pp. 4–5. See F. Houang, *Le Néo-Hegelianisme en Angleterre*, pp. 107–108.

67. *The Principle of Individuality and Value*, p. 340.

68. W. James, *The Will to Believe* (New York: Longmans, 1932), p. IX.

69. Andrew Seth Pringle-Pattison, b. Edinburgh, 1856; d. Edinburgh, 1931. Educated at Edinburgh and in Germany; taught at Edinburgh, Cardiff, and St. Andrews. He assumed the name Pringle-Pattison in 1898 to satisfy a condition of succeeding to an estate.

Main works: *The Development from Kant to Hegel* (2nd ed.; New York: Stochert, 1924). *Hegelianism and Personality* (Edinburgh: Blackwood, 1887; 2nd ed., 1893). *The Idea of God in the Light of Recent Philosophy* (Oxford: Clarendon Press, 1917; 2nd ed., 1920). *The Idea of Immortality* (Oxford: Clarendon Press, 1922). *Studies in the Philosophy of Religion* (Oxford: Clarendon Press, 1930). *Balfour Lectures on Realism*, ed. G. F. Barbour (London: Blackwood, 1933).

Study: G. Watts Cunningham, *The Idealistic Argument in Recent British and American Philosophy* (New York: Century, 1933), pp. 149–168.

70. John Ellis McTaggart, b. London, 1866; d. London, 1925. Educated at Trinity College, Cambridge. After spending some years in New Zealand he returned to England and was appointed lecturer in moral philosophy at Cambridge.

Main works: *Studies in the Hegelian Dialectic* (Cambridge: University Press, 1896; 2nd ed., 1922). *Studies in the Hegelian Cosmology* (Cambridge: University Press, 1901; 2nd ed., 1918). *Some Dogmas of Religion* (London: Arnold, 1906; 2nd ed., 1930). *A Commentary on Hegel's Logic* (Cambridge: University Press, 1910; 2nd ed., 1931). *The*

Nature of Existence (2 vols.; Cambridge: University Press, 1921, 1927). *Philosophical Studies,* ed. S. V. Keeling (London: Arnold, 1934).

Studies: C. D. Broad, *Examination of McTaggart's Philosophy* (2 vols.; Cambridge: University Press, 1933, 1938). G. Watts Cunningham, op. cit., pp. 202–238.

71. James Ward, b. Hull, Yorkshire, 1843; d. Cambridge, 1925. Studied at Trinity College, Cambridge, and in Berlin and Göttingen. Professor at Trinity College from 1897.

Main works: *Naturalism and Agnosticism* (2 vols.; London: Macmillan, 1899; 4th ed., in one volume, 1915). *The Realm of Ends, or Pluralism and Theism* (Cambridge: University Press, 1911; 2nd ed., 1920). *A Study of Kant* (Cambridge: University Press, 1922). *Essays in Philosophy* (Cambridge: University Press, 1927).

Study: G. Watts Cunningham, op. cit., pp. 169–201.

72. *The Nature of Existence*, II, 479. "All true philosophy must be mystical, not indeed in its methods, but in its final conclusions" (*Studies in the Hegelian Dialectic*, p. 255).

XIX. Pragmatic Humanism: F. C. S. Schiller

1. Ferdinand Canning Scott Schiller, b. Altona, Schleswig-Holstein (on the Danish side of the border), in 1864; d. Los Angeles, 1937. His early years were spent in Switzerland. After studying at Balliol College, Oxford, he taught German at Eton, then returned to Oxford and obtained his M. A. degree. In 1893 he traveled to the United States and continued his graduate studies in philosophy at Cornell and taught logic and metaphysics. He became acquainted with William James, who influenced his philosophy. In 1897 he returned to Oxford and taught there until his retirement in 1926. From then on he lectured for part of the year at the University of Southern California in Los Angeles. He made his permanent home there in 1935.

Works: *Riddles of the Sphinx: A Study in the Philosophy of Evolution* (London: Macmillan, 1891; 3rd rev. ed., 1910). *Humanism: Philosophical Essays* (2nd ed.; London: Macmillan, 1912). *Studies in Humanism* (2nd ed.; London: Macmillan, 1912). *Formal Logic: A Scientific and Social Problem* (London: Macmillan, 1912). *Problems of Belief* (London: Hodder & Stoughton, 1924). *Logic for Use: An Introduction to the Voluntarist Theory of Knowledge* (London: G. Bell, 1929). *Must Philosophers Disagree? and other Essays in Popular Philosophy* (London: Macmillan, 1934). *Our Human Truths* (New York: Columbia University Press, 1939).

Studies: D. Parodi, "Le pragmatisme d'après Messrs. W. James et Schiller," *Revue de Métaphysique et Morale*, 16 (1908), pp. 93–112. M. Hebert, *Le pragmatisme. Etude de ses diverses formes anglo-américaines* (Paris, 1909). R. B. Perry, "Dr. Schiller on William James and on Realism," *Mind*, 24 (1915), pp. 240–249. R. Abel, *The Pragmatic Humanism of F. C. S. Schiller* (New York: Columbia University Press, 1955).

2. William James, *The Meaning of Truth* (New York: Longmans, 1909), p. 169. For the relationship of Schiller to James, see R. B. Perry, *The Thought and Character of William James* (Boston: Little, Brown, 1935), II, 494–513.

3. *Humanism*, p. xix.

4. Ibid., pp. xxvi–xxvii; *Studies in Humanism*, p. 12.

5. *Humanism*, p. xxi.

6. Ibid. See "From Plato to Protagoras," in *Studies in Humanism*, pp. 22–70.

7. *Our Human Truths*, p. 283.

8. *Formal Logic*, p. 72.

9. *Humanism*, p. xxv.

10. *Studies in Humanism*, pp. 181–182.

11. *Logic for Use*, pp. 147–148.

12. *Humanism*, p. 61. For Schiller's difficulties in solving the problem of truth, see R. Abel, *The Pragmatic Humanism of F. C. S. Schiller*, pp. 101ff.

13. *Studies in Humanism*, p. 195.

14. Ibid., p. 422.

15. Ibid., p. 429.

16. Ibid., p. 188. Thus Schiller writes that "the 'realities' of civilized life are the embodiments of the ideas and desires of civilized man..." ibid., p. 199).

17. Axioms such as the principles of identity, contradiction, excluded middle, and causality are "essentially postulates, made with an ultimately practical end." They are not derived from the external world as the old empiricism maintained, nor are they necessary *a priori* laws as Kant claimed. They are ways we devise to organize our experience for practical purposes. See "Axioms as Postulates," in *Personal Idealism: Philosophical Essays by Eight Members of the University of Oxford* (London: Macmillan, 1902), pp. 47–133.

18. *Studies in Humanism*, p. 202.

19. See A. K. Rogers, *English and American Philosophy Since 1800* (New York: Macmillan, 1923), pp. 364–365.

20. *Studies in Humanism*, p. 483.

21. Ibid., pp. 422–444. "We need not shrink from words like 'hylozoism,' or (better) 'panpsychism,' provided that they stand for interpretations of the lower in terms of the higher. For at bottom they are merely forms of Humanism—attempts, that is, to make the human and the cosmic more akin, and to bring them closer to us, that we may act upon them more successfully" ibid., p. 443).

22. Ibid., p. 445.

23. For Schiller's notion of primary reality, see ibid., pp. 220–221. For his notion of matter, see ibid., p. 434. See also A. R. Gifford, "The Pragmatic *HULÉ* of Mr. Schiller," *Journal of Philosophy*, 5 (1908), pp. 99–104; H. M. Kallen, "The Pragmatic Notion of *HULÉ*," ibid., pp. 293–297.

Schiller sometimes regards *hulé* metaphysically as the objectively real chaos out of which the world is made, and sometimes epistemologically as the ever-receding limitation of our knowledge. See R. Abel, op. cit., pp. 118–119.

24. *Studies in Humanism*, p. 447.

25. Ibid., pp. 285–286. On God as the finite initiator of the evolution of the universe, see *Riddles of the Sphinx*, pp. 302–361.

26. Schiller had Daniel Alexander Murray as a disciple. See the latter's *Pragmatism*, 1912.

XX. Return to Realism

1. A. N. Whitehead, *Process and Reality* (New York: Social Science Book Store, 1929), p. 16.

2. *The Philosophy of Bertrand Russell*, ed. P. A. Schilpp (Evanston: The Library of Living Philosophers, V, 1946), p. 12. Moore modestly denied that Russell owed anything of value to him and claimed Russell as his teacher. See *The Philosophy of G. E. Moore*, ed. P. A. Schilpp (2nd ed.; Evanston and Chicago: Northwestern University Press, 1952; The Library of Living Philosophers, IV), p. 15.

3. George Edward Moore, b. London, 1873; d. Cambridge, 1958. He entered Trinity College, Cambridge, in 1892 and remained there as a student and Fellow until 1904.

After an absence of seven years he returned and lectured until 1939. On his retirement from Cambridge he visited the United States, lecturing at Smith College, Princeton, and Columbia University.

Works: *Principia Ethica* (Cambridge: University Press, 1903). *Ethics* (New York: Henry Holt, 1912). *Philosophical Studies* (London: Routledge & Kegan Paul, 1922). *Some Main Problems of Philosophy* (New York: Macmillan, 1953). *Philosophical Papers* (New York: Macmillan, 1959). *The Commonplace Book 1919–1953*, ed. C. Lewy (London: Allen & Unwin, 1963).

Studies: *The Philosophy of G. E. Moore*, ed. P. A. Schilpp (2nd ed.; Evanston and Chicago: Northwestern University Press, 1952; The Library of Living Philosophers, IV). J. Passmore, *A Hundred Years of Philosophy* (London: Duckworth, 1957), pp. 203–216. A. R. White, *G. E. Moore, a Critical Exposition* (Oxford: Blackwell, 1958). G. J. Warnock, *English Philosophy Since 1900* (London: Oxford University Press, 1958), pp. 12–29. M. Warnock, *Ethics Since 1900* (London: Oxford University Press, 1960), pp. 16–55.

4. *The Philosophy of G. E. Moore*, p. 14.

5. Originally printed in *Mind*, N. S. Vol. XII, 1903, this paper was published in *Philosophical Studies*, pp. 1–30.

6. Ibid., p. 30.

7. "A Defence of Common Sense," *Philosophical Papers*, pp. 33–34.

8. Moore's method of analysis involves holding before the mind an intelligible object in order to inspect it; dividing it, if possible, into its constituent concepts; and distinguishing it from other objects with which it might be confused. See A. R. White, *G. E. Moore*, pp. 66–83.

9. "A Defence of Common Sense," pp. 35–36. See "True and False Beliefs," *Some Main Problems of Philosophy*, pp. 284–287.

10. For Moore's notion of common sense, see A. R. White, op. cit., pp. 9–20. Moore's relation to Reid is discussed ibid., pp. 192–199, his relation to Berkeley on this point, pp. 191–192.

11. "Hume's Philosophy," *Philosophical Studies*, pp. 158–159.

12. "Proof of an External World," *Philosophical Papers*, pp. 148–150. See "Hume's Theory Explained," *Some Main Problems of Philosophy*, p. 125.

13. "Is Time Real?," *Some Main Problems of Philosophy*, p. 211.

14. See A. R. White, op. cit., p. 34. Moore does not take ordinary language as an infallible guide. Language in many instances, he says, has grown up "as if it were expressly designed to mislead philosophers." "The Concept of Reality," *Philosophical Studies*, p. 217.

15. *Reid's Essays on the Intellectual Powers of Man*, ed. W. Hamilton (London: Longmans, 1864), p. 362a.

16. "Though the idea of sense-data is at least as old as Locke and Berkeley, and Moore himself was using it by 1903, the introduction of the term is probably due to Moore's 1910/11 lectures and its publication to Russell's *The Problems of Philosophy* in 1912" (A. R. White, op. cit., p. 153). See K. T. Gallagher, "Some Recent Anglo-American Views on Perception," *International Philosophical Quarterly*, IV (1964), 122–141.

Moore defines sense-data as the direct objects of sensations or perceptions. He sometimes calls them "sensibles," "sense-qualities," "sense contents," or "appearances." Examples are a patch of white color, a sound, pain, or ache. At first he called color, size, and shape sense-data; but later he restricted the sense-data of sight to a "patch" which is of a certain color, size, and shape. See "Sense-Data," *Some Main Problems of Philosophy*, p. 30, and n. 2.

17. "A Defence of Common Sense," *Philosophical Papers*, p. 58.

18. "A Reply to *My* Critics," *The Philosophy of G. E. Moore*, p. 653. Moore refers to his early paper "The Refutation of Idealism," in *Philosophical Studies*, pp. 1–30.

19. "A Reply to My Critics," p. 658.

20. Ibid., p. 653.

21. Ibid., p. 659.

22. "Being, Fact and Existence," *Some Main Problems of Philosophy*, p. 291.

23. Ibid., p. 300. "Abstractions and Being," *Some Main Problems of Philosophy*, p. 372. In his early book *Principia Ethica* (pp. 110–111) Moore denies that numbers and universal truths exist; only things having temporal duration exist.

24. "Is Time Real?" pp. 212–214. See "The Conception of Reality," *Philosophical Studies*, pp. 211–219.

25. "Is Existence a Predicate?" *Philosophical Papers*, p. 125. For Moore's criticism of Russell's view that existence is essentially a property of a propositional function, see p. 123. For his analysis of "reality" as a predicate, see "The Conception of Reality," pp. 197–219.

26. *Principia Ethica*, pp. 16–17. Later, Moore expresses doubt whether goodness is really indefinable; in any case, he says that all his proofs to show that it is are fallacious. See "Is Goodness a Quality?" *Philosophical Papers*, p. 98. Moore insists that goodness is an intrinsic, absolute quality; it is not a relational property. That something is or would be good does not depend on the existence of a rational will. See "A Reply to My Critics," *The Philosophy of G. E. Moore*, p. 617.

27. *Principia Ethica*, p. 73. In the broad sense Moore calls the naturalistic fallacy the attempt to define the good by reference to some other object, whether this be natural or supersensible. In this extended meaning of the fallacy, metaphysical systems of ethics are also guilty of it. See ibid., pp. 38–39.

28. Ibid., p. 71.

29. Ibid., p. 128.

30. Ibid., p. 166.

31. Ibid., p. 188.

32. Bertrand Russell, b. Ravenscroft near Trellcck, Monmouthshire, England, 1872. J. S. Mil] was his godfather. First educated by private tutors. By the age of eighteen he abandoned belief in free will, immortality, and God. Attended Trinity College, Cambridge, 1890–1894, studying mathematics the first three years and philosophy in the fourth. Became an Hegelian and admirer of Bradley. Attaché at British Embassy in Paris, 1894. In 1895 he studied economics and social democracy in Berlin. Abandoned Hegelianism with G. E. Moore in 1898. In 1900 attended International Congress of Philosophy in Paris with Whitehead and became acquainted with the work of Peano. Lectured at Cambridge 1910–1916. Visited Russia, Japan, China, and lectured in the United States extensively from 1924 to 1944 and again in 1951.

Main works: *A Critical Exposition of the Philosophy of Leibniz* (Cambridge: University Press, 1900). *The Principles of Mathematics* (Cambridge: University Press, 1903; 2nd ed., New York: Norton, 1937). *Principia Mathematica* (with A. N. Whitehead) (3 vols.; Cambridge: University Press, 1910–1913; 2nd ed., 1925–1927). *The Problems of Philosophy* (London: Thornton Butterworth, 1912). *Our Knowledge of the External World* (London: Allen & Unwin, 1914; rev. ed., 1926). *Mysticism and Logic* (London: Allen & Unwin, 1917). *Introduction to Mathematical Philosophy* (London: Allen & Unwin, 1919; 2nd ed., 1920). *The Analysis of Mind* (London: Allen & Unwin, 1921). *Why I Am Not a Christian* (London: Watts & Co., 1927). *The Analysis of Matter* (New York: Harcourt, Brace, 1927). *Philosophy* (New York: Norton, 1927). *Sceptical Essays* (London: Allen & Unwin, 1935). *An Inquiry into Meaning and Truth* (New York: Norton, 1940). *A History of Western Philosophy* (New York: Simon and Schuster, 1945). *Human Knowledge, Its Scope and Limits* (London: Allen & Unwin, 1948). *Human Society in Ethics and Politics* (London: Allen & Unwin, 1954). *Logic and Knowledge, Essays*

1901–1950, ed. R. C. Marsh (London: Allen & Unwin, 1956). *My Philosophical Development* (London: Allen & Unwin, 1959). *The Basic Writings of Bertrand Russell*, ed. R. E. Egner and L. E. Denonn (London: Allen & Unwin, 1961). *Political Ideals* (New York: Simon & Schuster, 1964).

Studies: P. E. Jourdain, *The Philosophy of Mr. Bertrand Russell* (London: Allen & Unwin, 1918). *The Philosophy of Bertrand Russell*, ed. P. A. Schilpp (Evanston: The Library of Living Philosophers, V, 1946; bibliography). C. A. Fritz, *Bertrand Russell's Construction of the External World* (London: Routledge, 1952). J. O. Urmson, *Philosophical Analysis* (Oxford: Clarendon Press, 1956). J. A. Passmore, *A Hundred Years of Philosophy* (London: Duckworth, 1957, pp. 215–241). G. J. Warnock, *English Philosophy since 1900* (London: Oxford University Press, 1958, pp. 30–42).

33. *My Philosophical Development*, p. 62.

34. Ibid., p. 217.

35. For Russell's theory of analysis, see "The Philosophy of Logical Atomism," in *Logic and Knowledge*, pp. 177–281; *Inquiry into Meaning and Truth*, chap. xxiv. Also M. Weitz, "The Unity of Russell's Philosophy," *The Philosophy of Bertrand Russell*, ed. P. A. Schilpp, pp. 110–121; J. O. Urmson, *Philosophical Analysis.*

36. *Our Knowledge of the External World*, p. 42. Russell calls logic the essence of philosophy in the sense that it enables the philosopher to analyze complex particulars and to reach their logical form. But when he speaks of philosophy as a realism, he denies that logic is any part of philosophy. See *My Philosophical Development*, pp. 276–277.

37. See "The Philosophy of Logical Atomism" and "Logical Atomism," in *Logic and Knowledge*, pp. 175–281, 323–343.

38. For Russell's criticism of monism as based on the doctrine of internal relations, see *Our Knowledge of the External World*, pp. 54–61; *My Philosophical Development*, pp. 54–64.

39. *My Philosophical Development*, p. 55.

40. *Our Knowledge of the External World*, p. 59.

41. In his early theory Russell thought that particulars are diverse because of their spatial and temporal relations; in short, that a particular is defined by its spatio-temporal position. See "On the Relation of Universals to Particulars," *Logic and Knowledge*, pp. 123–124. In a note appended in 1955 Russell abandons this view in favor of the Leibnizian conception that a particular is constituted of qualities (p. 124). See *Human Knowledge, Its Scope and Limits*, p. 310. For Russell's early view on universals and

particulars, see *The Problems of Philosophy*, chaps. viii–x. See also A. Donagan, "Universals and Metaphysical Realism," *The Monist*, 47 (1963), pp. 211–246.

42. *Human Knowledge, Its Scope and Limits*, p. 128. See *Our Knowledge of the External World*, p. 60.

43. *Our Knowledge of the External World*, p. 63. Atomic facts are usually known empirically; Russell thinks it very doubtful if one such fact can be inferred from another. Pure logic, on the other hand, is wholly *a priori* (ibid.). On atomic and molecular propositions, see *Principia Mathematica*, I, xv–xix; *Logic and Knowledge*, pp. 203–216.

44. In his later works Russell questions whether we can reach atomic facts incapable of further analysis. It is perfectly possible, he says, that complex things are capable of analysis *ad infinitum*, without reaching what is truly simple. But even if there are no atomic facts, there are atomic propositions. These are sentences that do not contain the word "all" or "some" and have no parts that are sentences. See *My Philosophical Development*, pp. 222–223.

45. *Tractatus Logico-Philosophicus*, 2.0201. Quoted in *My Philosophical Development*, p. 118.

46. *An Inquiry into Meaning and Truth*, pp. 328–342.

47. *Human Knowledge*, p. 131. See *My Philosophical Development*, p. 113.

48. *My Philosophical Development*, pp. 113–114. In 1948 Russell wrote, "And to allow grammar to dictate our metaphysic is now generally recognized to be dangerous." *Human Knowledge, Its Scope and Limits*, p. 311.

49. *An Inquiry into Meaning and Truth*, p. 438. As late as *My Philosophical Development* (1959) he writes that "syntax—i.e., the structure of sentences—must have some relation to the structure of facts, at any rate in those aspects of syntax which are unavoidable and not peculiar to this or that language" (p. 157).

50. *The Problems of Philosophy*, pp. 202–203. Russell expresses the correspondence of belief to fact that is truth in terms of a picture: "Every belief which is not merely an impulse to action is in the nature of a picture, combined with a yes-feeling or a no-feeling; in the case of a yes-feeling it is 'true' if there is a fact having to the picture the kind of similarity that a prototype has to an image; in the case of a no-feeling it is 'true' if there is no such fact." *Human Knowledge, Its Scope and Limits*, p. 170. Like Moore, Russell criticizes the pragmatic notion of truth. See *My Philosophical Development*, pp. 176–181. For a general discussion of the nature of truth, see *An Inquiry into Meaning and Truth*, especially chap. xxi.

51. *An Inquiry into Meaning and Truth*, p. 430.

52. For the theory of descriptions, see *Logic and Knowledge*, pp. 41–56, 241–254; *Principia Mathematica*, I, 66–71, 173–186; *Introduction to Mathematical Philosophy*, pp. 167–180; *My Philosophical Development*, pp. 83–85.

53. *My Philosophical Development*, p. 84.

54. *Introduction to Mathematical Philosophy*, p. 179.

55. *My Philosophical Development*, p. 85. See *Logic and Knowledge*, pp. 232–234. *Introduction to Mathematical Philosophy*, p. 179. In his *Principles of Mathematics* Russell distinguishes between being and existence. "*Being* is that which belongs to every conceivable term, to every possible object of thought.... Numbers, the Homeric gods, relations, chimeras and four-dimensional space all have being, for if they were not entities of a kind, we could make no propositions about them.... *Existence*, on the contrary, is the prerogative of some only amongst beings. To exist is to have a specific relation to existence..." (p. 449). In *My Philosophical Development*, however, "being" is declared to be a useless word (p. 69).

56. G. E. Moore, *Philosophical Papers*, pp. 123–126.

57. *My Philosophical Development*, p. 85; *Logic and Knowledge*, p. 241; *Introduction to Mathematical Philosophy*, pp. 178–179.

58. *My Philosophical Development*, p. 158. In his *Introduction to Mathematical Philosophy*, p. 167 (1919), Russell wrote that in a sense logic is also concerned with reality: "Logic, I should maintain, must no more admit a unicorn than zoology can; for logic is concerned with the real world just as truly as zoology, though with its more abstract and general features."

59. *Logic and Knowledge*, p. 193.

60. *My Philosophical Development*, p. 134. See "Knowledge by Acquaintance and Knowledge by Description," *Mysticism and Logic*, pp. 209–232; "On the Nature of Acquaintance," *Logic and Knowledge*, pp. 127–174.

61. *My Philosophical Development*, pp. 135–139. See *Philosophy*, pp. 206–209, 210, 292.

62. *Philosophy*, p. 281.

63. *Human Knowledge, Its Scope and Limits*, pp. 98, 310–325.

64. *Philosophy*, p. 281.

65. "We cannot, however, infer that the sun is *not* bright—meaning by 'brightness' the quality that we know in perception. The only legitimate inferences as regards the physical sun are structural; concerning a property that is not structural, such as brightness, we must remain completely agnostic." *Human Knowledge, Its Scope and Limits*, pp. 245–246.

66. *My Philosophical Development*, p. 208.

67. *Philosophy*, pp. 229–235; *Human Society in Ethics and Politics*, pp. no-118.

68. Alfred North Whitehead, b. Ramsgate in the Isle of Thanet, Kent, 1861; d. Cambridge, Massachusetts, 1947. He was raised in southern England, where the remains of the medieval past stirred his imagination. After classical studies at Sherborne in Dorsetshire, he entered Trinity College, Cambridge, in 1880, to study mathematics. In 1885 he was elected Fellow of Trinity College. Resigned as Senior Lecturer in 1910; went to London and taught mathematics at University College. From 1914 to 1924 he was professor at the Imperial College of Science and Technology in Kensington; during the later years of this period he was Dean of the Faculty of Science at the University of London. He was professor of philosophy at Harvard University from 1924 to his retirement in 1936.

Works: A complete bibliography is contained in *The Philosophy of Alfred North Whitehead*, ed. P. A. Schilpp (2nd ed.; New York: Tudor, 1951, The Library of Living Philosophers), pp. 745–778. See also W. E. Stokes, "A Select and Annotated Bibliography of Alfred North Whitehead," *The Modern Schoolman*, 39 (1963), pp. 135–151.

Principal writings: *Principia Mathematica* (with B. Russell) (3 vols.; Cambridge: University Press, 1910–1913; 2nd ed., 1925–1927). *An Enquiry Concerning the Principles of Natural Knowledge* (Cambridge: University Press, 1919; 2nd ed., 1925). *The Concept of Nature* (Cambridge: University Press, 1920). *Science and the Modern World* (New York: Macmillan, 1925). *Religion in the Making* (New York: Macmillan, 1926). *Symbolism, Its Meaning and Effect* (New York: Macmillan, 1927). *The Aims of Education and Other Essays* (New York: Macmillan, 1929). *Adventures of Ideas* (New York: Macmillan, 1933). *Process and Reality* (New York: Macmillan, 1929). *Modes of Thought* (New York: Macmillan, 1938). *Essays in Science and Philosophy* (New York: Philosophical Library, 1947). *The Wit and Wisdom of Whitehead*, ed. A. H. Johnson (Boston: Beacon Press, 1947). *Alfred North Whitehead, an Anthology*, selected by F. S. C. Northrop and M. W. Gross (Cambridge: University Press, 1953). *Dialogues of Alfred North Whitehead*, recorded by L. Price (London: Max Reinhardt, 1954).

Studies: P. Ushenko, *The Logic of Events* (Berkeley: University of California Press, 1929). J. Wahl, *Vers le concret* (Paris: Vrin, 1932), pp. 127–221. D. Emmet, *Whitehead's Philosophy of Organism* (London: Macmillan, 1932). E. J. Lintz, *The Unity of the Universe according to Alfred North Whitehead* (Fribourg, Switzerland: University of Fribourg Dissertation, 1939). W. W. Hammerschmidt, *Whitehead's Philosophy of Time* (New York: King's Crown Press, 1947). *The Philosophy of Whitehead*, ed. P. A. Schilpp (2nd ed.; New York: Tudor, 1951, The Library of Living Philosophers). C.

Hartshorne, *The Divine Relativity* (New Haven: Yale University Press, 1948). A. H. Johnson, *Whitehead's Theory of Reality* (Boston: Beacon Press, 1953). N. Lawrence, *Whitehead's Philosophical Development* (Berkeley: University of California Press, 1956). L. Bright, *Whitehead's Philosophy of Physics* (New York: Sheed & Ward, 1958). A. H. Johnson, *Whitehead's Philosophy of Civilization* (Boston: Beacon Press, 1958). I. Leclerc, *Whitehead's Metaphysics* (New York: Macmillan, 1958). W. Mays, *The Philosophy of Whitehead* (New York: Macmillan, 1959). R. M. Palter, *Whitehead's Philosophy of Science* (Chicago: University of Chicago Press, 1960). *The Relevance of Whitehead*, ed. I. Leclerc (New York: Macmillan, 1961). D. W. Sherburne, *A Whiteheadian Aesthetic* (New Haven: Yale University Press, 1961).

69. *The Philosophy of A. N. Whitehead*, ed. P. A. Schilpp, p. 11.

70. *Science and the Modern World*, p. 122. See *Adventures of Ideas*, p. 187.

71. *Dialogues of Alfred North Whitehead*, pp. 4–5.

72. *Science and the Modern World*, pp. 69, 81. See A. O. Lovejoy, *The Revolt against Dualism* (Open Court, 1930), Lecture V: "Mr. Whitehead and the Denial of Simple Location."

73. *Science and the Modem World*, p. 71.

74. "Modern physics has abandoned the doctrine of Simple Location. The physical things which we term stars, planets, lumps of matter, molecules, electrons, protons, quanta of energy, are each to be conceived as modifications of conditions within space-time, extending throughout its whole range. There is a focal region, which in common speech is where the thing is. But its influence streams away from it with finite velocity throughout the utmost recesses of space and time" (*Adventures of Ideas*, pp. 201–202).

75. *Science and the Modern World*, p. 72. See *Process and Reality*, pp. 11, 142. An abstraction may be grounded in reality: "Now an abstraction is nothing else than the omission of part of the truth. The abstraction is well-founded when the conclusions drawn from it are not vitiated by the omitted truth" (*Modes of Thought*, p. 189).

76. *Science and the Modern World*, p. 77. See *Modes of Thought*, pp. 180–182. Sense qualities, such as colors, sounds, tastes, "can with equal truth be described as our sensations or as the qualities of the actual things which we perceive. These qualities are thus relational between the perceiving subject and the perceived things." *Symbolism, Its Meaning and Effect*, pp. 21–22.

77. *The Concept of Nature*, pp. 30–31.

78. *Science and the Modern World*, p. 79.

79. *Process and Reality*, p. x.

80. *Adventures of Ideas*, p. 202.

81. *Modes of Thought*, p. 188. The relations of an event to other events and to eternal objects are internal relations, entering into the essence of the event. "Each relationship enters the essence of the event; so that, apart from the relationship, the event would not be itself" (*Science and the Modern World*, p. 174). Through his doctrine of internal relations Whitehead conies close to the philosophy of Hegel and Bradley. Referring to *Process and Reality* he writes: "Finally, though throughout the main body of the work I am in sharp disagreement with Bradley, the final outcome is after all not so greatly different. Indeed, if this cosmology be deemed successful, it becomes natural at this point to ask whether the type of thought involved be not a transformation of some main doctrines of Absolute Idealism onto a realistic basis" (*Modes of Thought*, pp. vii, viii). See p. 254.

82. *Science and the Modern World*, p. 128. Each actual event "is a microcosm representing in itself the entire all-inclusive universe" (*Religion in the Making*, p. 91).

83. *Principles of Natural Knowledge*, pp. 62–63.

84. Ibid., p. 66.

85. Ibid., pp. 82ff.

86. Ibid., p. 88.

87. *The Concept of Nature*, p. 45. This realist attitude toward science is seen in his conception of the laws of physics. "The laws of physics are the laws declaring how the entities mutually react among themselves" (*Science and the Modern World*, p. 150).

88. Ibid., p. 168.

89. *Process and Reality*, p. 65.

90. Ibid., p. 43. For James' doctrine of experience, see above, p. 636.

91. Whitehead likens his notion of "prehension" to the Leibnizian notion of "perception but without the latter's association with consciousness and representative perception. Accordingly, on the Leibnizian model, I use the term 'prehension' for the general way in which the occasion of experience can include, as part of its own essence, any other entity, whether another occasion of experience or an entity of another type. This term

is devoid of suggestion either of consciousness or of representative perception" (*Adventures of Ideas*, p. 300).

92. Whitehead attributes to James the inauguration of a new stage in philosophy through his essay "Does Consciousness Exist?" which argues, against Descartes, that consciousness is not an entity but a function. See *Science and the Modern World*, pp. 199–200. Whitehead greatly admired James, listing him with Plato, Aristotle, and Leibniz as one of the four great thinkers in Western philosophy. See *Modes of Thought*, pp. 3–4.

93. *Process and Reality*, pp. 135–136.

94. *Science and the Modern World*, pp. 130, 142ff.

95. For Whitehead's account of the categories, see *Process and Reality*, pp. 30ff.

96. Ibid., pp. 31–32.

97. Ibid., pp. 46–47, 146.

98. "It (i.e., creativity) can thus be termed a 'real potentiality.' The 'potentiality' refers to the passive capacity, the term 'real' refers to the creative activity, where the Platonic definition of 'real' in the *Sophist* is referred to" (*Adventures of Ideas*, p. 230). See *Sophist*, 247E.

99. *Process and Reality*, pp. 374, 523.

100. Ibid., p. 47. On eternal objects, see Ibid., pp. 34, 70, 445.

101. Ibid., p. 392.

102. Ibid., pp. 521–523.

103. Ibid., p. 525. "Thus all attainment is immortal in that it fashions the actual ideals which are God in the world as it is now" (*Religion in the Making*, p. 159). God is finite and limited because his goodness excludes evil (ibid., p. 153). For Whitehead's notion of a finite God, see C. Fabro, *Introduzione all' Ateismo Moderno* (Rome: Editrice Studium, 1964), pp. 767–799.

104. *Adventures of Ideas*, p. 301.

105. Ibid., p. 324.

106. Ibid., p. 348.

107. Ibid., pp. 353, 360.

108. Ibid., p. 369.

Robin George Collingwood, b. 1889; d. 1943. Professor of metaphysics, Magdalen College, Oxford. Trained in the principles and methods of realism, he became critical of thorn and rejected the realist position. He attempted to reform metaphysics by making it a thoroughly historical and empirical science. His main works include: *Speculum Mentis* (Oxford: Clarendon Press, 1924); *Outlines of a Philosophy of Art* (London: Oxford University Press, 1925); *An Essay on Philosophical Method* (Oxford: Clarendon Press, 1933); *The Principles of Art* (Oxford: Clarendon Press, 1938); *An Autobiography* (London: Oxford University Press, 1939); *An Essay on Metaphysics* (Oxford: Clarendon Press, 1940); *The New Leviathan* (Oxford: Clarendon Press, 1942); *The Idea of Nature* (Oxford: Clarendon Press, 1945); *The Idea of History* (Oxford: Clarendon Press, 1946); *Essays in the Philosophy of Art*, ed. A. Donagan (Bloomington: Indiana University Press, 1964). Study: A. Donagan, *The Later Philosophy of R. G. Collingwood* (Oxford: Clarendon Press, 1962).

XXI. Language and Metaphysics

1. F. H. Bradley, *Appearance and Reality*, London, 1897, pp. x, 1.

2. Charlie Dunbar Broad, b. Harlesden in Middlesex, 1887–. Studied at Dulwich College and Trinity College, Cambridge; elected Fellow of Trinity in 1911. Taught at St. Andrews 1914–1920 and at Bristol 1920–1923. Returned to Trinity College, where he occupied the Chair of Moral Philosophy in 1933.

Main works: *Perception, Physics, and Reality* (Cambridge: University Press, 1914). *Scientific Thought* (London: Kegan Paul, 1923). *Mind and Its Place in Nature* (London: Kegan Paul, 1925). *Five Types of Ethical Theory* (London: Kegan Paul, 1930). *Examination of McTaggart's Philosophy* (2 vols.; Cambridge: University Press, 1933, 1938). *Ethics and the History of Philosophy* (London: Routledge & Kegan Paul, 1952). *Religion, Philosophy and Psychical Research* (London: Routledge & Kegan Paul, 1953).

Studies: M. Lean, *Sense-Perception and Matter: A Critical Analysis of C. D. Broad's Theory of Perception* (London; Routledge, 1953). J. Wild, "An Examination of Critical Realism with Special Reference to C. D. Broad's Theory of Sense," *Philosophy and Phenomenological Research*," 1953–1954, pp. 143–161. *The Philosophy of C. D. Broad*, in The Library of Living Philosophers, ed. P. A. Schilpp (New York: Tudor, 1959).

3. C. D. Broad, "Critical and Speculative Philosophy," *Contemporary British Philosophy* (First Series), ed. J. H. Muirhead (New York: Macmillan, 1924), p. 78.

4. C. D. Broad, *Scientific Thought*, p. 16.

5. Ibid., p. 20.

6. Ludwig Wittgenstein, b. Vienna, 1889; d. Cambridge, England, 1951. Studied engineering at the Technische Hochschule in Berlin-Charlottenburg and the University of Manchester. Experimented with kites, jet engines, and propeller design. Became interested in pure mathematics and then in the philosophy of mathematics. Read Russell's *Principles of Mathematics* and the works of Frege, which introduced him to philosophy. Studied under Russell at Trinity College, Cambridge, 1912–1913; at the same College he became acquainted with G. E. Moore and Whitehead. Served in the Austrian army during the war. From 1919 to 1920 he studied at the Teachers' Training College in Vienna and taught in elementary schools from 1920 to 1926. Designed a mansion in Vienna for one of his sisters. Through his acquaintance with Moritz Schlick and Friedrich Waismann he influenced the Vienna Circle. He returned to Cambridge as a student in 1929; received the doctorate the same year. The following year he was elected Fellow of Trinity College. With some interruptions he lectured at Cambridge from 1930 to 1947.

   For biographical material, see Norman Malcolm, *Ludwig Wittgenstein, a Memoir, with a Biographical Sketch by Georg Henrik von Wright* (London: Oxford University Press, 1958).

   Works: *Tractatus Logico-Philosophicus,* trans. C. K. Ogden (London: Kegan Paul, 1922); new translation by D. F. Pears and B. F. McGuinness (New York: The Humanities Press, 1961). *Philosophical Investigations*, trans. G. E. M. Anscombe (New York: Macmillan, 1953). *Remarks on the Foundations of Mathematics*, trans. G. E. M. Anscombe (Oxford: Blackwell, 1956). *Preliminary Studies for the "Philosophical Investigations": Generally Known as the Blue and Brown Books* (New York: Harper, 1958). *Notebooks, 1914–1916*, ed. G. H. von Wright and G. E. M. Anscombe (New York: Harper, 1961).

   Studies: M. Black, *Language and Philosophy* (Ithaca: Cornell University Press, 1949), pp. 141–165. J. O. Urmson, *Philosophical Analysis* (Oxford: Clarendon Press, 1956). G. J. Warnock, *English Philosophy Since 1900* (London: Oxford University Press, 1958), pp. 62–93. D. Pole, *The Later Philosophy of Wittgenstein* (University of London: Athlone Press, 1958). G. E. M. Anscombe, *An Introduction to Wittgenstein's "Tractatus"* (London: Hutchinson University Library, 1959). M. J. Charlesworth, *Philosophy and Linguistic Analysis* (Louvain: Nauwelaerts, 1959), pp. 74–125. E. Stenius, *Wittgenstein's 'Tractatus"* (Oxford: Blackwell, 1960). G. K. Plochmann and J. B. Lawson, *Terms in Their Propositional Contexts in Wittgenstein's Tractatus* (Carbondale: Southern Illinois University Press, 1962). G. Pitcher, *The Philosophy of Wittgenstein* (Englewood Cliffs, NJ: Prentice-Hall, 1964). J. Griffin, *Wittgenstein's Logical Atomism* (Oxford: Clarendon Press, 1964). V. Mehta, *Fly and the Fly-Bottle* (Boston: Little, Brown, 1962). M. Black, *A Companion to Wittgenstein's Tractatus* (Cambridge: University Press, 1964).

7. *Tractatus*, 4.112.

8. Ibid., 4.003.

9. Ibid., 3.323.

10. Ibid., 4.01, 4.021, 4.022.

11. Ibid., 2.1511, 2.1512.

12. N. Malcolm, *Ludwig Wittgenstein, a Memoir*, pp. 68–69.

13. *Tractatus*, 6.124.

14. Ibid., 6.2.

15. Ibid., 4.11.

16. Ibid., 4.113ff. In the preface (p. 3) Wittgenstein says, "Thus the the aim of the book is to set a limit to thought, or rather—not to thought, but to the expression of thoughts: for in order to be able to set a limit to thought, we should have to find both sides of the limit thinkable (i.e., we should have to be able to think what cannot be thought). It will therefore only be in language that the limit can be set, and what lies on the other side of the limit will simply be nonsense (*Unsinn*)." Consequently, "*The limits of my language* mean the limits of my world" (ibid., 5.6).

17. Ibid., *6.52,* 6.521.

18. Ibid., 6.53.

19. Ibid., *5.61.*

20. Ibid., 6.432.

21. This structure is the one described by logical atomism, as is clear from the opening propositions of the *Tractatus.*

22. Ibid., 6.54. Brand Blanshard's comment underlines the paradox of Wittgenstein's statement: "But if the rungs of the ladder make no sense, how can he climb up on them? Wittgenstein is in a dilemma from which he can hardly escape by a metaphor." B. Blanshard, *Reason and Analysis* (London: Allen & Unwin, 1962), p. 148.

23. *Philosophical Investigations*, 11 (references are to paragraph numbers).

24. Ibid., 7.

25. Ibid., 115, 1.

26. Ibid., 339.

27. Ibid., 124.

28. Ibid., 109.

29. Ibid., 119.

30. Ibid., 116.

31. Ibid., 309.

32. Ibid., 111.

33. Ibid., 116. "When philosophers use a word—'knowledge,' 'being,' 'object,' 'I,' 'proposition,' 'name'—and try to grasp the *essence* of the thing, one must always ask oneself: is the word ever actually used in this way in the language-game which is its original home?—What *we* do is to bring words back from their metaphysical to their everyday usage." Philosophy does not advance any kind of theory or offer explanations; its role is descriptive. See Ibid., 109. "Philosophers are constantly tempted to ask and answer questions in the way science does. This tendency is the real source of metaphysics, and leads the philosopher into complete darkness. I want to say here that it can never be our job to reduce anything or to explain anything. Philosophy really is 'purely descriptive,'" *The Blue and the Brown Books*, p. 18.

34. See G. E. Moore, "Wittgenstein's Lectures in 1930–33," *Mind*, 1954, p. 26; *Philosophical Papers*, p. 322.

35. For examples of the merging of these two types of analysis, see H. Feigl and W. Sellars, introduction to *Readings in Philosophical Analysis* (New York: Appleton-Century-Crofts, 1949), p. vi; and A. J. Ayer, Introduction to *Logical Positivism* (Glencoe, IL: The Free Press, 1959), pp. 3–10.

For the history of the Vienna Circle and the philosophy of logical-positivism, see V. Kraft, *The Vienna Circle. The Origin of Neo-Positivism* (New York: Philosophical Library, 1953). O. Neurath, *Le* développement du Cercle de Vienne *et l'avenir de l'empirisme logique* (Paris: Hermann, 1935). A. J. Ayer, The Vienna Circle," *The Revolution in Philosophy* (London: Macmillan, 1956), pp. 70–87; same author, *Logical Positivism* (Glencoe, IL: The Free Press, 1959), pp. 3–10. J. R. Weinberg, *An Examination of Logical Positivism* (London: Kegan Paul, 1936). O. Neurath and C. W. Morris, *Logical Positivism, Pragmatism and Scientific Empiricism* (Paris: Hermann, 1937). H. Feigl, "Logical Empiricism," *Twentieth Century Philosophy*, ed. D. D. Runes (New York: Philosophical Library, 1943), pp. 373–416. P. Frank, *Between Physics and Philosophy* (Cambridge, MA: Harvard University Press, 1941); same author, *Introduction to Modern Science and Its Philosophy* (Cambridge, MA: Harvard University Press, 1949). C. E. M. Joad, *A Critique of Logical Positivism* (Chicago: University of Chicago Press, 1950). J. Joergesen, *The Development of Logical Empiricism, International Encyclopedia of Unified Science*, II, 9 (Chicago: University of Chicago Press, 1951). H. Reichenbach, *The Rise of Scientific Philosophy* (Berkeley: University of California Press, 1953). F. Barone, *Il neopositivismo logico* (Turin, 1953). G. Bergmann, *The Metaphysics of Logical Positivism* (New York: Longmans, 1954). R. von Mises, *Positivism: A Study in Human Understanding* (New York: George Braziller, 1956).

7. Moritz Schlick, b. Berlin, 1882; d. Vienna, 1936, murdered by a student. Studied physics at Lausanne, Heidelberg, and Berlin, where he took the doctorate under Max Planck in 1904. Taught physics at the University of Kiel and in 1922 became professor of philosophy at Vienna.

Philosophical works: *Allgemeine Erkenntnislehre* (Berlin: J. Springer, 1918; 2nd ed., 1925); *Kritizistische oder empiristische Deutung der modernen Physik?*, in *Kant-Studien*, 1921; *Erleben, Erkennen, Metaphysik*, in *Kant-Studien*, 1926; *Gesammelte Aufsätze 1926–36* (Vienna: Gerold, 1938); *Fragen der Ethik* (Vienna: 1930); *Problems of Ethics*, trans. D. Rynin (New York: Prentice-Hall, 1939); J. Springer, *Philosophie der Natur* (Vienna: Gerold, 1948); *Natur und Kultur*, ed. J. Rauscher (Vienna: 1952); *Les Enoncés scientifiques et la réalité du monde extérieur* (Paris: Hermann & Cie, 1934).

38. Ernst Mach, b. Turas, Moravia, 1838; d. Haar in Bavaria, 1916. Taught physics and philosophy at the University of Vienna. Published *Erkenntnis und Irrtum* (Leipzig, 1905). See C. B. Weinberg, *Mach's Empirio-Pragmatism in Physical Science* (New York, 1937); P. Frank, "Ernst Mach—The Centenary of His Birth," *Erkenntnis*, 7 (1938), pp. 17–56; same author, *Between Physics and Philosophy* (Cambridge, MA: Harvard University Press, 1941), chap. x: "Ernst Mach and the Unity of Science."

Frank explains that Mach's antipathy to metaphysics was not "a demand arising from some anti-metaphysical mood, but the only means of making possible the unification of science. According to Mach, metaphysics must be eliminated 'because it is contradictory to the economical function of science.'" For the unification of the sciences into a coherent logical system, propositions of a homogeneous type are needed. Because the propositions of metaphysics are not of the type found in the empirical sciences, all of which are reducible to sentences containing only perception terms as predicates, they must be eliminated (ibid., p. 219).

39. A. J. Ayer, *Logical Positivism*, p. 7.

40. Rudolf Carnap, b. Wuppertal, 1891–. Professor at Vienna, then held chair of philosophy of nature in the German University of Prague from 1931 to 1936. In the United States he has taught at Chicago and is currently at the University of California in Los Angeles.

Main Works: *Ler logische Aufbau der Welt* (Berlin, 1928); *Schein—probleme in der Philosophie* (Berlin, 1928). *The Unity of Science* (*Psyche Miniatures*), trans. M. Black (London: Kegan Paul, 1934). *Philosophy and Logical Syntax* (London: Kegan Paul, 1935). *Foundations of Logic and Mathematics, International Encyclopedia of Unified Science*, I, 3 (Chicago: University of Chicago Press, 1939). *Introduction to Semantics*

(Cambridge, MA: Harvard University Press, 1942). *The Logical Syntax of Language* (New York: Humanities Press, 1951). *Meaning and Necessity* (2nd ed.; Chicago: University of Chicago Press, 1956). *Logical Foundations of Probability* (Chicago: University of Chicago Press, 1950). *The Continuum of Inductive Methods* (Chicago: University of Chicago Press, 1952).

Study: *The Philosophy of Rudolf Carnap*, ed. P. A. Schilpp (La Salle, IL: Open Court Publishing Co., 1964).

41. "The Physical Language as the Universal Language of Science," *Readings in Twentieth-Century Philosophy*, ed. W. P. Alston and G. Nakhnikian (Glencoe, IL: The Free Press, 1963), p. 393. See "The Elimination of Metaphysics through Logical Analysis of Language," *Logical Positivism*, ed. A. J. Ayer, p. 77.

42. The logical positivists appealed to Wittgenstein's *Tractatus* for this principle, though Wittgenstein denied teaching it as a theory of meaning. See J. Passmore, *A Hundred Years of Philosophy* (London: Duckworth, 1957), p. 371.

43. The meaning of the verification principle has undergone a considerable development and liberalization in Carnap's thought. At first he held that sentences are empirically meaningful only if they can actually be translated into the language of observation or experience. See "The Methodological Character of Theoretical Concepts," *The Foundations of Science and the Concepts of Psychology and Psychoanalysis*, ed. H. Feigl and M. Scriven (Minneapolis: University of Minnesota Press, 1956), p. 39. Later, in *Philosophy and Logical Syntax*, he distinguished between direct and indirect verification. Only basic, protocol sentences, which record an experience (e.g., "I feel a headache") are directly verifiable. Other propositions, such as the general laws of physics, are only indirectly verifiable by deducing from them directly verifiable propositions. Still later, in "Testability and Meaning," he preferred to use the terms "testable" and "confirmable" for propositions only indirectly verifiable (*Philosophy of Science*, Vol. III [1936], Vol. IV [1937]).

44. *Philosophy and Logical Syntax*, pp. 89–90; *Readings in Twentieth-Century Philosophy*, pp. 455–456.

45. *The Logical Syntax of Language*, p. 8.

46. "The Elimination of Metaphysics through Logical Analysis of Language," *Logical Positivism*, ed. A. J. Ayer, p. 80.

47. *Tractatus*, 4.121.

48. *The Logical Syntax of Language*, p. 284.

49. "Empiricism, Semantics, and Ontology," *Semantics and the Philosophy of Language*, ed. L. Linsky (Urbana: University of Illinois Press, 1952), pp. 209–212.
It is in this empirical and non metaphysical sense of "real" that Carnap speaks of "confronting" statements with observed facts or reality and thereby confirming them. See "Truth and Confirmation," *Readings in Philosophical Analysis*, ed. H. Feigl and W. Sellars (New York: Appleton-Century-Crofts, 1949), pp. 119–127.
Moreover, it is a matter of convention as to whether directly established statements (protocol statements) are understood to refer to observed things and processes or to acts of perception (ibid., p. 124, n. 13).

50. *Tractatus*, 6.522.

51. Alfred Jules Ayer, b. 1910–. Studied at Oxford and Vienna, where he had personal contact with the founders of logical positivism, Schlick and Carnap. In 1946 he became Professor of Mind and Logic at the University of London, and in 1960 Professor of Logic at Oxford.
Main works: *Logic, Truth and Language* (1st ed.; London: Victor Gollancz, 1936; 2nd ed., 1946). *The Foundation of Empirical Knowledge* (London: Macmillan, 1940). *Thinking and Meaning* (London: Macmillan, 1947). *Philosophical Essays* (London: Macmillan, 1954). *The Problem of Knowledge* (London: Macmillan, 1956). *The Concept of a Person and Other Essays* (London: Macmillan, 1963).

52. *Language, Truth and Logic* (2nd ed.), p. 32.

53. T. E. Hill, *Contemporary Theories of Knowledge* (New York: Ronald Press, 1961), p. 407.

54. *Language, Truth and Logic*, ibid.

55. Ibid., pp. 152–153.

56. Ibid., p. 26.

57. Ibid., p. 78.

58. Ibid., p. 31.

59. Ibid., p. 17.

60. Ibid., pp. 9–12, 36–37. In the first edition of *Language, Truth and Logic* Ayer claimed that no empirical propositions can be conclusively verified (p. 38). In the preface to the second edition he makes an exception of basic propositions (p. 10). See "Basic Propositions," *Philosophical Essays*, p. 121.

In the second edition Ayer defines more precisely his use of the words "sentence," "statement," and "proposition." A sentence is "any form of words that is grammatically significant." A statement is that which is expressed by every indicative sentence, whether it is literally meaningful or not. Two sentences mutually translatable express the same statement. A proposition is what is expressed by sentences that are literally meaningful (ibid., p. 8).

61. Ibid., p. 38.

62. Ibid., pp. 36, 115. To the argument that the order observed in nature is sufficient evidence for the existence of God, Ayer replies that to assert the existence of God on this ground is simply equivalent to asserting that there is a certain regularity in nature. This would be to define God in terms of observable facts and not as a transcendent being (ibid., p. 115).

63. Ibid., pp. 107–113. This is called the "emotive theory" of ethics. See M. Warnock, *Ethics Since 1900* (London: Oxford University Press, 1960), pp. 79–118. The American philosopher C. L. Stevenson was the first to develop this doctrine in detail. See his *Ethics and Language* (New Haven: Yale University Press, 1945).

64. *Language, Truth and Logic*, pp. 20–22.

65. "On the Analysis of Moral Judgments," *Philosophical Essays*, p. 237. But in the last analysis, Ayer says, there can be no guarantee of the correctness of a moral attitude "because nothing counts as a guarantee" (ibid., p. 244).

66. "The Vienna Circle," *The Revolution in Philosophy* (London: Macmillan, 1956), pp. 75–76.

67. *Language, Truth and Logic*, p. 16.

68. John Wisdom, "Note on the New Edition of Professor Ayer's *Language, Truth and Logic*," *Philosophy and Psycho-Analysis* (Oxford: Blackwell, 1953), p. 245. Wisdom continues: "The fact is, the verification principle is a metaphysical proposition—a 'smashing' one if I may be permitted the expression. After study of it we come to its complementary platitude 'Every sort of statement has its own sort of meaning' which by the verification principle itself becomes 'Every sort of statement has its own sort of logic'" (ibid., pp. 245–246).

69. *The Problem of Knowledge*, pp. 238–239. See *The Concept of a Person*, pp. 36–81.

70. *The Foundations of Empirical Knowledge*, pp. 113–114, 231. By "sense data" Ayer simply means "what is observed"; he does not defend any special theory about the nature of sense data (ibid., pp. 116–117). Although Ayer holds that statements about physical

objects can be verified or falsified only through the occurrence of sense data, he insists that they cannot be reducible to statements about sense data. Thus a statement such as "There is a cigarette case on this table" cannot be reduced to "a set of statements about one's sense experiences, that is, to a set of statements about the way that things would seem" (*The Problem of Knowledge*, pp. 144–148).

71. *The Concept of a Person*, p. 21.

72. John Wisdom, *Problems of Mind and Matter* (Cambridge: University Press, 1934). Other works by Wisdom are: *Other Minds* (Oxford: Blackwell, 1952). *Philosophy and Psycho-Analysis* (Oxford: Blackwell, 1953). For his philosophy, see D. A. T. Gasking, "The Philosophy of John Wisdom," *The Australasian Journal of Philosophy*, 1954, pp. 136–156, 185–212; M. J. Charlesworth, *Philosophy and Linguistic Analysis* (Louvain: Nauwelaerts, 1959), pp. 151–167.

73. *Philosophical Investigations*, 255.

74. J. Wisdom, *Philosophy and Psycho-Analysis*, pp. 169–181.

75. M. Lazcrowitz, "The Positivist Use of Nonsense," *Mind*, 1946, p. 250; A. Farrell, "An Appraisal of Therapeutic Positivism," *Mind*, 1946, pp. 25–48, 133–150.

76. J. Wisdom, op. cit., p. 174.

77. Ibid., p. 41.

78. See M. Weitz, "Oxford Philosophy," *The Philosophical Review*, 1953, pp. 187—233, and M. J. Charlesworth, op. cit., pp. 168–193.

79. B. Blanshard, *Reason and Analysis* (London: Allen & Unwin, 1962), p. 340.

80. G. Ryle, "Systematically Misleading Expressions," *Logic and Language*, ed. A. Flew (1st series; Oxford: Blackwell, 1951), p. 36.

81. P. F. Strawson, "On Referring," *Mind*, 1953, pp. 320–344.

82. J. Austin, *How to Do Things with Words* (Cambridge, MA: Harvard University Press, 1962). Other writings: "Other Minds," *Logic and Language*, ed. A. Flew (2nd series, 1953), pp. 123–158; *Philosophical Papers* (Oxford: Clarendon Press, 1961); *Sense and Sensibilia* (Oxford: Clarendon Press, 1962).

83. G. Ryle, "Categories," *Logic and Language* (2nd series), pp. 65–87.

84. G. Ryle, *The Concept of Mind* (New York: Barnes & Noble, 1949).

85. G. Ryle, "Systematically Misleading Expressions," p. 36.

86. R. M. Hare, *The Language of Morals* (Oxford: Clarendon Press, 1952), p. 3. See R. M. Hare, *Freedom and Reason* (Oxford: Clarendon Press, 1963). For Oxford ethical thinkers, see M. Warnock, *Ethics Since 1900* (London: Oxford University Press, 1960), pp. 119–161; M. J. Charlesworth, *Philosophy and Linguistic Analysis*, pp. 185–190.

87. R. M. Hare, *The Language of Morals*, p. 172.

88. Ibid., p. 69.

89. P. Nowell-Smith, *Ethics* (Harmondsworth, Middlesex: Penguin Books, 1959). See S. E. Toulmin, *An Examination of the Place of Reason in Ethics* (Cambridge: University Press, 1950).

90. G. E. M. Anscombe, "What Wittgenstein Really Said," *The Tablet*, April 17, 1954, p. 373.

91. P. F. Strawson, "Critical Notice of 'Philosophical Investigations,'" *Mind*, 1954, p. 68. Among recent books on metaphysics, see *The Nature of Metaphysics*, ed. D. F. Pears (London: Macmillan, 1957); D. M. Emmet, *The Nature of Metaphysical Thinking* (New York: Macmillan, 1957); S. E. Toulmin, R. W. Hepburn, A. MacIntyre, *Metaphysical Beliefs* (London: SCM Press, 1957); *Prospect for Metaphysics*, ed. I. Ramsey (London: Allen & Unwin, 1961); *Freedom and the Will*, ed. D. F. Pears (London: Macmillan, 1963); *Clarity Is Not Enough: Essays in Criticism of Linguistic Philosophy*, ed. H. D. Lewis (London: Allen & Unwin, 1963). *The Monist*, Vol. XLVII, No. 2, 1963: *Metaphysics Today* (essays by J. N. Findlay, C. Hartshorne, A. Donagan, N. Malcolm, S. C. Pepper, R. Taylor). F. Zabech, "Oxford and Metaphysics; a New Page in Contemporary Philosophy," *International Philosophical Quarterly*, III (1963), 307–320.

92. P. F. Strawson, *Individuals: An Essay in Descriptive Metaphysics* (London: Methuen, 1959). See P. F. Strawson, "Analyse, Science et Métaphysique," *La philosophie analytique* (Paris: Editions de Minuit, 1962), pp. 105–118.

93. See J. Macquarrie, *Twentieth Century Religious Thought: The Frontiers of Philosophy and Theology*, 1900–1960 (New York: Harper & Row, 1963), pp. 304–305; A. N. Prior, "Can Religion Be Discussed?" *New Essays in Philosophical Theology*, ed. A. Flew and A. C. MacIntyre (London: SCM Press, 1963); P. Munz, *Problems of Religious Knowledge* (London: SCM Press, 1959); W. N. Clarke, "Linguistic Analysis and Natural Theology," *Proceedings of the American Catholic Philosophical Association*, 34 (1960); M. J. Charlesworth, "Linguistic Analysis and Language about God," *International Philosophical Quarterly*, I (1961), pp. 139–167; F. Ferré, *Language, Logic and God* (New York: Harper, 1961); I. Ramsey, *Models and Mystery* (London: Oxford University Press, 1964). *The Monist*, Vol. XLVII, n. 3, 1963; *Religious Language and Philosophy*.

94. See *Clarity Is Not Enough: Essays in Criticism of Linguistic Philosophy*, ed. H. D. Lewis (London: Allen & Unwin, 1963). The leading article "Clarity Is Not Enough" is by H. H. Price. See also the review by H. B. Acton, entitled "The Return to Metaphysics," in the *Listener*, May 30, 1963, pp. 931–932.

Henry Habberley Price, b. at Neath in South Wales in 1899, is a Fellow of Trinity College, Oxford. He belongs to the English neorealist movement begun by Moore and Russell. His principal work *Perception* (London: Methuen, 1932) is a phenomenological study of sense perception. He strongly opposes the notion that in perception an object is known by means of an inference from effect to cause. Rather, material objects are immediately present to our sense powers. Other works: *Hume's Theory of the External World* (Oxford: Clarendon Press, 1940), and *Thinking and Representation* (Oxford: Clarendon Press, 1946).

PART FOUR: AMERICAN PHILOSOPHY

XXII. The Beginnings

1. For the intellectual life of the New England colonies, see H. W. Schneider, *The Puritan Mind* (New York: Henry Holt, 1930; Ann Arbor Paperback, 1958); P. Miller, *The New England Mind; the Seventeenth Century* (New York: Macmillan, 1939); P. Miller, *The New England Mind: from Colony to Province* (Cambridge, MA: Harvard University Press, 1933); S. E. Morison, *The Intellectual Life of Colonial New England* (2nd ed.; New York: New York University Press, 1956); L. B. Wright, *The Cultural Life of the American Colonies 1607–1763* (New York: Harper, 1957); D. J. Boorstin, *The Americans: The Colonial Experience* (New York: Random House, 1958).

2. See P. Miller, *The New England Mind: from Colony to Province*, p. 437.

3. See Berkeley's *Verses on the Prospect of Planting Arts and Learning in America*, quoted by H. W. Schneider, *A History of American Philosophy* (2nd ed.; New York: Columbia University Press, 1963), p. 100.

4. Cotton Mather, b. Boston, 1663; d. Boston, 1728. After studying at Harvard he was appointed minister of the Second Congregationalist Church. His fame as a writer was international and he was elected to the Royal Society in 1713.

Works: Of his many published writings the following are most important: *Magnalia Christi Americana; or, The Ecclesiastical History of New England, from Its First Planting in the Year 1620, unto the Year of Our Lord 1698* (London, 1702). *Essays to Do Good* (Boston, 1710 and 1808). *Religio Philosophica; or The Christian Philosopher* (London, 1721). Kenneth D. Murdock, *Selections from Cotton Mather* (New York: Harcourt, Brace, 1926; reprinted by Hafner Publ. Co., New York). Contains selections from *The*

Christian Philosopher.
Study: R. P. Boas and L. Boas, *Cotton Mather, Keeper of the Puritan Conscience* (New York: Harper, 1928).

5. Quoted by P. Miller, *The New England Mind: from Colony to Province*, p. 422.

6. For Dryden's denunciation of "philosophizing divines," see P. Miller, op. cit., pp. 441–442. For the medieval notion of "philosophizing theologian," see É. Gilson, *Elements of Christian Philosophy* (New York: Doubleday, 1960), p. 12; "Les 'Philosophantes,'" *Archives d'histoire doctrinale et littéraire du moyen âge*, 19 (1952), 135–140.

7. *The Christian Philosopher*, p. 1.

8. Ibid., p. 8.

9. Ibid., p. 13.

10. Ibid., p. 291.

11. Ibid.

12. Ibid., p. 82.

13. *Essays to Do Good* (London, 1808), p. 19.

14. On "Do-Good," see P. Miller, op. cit., pp. 395–416.

15. Samuel Johnson, b. Guilford, Connecticut, 1696; d. 1772. He was raised a Congregationalist and trained at Yale for the ministry, but he was converted to the Church of England in 1722. He was rector of the church at Stratford, Connecticut, tutor at Yale, and first President of King's College, now Columbia University. Most complete biography: E. È. Beardsley, *Life and Correspondence of Samuel Johnson, D.D.* (New York, 1873). See also *Samuel Johnson, President of King's College, His Career and Writings*, ed. by H. and C. Schneider (New York: Columbia University Press, 1929), Vol. I.
Works: His philosophical works are contained in *Samuel Johnson, President of King's College*..., Vol. II. Most important are the *Elementa Philosophica*, divided into *Noetica* and *Ethica* (1752), and his correspondence with Berkeley (1729–1730) and Cadwallader Colden (1744–1753). The *Ethica* appeared in 1746 under the title *A System of Morality*.
Studies: "The Mind of Samuel Johnson," by H. W. Schneider, in *Samuel Johnson, President of King's College*..., I, 3–22.

6. *Autobiography*, ed. Schneider, I, 5–6. Pierre de la Ramée, or Peter Ramus (1515–15 72), a French Protestant humanist and professor of philosophy at the Collège de France.

A violent critic of Aristotle, he selected as the title of his thesis: "Everything that Aristotle taught is false." Ramus' logic enjoyed great popularity. See W. J. Ong, *Ramus, Method, and the Decay of Dialogue* (Cambridge, MA: Harvard University Press, 1958). For a detailed study of Ramus' influence on New England thought, see P. Miller, *The New England Mind: the Seventeenth Century* (New York: Macmillan, 1939). Johann Heinrich Alsted (1588–1638), a German, Protestant divine. His *Encyclopedia* was one of the largest and most successful in its day. For its influence, see S. E. Morison, *Harvard College in the Seventeenth Century* (Cambridge, MA: Harvard University Press, 1936), pp. 147, 158–159, 162, 209, 222. This work should be consulted for the teaching of philosophy at Harvard in the seventeenth century.

17. *Autobiography*, II, 27.

18. Ibid., p. 364, n. 10.

19. Ibid., p. 373, n. 3. "I am a mind; the body is not properly myself or a part of myself. The body is a machine to which I am at present confined." See p. 479, n. 15.

20. Ibid., pp. 375–376, n. 8. Johnson owes this identification of sensible reality with our perception of it to Berkeley, whom he met during the latter's visit to New England. Johnson wrote two letters to him while he was living in Rhode Island, asking for clarification of his idealist philosophy. In the first, Johnson avows that he is almost convinced of Berkeley's stand, though he has some difficulties with it. One of the most important is the possibility of reconciling idealism with Newton's physics. Berkeley, in reply, assured him that Newton's physics is not inconsistent with the principles of idealism. In his second letter of 1730 and in his later *Elementa*, Johnson has been won over to Berkeley's side. For this correspondence, see Vol. II, pp. 263–284.

21. Vol. II, p. 379, n. 13. See John 1:9.

22. Ibid., p. 380, n. 14.

23. Ibid., p. 381, n. 2.

24. The correspondence between Johnson and Colden is published in Vol. II, pp. 287–305.

25. Vol. II, p. 383, n. 3. Further arguments for God's existence are found on pp. 460–469.

26. Ibid., p. 390, n. 13. For the history of infinity as a positive notion, see É. Gilson, "Theology and the Unity of Knowledge," *The Unity of Knowledge* (Columbia University Bicentennial Conference, 1955); *History of Christian Philosophy in the Middle Ages* (New York: Random House, 1955), pp. 448–449.

27. Vol. II, p. 382, n. 3.

28. Ibid., pp. 387–388, n. 9. See Exodus 3:14. Johnson refers to the English scholar John Hutchinson (1674–1737), author of *Moses's Sine Principio*. See *Dictionary of National Biography*, X, 342.

29. For medieval interpretations of the divine name "I AM WHO AM" (Exodus 3:14) see É. Gilson, op. cit., pp. 368–369.

30. Vol. II, p. 421, n. 6.

31. Ibid., p. 421, n. 5.

32. Ibid., pp. 479–480, n. 16.

33. Jonathan Edwards, b. at East Windsor, Connecticut, in 1703; d. Princeton, 1758. After graduating from Yale in 1720 he spent a brief residency at a Presbyterian church in New York, then returned to Yale in 1724 as senior tutor. In 1727 he was ordained assistant minister to his grandfather, Solomon Stoddard, pastor of the Congregationalist Church at Northampton. At Stoddard's death in 1729 Edwards became pastor. Dismissed from the parish in 1748 because of his rigorous stand on the need of experienced "conversion" to be a church member, he was appointed pastor at Stockbridge, Massachusetts, in 1751. He was elected president of the College of New Jersey (now Princeton) in 1757.

Works: *The Works of President Edwards, with a Memoir of His Life*, ed. by Sereno E. Dwight (10 vols.; New York: G. & C. & H. Carvill, 1829–1830). Vol. I contains the Life of Edwards. *Jonathan Edwards, Representative Selections*, by C. H. Faust and T. H. Johnson (New York: American Book Co., 1935; excellent bibliography), *Images or Shadows of Divine Things by Jonathan Edwards*, ed. P. Miller (New Haven: Yale University Press, 1948). *Puritan Sage: Collected Writings of Jonathan Edwards*, ed. V. Ferm (New York: Philosophical Library, 1953). *Freedom of the Will*, ed. P. Ramsey (New Haven: Yale University Press, 1957). *The Nature of True Virtue*, ed. W. K. Frankena (Ann Arbor Paperbacks, 1960).

34. *Works*, I, 30.

35. Quoted by P. Miller, *Images or Shadows of Divine Things by Jonathan Edwards*, p. 1.

36. *Representative Selections*, p. 18.

37. Ibid., p. 19.

38. Ibid., p. 31.

39. Ibid., p. 27.

40. *Representative Selections*, p. 29.

41. Ibid., pp. 28–29. Edwards identifies the idea and the reality of a being. "Seeing the perfect idea of a thing, is, to all intents and purposes, the same as seeing the thing. It is not only equivalent to seeing it, but it is seeing of it; for there is no other seeing but having an idea. Now, by seeing a perfect idea, so far as we see it, we have it." *Miscellanies*, n. 200, quoted by P. Miller, *Images or Shadows of Divine Things by Jonathan Edwards*, p. 22.

42. For a discussion and bibliography on this subject, see *Representative Selections*, p. xxvii and n. 44.

43. Ibid., p. 337.

44. *Works*, III, 3.

45. Ibid., p. 10.

46. Ibid., p. 71.

47. Ibid., II, pp. 3–4.

48. See *Representative Selections*, pp. 349–371.

49. Cadwallader Colden, b. in Ireland of Scottish parents in 1688; d. New York, 1776. He studied at Edinburgh, receiving his bachelor's degree in 1705. From 1705 to 1710 he studied medicine at London. Having emigrated to the American colonies in 1710, he first practiced medicine in Philadelphia, then pursued a career in public administration in New York.

Works: Most of his philosophical works are unpublished. His brief *Introduction to Philosophy* is printed in J. L. Blau, *American Philosophic Addresses 1700–1900* (New York: Columbia University Press, 1946), pp. 289–311. His correspondence with Samuel Johnson is found in H. W. and C. Schneider, *Samuel Johnson, President of King's College: His Career and Writings* (New York: Columbia University Press, 1929), Vol. II, pp. 286–305. *An Explication of the First Causes of Action in Matter, and of the Cause of Gravitation* (New York, 1745). *The Principles of Action in Matter, the Gravitation of Bodies, and the Motion of the Planets, Explained from Those Principles* (London, 1751).

50. *American Philosophic Addresses*, p. 292.

51. Ibid., p. 294.

52. In *Samuel Johnson, His Career and Writings*, p. 297.

53. *American Philosophic Addresses*, p. 296.

54. Ibid., p. 298.

55. See É. Gilson, *Les Métamorphoses de la Cité de Dieu* (Louvain: Publications Universitaires, 1952).

56. Quoted by H. Schneider, *The Puritan Mind*, p. 15.

57. See H. Schneider, op. cit., p. 25, n. 15.

58. See P. Miller, *Roger Williams: His Contribution to the American Tradition* (Indianapolis: Bobbs-Merrill, 1953).

59. Thomas Jefferson, b. Shadwell, Virginia, 1743; d. Monticello, Virginia, 1826. He attended the College of William and Mary. He was an excellent scholar in the languages and natural sciences. He was Governor of Virginia and third president of the United States. In his last years he founded the University of Virginia.

Works: *Writings*, 20 vols., ed. by A. A. Lipscomb (Washington, DC: Thomas Jefferson Memorial Association, 1905). *The Life and Selected Writings of Thomas Jefferson*, ed. by Adrienne Koch and William Peden (New York: Knopf, 1944). *The Living Thoughts of Thomas Jefferson*, ed. by John Dewey (New York: Longmans, 1940). *Alexander Hamilton and Thomas Jefferson, Representative Selections*, ed. by F. C. Prescott (New York: American Book Co., 1934). *The Political Writings of Thomas Jefferson*, ed. T. Dumbauld (New York: Liberal Arts, 1955).

Studies: Adrienne Koch, *The Philosophy of Thomas Jefferson* (New York: Columbia University Press, 1943). D. J. Boorstin, *The Lost World of Thomas Jefferson* (New York: Henry Holt, 1948).

XXIII. New England Transcendentalism

1. On Transcendentalism, see O. B. Frothingham, *Transcendentalism in New England* (New York: Putnam, 1876); H. C. Goddard, *Studies in New England Transcendentalism* (New York: Columbia University Press, 1908; reprint: Hillary House, 1960); Van Wyck Brooks, *The Flowering of New England, 1815–1865* (rev. ed.; New York: Dutton, 1941); F. O. Matthiessen, *American Renaissance; Art and Expression in the Age of Emerson and Whitman* (London & New York: Oxford University Press, 1941). P. Miller, *The Transcendentalists: An Anthology* (Cambridge, MA: Harvard University Press, 1950; excellent bibliography).

2. W. H. Channing, *The Life of William Ellery Channing* (2nd ed.; Boston: American Unitarian Association, 1887), p. 276. Brownson makes a similar complaint against Unitarianism. See P. Miller, op. cit., p. 46.

3. This is Orestes Brownson's summary of the situation. See P. Miller, op. cit., p. 242. Locke did not lack defenders among Unitarians. See, for example, the passage from Alexander H. Everett (1790–1847) in P. Miller, op. cit., pp. 29–33.

4. P. Miller, op. cit., p. 242.

5. "The Transcendentalism" in R. W. Emerson, *Complete Works*, ed. E. W. Emerson (Boston: Houghton Mifflin, 1903–1904), Vol. I, p. 340.

6. P. Miller, op. cit., p. 246.

7. For Emerson's relations to Kant and other German philosophers, see R. Wellek, "Emerson and German Philosophy," *New England Quarterly*, 16 (1943), 41–63.

8. Ralph Waldo Emerson, b. Boston, 1803; d. Concord, 1882. He was born and raised in Boston and attended Harvard, graduating in 1821. Having studied for the ministry, he was appointed pastor of the Second Church (Unitarian) in Boston. In 1832 he went to England, where he met Coleridge, Carlyle, and Wordsworth. He formed a lifelong friendship with Carlyle and first published his works in America. Carlyle in turn published Emerson's in England. On his return to America he lived at the old manse in Concord, Massachusetts, and pursued a career of writing and lecturing. In 1847 he again visited England and lectured there. A third journey in 1872 took him to Egypt.

Works: *The Complete Works of Ralph Waldo Emerson*, ed. E. W. Emerson (12 vols.; Boston: Houghton Mifflin Co., 1903–1904). Unless otherwise specified, references are to this edition. *Ralph Waldo Emerson, Representative Selections*, ed. F. I. Carpenter (New York: American Book Co., 1934). *Selections front Ralph Waldo Emerson*, ed. S. E. Whicher (Boston: Houghton Mifflin Co., 1957).

Studies: Definitive biographical study: R. L. Rusk, *Life of Ralph Waldo Emerson* (New York: Scribner's Sons, 1949). F. I. Carpenter, *Emerson Handbook* (New York: Hendricks House, 1953; excellent bibliography). K. W. Cameron, *Emerson the Essayist: An Outline of His Philosophical Development through 1836* (Raleigh, NC: Thistle Press, 1945). J. Bishop, *Emerson on the Soul* (Cambridge, MA: Harvard University Press, 1904).

9. "The Transcendentalist," I, 329, 337. For the influence of Eastern thought on Emerson, see F. I. Carpenter, *Emerson and Asia* (Cambridge, MA: Harvard University Press, 1930). A. Christy, *The Orient in American Transcendentalism* (New York: Columbia University Press, 1932).

10. Ibid., p. 334.

11. Ibid., pp. 334, 335.

12. Ibid., p. 334.

13. Ibid., p. 359.

14. For the philosophy of Charles Fourier, see above, p. *266*.

15. "Life and Letters in New England," X, 352.

16. "Nature," I, 10.

17. Ibid., pp. 4, 5.

18. For Emerson's estimate of Plato and the Platonists, see his essay "Plato; or, the Philosopher." On his knowledge of the Platonists, see S. G. Brown, "Emerson's Platonism," *New England Quarterly*, 18 (1945), 325–345.

19. "The Over-Soul," II, 269.

20. "Nominalist and Realist," III, 231. Although Emerson did not subscribe to any particular religion, he preferred the Catholic to the Protestant, not only because of his romantic delight in the Catholic liturgy, but because of its universality. See the remarkable passages from his Letters published in S. E. Whicher, *Selections from Ralph Waldo Emerson* (Boston: Houghton Mifflin Co., 1957), pp. 217–218, 312.

21. "Nature," I, 10.

22. "The Over-Soul," II, 282. For the history of the notion of "enthusiasm" in the seventeenth and eighteenth centuries, see R. A. Knox, *Enthusiasm: A Chapter in the History of Religion* (Oxford: University Press, 1950; paperback: Galaxy Book, 1961).

23. Ibid., II, p. 287.

24. See E. W. Todd, "Philosophical Ideas at Harvard College, 1817–1837," *New England Quarterly*, 16 (1943), 63–90.

25. See P. Miller, *Errand into the Wilderness* (Cambridge, MA: Harvard University Press, 1956), chap. viii: From Edwards to Emerson. A. R. Capronigri compares and contrasts Emerson's and Brownson's initial intuition of God or the "Over-Soul" in "Brownson and Emerson," *New England Quarterly Review*, 18 (1945), 368–390.

26. Orestes A. Brownson, b. Stockbridge, Vermont, 1803; d. Detroit, 1876. His body lies in the chapel of Notre Dame, Indiana. Born of Puritan stock and raised in the

Congregationalist religion; he had little formal education. In 1822 he joined the Presbyterian Church but became displeased with the Calvinist depreciation of reason and its doctrine of predestination. In 1824 he became a member of the Universalist Church, which teaches the salvation of all men. Five years later he denounced Christianity and joined the socialist sect of Robert Dale Owen and Fanny Wright. In 1832 he joined the Unitarians and came under the influence of Channing. The next year he read Victor Cousin, who introduced him to philosophy. For ten years he was a follower of Cousin. His reading of Kant and especially of Gioberti (the latter in 1849) helped him to give final form to his philosophy. In 1838 he started *The Boston Quarterly Review*, which in 1842 was merged with *The U.S. Democratic Review of New York*. In 1844 he was received into the Catholic Church. The same year he started *Brownson's Quarterly Review*, which he published, until 1875, except from 1865 to 1872.

Works: *The Works of Orestes A. Brownson*, ed. H. F. Brownson (20 vols.; Detroit: Thorndike Nourse, 1882–1907). Selected essays in P. Miller, *The Transcendentalists. An Anthology* (Cambridge, MA: Harvard University Press, 1950); *Selected Essays*, ed. R. Kirk (Chicago: Henry Regnery, 1955). Selected correspondence in H. F. Brownson, *Orestes A. Brownson's Early, Middle, and Latter Life* (3 vols.; Detroit: T. Nourse, 1882–1907).

Studies: S. A. Raemers, *America's Foremost Philosopher* (Washington, DC: St. Anselm's Priory, 1931). A. M. Schlesinger, Jr., *Orestes A. Brownson: A Pilgrim's Progress* (Boston: Little, Brown & Co., 1939). T. Maynard, *Orestes Brownson: Yankee, Radical, Catholic* (New York: Macmillan Co., 1943). B. Farrell, *Orestes Brownson's Approach to the Problem of God* (Washington, DC: Catholic University Press, 1950). M. A. Fitzsimons, "Brownson's Search for the Kingdom of God: The Social Thought of an American Radical," *Review of Politics*, 16 (1954), 22–36.

27. Isaac Thomas Hecker, b. New York, 1819; d. New York, 1888. Like Brownson, he was a student of German philosophy and a social reformer. For a while he associated with the Transcendentalists, but thought they over-exalted human nature. A convert to the Catholic Church in 1844, he was ordained a priest of the Redemptorist Order and later founded the Missionary Society of St. Paul the Apostle (the Paulist Fathers).

28. For Brownson's mature evaluation of Cousin, see his essay "Victor Cousin and his Philosophy" (1867), II, 307–329.

29. P. Miller, *The Transcendentalists*, p. 243.

30. "Rationalism and Traditionalism" (1860), I, 490.

31. Ibid., p. 502.

32. Ibid., p. 494.

33. Ibid., p. 519.

34. The total separation of philosophy from revelation, Brownson says, dates from Descartes; both Greek and medieval philosophy made use of revelation. See "The Giobertian Philosophy" (1864), II, 235–236; "Schools of Philosophy" (1854), I, 280; "Essay in Refutation of Atheism" (1873–1874), II, 40.

35. "Refutation of Atheism," pp. 46–47. Brownson was much indebted to Pierre Leroux, a disciple of Cousin, for his analysis of thought. See ibid., p. 44.

36. Ibid., p. 44.

37. Ibid., p. 47.

38. Ibid., p. 48. See "An Old Quarrel" (1867), II, 295–296. Brownson's most extensive examination and critique of Kant is contained in his essay "Kant's Critic of Pure Reason" (1844), I, 130–213.

39. "Refutation of Atheism," II, 56–61. On the distinction between Being and existence, see "The Existence of God" (1852), I, 269.

40. "Refutation of Atheism," II, 61.

41. Ibid., p. 73.

42. Ibid., p. 76. See "The Giobertian Philosophy," II, 265.

43. "The Giobertian Philosophy," II, 257.

44. "The Existence of God," I, 262.

45. Ibid., p. 269.

46. "An Old Quarrel," II, 303. Brownson thinks that St. Thomas is essentially in agreement with St. Augustine and St. Anselm. See ibid., pp. 304–306. For his attitude toward the proofs of St. Thomas and St. Anselm, see "Maret on Reason and Revelation" (1857–1858), I, 443–444.

47. Denzinger, *Enchiridion Symbolorum* (Herder, 1957), p. 465, n. 1659.

48. Brownson ascribes the condemned proposition to unnamed "Louvain professors" and denies that he himself teaches it in the sense in which it was condemned. "Refutation of Atheism," II, 52. See "The Giobertian Philosophy," II, 260–261. For the identity of these professors, see below, note 50.

49. "An Old Quarrel," II, 304. In a reply to a letter by H. S. McMurdie, Brownson comments on each of the seven propositions concerning ontologism and pantheism condemned by Pius IX in 1861, and he denies that he teaches them. See T. T. McAvoy, "Brownson's Ontologism," *The Catholic Historical Review*, 28 (1943), 376–381.

50. "Rationalism and Traditionalism," I, 506. Brownson denies that we have an innate idea of God, contrary to the "professors of Louvain," represented by Abbé Lefebve. See pp. 505, 506.

51. "The Existence of God," I, 274–275; "An Old Quarrel," II, 303–304.

52. "Rationalism and Traditionalism," I, 520.

53. "The Laboring Classes," in P. Miller, *The Transcendentalists*, p. 438.

54. For Channing's reaction, see P. Miller, op. cit., pp. 446–449. For Parker's views on the present condition of society, see pp. 449–457.

55. "The Democratic Principle" (1873), XVIII, 223.

56. Ibid., p. 225.

57. "Liberalism and the Church" (1869), XIII, 45. Brownson's views on the American Constitution are best expressed in one of his finest works, *The American Republic: Its Constitution, Tendencies and Destiny* (1865), XVIII, 1–222. On his political philosophy, see T. I. Cook and A. B. Leavelie, "Orestes A. Brownson's The American Republic," *Review of Politics*, 4 (1942), 77–90, 173–193; J. Donovan, "Brownson, the Philosophical Expounder of the Constitution," *Proceedings of the American Catholic Philosophical Association* (1931), 148–165. S. J. Parry, "The Premises of Brownson's Political Theory," *Review of Politics*, 16 (1954), 194–211.

58. "The Church and the Republic" (1856), XII, 9.

59. "The Spiritual not for the Temporal" (1853), XI, 43. See F. E. McMahon, "Orestes Brownson on Church and State," *Theological Studies*, 15 (1954), 175–228.

60. "Temporal Power of the Popes" (1854), XI, 123.

61. Ibid., pp. 127–128.

62. "The Church and the Republic," XII, 31; "Union of Church and State," (1867) XIII, 142.

XXIV. Idealism of the Schools

1. James McCosh, b. Carskeoch, Scotland, 1811; d. Princeton, 1894. He was the main exponent of Reid's common-sense philosophy in the United States. He studied under Hamilton in Scotland but was repelled by his skepticism and agnosticism. Reid's common-sense philosophy, with its assurance of an intuition of reality, seemed to him a better support for his orthodox Presbyterian religion. In 1868 he was called to America to become president of the College of New Jersey at Princeton. He taught there until his death. His teachings and writings were highly influential in spreading the Scottish philosophy in the many Presbyterian and Congregationalist colleges in the States, where for a time it held almost complete sway. Its popularity was not due, however, to its vitality or originality; as H. W. Schneider says, "...McCosh and his Presbyterian colleagues restored to the evangelical churches a philosophical grounding for their faith which they had lost since Edwards" (*A History of American Philosophy* [2nd ed.; New York: Columbia University Press, 1963], p. 249).

2. For a detailed account of the St. Louis Movement and its members, see H. A. Pochmann, *German Culture in America: Philosophical and Literary Influences 1600–1900* (Madison: University of Wisconsin Press, 1957), pp. 257–294. Source materials on the School are edited by C. M. Perry, *The St. Louis Movement in Philosophy* (Norman, Oklahoma: University of Oklahoma Press, 1930). See P. R. Anderson, *Platonism in the Midwest* (New York: Temple University Publications, 1963).

3. For the Concord School, see H. A. Pochmann, op. cit., pp. 294–304.

4. Borden Parker Bowne, b. Leonardsville, New Jersey, 1847; d. Boston, 1910. While studying at New York University he developed an interest in philosophy. After teaching for two years he became pastor of a Methodist church in Whitestone, New York, but he gave up this position after a short time in order to devote himself to philosophy. In an early work, *The Philosophy of Herbert Spencer*, he criticizes Spencer's evolutionary philosophy and his theory of knowledge because it contradicts the notion of a substantial self. Before publishing the book, he left to study in Germany (1871–1873), where he came under the influence of the objective idealism of Lotze. On his return to the United States he turned to journalism for a time, then taught philosophy at Boston University until his death.

   Works: His numerous works include *Metaphysics* (New York: Harper, 1882; Boston: Boston University Press, 1943); *Principles of Ethics* (New York: Harper, 1892); *The Theory of Thought and Knowledge* (New York: Harper, 1897); *The Immanence of God* (Boston: Houghton Mifflin, 1905); *Personalism* (Boston: Houghton Mifflin, 1908). *Kant and Spencer: A Critical Exposition* was published posthumously (Boston: Houghton Mifflin, 1912).

Studies: F. J. McConnell, *Borden Parker Bowne* (New York: The Abingdon Press, 1929). A. C. Knudson, "Bowne as Teacher and Author," *The Personalist*, I (1920), 5–14. On the personalism of Bowne's pupil, Edgar Sheffield Brightman, see A. J. Reck, *Recent American Philosophy* (New York: Pantheon Books, 1964), pp. 311–336.

5. *The Theory of Thought and Knowledge*, p. 3.

6. Ibid., p. 319.

7. Ibid., p. 321.

8. Ibid., p. 322.

9. Ibid., p. 325.

10. *Metaphysics*, p. 450. "Everyone knows that in sensation he is conditioned by something not himself. If asked how we know it, the answer is that no one knows how he knows it, but everyone knows that he knows it." "No one can regard himself as the universe" (ibid., pp. 451–452). And yet for Bowne our thought of the universe "is made up entirely of subjective elements." The sense elements of knowledge are only objectified affections of the soul. The rational elements are entirely contributed by the mind itself. "The mind must build the world out of its own states and ideas" (ibid., p. 450).

11. *The Theory of Thought and Knowledge*, p. 342.

12. Ibid., pp. 328–329.

13. *Metaphysics*, pp. 27, 28.

14. Ibid., p. 31.

15. Ibid., pp. 55, 163.

16. Ibid., p. 37.

17. Ibid., p. 41.

18. Ibid., p. 50.

19. Ibid., p. 96.

20. Ibid., p. 97.

21. Ibid., pp. 99, 100.

22. Josiah Royce, b. Grass Valley, California, 1855; d. Cambridge, Massachusetts, 1916. In 1871 he entered the newly founded University of California at Berkeley. Although philosophy was not vet on the curriculum, he read Mill and Spencer. On obtaining his B.A. he won a scholarship to study in Germany. There he read the German philosophers and followed the courses of Lotze, Wundt, and Windelband at Gottingen. Back in the United States, Johns Hopkins University offered him a scholarship. There he met William James, who encouraged him to continue in philosophy. He studied under G. S. Morris and C. S. Peirce. Having obtained his Ph.D. at Johns Hopkins in 1878, he returned to teach at the University of California. Four years later, in 1882, he was offered a chair at Harvard. He taught there until his death.

Works: Bibliographical: F. M. Oppenheim, "A Critical Annotated Bibliography of the Published Works of Josiah Royce," *The Modern Schoolman*, 41 (1964), pp. 339–365. His main works are *The Religious Aspect of Philosophy* (Boston: Houghton Mifflin, 1885; Harper Torchbook, 1958); *The Spirit of Modern Philosophy* (Boston: Houghton Mifflin, 1892; reprinted: New York: George Braziller, 1955). *The Conception of God* (New York: Macmillan, 1898); *The World and the Individual* (2 vols.; New York: Macmillan, 1900–1901; reprint: Dover edition, 1959); *The Philosophy of Loyalty* (New York: Macmillan, 1908); *The Problem of Christianity* (2 vols.; New York: Macmillan, 1913).

Studies: *Papers in Honor of Josiah Royce on His Sixtieth Birthday*, ed. J. E. Creighton (New York 1916). J. H. Muirhead, *The Platonic Tradition in Anglo-Saxon Philosophy* (New York: Macmillan, 1931), pp. 347–412. G. Marcel, *Royce's Metaphysics,* trans. V. and G. Ringer (Chicago: Henry Regnery, 1956). J. E. Smith, *Royce's Social Infinite* (New York: Liberal Arts Press, 1950). J. H. Cotton, *Royce on the Human Self* (Cambridge, MA: Harvard University Press, 1954).

23. *The Religious Aspect of Philosophy*, p. 8.

24. Ibid., p. 25.

25. Ibid., p. 26.

20. Ibid., p. 27.

27. Ibid., p. 38.

28. Ibid., p. 42.

29. Ibid., p. 139.

30. Ibid., pp. 148–149.

31. Ibid., p. 2 16.

32. Ibid., p. 387.

33. Ibid., p. 389.

34. Ibid., pp. 398–399.

35. Ibid., p. 411.

36. Ibid., p. 419.

37. Ibid., p. 424.

38. Ibid., p. 431. "An error, we reply, is an incomplete thought, that to a higher thought, which includes it and its intended object, is known as having failed in the purpose that it more or less clearly had, and that is fully realized in this higher thought" (ibid., p. 425).

39. Ibid., pp. 424–425. "The idea of the barely possible, in which there is no actuality, is an empty idea. If anything is possible, then, when we say so, we postulate something as actually existent in order to constitute this possibility. The conditions of possible error must be actual. Bare possibility is blank nothingness. If the nature of error necessarily and with perfect generality demands certain conditions, then these conditions are as eternal as the erroneousness of error itself is eternal. And thus the inclusive thought, which constitutes the error, must be postulated as existent" (ibid., pp. 429–430).

40. *The Spirit of Modern Philosophy*, p. 373.

41. *The Conception of God*, pp. 43–44.

42. *The World and the Individual*, I, 325.

43. Ibid., p. 332.

44. Ibid., p. 75.

45. *The Religious Aspect of Philosophy*, p. 442.

46. Ibid., pp. 433–444.

47. James E. Creighton, *Studies in Speculative Philosophy* (New York: Macmillan, 1925), p. 51. Creighton's former students at the Sage school contributed to *Philosophical Essays in Honor of James Edwin Creighton*, ed. G. H. Sabine (New York: Macmillan, 1917). For his thought, see G. H. Sabine, "The Philosophy of James Edwin Creighton," *Philosophical Review*, 34 (1925), 230–245.

48. Brief sketches of the philosophies of these men are contained in A. R. Reck, *Recent American Philosophy* (New York: Pantheon Books, 1964).

49. Among Blanshard's works are: *The Nature of Thought* (2 vols.; London: Allen & Unwin, 1939); *On Philosophical Style* (Manchester: Manchester University Press, 1954); *The Impasse in Ethics and a Way Out* (Berkeley: University of California Press, 1955); *Reason and Goodness* (London: Allen & Unwin, 1961); *Reason and Analysis* (London: Allen & Unwin, 1962).
For the history of American and English idealism, see A. C. Ewing, *The Idealist Tradition front Berkeley to Blanshard* (Glencoe, IL: The Free Press, 1957). This book contains selections from the idealists, with an introduction, commentary, and excellent bibliography. See also A. C. Ewing, *Idealism: A Critical Survey*, 3rd ed. (London: Methuen, 1961); H. W. Schneider, *A History of American Philosophy*, 2nd ed. (New York: Columbia University Press, 1963), pp. 454–510.

XXV. Resurgence of Realism

1. William James, *Essays in Radical Empiricism* (New York: Longmans, 1912), p. 39.

2. Ibid., p. 40.

3. W. P. Montague, "The Story of American Realism," *The Ways of Things* (New York: Prentice-Hall, 1940), p. 230.

4. *The New Realism: Co-operative Studies in Philosophy* (New York: Macmillan, 1912). The Program of the New Realists is printed as an Appendix, pp. 471–480. For the New Realism, see R. Kremer, *Le Néo-Réalisme Américain* (Louvain: Institut Supérieur, 1920); Sister Mary Verda, *New Realism in the Light of Scholasticism* (New York: Macmillan, 1926).

5. W. P. Montague, "Professor Royce's Refutation of Realism," *Philosophical Review*, 11 (1902), pp. 446–458. R. B. Perry, "Prof. Royce's Refutation of Realism and Pluralism," *The Monist*, 12 (1902), pp. 43–55.

6. W. P. Montague, "The Story of American Realism," p. 235.

7. First published in *The Journal of Philosophy, Psychology, and Scientific Methods*, 7 (1910), 5–14, this article is reprinted in *The Development of American Philosophy*, ed. W. G. Muelder and L. Sears (Boston: Houghton Mifflin, 1940), pp. 304–310. See *The New Realism*, pp. 11–12; R. B. Perry, *Present Philosophical Tendencies* (New York: Longmans, 1929), pp. 129–132. For Perry's philosophy, see A. J. Reck, *Recent American Philosophy* (New York: Pantheon Books, 1964), pp. 3–41.

8. W. P. Montague, op. cit., pp. 237–238.

9. R. B. Perry, "A Realistic Theory of Independence," *The New Realism*, pp. 99–151; R. B. Perry, *Present Philosophical Tendencies*, pp. 313–319.

10. R. B. Perry, *Present Philosophical Tendencies*, p. 308.

11. Ibid., p. 310. According to Perry, epistemological monism "means that when things are known they are identical, element for element, with the idea, or content of the knowing state. According to this view, instead of there being a fundamental dual division of the world into ideas and things, there is only the class of things; ideas being the subclass of those things that happen to be known" (ibid., p. 126).

12. *The New Realism*, p. 35.

13. W. P. Montague, "A Realistic Theory of Truth and Error," *The New Realism*, p. 255. See W. P. Montague, "The Story of American Realism," p. 238.

14. See É. Gilson, *Being and Some Philosophers* (Toronto: Pontifical Institute of Mediaeval Studies, 1952), pp. 74–107.

15. R. B. Perry, "A Realistic Theory of Independence," *The New Realism*, pp. 100–103.

16. W. P. Montague, "The Story of American Realism," pp. 238–240; *The New Realism*, Introduction, pp. 4–6.

17. *The New Realism*, pp. 482–483.

18. E. B. Holt, "The Place of Illusory Experience in a Realistic World," *The New Realism*, pp. 303–373.

19. W. P. Montague, "A Realistic Theory of Truth and Error," *The New Realism*, p. 253; "Note on Professor Holt's Essay," ibid., pp. 480–481.

20. W. P. Montague, "A Realistic Theory of Truth and Error," pp. 291–292.

21. W. P. Montague, "The Story of American Realism," *The Ways of Things*, pp. 248–249.

22. *Essays in Critical Realism: A Co-operative Study of the Problem of Knowledge* (New York: Macmillan, 1920). For Critical Realism, see J.-A. Ryan, "Two Essays on American Critical Realism," *Revue de l'Université d'Ottawa*, 6 (1936), 102*–128*, 202*–296*.

23. D. Drake, "The Approach to Critical Realism," *Essays in Critical Realism*, p. 15.

24. Ibid., p. 21.

25. Ibid., p. 6.

20. C. A. Strong, "On the Nature of the Datum," *Essays in Critical Realism*, pp. 223–224. In note 1, p. 224, Strong acknowledges his indebtedness to Santayana for this "precious conception" of data as essences.

27. D. Drake, op. cit., p. 25.

28. A. K. Rogers, "The Problem of Error," *Essays in Critical Realism*, pp. 117–118.

29. D. Drake, op. cit., p. 20.

30. Ibid., pp. 23–24.

31. R. W. Sellars, "What is the Correct Interpretation of Critical Realism?" *Journal of Philosophy*, 24 (1921), 240. "No motive has entered to cause us to doubt the existence of a physical realm co-existent with the percipient; but reflection has discovered that the content with which we automatically clothe these acknowledged realities is subjective." "Knowledge and Its Categories" (*Essays in Critical Realism*, p. 197). For Sellar's critical realism, see A. J. Reck, op. cit., pp. 208–242; for Lovejoy, see pp. 243–275.

32. B. H. Bode, "Critical Realism," *Journal of Philosophy*, 19 (1922), 68–78; W. P. Montague, "The Story of American Realism," *The Ways of Things*, pp. 258–259. For the position of J. B. Pratt, see "Critical Realism and the Possibility of Knowledge," *Essays in Critical Realism*, pp. 85–113.

33. C. E. M. Joad, "A Criticism of Critical Realism," *Monist*, 32 (1922), 520–529; A. W. Moore, "Some Logical Aspects of Critical Realism," *Journal of Philosophy*, 19 (1922), 589–596; S. P. Lamprecht, "Critical Realism and the External World," *Journal of Philosophy*, 19 (1920), 651–661; M. Ten Hoor, "George Santayana's Theory of Knowledge," *Journal of Philosophy*, 20 (1923), 197–211; W. P. Montague, ibid., p. 259.

34. George Santayana, b. Madrid, 1863 of Spanish parents; d. Rome, 1952. In 1872 he was reunited with his mother, who was then living in Boston with her children by her first husband, an American named George Sturgis. Santayana followed the courses of Royce and lames at Harvard, then studied philosophy in Germany from 1886 to 1888. Having returned to Harvard, he obtained the doctorate in philosophy and immediately began teaching at the University. A sabbatical year in 1896–1897 was spent at Cambridge, England, systematically reading Plato and Aristotle. On his retirement in 1912 he returned to Europe and lived in solitude, chiefly in Rome. Autobiographical material will be found in "A General Confession" (Part 1 originally appeared as "A Brief History of My Opinions") in *The Philosophy of George Santayana*, ed. P. A.

Schilpp (Evanston and Chicago: Northwestern University Press, 1940), pp. 3–30. Also in G. Santayana, *Persons and Places, The Background of My Life* (New York: Scribner's, 1944); *The Middle Span* (New York: Scribner's, 1947); *My Host the World* (New York: Scribner's, 1953), collected in one volume, *Persons and Places: The Autobiography in One Volume of George Santayana*, ed. D. Cory (New York: Scribner's, 1963). D. Cory, *Santayana: The Later Years. A Portrait with Letters* (New York: George Braziller, 1963).

Works: *The Works of George Santayana* (15 vols.; New York: Scribner's, 1936–1940). Main philosophical writings: *The Life of Reason, or the Phases of Human Progress* (5 vols.: *Reason in Common Sense, Reason in Society, Reason in Religion, Reason in Art, Reason in Science* [New York: Scribner's, 1905–1906; new ed., New York: Scribner's, 1954]). His more mature thought is contained in *Scepticism and Animal Faith* (New York: Scribner's, 1923); and *Realms of Being: The Realm of Essence, The Realm of Matter, The Realm of Truth, The Realm of Spirit,* one-volume edition (New York: Scribner's, 1942). Selections in *The Philosophy of Santayana*, ed. I. Edman (The /Modern Library, New York: Random House, 1942). In his novel *The Last Puritan* (New York: Scribner's, 1935) the two main characters, Oliver and Mario, represent the conflict between the Puritan and Latin elements of his thought.

Studies: G. W. Howgate, *George Santayana* (Philadelphia: University of Pennsylvania Press, 1938). M. R. Munitz, *The Moral Philosophy of Santayana* (New York: Columbia University Press, 1939). *The Philosophy of George Santayana*, The Library of Living Philosophers, vol. II, ed. P. A. Schilpp (Chicago: Northwestern University Press, 1940; good bibliography). J. Duron, *La Pensée de George Santayana* (Paris: Nizet, 1949). N. Bosco, *Il Realismo Critico di Giorgio Santayana* (Turin: Edizioni di "Filosofia," 1951). W. E. Arnett, *Santayana and the Sense of Beauty* (Bloomington: Indiana University Press, 1955). I. Singer, *Santayana's Aesthetics* (Cambridge, MA: Harvard University Press, 1957). R. Butler, *The Mind of Santayana* (Chicago: Regnery, 1955). R. Butler, *The Life and World of George Santayana* (Chicago: Regnery, 1960).

35. "General Confession," *The Philosophy of George Santayana*, p. 17.

36. Ibid., p. 8.

37. *Scepticism and Animal Faith*, p. 3.

38. Ibid., p. 92.

39. Ibid., p. 39.

40. Ibid., pp. 14–18.

41. Ibid., p. 69.

42. Ibid., pp. 38–39.

43. Ibid., p. 41; "A General Confession," p. 19.

44. *Scepticism and Animal Faith*, pp. 289–293. In his essay "Three Proofs of Realism" (*Essays in Critical Realism*, pp. 163–184) he does not deduce the existence of the external world from the immediate data of consciousness but shows "that all reasonable human discourse makes realistic assumptions" (p. 183).

45. In *The Sense of Beauty* Santayana calls beauty "objectified pleasure" (ed., 1936, p. 41). Thirty years later he repudiated this description because it appears to make beauty a subjective experience. In his later formulation he describes beauty as an essence or quality, "a vital harmony felt and fused into an image under the form of eternity." "The Mutability of Esthetic Categories," *The Philosophical Review*, 34 (1925), p. 284, n. 2. A beautiful essence, accordingly, is a complex essence, embracing an essence or image and also a "viral harmony" or pleasure felt and made the object of intuition. On this point, and on the dispute over the possibility of a radical change in Santayana's view of beauty, see I. Singer, *Santayana's Aesthetics*, pp. 33–44. Santayana himself denied any fundamental change in doctrine. See his "Apologia Pro Mente Sua," *The Philosophy of George Santayana*, p. 538. In *Realms of Being*, p. 8, he writes: "The beautiful is itself an essence, an indefinable quality felt in many things which, however disparate they may be otherwise, receive this name by virtue of a special emotion, half wonder, half love, which is felt in their presence."

46. *Realms of Being*, pp. 3–11.

47. Some essences are simple, some complex. Examples of the former are Pure Being (which is the self-identity found in all essences), qualities such as blueness, roundness; examples of the latter are an individual person such as Socrates or a landscape. The complexity of an essence can be infinite: "There is no limit to this complexity in unity: the system of any world is one essence; the whole realm of essence is one essence" (*Realms of Being*, p. 71).

48. Ibid., p. 41.

49. Ibid., p. 44.

50. Ibid., p. 189.

51. Just as data or essences are projected by the organism, or more exactly by its central part the psyche, into the place where it feels some agent is acting upon it, so existence is added to the data by ourselves because of the impact of things upon us. Existence is "the finding, the occurrence, the assault, the impact" of things here and now. See "Three Proofs of Realism," *Essays in Critical Realism*, pp. 179–180; *Scepticism and Animal Faith*, p. 37.

52. *Realms of Being*, p. 292.

53. G. W. Howgate, *George Santayana*, p. 243.

54. *The Unknowable* (Oxford: Clarendon Press, 1923), pp. 8–9.

55. *Realms of Being*, pp. 445–446. Truth accordingly is a form or essence that adds "an eternal dimension to transitory being." Beauty and goodness are likewise essences, but unlike truth, which attends every event, beauty and goodness "arise only at certain junctures, when various streams of events, already flowing in definite tropes, meet and mingle in a temporary harmony; a harmony which such of these streams as are organized into psyches may feel and rejoice in" (ibid., p. 445).

56. *Scepticism and Animal Faith*, p. 267.

57. Ibid., p. 269.

58. *Realms of Being*, p. 446.

59. Ibid., pp. 402, 406.

60. Ibid., p. 540.

61. Ibid., p. 572.

62. Ibid., p. 567.

63. *Scepticism and Animal Faith*, pp. 273–274.

64. "A General Confession," p. 23.

65. *Life of Reason*, V, 319.

66. *Platonism and the Spiritual Life* (New York: Scribner's, 1927), pp. 28–29.

67. M. K. Munitz, *The Moral Philosophy of Santayana*, p. 106.

XXVI. Pragmatism

1. R. B. Perry, *The Thought and Character of William James* (Boston: Little, Brown, 1935), I, 814.

2. See P. P. Wiener, *Evolution and the Founders of Pragmatism* (Cambridge, MA: Harvard University Press, 1949), pp. 18–30.

3. See P. P. Wiener, op. cit. This work contains important studies on the origin of pragmatism and the relations of the members of the Metaphysical Club to the theory of evolution. See also E. H. Madden, *Chauncey Wright and the Foundation of Pragmatism* (Seattle: University of Washington Press, 1963); R. Hofstadter, *Social Darwinism in American Thought* (rev. ed.; Boston: Beacon Press, 1955); *Evolutionary Thought in America*, ed. S. Persons (New Haven: Yale University Press, 1950).

4. Peirce, *Collected Papers*, 5, 12.

5. This is according to the testimony of William James, "Philosophical Conceptions and Practical Results," *Collected Essays and Reviews*, ed. R. B. Perry (New York: Longmans, 1920), p. 410.

The term "pragmatism" probably originated with Peirce. James states incorrectly that Peirce introduced it in his essay "How to Make Our Ideas Clear" (*Pragmatism*, p. 46). In a letter to James, Peirce is uncertain whether he or James coined the term. He writes, "Who originated the term 'pragmatism,' I or you? Where did it first appear in print?" (See R. B. Perry, *The Thought and Character of William James*, II, 407, n. 5. The term "pragmatic belief" appears in Kant's *Critique of Pure Reason*, A 824–B 852. On this basis Peirce appears to have coined the term "pragmatism" and used it in oral discussions of his theory at the Metaphysical Club in the 1870s. When James made the term well known in his Pragmatism lectures, Peirce began employing it in print. See M. G. Murphey, *The Development of Peirce's Philosophy*, p. 150, n. 7.

6. A. Bain, *The Emotions and the Will* (3rd ed.; London: Parker, 1875), p. 505.

7. Peirce, *Collected Papers*, 5, 12.

8. See Max H. Fisch, "Alexander Bain and the Genealogy of Pragmatism," *Journal of the History of Ideas*, 15 (1954), 40–444.

9. Charles Sanders Peirce, b. Cambridge, Massachusetts, 1839; d. Milford, Pennsylvania, 1914. He owed his early training in mathematics, science, and philosophy to his father, Benjamin Peirce, who taught mathematics at Harvard. He attended Harvard, specializing in science, and graduated in 1859. He held a position with the United States Coastal and Geodesic Survey from 1861 to 1891. Although he did not obtain a permanent teaching post at Harvard, he lectured there occasionally. For five years he held a lectureship in logic at Johns Hopkins. After 1891, he lived in retirement and poverty in Milford, Pennsylvania.

Works: Peirce wrote almost eighty original philosophical papers, mainly on logic and metaphysics, and twenty papers and one small volume in physics, astronomy, and the theory of measurement. After his death, many of his unpublished manuscripts were printed, with his already published papers, under the title *Collected Papers of Charles Sanders Peirce*, Vols. 1–6 eds. C. Hartshorne and P. Weiss, Vols. 7–8 ed. A. W. Burks (Cambridge, MA: Harvard University Press, 1931–1935, 1958). Useful selections: *Chance, Love and Logic*, ed. M. R. Cohen (New York: Harcourt, Brace, 1923). *The Philosophy of Peirce: Selected Writings*, ed. J. Buehler (New York: Harcourt, Brace, 1940; paperback ed. Dover Publications, 1955). *Values in a Universe of Chance: Selected Writings of Charles S. Peirce*, ed. P. P. Wiener (Stanford: Stanford University Press, 1958).

Studies: J. Buehler, *Charles Peirce's Empiricism* (New York: Harcourt, Brace, 1939). J. K. Feibleman, *An Introduction to Peirce's Philosophy* (New York: Harper & Bros., 1946). T. A. Goudge, *The Thought of C. S. Peirce* (Toronto: Toronto University Press, 1950). W. B. Gallie, *Peirce and Pragmatism* (Penguin Books, 1952). *Studies in the Philosophy of Charles Sanders Peirce*, ed. P. P. Wiener and F. H. Young (Cambridge, MA: Harvard University Press, 1952). M. Thompson, *The Pragmatic Philosophy of C. S. Peirce* (Chicago: University of Chicago Press, 1953). M. G. Murphey, *The Development of Peirce's Philosophy* (Cambridge, MA: Harvard University Press, 1961). *Classic American Philosophers: Peirce, James, Royce, Santayana, Dewey, Whitehead*; selections from their writings, with introductory essays by Max H. Fisch, general editor, and others (New York: Appleton-Century-Crofts, 1951).

10. 1. 1. (Unless otherwise indicated, all references to Peirce are to his *Collected Papers* by volume and paragraph. 1. 1. refers to volume 1, paragraph 1.) Peirce wrote these lines about 1898. Writing to James in 1909, his description of his purpose in philosophizing is different and more in accord with his actual accomplishment: "The only thing I have ever striven to do in philosophy has been to analyze sundry concepts with exactitude..." Quoted in T. A. Goudge, *The Thought of C. S. Peirce*, p. 325.

11. 2. 148, 4. 53.

12. 5. 265, 5. 376.

13. For Peirce's criticism of intuition, see 5. 213–5. 263.

14. 5. 376.

15. 5. 388–5. 392.

16. 5. 402. See 5. 9.

17. 5. 412.

18. 5. 414. See 6. 482.

19. 5. 425. Peirce continues: "The phenomenon consists in the fact that when an experimentalist shall come to *act* according to a certain scheme that hc has in mind, then will something else happen, and shatter the doubts of sceptics, like the celestial fire upon the altar of Elijah" (ibid.).

20. 5. 423.

21. 5. 380.

22. 5. 383.

23. 5. 384.

24. 6. 485. Peirce identifies the true with the satisfactory, but he insists that the satisfactory is not "whatever excites a certain peculiar feeling of satisfaction." This would be pure hedonism. Rather, "to say that an action or the result of an action is Satisfactory is simply to say that it is congruous to the aim of that action" (5. 560).

25. 5. 565.

20. 6. 1.

27. 6. 6, 6. 5.

28. 6. 2.

29. 6. 3.

30. 6. 5.

31. 1. 284. See 5. 37. Peirce admitted three categories of phenomena, called Firstness, Secondness, and and Thirdness. Firstness is the original, fresh, and unique quality of every phenomenon; for example, "the color of magenta, the odor of attar, the sound of a railway whistle, the taste of quinine" (1. 304). Secondness is the hard fact of any phenomenon, its thisness or haecceity. This includes its individuality and existence or occurrence here and now. Since the experience of individuality involves shock, rceistance, or interruption, the category of Secondness implies a duadic relation, unlike Firstness, which is monadic. Thirdness is the element of generality inherent in every phenomenon. Because of this element the phenomenon is subject to law and is capable of being represented by a general sign or concept. This is the category of rationality or intelligibility, unlike the first two categories which are irrational. Thirdness involves a triadic relation between several items of experience and their interpreter. See T. A. Goudge, *The Thought of C. S. Peirce*, pp. 85–95; M. G. Murphey, *The Development of Peirce's Philosophy*, pp. 296–378.

32. "In short, *cognizability* (in its widest sense) and *being* are not merely metaphysically the same, but are synonymous terms." 5. 257. Peirce's basic idealism is clear from his statement that anything that can be experienced "is of the nature of cognition" (ibid.).

33. 1. 548, 5. 294.

34. 6. 352.

35. Ibid.

36. 6. 318. For Peirce's relations to Scotus, see M. G. Murphey, *The Development of Peirce's Philosophy*, pp. 120–134, 138–140, 309–311. R. P. Goodwin, "Charles Sanders Peirce: A Modern Scotist?" *The New Scholasticism*, 35 (1961), 478–509. J. F. Boler, *Charles Peirce and Scholastic Realism. A Study of Peirce's Relation to John Duns Scotus* (Seattle: University of Washington Press, 1963).

37. 6. 335, 6. 336, 6. 495.

38. 1. 19.

39. "Even Duns Scotus is too nominalistic when he says that universals are contracted to the mode of individuality in singulars, meaning, as he does, by singulars, ordinary existing things. The pragmaticist cannot admit that. I myself went too far in the direction of nominalism when I said (5. 403) that it was a mere question of the convenience of speech whether we say that a diamond is hard when it is not pressed upon, or whether we say that it is soft until it is pressed upon. I *now* say that experiment will prove that the diamond is hard, as a positive fact. That is, it is a real fact that it *would* resist pressure, which amounts to extreme scholastic realism" (8. 208). This shows the distance separating the realism of Duns Scotus and the phenomenalism of Peirce. Whatever Peirce borrowed from Scotus he transformed in his own philosophy.

40. *North American Review*, 113 (1871), p. 452.

41. 6. 368.

42. 5. 121. Peirce can also say that "metaphysical conceptions are primarily and at bottom thoughts about words, or thoughts about thoughts..." (5. 294).

43. 1. 115.

44. 6. 495.

45. 5. 316.

46. 5. 407.

47. 6. 491.

48. 6. 502.

49. 6. 503.

50. 6. 493. "...one cannot logically infer the existence of God; one can only know Him by direct perception" (6. 653). See Pascal, "The heart has its own reasons which Reason does not know" (*Pensées*, ed. and trans. H. F. Stewart [New York: Pantheon Books, 1950], p. 343. n. 6.20).

51. 1. 653. Vitally important beliefs are those that commit us to act, e.g., the existence of God and the immortality of the soul. Pure theoretical knowledge, or science, on the other hand, "has nothing directly to say concerning practical matters, and nothing even applicable at all to vital crises...matters of vital importance must be left to sentiment, that is, to instinct" (1. 637).

52. 6. 102. For the conflict between the scientific, naturalistic side of Peirce's thought and his transcendentalism, see T. A. Goudge, *The Thought of C. S. Peirce*, pp. 253–254. For the importance of metaphysics in Peirce's philosophy and for his criticism of positivism, see M. F. Fairbanks, "C. S. Peirce and Positivism," *The Modern Schoolman*, 41 (1964), pp. 323–337.

53. 6. 465.

54. 6. 489, 6. 490.

55. William James, b. New York City, 1842; d. Chocorua, New Hampshire, 1910. His father, Henry James, Sr., was a friend of Emerson and Thoreau and a philosopher in his own right. (For his father's philosophy, see F. H. Young, *The Philosophy of Henry James, Sr.* [New York: Bookman Associates, 19501). His brother, Henry James, Jr., was the famous novelist. William James received his early schooling both in New York and abroad. For a while he studied art in Newport, Rhode Island, then science at the Lawrence Scientific School and the Harvard Medical School. In 1865 he accompanied the naturalist Louis Agassiz on an expedition to the Amazon; he returned in poor health and with a distaste for natural history. He continued his medical studies in Germany, became interested in psychology, and proposed to establish it as a science. At this period he read Renouvier, whose philosophy and psychology greatly influenced him. Still suffering from ill-health, he returned home in 1868 and took his medical degree at Harvard in 1869. In 1872 he was appointed instructor in physiology at Harvard. He added psychology to his course and formed one of the first psychology laboratories in the United States. He lectured extensively and with great success both in America and abroad.

Works: His most important works include: *The Will to Believe and Other Essays in Popular Philosophy* (New York: Longmans, 1897; new ed., 1932). *The Principles of Psychology* (2 vols.; New York: Henry Holt, 1890; Dover Publications, 1950). *Psychology, the Briefer Course* (Harper Torchbooks, 1961). *Pragmatism* (New York: Longmans, 1907). *The Varieties of Religious Experience* (New York: Longmans, 1902; Mentor Books, 1958). *The Meaning of Truth* (New York: Longmans, 1909). *A Pluralistic Universe* (New York: Longmans, 1909). *Some Problems of Philosophy* (New York: Longmans, 1911). *Essays in Radical Empiricism* (New York: Longmans, 1912). *Collected Essays and Reviews* (New York: Longmans, 1920). See R. B. Perry, *Annotated Bibliography of the Writings of William James* (New York: Longmans, 1920).

Studies: Indispensable for the life and thought of James, R. B. Perry, *The Thought and Character of William James* (2 vols.; Boston: Little, Brown, 1935). Same author, *Present Philosophical Tendencies* (New York: Longmans, 1929, Appendix: The Philosophy of William James, pp. 349–378); *In the Spirit of William James* (New Haven: Yale University Press, 1938). Various authors, *In Commemoration of William James 1842–1942* (New York: Columbia University Press, 1942); *William James, the Man and the Thinker* (Madison: University of Wisconsin Press, 1942). Lloyd Morris, *William James* (New York: Scribner's, 1950). B. P. Brennan, *The Ethics of William James* (New York: Bookman Associates, 1961).

56. For Peirce's relations with James, see R. B. Perry, *The Thought and Character of William James*, I, 533–542.

57. *Pragmatism*, pp. 3–40.

58. *Essays in Radical Empiricism*, p. 41. See *A Pluralistic Universe*, pp. 7–8.

59. *The Meaning of Truth*, p. xii. See *A Pluralistic Universe*, pp. 279–280; *Essays in Radical Empiricism*, p. 42. For a defense of the reality of relations directed against F. H. Bradley, see *A Pluralistic Universe*, pp. 347–369.

60. Ibid., p. 348. Experience is "pure" when it is taken on a primitive level, before it is distinguished into its physical and mental components. "The instant field of the present is always experience in its 'pure' state, plain unqualified actuality, a simple *that*, as yet undifferentiated into thing and thought, and only virtually classifiable as objective fact or as some one's opinion about fact" (*Essays in Radical Empiricism*, p. 74).

For James' relations with Bergson, see R. B. Perry, *The Thought and Character of William James*, II, 599–636. Bergson wrote to James that American pragmatism and his own "new philosophy" in France have been established independently of one another, with different points of departure and different methods, and yet they "tend to coincide" (ibid., pp. 616–617). James saw a close agreement between Bergson's fundamental ideas and the general system of metaphysics he proposed to write but never did (ibid., p. 606). See W. James, *A Pluralistic Universe*, VI: Bergson and his Critique of Intellectualism, pp. 225–273.

61. *Essays in Radical Empiricism*, p. 27. James quotes this passage from the English philosopher Shadworth Hodgson (1832–1912). Hodgson's empiricism greatly influenced James. For the relations between the two men, see R. B. Perry, *The Thought and Character of William James*, I, 611–653.

62. *Collected Essays and Reviews*, p. 374.

63. *The Meaning of Truth*, pp. 1–42, 127.

64. *Collected Essays and Reviews*, p. 328.

65. *Essays in Radical Empiricism*, p. 22.

66. *Collected Essays and Reviews*, p. 376. See *The Meaning of Truth*, pp. 43–50.

67. See C. S. Peirce, *Collected Papers, 5.* 3; 5. 414; 6.482.

68. *Pragmatism*, p. 45.

69. Ibid., pp. 49–50.

70. Ibid., pp. 54–55.

71. C. S. Peirce, *Collected Papers*, 2. 430.

72. *The Meaning of Truth*, pp. 201–202.

73. Ibid., p. 304.

74. H. Bergson, "Sur le pragmatisme de William James, vérité et réalité," written as a preface to James' *Pragmatism*, trans. E. LeBrun (Paris: Flammarion, 1911).

75. *Pragmatism*, p. 203.

76. *The Will to Believe*, p. 114.

77. *Pragmatism*, p. 76.

78. Ibid., p. 75. James does not deny theoretic interests and satisfactions, but he does not want to separate them from the practical "profits" to which they lead. He describes theoretic satisfactions as the feeling of the inner consistency among our judgments, objects, and reactions, all of which are in the mind. (Theoretic truth does not consist in the mind's correctly copying an archetypal reality.) This feeling of satisfaction, however, and the speculative life in general, are an aid to the satisfactory adaptation to our

environment. James sees little point in pursuing inner consistency among our ideas for its own sake, without regard for the "collateral proofs" to be reached from them in the satisfactory adjustment to our surroundings. See his reply to the English philosopher H. W. B. Joseph: "Humanism and Truth Once More," *Mind*, N. S. 14 (1905), 190–198.

79. *Pragmatism*, p. 204.

80. J. Royce, *The Philosophy of Loyalty* (New York: Macmillan, 1908), pp. 346–347.

81. *Pragmatism*, p. 58.

82. Ibid., p. 61.

83. Ibid., p. 223.

84. Clifford's "The Ethics of Belief" appeared in the *Contemporary Review* of January 18, 1877, and was reprinted in his *Lectures and Essays* (London: Macmillan, 1879). James' review of the *Lectures* is printed in his *Collected Essays and Reviews*, pp. 137–146.

85. *The Will to Believe*, p. 14.

86. "That Renouvier's was the greatest individual influence upon James' thought cannot be doubted. Renouvier's phenomenalism, his pluralism, his fideism, his moralism, and his theism were all congenial to James' mind, and in them James found support and confirmation. On the other hand, he dissented from Renouvier's intellectualism, from his monadism, and from certain of his speculative extravagances." R. B. Perry, *The Thought and Character of William James*, I, p. 655.

87. Quoted ibid., pp. 323, 658.

88. *Collected Essays and Reviews*, p. 34.

89. Quoted by R. B. Perry, op. cit., p. 323.

90. *The Will to Believe*, p. 22.

91. Ibid., p. 102.

92. Ibid., p. 109.

93. Ibid., pp. 25–27.

94. Ibid., p. 127.

95. Ibid., p. 40.

96. *The Varieties of Religious Experience* (Mentor edition), p. 384. James uses Frederick W. H. Myers' theory of the subliminal self to explain this communication between our finite selves and a wider world of being. Myers writes, "Each of us is in reality an abiding psychical entity far more extensive than he knows—an individuality which can never express itself completely through any corporeal manifestation. The Self manifests through the organism; but there is always some part of the Self unmanifested; and always, as it seems, some power of organic expression in abeyance or reserve." Quoted by James, ibid., p. 386.

97. Ibid., p. 389.

98. Ibid., p. 395. For the distinction between metaphysical and moral attributes of God, see pp. 339ff. See also C. Fabro, *Introduzione all' Ateismo Moderno* (Rome: Studium, 1964), pp. 721–728.

99. Ibid., p. 395. For James' views on immortality, see R. B. Perry, *The Thought and Character of William James*, II, 355–357.

100. W. James, "Human Immortality," published in *The Will to Believe, Human Immortality, and other Essays in Popular Philosophy* (Dover Publications, 1956), p. 30.

101. "The Thirteen Pragmatisms," *Journal of Philosophy*, 5 (1908), 5–39. Part II is reprinted in *The Development of American Philosophy*, ed. Muelder and Sears (Boston: Houghton, Mifflin, 1940), pp. 404–410.

102. *The Will to Believe*, p. 95.

103. *The Varieties of Religious Experience*, p. 392.

104. John Dewey, b. Burlington, Vermont, 1859; d. New York, 1952. He graduated from the University of Vermont in 1879. After teaching high school for three years he entered Johns Hopkins University to do graduate work in philosophy. There he followed Peirce's courses in logic and studied under the Hegelian George S. Morris. He graduated from Johns Hopkins in 1884, having written a thesis on the psychology of Kant. Traveling west, he taught at the University of Michigan (1884–1888) and the University of Minnesota (1888–1889), then returned to head the Department of Philosophy at Michigan (1889–1894). In 1894 he became head of the Department of Philosophy and Psychology at the University of Chicago; in 1896 he founded the Laboratory School or Dewey School of Education. At Chicago he was associated with George Herbert Mead (I 863–1931), who, under Dewey's influence, applied pragmatism to social psychology. For two years Dewey lectured in Peking, China, and for shorter periods he was in Turkey, Mexico, and Russia. In 1905 he joined the faculty

of Columbia University, retiring in 1929. See "Biography of John Dewey," ed. Jane M. Dewey (his daughter), in *The Philosophy of John Dewey*, ed. P. A. Schilpp (Evanston and Chicago: Northwestern University Press, 1939), pp. 3–45. Dewey tells the story of his philosophical development in "From Absolutism to Experimentalism," *Contemporary American Philosophy*, ed. G. P. Adams and W. P. Montague (New York: Macmillan, 1930), II, 13–27. For Mead's pragmatism, see A. J. Reck, *Recent American Philosophy* (New York: Pantheon Books, 1964), pp. 84–122.

Works: See M. H. Thomas, *A Bibliography of John Dewey, 1882–1939* (New York: Columbia University Press, 1939). Among his most important writings are: *The Study of Ethics* (Ann Arbor: Register, 1894). *The School and Society* (Chicago: University of Chicago Press, 1900). *The Child and the Curriculum and The School and Society* (Phoenix Books, University of Chicago Press, 1956). *Studies in Logical Theory* (Chicago: University of Chicago Press, 1903). *Ethics:* with James H. Tufts (New York: Henry Holt, 1908, 2nd ed., 1932). *The Influence of Darwin on Philosophy* (New York: Henry Holt, 1910). *Democracy and Education* (New York: Macmillan, 1910). *Essays in Experimental Logic* (Chicago: University of Chicago Press, 1916). *Reconstruction in Philosophy* (New York: Henry Holt, 1920; Mentor Book, 1950). *Human Nature and Conduct* (New York: Henry Holt, 1922). *Experience and Nature* (Chicago: Open Court, 1925; Dover Publications, 1950). *The Quest for Certainty* (New York: Minton, Balch, 1929; Capricorn Books, 1900). *Philosophy and Civilization* (New York: Minton, Balch, 1931). *Art as Experience* (New York: Minton, Balch, 1934). *A Common Faith* (New Haven: Yale University Press, 1934). *Logic: The Theory of Inquiry* (New York: Henry Holt, 1938). *Theory of Valuation* (Chicago: University of Chicago Press, 1939). *Problems of Men* (New York: Philosophical Library, 1946). *Knowing and the Known*, with A. F. Bentley (Boston: Beacon Press, 1949). *Intelligence in the Modern World*, selections, ed. J. Ratner (New York: Modern Library, 1939).

Studies: *John Dewey, the Man and His Philosophy* (Cambridge, MA: Harvard University Press, 1930). *The Philosophy of John Dewey*, ed. P. A. Schilpp (Evanston and Chicago: Northwestern University Press, 1939). Sidney Hook, *John Dewey: An Intellectual Portrait* (New York: Day, 1939). *The Philosopher of the Common Man: Essays in Honor of John Dewey to Celebrate His Eightieth Birthday* (New York, 1940). M. G. White, *The Origin of Dewey's Instrumentalism* (New York: Columbia University Press, 1943). *John Dewey: Philosopher of Science and Freedom*, ed. Sidney Hook (New York: Dial, 1950). G. R. Geiger, *John Dewey in Perspective* (Oxford University Press, 1958). E. C. Moore, *American Pragmatism: Peirce, James, and Dewey* (New York: Columbia University Press, 1961).

105. For the early development of Dewey's thought, see M. G. White, *The Origin of Dewey's Instrumentalism*; J. Collins, "The Genesis of Dewey's Naturalism," *John Dewey: His Thought and Influence*, ed. J. Blewett, pp. 1–32; B. H. Zedier, "Dewey's Theory of Knowledge," ibid., pp. 59–84; G. Dykhuizen, "John Dewey: The Chicago Years," *Journal of the History of Philosophy*, II (1964), 227–253.

106. Dewey's contribution to *Studies in Logical Theory* (1903) "marks a final and complete break with his early Hegelian idealism and launches his instrumental theory of reflective thought." "Biography of John Dewey," *The Philosophy of John Dewey*, ed. P. A. Schlipp, p. 33.

107. *Reconstruction in Philosophy*, pp. 8–9.

108. Ibid., p. 17.

109. Ibid., p. 18.

110. Ibid., p. 20.

111. Ibid., p. 21.

112. Quoted by J. Ratner, "Dewey's Conception of Philosophy," *The Philosophy of John Dewey*, p. 50.

113. *The Influence of Darwin on Philosophy*, pp. 17–18. For Dewey's atheism, see C. Fabro, *Introduzione all' Ateismo Moderno* (Rome: Editrice Studium, 1904), pp. 800–820.

114. *Logic: The Theory of Inquiry*, pp. 84–87; *The Influence of Darwin on Philosophy*, pp. 5–6.

115. *Logic: The Theory of Inquiry*, p. 92; *The Quest for Certainty*, pp. 98–99.

116. *Reconstruction in Philosophy*, pp. 28–38.

117. *Logic: The Theory of Inquiry*, pp. 104–105.

118. *The Influence of Darwin on Philosophy*, pp. 132–133.

119. For this Thomistic distinction, see St. Thomas, *Summa Theologiae*, I, 79, 8. Dewey considers reason identical with the *intellectus* of the scholastics. See *The Quest for Certainty*, p. 203. Since, for the Thomists, all reasoning begins and ends with insight or understanding, from their point of view Dewey's rejection of the latter entails the denial of the former. As a result, his philosophy appears as an "irrationalism." See A. C. Pegis, "Man and the Challenge of Irrationalism," *Race, Nation, Person: Social Aspects of the Race Problem* (New York: Barnes & Noble, 1944), pp. 69–93.

120. *Logic: The Theory of Inquiry*, p. 143. By his distinction between experience and knowledge, Dewey differs from William James. As we have seen, James distinguishes between "knowledge of acquaintance" and "knowledge about." The former is direct and intuitive, the latter conceptual and representative. Dewey in effect denies knowledge

of acquaintance. Commenting on James' phrase "knowledge of acquaintance," Dewey says that acquaintance implies recognition and recognition familiarity. To this, Santayana shrewdly rejoins that "we are left with an uncomfortable suspicion that it is impossible to inspect anything for the first time." See Santayana, "Dewey's Naturalistic Metaphysics," *Obiter Scripta* (London: Constable & Co., 1936), p. 166–167.

121. *The Quest for Certainty*, p. 110.

122. Ibid., pp. 24–26. "...the object of knowledge is eventual; that is, it is an outcome of directed experimental operations, instead of something in sufficient existence before the act of knowing" (ibid., pp. 163–164).

123. Ibid., pp. 129–130.

124. Ibid., p. 132.

125. Ibid., pp. 107–108, 121. See P. W. Bridgman, *The Logic of Modern Physics* (New York: Macmillan, 1929), p. 5. On the same point Dewey also cites A. Eddington, *The Nature of the Physical World* (New York: Macmillan, 1928), p. 255.

126. Thus, numbers are neither essences nor properties of existing things; they are designations of potential operations. See *The Quest for Certainty*, p. 153.

127. Ibid., pp. 107, 133.

128. Ibid., pp. 132, 159–161. "The test of ideas, of thinking generally, is found in the consequences of the acts to which the ideas lead, that is, in the new arrangements of things which are brought into existence" (ibid., p. 131).

129. "Experience, Knowledge and Value: A Rejoinder," *The Philosophy of John Dewey*, p. 572.

130. "What Does Pragmatism Mean by Practical?" *Journal of Philosophy*, 5 (1908), pp. 85–99. In this article (a review of James' *Pragmatism*), Dewey insists that "ideas are always working hypotheses concerning attaining particular empirical results, and are tentative programs (or sketches of method) for attaining them" (p. 93). He criticizes James for sometimes abandoning this strict rule and treating any good that flows from the acceptance of a belief as evidence of its truth. As Dewey points out, James appeals to this broader notion of pragmatic truth, particularly when dealing with theological notions. By applying the narrower rule, Dewey eliminates these notions.

131. *The Quest for Certainty*, p. 38. "Knowing is itself a mode of practical action and is *the* way of interaction by which other natural interactions become subject to directions" (ibid., p. 104).

132. Ibid., pp. 132–134.

133. Ibid., p. 244. For a critical evaluation of Dewey as an ethical thinker, see J. Maritain, *Moral Philosophy* (New York: Charles Scribner's Sons, 1964), pp. 399–418.

134. Ibid., p. 246.

135. *Theory of Valuation*, p. 32.

136. *Human Nature and Conduct*, pp. 11–13.

137. Ibid., p. 211.

138. *Reconstruction in Philosophy*, p. 177.

139. *Intelligence in the Modern World*, ed. J. Ratner, p. 1025.

140. *Reconstruction in Philosophy*, p. 186.

141. *Democracy and Education*, p. 115.

142. *Experience and Nature*, p. 202.

143. *Intelligence in the Modern World*, ed. J. Ratner, p. 400. "A democracy is more than a form of government; it is primarily a mode of associated living, of conjoint communicated experience" (*Democracy and Education*, p. 101).

144. *Reconstruction in Philosophy*, pp. 184–185.

145. Dewey tells the story of applying to a dealer for desks and chairs for his school. The dealer, "more intelligent than the rest," remarked: "I am afraid we have not what you want. You want something at which the children may work; these are all for listening!" *The School and Society* (2nd ed., 1915), p. 32.

146. *Experience and Education*, pp. 5–6.

147. *The School and Society*, p. 11.

Epilogue

1. The philosophical production has grown so large that several bibliographies are devoted to it. Leaving aside the countless specialized bibliographies, two at least should be mentioned. (1) *Répertoire bibliographique de la philosophie*, Editions de l'institut

Supérieur de Philosophie, Louvain, since 1934. Volume XIII (1901) lists over six thousand titles for that year. This does not include the recensions (117 pages of titles), nor does it pretend to cover the whole philosophical production in Europe; the only languages retained are, at least as a rule, German, English, Spanish, Catalan, French, Italian, Dutch, and Portuguese. Other systematic limitations are applied to the choice of subjects within certain particular philosophical disciplines, such as logic, psychology, etc.; see Introduction to the volume for 1961, pp. 4–5. Three hundred periodicals are listed for Europe and America, pp. 6–13. (2) *Bibliographie de la philosophie*, published by the International Institute of Philosophical Collaboration, Librairie Philosophique Joseph Vrin, 6 Place de la Sorbonne, Paris-6e, since 1937. This bibliography gives succinct information on the content of the works; it covers several languages, European or otherwise, omitted by the *Répertoire*.

Designed by Fiona Cecile Clarke, the CLUNY *logo depicts a monk at work in the scriptorium, with a cat sitting at his feet.*

The monk represents our mission to emulate the invaluable contributions of the monks of Cluny in preserving the libraries of the West, our strivings to know and love the truth.

The cat at the monk's feet is Pangur Bán, from the eponymous Irish poem of the 9th century. The anonymous poet compares his scholarly pursuit of truth with the cat's happy hunting of mice. The depiction of Pangur Bán is an homage to the work of the monks of Irish monasteries and a sign of the joy we at Cluny take in our trade.

"Messe ocus Pangur Bán,
cechtar nathar fria saindan:
bíth a menmasam fri seilgg,
mu memna céin im saincheirdd."

Made in the USA
Columbia, SC
08 November 2024